MW00581896

Screen Stories and Moral Understanding

Screen Stories and Moral Understanding

Interdisciplinary Perspectives

Edited by

Carl Plantinga

OXFORD
UNIVERSITY PRESS

OXFORD
UNIVERSITY PRESS

Oxford University Press is a department of the University of Oxford. It furthers
the University's objective of excellence in research, scholarship, and education
by publishing worldwide. Oxford is a registered trade mark of Oxford University
Press in the UK and certain other countries.

Published in the United States of America by Oxford University Press
198 Madison Avenue, New York, NY 10016, United States of America.

CIP data is on file at the Library of Congress

ISBN 978–0–19–766567–1 (pbk.)
ISBN 978–0–19–766566–4 (hbk.)

DOI: 10.1093/oso/9780197665664.001.0001

Paperback printed by Marquis Book Printing, Canada
Hardback printed by Bridgeport National Bindery, Inc., United States of America

Contents

IV. CHARACTER ENGAGEMENT

V. THE REFLECTIVE AFTERLIFE

Acknowledgments

This book was made possible by a grant from the Templeton Religion Trust for "Screen Stories and Moral Understanding," one of the projects in the Trust's "Art Seeking Understanding" initiative. The book emerged from a series of virtual seminars held in early 2021, in which all of this book's authors were participants. That the seminars were a success is due in part to the creative ideas and organizational acumen of Rebecca Sok of Blueprint 1543. Garrett Strpko cohosted the seminars with me, and John Rhym's engagement and assistance were invaluable as well. The seminar's authors and respondents hailed from media psychology, philosophy, communication, film and media studies, and other disciplines and joined us (virtually) from Europe, Australia, Asia, and the United States. All conference participants deserve thanks for their contributions: Katalin Balint, Anne Bartsch, Helena Bilandzic, Noël Carroll, Mathew Cipa, Anne Eaton, Allison Eden, Jeorg Fingerhut, Dan Flory, Cynthia Freeland, Matthew Grizzard, James Harold, Mette Hjort, Frederick Hopp, Eileen John, Sarah Kozloff, Dan Levin, Wyatt Moss-Wellington, Ted Nannicelli, Mary Beth Oliver, Karen Pearlman, John Rhym, Robert Sinnerbrink, Murray Smith, Jane Stadler, Paul C. Taylor, Malcolm Turvey, Tom Wartenberg, René Weber, and Nicholas Wolsterstorff. I'd like to thank Allison Eden and Nicholas Wolterstorff in particular, who provided helpful guidance as advisors for the grant project.

Finally, gratitude is due to the Templeton Religion Trust for its grant support of a subsequent three-year project, "Character Engagement and Moral Understanding in Screen Stories," to be undertaken from June 2022 through May 2025. Grantees Allison Eden, Dan Levin, Murray Smith, and I plan to extend the studies represented in this book, but focus on the relationship of the viewer's engagement with characters to the development of moral understanding. This work will also be interdisciplinary; the grantees hail from media psychology, psychology, and film and media studies.

Carl Plantinga

Introduction

Carl Plantinga

Moving-image fictions are engines of attention with the capacity to rivet the viewer's interest longer and more powerfully than any other medium. Whether we think of narrative fiction films as art or entertainment, one of the central functions of such "screen stories" is the provision of enjoyment. Beyond enjoyment, however, can the viewing screen stories also lead to moral understanding and reflection? If so, how and under what conditions might that occur? Would it occur in relation to "peak" experiences, those moviegoing encounters, often had when we are teenagers, that move us deeply and make a permanent imprint on our lives? Or does it occur gradually as a kind of long-term cultivation of perspectives, rooted in the repetition of paradigm scenarios, character types, and their associated affective charges (Plantinga 2009, 80–84)? How can screen stories stimulate the moral imagination? And how do moving-image and literary narratives function differently in this regard? How do the strong emotions that films elicit relate to their influence? Does thematic ambiguity, formal complexity, moral conflict, or the elicitation of contradictory emotions lead to moral and political questioning and reflection? These are the sorts of questions examined in this book.

Storytelling is a fundamental activity for human beings, with many diverse functions and roles to play in human life. Stories entertain, inspire, teach, catalyze, cajole, placate, and warn. The arts of storytelling—film, literature, theater, opera, etc.—often present us with stories that are fictive, or in other words, stories that aren't literally true. More than that, viewers *know* that they aren't literally true while they watch or read them. Yet all fictions correlate in various ways with the actual world around us. While Mookie of Spike Lee's *Do the Right Thing* (1989) and Marge Gunderson of the Coen brothers' *Fargo* (1996) are fictional characters, in many respects they are like real people. While the extraordinary events of *Pan's Labyrinth* (2006) and *Winter's Bone* (2010) are the products of somebody's imagination, they could spark the moral imagination of audience members and perhaps even prompt self-examination. Fictions may harbor truths, elicit questions and reflection, or foster journeys of discovery (see Smith in this volume). As bell hooks writes, we may say we attend movies to be entertained, but we also "go to movies to learn" (1996, 2).

J. Hillis Miller claims that stories are both "order giving" and "order finding" (1990, 68). This corresponds with the contention of media effects scholars that narrative media can both reinforce and alter our beliefs and perspectives. We construct and

Carl Plantinga, *Introduction* In: *Screen Stories and Moral Understanding.* Edited by: Carl Plantinga,
Oxford University Press. © Oxford University Press 2023. DOI: 10.1093/oso/9780197665664.003.0001

remember stories as a means of forging personal and group identities and of establishing values and principles. We read and tell stories to our children as a means of instruction. The sacred texts of various world religions couch their revelations in narrative form, offering stories that explain ultimate meaning and purpose. Historical narratives provide accounts of the past that solidify meaning for the present. Stories are also a means of exploration and imaginative play. As Miller writes, "We need fictions in order to experiment with possible selves and to learn to take our places in the real world, to play our parts there" (69). Fictions are also a relatively safe place from which to criticize or question the reigning assumptions of a culture or group. Narrative fictions can cultivate patterns of thinking and feeling and can deconstruct existing patterns, thus suggesting alternative ways of understanding the world.

Oral storytelling is likely as old as human society itself. The history of theatrical and literary forms of narrative extends back thousands of years. In the past century and a quarter new forms of storytelling on screens have *also* become extremely popular. The momentum for stories on screens grew with the invention of the motion pictures in the late 19th century and soon branched out to various media, including television, videotape, DVDs, and today all the various forms of digital dissemination, including streaming. Stories on screens have become central to our lives and to many world cultures.

Moral Understanding and Screen Stories

In this book we ask particular questions regarding screen stories: Can the viewing of screen stories lead to moral understanding? Can fictions on screens help us understand the ethical implications of complex situations, apply general principles to concrete circumstances, or develop empathy for others? Can screen stories teach us to ask the right questions, stimulate the moral imagination, generate significant reflection, lead to useful discussion? In this book leading scholars from various disciplines—communication, film and media studies, philosophy, and media psychology—consider these questions.

This might seem a rather odd pursuit in relation to film, given that various social forces have focused more squarely on the movies as a source of moral corruption. Beginning with its origins in the late 19th century, the influence of film has often been thought to be harmful. The art of cinema developed from what could fairly be called cheap entertainments: illusionistic toys, penny arcades, and vaudeville theaters transformed for the projection of movies. In their early years, films were thought to appeal primarily to the less savory corners of society. Early movies were often crude and primitive. The city of Chicago began censoring movies in 1907, and soon other municipalities and states followed suit. The U.S. Supreme Court ruled in 1915 that the movies, as a "business pure and simple" were not subject to the protections of the First Amendment and freedom of speech (Mast, 1982, 142). The Court compared the movies to "the theatre, the circus, and other shows and spectacles" (141).

During the 1920s and 1930s, questions about the social influence of this new medium led to the Payne Fund Studies, a wide-reaching and ambitious research project. Although the studies demonstrated that any effects of the movies were wholly subject to individual differences, the project nonetheless showed, as Garth Jowett puts it, that "prejudices for or against war, [attitudes] on race issues, and toward criminals, were significantly affected by viewing motion pictures on these subjects" (1976, 223). The findings of the Payne Fund Studies were generally measured and careful, but a book soon appeared that popularized the results with an imbalance toward the negative. *Our Movie Made Children* (Forman 1933) was an attack on the film industry that indicated harmful effects from viewing movies, arguing that the movies' central themes of love, sex, and crime had decisively negative effects on young minds (Jowett 1976, 225). It was concerns such as these, plus the fear of censorship, that led to the adoption of the Production Code of 1934 by the major Hollywood studios. The Code limited the topics movies could represent and dictated how various topics would be represented.

At the time of this writing, perceptions have changed dramatically. Concerns about the potential of movies to corrupt audiences have not entirely dissipated, with several countries worldwide regularly censoring the movies (Plantinga 2018, 15–21). Yet most readers in Western countries, at least, would agree that narrative film has taken its place among the world's great art forms. Aside from the question of art, it is undeniable that stories on screens have become ubiquitous, something like the air that we breathe or the food that we consume. Sure, some food is rotten, but who would condemn *all* food? Similarly, it would make little sense to condemn screen stories in toto.

Movies, as philosopher Noël Carroll (1996) has argued, are attentional engines with the power to maintain the focus of audiences through what he calls "intense engagement" and "widespread accessibility." Narrative films can be affectively powerful, suggesting that they have the potential to influence audiences because they greatly move them (Plantinga 2009, 2013; Plantinga and Smith 1999; Carroll, Oliver, and Sinnerbrink, all in this volume). Yet if narrative films have a potential to corrupt, then they should also have the facility to foster beneficial learning, or what we call in this book *moral understanding*. Moral understanding, as we see it, is not limited to matters of personal behavior and integrity but also encompasses the key social and political issues of the day, for example, calls for justice in various cultural contexts.

Various authors in this book, primarily Ted Nannicelli but also Mary Beth Oliver and Nicholas Wolterstorff, discuss the nature of moral understanding in detail. Thus it is sufficient here to introduce and briefly define the concept, with the assurance to readers that more discussion will follow in subsequent chapters. We do not operate here with a narrow or technical definition of moral understanding. To have moral understanding is to discern right and wrong and the moral implications of human action in a wide range of spheres of activity. Moral understanding goes beyond moral reflection and even moral knowledge. As Christoph Baumberger (2013) argues, understanding is a complex cognitive achievement that may consist of any or all of the following: categorization, the development of models, the asking of new questions, phenomenal knowledge, and propositional knowledge. Allison Hills defines moral understanding in part as "knowing why" in addition to "knowing that." (2010). Carroll argues that what he calls "clarification" occurs when we refine what we already know by drawing new connections between elements of our moral knowledge or become better able to apply moral knowledge to concrete situations (1998b, 319–342).

In harmony with this, Nannicelli provides in this volume what he calls an "abilities account" of moral understanding. And Oliver describes the development of moral understanding as a process toward which various spectator responses, such as "inspiration" and "elevation," may play a significant role. Thus although moral understanding may consist of cognitive abilities, it depends for its development on the right sort of motivation for the development those abilities. That motivation can result from emotions such as elevation and admiration (see the chapters by Oliver and Carroll). Thinking of moral understanding as a process also helps us to see the role of the cultivation of moral perspectives and habits of which Helena Bilandzic writes in this volume. That moral understanding is a complex cognitive achievement does not compromise the fact that its component parts, many of which are listed above, are concrete and subject to empirical testing.

The claim that *literary* fiction and especially the novel may lead to moral understanding would not be new or surprising. Many would say that we learn about misleading first impressions from Jane Austen's *Pride and Prejudice* and about empathy and understanding from Harper Lee's *To Kill a Mockingbird*. Philosopher and novelist Iris Murdoch (1970) claims that the right sort of literary fiction can bring about changes in the reader's capacities or dispositions, leading to an "unselfing" or blocking of our usual selfish dispositions. Reading novels may help us to see human situations in their morally salient respects. Such stories can even move us to "act rightly" (167–168). Martha Nussbaum (1990) similarly argues that the structure of the novel offers an experience for the reader that has the potential to be morally instructive. She writes that "literature is an extension of life not only horizontally, bringing the reader into contact with events or locations or persons or problems he or she has not otherwise met, but also, so to speak, vertically, giving the reader experience that is deeper, sharper, and more precise than much of what takes place in life" (48). Nussbaum is not alone in suggesting that novel reading can train readers to become morally sensitive or to exercise more sophisticated moral judgment. Psychologist Keith Oatley for example, writes that literary fiction enlarges empathy "in the context of a hundreds-year old march toward equality and humane treatment of others" (2011, 167).

What about stories on screens? Can movies or streamed series contribute to moral learning and understanding, and if so, how and under what conditions? Can films sometimes help us to imagine a situation more vividly, and thus more clearly discern its moral significance in relation to social justice, as Wolterstorff argues in his chapter? Does the presentation of screen stories in moving photographic images and recorded sound impact the potential for moral understanding (see Plantinga, this volume)? Can film characters serve as exemplars, and thus teach audiences something about what it means to be a virtuous person, as Carroll, Allison Eden and Mathew Grizzard, and Oliver suggest in their chapters? Could it be that we also can learn from a film's moral failures, such as the failure of *Hamilton* (2020) to represent Thomas Jefferson's rape of Sally Hemmings as morally serious, as Paul Taylor discusses in his chapter? Are we led to serious moral reflection by the representation of moral conflict, as René Weber and Frederic Hopp discuss in their chapter?

If films have the capacity to contribute to moral understanding, does this occur during the screening itself? Or, as several of the authors here argue, could it be that what we do with the film *after* the screening—how we think about, discuss, and incorporate it into individual thought and cultural discourse—plays a role in whatever moral learning it might engender? These are the issues dealt with in this book.

Interdisciplinary Challenges

The contributors to this book approach these issues from the disciplines of communication, media psychology, film and media, and philosophy, bringing with them the methodologies and fundamental assumptions of their respective fields of study. The move toward interdisciplinarity is born of the conviction that cooperation between disciplines, which needs to begin with simple familiarity with and acknowledgment of alternative research traditions, will eventually lead to better understanding of the issues. In this regard, this book is merely a beginning of what we hope will be an emerging interdisciplinary synergy.

The chapters here derive from virtual seminars conducted in early 2020 during which scholars from these disciplines were invited to speak and respond to each other's presentations. Even *within* the respective disciplines of the speakers/authors, there exist philosophical and methodological differences. Thus, for example, Robert Sinnerbrink, in this volume, discusses the very different cognitive/analytic and "Continental" understandings of affect within film and media studies. There is also the well-known division between continental and analytic approaches to philosophy, and the divide between "empirical" and "critical" approaches to media studies (Ang 2013).

The contributors to this volume share a sympathy for a common approach that to some extent transcends the disciplines—the cognitive/analytic approach and, more narrowly, aesthetic cognitivism (discussed further below). Thus it would be helpful to note that although the contributions here emerge from various disciplines, the contributors generally favor analytic, cognitive, and empirical methodologies. In film studies, cognitive/analytic film theory emerged in the 1990s as a reaction to what has been variously termed "screen theory," "subject position theory," or "Grand Theory" of the 1970s and "culturalism" of the 1980s (Bordwell and Carroll 1996). Cognitive/analytic film and media theory is not a methodology, as Ted Nannicelli and Paul Taberham write, so much as "a stance, a perspective, or an approach" to the study of screen narrative (2014, 3). It borrows from analytic philosophy, as the contributions of philosophers to this volume show. And it strongly values empirical work in the cognitive and social sciences, as the chapters by media psychologists attest.

This cognitive stance or approach potentially finds a central place for cultural influences and variation as well, as various chapters in this book demonstrate. What Lisa Zunshine calls "cognitive cultural studies" is an interdisciplinary field that examines the "relationship between the 'evolved human brain' and 'the particular interpretations carried by particular cultures'" (2010, 8). Thus both James Harold and Wyatt Moss-Wellington (this volume) discuss how various institutions affect postviewing discussion and thought about narrative. And Taylor, in his chapter, provides a clear demonstration of two divergent modes of understanding *Hamilton* that could be taken to represent subcultures and how they differently guide the viewer's attention.

What are the benefits interdisciplinarity could bring? One would hope that the strengths of each discipline would influence the others—the empirical research of media psychologists and communication scholars, the deep familiarity with the workings of film structure and style of film and media scholars, and the conceptual clarification and problem-solving of philosophers. Murray Smith writes that philosophy, and by extension film and media theory, assist not merely in conceptual clarification but also in theory construction (2017). Theory construction should emphasize, Smith writes, "the interplay between conceptual and empirical work" and recognize movement and possible mutual benefit in both directions (28). Empirical work may cause us to revise our concepts and frameworks, while conceptual analysis may sharpen our empirical investigations.

One would hope that interdisciplinarity could help scholars to develop a common language to discuss central elements of the viewing experience, this despite the differing and/or ambiguous definitions of key terms within the disciplines as much as between them. Two concepts are illustrative in this regard: "immersion" and "character engagement." Immersion refers to the viewer's rapt attention and absorption in the viewing experience (Green et al. 2020). Most scholars of narrative hold that such immersion is key to the persuasive power of fiction. Various terms for immersion (or something immersion-like) include the following:

absorption
transportation
illusion
twofoldness
simulation
flow
attention
interest

The second concept, character engagement, is a relatively neutral term that names any of the myriad ways in which the spectator "relates" to a fictional character. The number of terms for varieties of character engagement is daunting:

identification
assimilation
solidarity
allegiance
parasocial relationship
liking/disliking
sympathy/antipathy
empathy
vicarious distress
experience-taking
alignment
recognition
projection
interest
wishful identification
simulation (again)
twofoldness (again)

In addition, of course, there are the various emotions with which one can respond to characters.

What makes these terms confusing is that some are contested, and many have differing meanings depending on the researcher using them. The terms "empathy" and "sympathy," for example, are widely used in strikingly different ways (Plantinga 2018, 196–204). Perhaps the most controversial concept is "identification." On some accounts, identification is characterized by the spectator taking the role of a story's protagonist, taking on her or his perspective, feeling the emotions she or he would feel, and taking on her or his goals. The viewer may temporarily take on the position of a character. This sort of identification does not necessarily last through the entire viewing process. Such viewers may *temporarily* forget about themselves, take the perspective of that character, and feel the "same emotions" presumably felt by that character (Cohen 2001; Cohen, Oliver, and Raney 2009; Moyer-Gusé 2015).

Similar conceptions of identification were also held in film studies, primarily in relation to the "subject position" or "suture" theory of the 1970s–1980s, which took the concept further, arguing that in some sense the viewing "subject" was actually "constituted" in the process of viewing the film (Pribram 2004). The subject was taken to be a "position" that the actual spectator could occupy while viewing, but the relationship between the subject and the empirical spectator was ambiguous at best. At worst, the power of the theory depended on a kind of willful confusion of, or equivocation between, subject position and spectator (Bordwell and Carroll 1996, 15). That the subject position is a creation of the film is uncontroversial; that the actual spectator might be "constructed" (as opposed to influenced or affected) by the film seems unlikely.

The notion of identification as wholly taking the perspective of a fictional character is controversial, as Eden and Grizzard point out in their chapter (also see Carroll 1990,

88–96; Plantinga 2009, 102–106). Some notions of identification do not recognize or account for *twofoldness*. We can both enjoy a representation as though it has some purchase on our lives and *simultaneously* recognize that it is a representation and not reality. Richard Wollheim initially used the concept of twofoldness in relation to painting, but the concept is useful in relation to all the representational arts, including media narratives (1987). The sort of immersion and character engagement characteristic of film viewing, together with twofoldness, is seemingly key to the special power that moving-image narratives can hold over us. The phenomenological power of the moving image and sound is tempered, or deflected, by an implicit recognition that the experience is in some sense artificial and constructed by the filmmakers.

This brief discussion of the notion of identification is just an inkling of the complex issues involved in researching the relationship between narrative film viewing and possible moral understanding. In addition to addressing some of these theoretical differences, the development of a common terminology may accelerate the progress of research as well. One might hope that such interdisciplinarity will eventually lead to some consensus rather than a further proliferation of alternative theories and concepts. Yet the contestation of previous concepts and theories may also lead to progress in a kind of dialectical give and take.

Aesthetic Cognitivism and Moral Learning

Aesthetic cognitivism, as Nannicelli writes in this volume, holds that one source (among others) of the value of the arts is the cognitive benefits they bring (see also Baumberger 2013; Freeland 1997; Graham 2005, 52–75; Tooby and Cosmides 2001). There exist more extreme versions of the claim. Philosopher Nelson Goodman has famously written that the arts "[should be taken no less seriously than the sciences as modes of discovery, creation, and enlargement of knowledge in the broad sense of advancement of understanding" (1978, 102). The authors in this volume tend to assume a moderate version of aesthetic cognitivism, thus holding that cognitive benefits are one of the potential values of the arts, and that the arts lead to moral understanding only under certain conditions (see my chapter in this volume).

The word "moral" in "moral understanding" has various connotations in different disciplines. The word is commonly used in the disciplines of philosophy, communication, and media psychology but has until recently been avoided in film and media studies. Examinations of issues related to morality and moral understanding regularly appear in the work of Carroll (see, for example, 1998a; 1998b, 291–359; 2003), among others. Some use the terms "moral" and "ethical" as synonyms, while others draw a distinction between the two words (Gaut 2007, 41–48). The terms "moral" and "morality" appear regularly in the social sciences; at an annual Media and Morality (n.d.) conference empirical researchers discuss their methods and findings, often drawing from psychologist Jonathan Haidt's (2012) moral foundations theory. Fine examples of this approach can be found in Ron Tamborini's edited collection, *Media and the Moral Mind* (2013).

The ideological and cultural bent of film and media studies, on the other hand, has long presumed the word "moral" to direct attention away from cultures and institutions and toward simplistic critiques of personal behavior. An interest in morality might be thought to unduly focus on individualistic concerns, such as the virtues and vices, for example, at the expense of political formations and cultural ideologies. It might be thought, as Moss-Wellington notes in his book *Cognitive Film and Media Ethics*, to lead to "regressive or unthinking moralism," to carry the "post-colonial baggage of appeals to Eurocentric authority," or to reinforce a dominant and oppressive ideology (2021, 4–5). Yet much as these dangers do exist, there is no getting around issues of "ought" and normative human behavior. One effect of avoiding all discussion of "morality" and "ethics" is to resort to a confusingly expansive use of the term "ideology" to fill in the conceptual gaps. This has the potential to cause us to ignore the many ways in which ethics, politics, and morality are mutually implicated. The concerns of film theorists in relation to culture, gender, race, and sexuality all have their foundation in moral as well as political positions. Eliding discussions of morality and ethics also leads to a presumption, rather than acknowledgment, of ethical principles at work in much film theory and criticism.

This project focuses on the capacity of screen stories to lead to one sort of understanding: *moral* understanding. From the standpoints of both rationalist and intuitionist accounts of moral learning, there is reason to hypothesize that screen stories can foster such learning. From the rationalist perspective, Lawrence Kohlberg claimed that the most morally advanced young people were those who had frequent opportunities to consider moral dilemmas from both their own and others' perspectives (Kohlberg, Levin, and Hewer 1983). From the intuitionist perspective of moral foundations theory, Haidt (2012) argues that morality develops from evolved intuitions that are elaborated within particular cultural contexts. From either standpoint, screen stories would seem to offer opportunities for learning from the moral dilemmas of fictional characters.

A large body of research in media psychology has investigated the extent to which screen characters are used as moral exemplars by viewers (Tamborini 2013; see Eden and Grizzard in this volume and Eden et al. 2020 for an overview of the theory and empirical evidence). A parallel line of research in psychology and literary studies has investigated the role of fictional narrative as an arena for moral simulation (Mar and Oatley 2008; Kidd and Castano 2013). Screen stories might be called "thought experiments" in which viewers consider the moral choices and outcomes faced by characters. As an example of this type of research, media psychologist Allison Eden tested the moral deliberation engaged in by viewers of a popular television drama and found that viewers used the character's emotions and judgments as a starting point for their own moral rumination and deliberation (Eden et al. 2017). Media may also lead to moral rumination by eliciting elevation in viewers (Oliver, Hartmann, and Woolley

2012; Oliver, this volume), which is related in its parameters to the emotion of admiration as it is discussed by Carroll in this volume.

Aesthetic cognitivism is not universally accepted as the right perspective on the arts. Some believe that the arts are to be valued chiefly for their own sake, or simply for the pleasure that they bring, independent of their cognitive benefits (Lamarque 2006). Or one might think that what the arts have to offer is not increased knowledge but merely commonplaces, propositions we already know (Stolniz 1992; Diffey 1995). And some, like Gregory Currie, are somewhat skeptical of the possibility that we learn from fiction (in this case, literary fiction), holding that fiction "has a happier, deeper, and more stable relation to imagination than it does to knowledge" and suggesting that those who say that fiction leads to learning sometimes "claim results without doing the hard work necessary to get them" (2020, 217–218).

The hypothesis that screen fiction may lead to moral understanding ought to be empirically tested. Currie, Heather Jane Ferguson, and Stacie Friend identify three "key knowledge gaps" in the scientific and humanities research on the cognitive benefits of literature (n.d.). First there exists little interaction between theoretical and empirical approaches. In this regard, the interdisciplinary interaction this book encourages suggests the right strategy. Second, they see insufficient attention to distinctions between fiction, literature, and narrative, suggesting a closer attention to conceptual clarification. Third, researchers need to decide what constitutes genuine learning, by which they mean cognitive and/or moral improvement. Again, conceptual clarity is key to designing effective measures for empirical work. Any empirical testing would require the clarity and specificity that such distinctions and fine-grained definitions would supply.

The Book's Organization

Moral Understanding

Moral understanding goes beyond moral deliberation or even moral knowledge. This first part of the book contains two chapters, the first developing a conception of moral understanding and the second describing a personalist approach to attaining it.

In Chapter 1, "Clarifying Moral Understanding," Nannicelli claims that moral understanding is a distinctive cognitive good, as he illustrates with a discussion of Carroll's notion of "clarification" in relation to moral persuasion. Clarification occurs when we refine what we already know by drawing new connections between elements of our moral knowledge or become better able to apply our moral knowledge to concrete situations. A screen narrative that increases the viewer's capacities in any of these areas, then, has the potential to increase moral understanding. And although nothing guarantees that increased understanding leads to changes in motivation and action, Nannicelli argues that understanding "exerts a kind of rational force that is action-motivating in a way that knowledge does not."

In Chapter 2, "Understanding (Mis)understanding: Sally Be a Lamb," Taylor argues for a personalist perspective on "ethical" understanding and identifies significant impediments that can block such understanding. He shows that the Sally Hemmings cameo in the filmed version of *Hamilton* (2020) exhibits a limited feeling for the female characters and an inability to see her rape by Jefferson as morally serious. Taylor advocates a self-critical turn in the ethical criticism of artworks. For the filmmaker, this is a duty to attend to the ethical dimension of her or his work. This attention soon turns to self-criticism, the goal being moral improvement. For both filmmakers and audiences, the quest for moral understanding "requires a strenuous regime of self-critique and self-correction, and the humility to accept that this discipline can always call our most cherished assumptions into question."

Transfer and Cultivation

The four chapters in Part II examine the means by which viewing screen stories can transfer beliefs or cultivate response patterns and sensitivities. "Transfer" refers to the capacity of narratives to inspire beliefs about the fictional world and then transfer those beliefs to the actual world. For example, a viewer might take the fictional character Ripley (Sigourney Weaver) of *Alien* (1979) or Clarice Starling (Jodie Foster) of *The Silence of the Lambs* (1992) as an exemplar of moral courage in her fictional world, thus forming the viewer's conception of actual moral courage. Or perhaps moral learning in some cases occurs in a less direct fashion, only after contemplating the morally ambiguous actions of Mookie (Spike Lee) in *Do the Right Thing* (1989) or Will Munny (Clint Eastwood) in *Unforgiven* (1992), neither of whom is meant as a clear exemplar of right action. Aside from such direct effects, much of the influence of stories on screens is gradually cultivated in ways we may not notice, through the repetition of common plot patterns, event structures, character behaviors, and character types.

In Chapter 3, "Phenomenal Experience and Moral Understanding: A Framework for Assessment," I consider the ways in which the visual and aural nature of motion picture representation may lead to moral understanding. I discuss four ways this might occur: (1) illustrative representation, (2) the simulation of looking and being looked at, (3) the phenomenal aspects of social cognition, and (4) audiovisual metaphors. In Chapter 4, "The Slow, Subtle, Small Effects of Filmic Narrative on Moral Understanding," Bilandzic considers the "slow, subtle, small" and long-term effects of filmic narrative on moral understanding. Bilandzic calls this "cultivation analysis." She defines moral cultivation as "the long-term, cumulative shaping of the audience's perceptions, expectations, and thinking about good and bad behavior." In Chapter 5, "Moral Conflict, Screen Stories, and Narrative Appeal," media psychologists Weber and Hopp posit that the moral conflict that undergirds all appealing storytelling leads to perspective-taking and mentalizing, and is thus an important catalyst for moral understanding. They discuss the Model of Intuitive Morality and Exemplars as supporting methods of evaluating moral conflicts in screen stories. In Chapter 6, "How Screen Stories Can Contribute to the Formation of Just Persons," philosopher Wolterstorff distinguishes between moral understanding, moral formation, and moral commitment, further claiming that any moral formation effected by screen stories is viewer-and-occasion-specific. One means through which moral formation could occur, he writes, is through *enhancement*, by which a film can assist us in imagining more vividly in such a way that the viewer can discern the moral significance of an action or scene.

Affect

Screen stories often elicit strong emotions and create powerful moods. The two chapters of Part III show how the affective nature of film viewing relates to moral understanding. In Chapter 7, "Affect and Moral Understanding," film and media scholar Sinnerbrink provides an overview of the relationship between affect and moral understanding in film. He also argues that the moral cognitive dissonance effect, by eliciting contradictory or ambiguous emotions and evaluations, can lead to enhanced moral understanding (as Weber and Hopp also imply in Chapter 5). Sinnerbrink illustrates this with an analysis of Michael Haneke's *Amour* (2012) and its remarkable and at times disturbing treatment of the ethics of euthanasia. In Chapter 8, "Morality and Media: The Role of Elevation/Inspiration," media psychologist Oliver describes "positive media psychology," which focuses on the prosocial functions of media. In this regard, one particular emotion that can be elicited by screen stories is *elevation*, which may arise when one witnesses unusual and striking acts of moral goodness. While noting the difficulties in finding clear empirical verification, Oliver suggests that research does imply that media-elicited emotions such as elevation are capable of leading to long-term changes in moral understanding in viewers.

Character Engagement

From a psychological perspective, one of the most remarkable features of narratives is their capacity to enact a kind of *parasocial relationship* between viewers and fictive characters. In his book on the subject, Smith has called this "character engagement" (1995). In Chapter 9, "Media Characters and Moral Understanding: Perspectives from Media Psychology," media psychologists Eden and Grizzard provide an overview of how character engagement in relation to moral understanding is conceived of in media psychology. They discuss numerous psychological processes involved in character engagement, but focus on viewers taking characters as moral exemplars. They claim that screen stories can become a kind of "moral laboratory," portraying dramatic conflicts with a clarity not seen in the actual world, with the potential to lead to moral rumination and change.

In Chapter 10, "Movies, Examples, and Morality: The Rhetoric of Admiration," Carroll argues that through the viewer's admiration for characters, fiction can engender moral learning. Carroll discusses admiration as an occurrent emotion; thus his chapter would also fit well into the preceding section on affect. Yet it has obvious connections to character engagement as well, as admiration for a fictional character is a form of engagement. Using the example of Jo (Saoirse Ronan) in *Little Women* (2019), Carroll shows that movies are *criterially prefocused* to elicit admiration for certain characters (see also Carroll 2003, 69–70) and that narratives often create *virtue wheels* whereby characters are explicitly designed to be compared and contrasted with one another vis-à-vis the human virtues. In this way, narratives are often explicitly designed to elicit moral rumination.

The Reflective Afterlife

If and when screen stories affect moral understanding, it would seem implausible to suggest that this would occur solely *during* the actual viewing of the work. If a film makes an impression on us, if it is being viewed in some sort of institutional context such as a university course or discussion group, or if it is seen with a group of friends, then you may reflect on it, discuss it, and perhaps learn from that reflection. Philosopher Peter Kivy (2006) calls this the "reflective afterlife" of a work. The final three chapters of this book examine this issue.

Harold, in Chapter 11, "Audiences' Role in Generating Moral Understanding?," reviews Jacqueline Bobo's (1993) study of Black women audience members' responses to the 1985 film *The Color Purple*. This is a case study in what bell hooks has called the "oppositional gaze," and shows that audiences can learn from morally flawed movies within various interpretative communities. Harold goes on to examine the implications of interpretative communities for moral rumination. Next comes Moss-Wellington, who in Chapter 12, "On Reflecting on Reflections: The Moral Afterlife and Screen Studies," considers the influence of one particular institution in encouraging moral reflection about screen stories: academia, and in particular academic scholarship. He considers film and screen media scholarship as one of these reflective institutions comprising an important component in the moral afterlife of screen stories, leading to moral rumination in classroom discussions, critical and hermeneutical writing, and the empirical study of our varied relationships with screen narratives. Smith's Chapter 13, "The Reflective Afterlife and the Ends of Imagining," ends the book with a discussion of the distinction between fiction and nonfiction in relation to the "mood-stance" approach. While the assertion of truths or propositions is often taken to be characteristic of nonfiction, and the invitation to the free play of the imagination with fiction, the boundaries between the two modes of narrative are actually quite porous. Nonfictions invite imaginative activity, and fictions have important connections to the actual world, sometimes inviting viewers to consider or even accept beliefs about the actual world. Smith suggests that in relation to moral understanding, one of the chief functions of fiction is to initiate the discovery of possibilities through imaginative exploration.

All of the chapters in this book address the relationship of screen stories to moral understanding in viewers. They do so, however, from varied academic traditions and often using distinct terminologies and methodologies. All agree that screen fictions can play a significant role in moral learning. The challenge at this point is not only to progress in determining how and when this occurs, but to do so through the synergies that may arise from cooperation between the disciplines and approaches. May the discussion continue.

Works Cited

Ang, Ian. 2013. "The Politics of Empirical Audience Research." In *The Media Studies Reader*, edited by Laurie Ouellete, 443–457. New York: Routledge.

Baumberger, Christoph. 2013. "Art and Understanding. In Defense of Aesthetic Cognitivism." In *Bilder sehen: Perspektiven der Bildwissenschaft*, edited by Marc Greenlee, Rainer Hammwöhner, Bernd Köber, Christoph Wagner, and Christian Wolff, 41–67. Regensburg: Schnell + Steiner.

Bobo, Jacqueline. 1993. "Reading through the Text: The Black Woman as Audience." In *Black American Cinema*, edited by Manthia Diawara, 272–287. New York: Routledge.

Bordwell, David, and Noël Carroll, eds. 1996. *Post-Theory: Reconstructing Film Studies*. Madison: University of Wisconsin Press.

Carroll, Noël. 1990. *The Philosophy of Horror*. New York: Routledge.

Carroll, Noël. 1996. *Theorizing the Moving Image*. Cambridge: Cambridge University Press.

Carroll, Noël. 1998a. "Morality and Aesthetics." In *Encyclopedia of Aesthetics*, vol. 3, edited by Michael Kelly, 278–282. New York: Oxford University Press.

Carroll, Noël. 1998b. *A Philosophy of Mass Art*. Oxford: Clarendon Press.

Carroll, Noël. 2002. "The Wheel of Virtue: Art, Literature, and Moral Knowledge." *Journal of Aesthetics and Art Criticism* 60, no. 1 (Winter): 3–26.

Carroll, Noël. 2003. *Engaging the Moving Image*. New Haven, CT: Yale University Press.

Cohen, Jonathan. 2001. "Defining Identification: A Theoretical Look at the Identification of Audiences with Media Characters." *Mass Communication & Society* 4, no. 3: 245–264.

Cohen, J., Mary Beth Oliver, and Arthur A. Raney. 2009. *Media and Social Life*. New York: Routledge.

Currie, Gregory. 2020. *Imagining and Knowing: The Shape of Fiction*. Oxford: Oxford University Press.

Currie, Gregory, Heather Jane Ferguson, and Stacie Friend. n.d. "Learning from Fiction: A Philosophical and Psychological Study." University of York. Accessed January 27, 2023. https://www.york.ac.uk/philosophy/research/theoretical-philosophy/aesthetics-art-literature/learning-from-fiction/.

Diffey, T. J. 1995. "What Can We Learn from Art?" *Australasian Journal of Philosophy* 73, no. 2: 204–211. https://doi.org/10.1080/00048409512346541.

Eden, Allison, Serena Daalmans, Merel Van Ommen, and Addy Weljers. 2017. "Melfi's Choice: Morally Conflicted Content Leads to Moral Rumination in Viewers." *Journal of Media Ethics* 32, no. 3: 142–153.

Eden, A. L., R. C. Tamborini, M. Aley, and H. Goble. 2020. "Advances in Research on the Model of Intuitive Morality and Exemplars (MIME)." In *The Oxford Handbook of Entertainment*

Theory, edited by A. L. Eden, R. C. Tamborini, M. Aley, and H. Goble, 231–249: Oxford: Oxford University Press.

Forman, Henry James. 1933. *Our Movie Made Children*. New York: Macmillan.

Freeland, Cynthia. 1997. "Art and Moral Knowledge." *Philosophical Topics* 25, no. 1: 11–36.

Gaut, Berys. 2007. *Art, Emotion, and Ethics*. Oxford: Oxford University Press.

Goodman, Nelson. 1978. *Ways of Worldmaking*. Indianapolis, IN: Hackett.

Graham, Gordon. 2005. *Philosophy of the Arts*. 3rd ed. London: Routledge.

Green, Melanie, Helena Bilandzic, Kaitlin Fitzgerald, and Elaine Paravati. 2020. *Media Effects: Advances in Theory and Research*. Edited by Mary Beth Oliver, Arthur A. Raney, and Jennings Bryant. New York: Routledge.

Haidt, Jonathan. 2012. *The Righteous Mind: Why Good People Are Divided by Politics and Religion*. New York: Pantheon Books.

Hills, Allison. 2010. *The Beloved Self: Morality and the Challenge of Egoism*. Oxford: Oxford University Press.

hooks, bell. 1996. *Reel to Real: Race, Sex, and Class at the Movies*. New York: Routledge.

Jowett, Garth. 1976. *Film: The Democratic Art*. Boston: Little, Brown.

Kidd, D. C., and E. Castano. 2013. "Reading Literary Fiction Improves Theory of Mind." *Science* 342: 377–380.

Kivy, Peter. 2006. *The Performance of Reading: An Essay in the Philosophy of Literature*. Malden, MA: Blackwell.

Kohlberg, L., C. Levine, and A. Hewer. 1983. *Moral Stages: A Current Formulation and Response to Critics*. Basel: Karger. doi:10.1159/isbn.978-3-318-03252-9.

Lamarque, P. 2006. "Cognitive Values in the Arts: Marking the Boundaries." In *Contemporary Debates in Aesthetics and the Philosophy of Art*, edited by M. Kieran, 127–139. Hoboken, NJ: Wiley-Blackwell.

Mar, Raymond A., and Keith Oatley. 2008. "The Function of Fiction Is the Abstraction and Simulation of Social Experience." *Perspectives on Psychological Science* 3, no. 3: n.p. https://doi.org/10.1111/j.1745-6924.2008.00073.x.

Mast, Gerald. 1982. *The Movies in Our Midst*. Chicago: University of Chicago Press.

Media and Morality. n.d. Accessed April 13, 2022. https://moralmedia.org/annual-meeting/.

Miller, J. Hillis. 1990. "Narrative." In *Critical Terms for Literary Study*, edited by Frank Lentricchia and Thomas McLaughlin, 66–79. Chicago: University of Chicago Press.

Moss-Wellington, Wyatt. 2021. *Cognitive Film and Media Ethics*. New York: Oxford University Press.

Moyer-Gusé, Emily. 2015. "Extending the Examination of Audience Involvement with Media Personae: Response to Brown." *Communication Theory* 25, no. 3: 284.

Murdoch, Iris. 1970. *The Sovereignty of Good*. London: Routledge.

Nannicelli, Ted, and Paul Taberham, eds. 2014. *Cognitive Media Theory*. New York: Routledge.

Nussbaum, Martha. 1990. *Love's Knowledge*. Oxford: Oxford University Press.

Oatley, Keith. 2011. *Such Stuff as Dreams: The Psychology of Fiction*. Oxford: Wiley-Blackwell.

Oliver, Mary Beth, Tilo Hartmann, and Julia K. Woolley. 2012. "Elevation in Response to Entertainment Portrayals of Moral Virtue." *Human Communication Research* 38: 360–378. doi:10.1111/j.1468-2958.2012.01427.x.

Plantinga, Carl. 2009. *Moving Viewers: American Film and the Spectator's Experience*. Berkeley: University of California Press.

Plantinga, Carl. 2013. "The Affective Power of Movies." In *Psychocinematics: Exploring Cognition at the Movies*, edited by Arthur P. Shimamura, 94–111. Oxford: Oxford University Press.

Plantinga, Carl. 2018. *Screen Stories: Emotion and the Ethics of Engagement*. Oxford: Oxford University Press.

Plantinga, Carl, and Greg M. Smith, eds. 1999. *Passionate Views: Film, Cognition, and Emotion.* Baltimore, MD: Johns Hopkins University Press.

Pribram, E. Deirdre. 2004. "Spectatorship and Subjectivity." In *A Companion to Film Theory,* edited by Toby Miller and Robert Stam, 146–164. Malden, MA: Blackwell.

Smith, Murray. 1995. *Engaging Characters: Fiction, Emotion, and the Cinema.* Oxford: Clarendon Press.

Smith, Murray. 2017. *Film, Art, and the Third Culture: A Naturalized Aesthetics of Film.* Oxford: Oxford University Press.

Stolniz, Jerome. 1992. "On the Cognitive Triviality of Art."

Tamborini, Ron, ed. 2013. *Media and the Moral Mind.* New York: Routledge.

Tooby, John, and Leda Cosmides. 2001. "Does Beauty Build Adapted Minds? Toward an Evolutionary Theory of Aesthetics, Fiction, and the Arts." *SubStance* 30, no. 1: 6–27.

Wollheim, Richard. 1987. *Painting as an Art.* London: Thames and Hudson.

Zunshine, Lisa. 2010. "Introduction: What Is Cognitive Cultural Studies?" In *Introduction to Cognitive Cultural Studies,* edited by Lisa Zunshine, 1–33. Baltimore, MD: Johns Hopkins University Press.

PART I
MORAL UNDERSTANDING

1
Clarifying Moral Understanding

Ted Nannicelli

Introduction

This project, *Screen Stories and Moral Understanding,* seeks to contribute to the development of one of the most influential versions of a view known as aesthetic cognitivism. Aesthetic cognitivism holds, roughly speaking, that at least part of an artwork's value *as an artwork* is some sort of cognitive value that it affords. This way of putting things combines two claims: that we can learn from art and that an artwork's capacity to engender learning is part of its value qua artwork. I have used the somewhat neutral terms "cognitive value" and "learning" here because aesthetic cognitivists disagree about how best to conceive of those concepts in more specific terms. Traditionally, aesthetic cognitivism was the view that art offered knowledge—and then further debates ensued about how to conceive of knowledge.

But the influential version of aesthetic cognitivism that has emerged in recent decades broadens its conception of cognitive value to include other sorts of cognitive goods. John Gibson helpfully describes this version of aesthetic cognitivism as "neo-cognitivism," which is "a motley of arguments that have in common only one thing: the denial that cognitive value is always a matter of truth and knowledge" (2008, 585). The cognitive good that has seemed the most promising in developing this line of inquiry, championed in different ways by various contemporary philosophers, is *understanding* (e.g., Nussbaum 1990; Elgin 1993, 2002; Baumberger 2013). And, as the *Screen Stories and Moral Understanding* project indicates, neo-cognitivism has seemed particularly illuminating and plausible in relationship to *moral* understanding in particular.

Upon examining the literature across a number of disciplines, however, one quickly finds that "moral understanding" is a contested concept, one that seems to mean different things to different people in distinct contexts. Thus, the aim of this chapter is to reinforce the foundation of the neo-cognitivist project by clarifying the concept of moral understanding and, moreover, defending an account of moral understanding that illuminates its particular value as a distinctive cognitive good.

Ted Nannicelli, *Clarifying Moral Understanding* In: *Screen Stories and Moral Understanding.* Edited by: Carl Plantinga, Oxford University Press. © Oxford University Press 2023. DOI: 10.1093/oso/9780197665664.003.0002

Moral Knowledge and Moral Understanding: An Initial Distinction

For a relatively brief illustration of the idea that moral understanding is plausibly a distinctive cognitive good with a particular value, consider the contrast between two accounts of moral transformation plausibly afforded by screen stories. Both accounts come from philosopher of art and film theorist Noël Carroll (1998a, 1998b). The first is called "clarificationism." Clarificationism is, roughly speaking, the idea that artworks like screen stories (and from here I shall just refer to "screen stories") afford moral learning not necessarily by conferring new moral knowledge but by clarifying and enhancing moral knowledge that we already possess. In his original statement of the position, Carroll writes, "Clarificationism does not claim that, in the typical case, we acquire new propositional knowledge from artworks, but rather that the artworks in question can deepen our *moral understanding* by, among other things, encouraging us to apply our moral knowledge and emotions to specific cases"[1] (1998b, 326, my italics).

The second account of moral change offered by Carroll might be described as "moral persuasion." By moral persuasion, I mean the process of inducing someone to believe a moral proposition (whether true or false). In a 2013 paper, "Moral Change: Fiction, Film, and Family," Carroll expands upon one of his original examples, *Philadelphia* (1993), with a greater emphasis on the psychological processes that underpin our ability to grasp the film's moral argument. And because the emotions are centrally involved in the psychological process Carroll describes, he offers a more robust account of them and their process of moral learning. In his words, "*Uncle Tom's Cabin* [which is his other primary example in the paper] and *Philadelphia* appear to succeed in recalibrating moral attitudes towards certain abominated groups by recalibrating representatives of those groups in terms of paradigm scenarios regarding the family. In this, they show how moral change is possible in popular fictions, by building on moral sentiments that are already firmly in place" (54).

So far, so familiar. But then Carroll concludes with a passage that displays an interesting difference from his earlier account: "I have proposed that one way in which moral change can be engineered in movies and other popular fictions is to emotively recalibrate the targets of the desired moral sentiments in terms of antecedently positive paradigm scenarios—ones already in the audience's ethico-emotive repertoire. In such cases, where the audience comes to an issue with a bias (such as racism or homophobia), the fiction writers and movie makers will attempt to outweigh that bias with an even more entrenched one" (2013, 54).

The moral change Carroll describes as being offered by *Philadelphia* might be characterized as involving the acquisition of moral knowledge (i.e., the true belief that people with AIDS and/or gay men are not fitting objects of moral abomination). And yet something about the audience's route to this knowledge might—indeed, I think *should*—strike us as lacking in an important way. For one thing, it seems as if, in this case, the audience is led to have the right moral view but remains ignorant of *why* the view is right. In other words, although the film may successfully persuade the audience that people with AIDS or gay men are unfitting objects of moral disgust, it does so, in Carroll's terms, by replacing one bias with another. That is, the film does not facilitate the audience's appreciation of the reasons *why* people with AIDS or gay men are not appropriate objects of moral disgust; it persuades the audience that they are morally considerable because they have families just like the (target) audience.

But evidently people with AIDS and gay men are morally considerable whether or not they have the sort of familiar, loving family that Andrew Beckett (Tom Hanks) has in *Philadelphia*. They are morally considerable because they are human beings, no less deserving of moral respect than any other human beings. Yet this is not something that the film, on Carroll's account of it, at least, is designed to help them understand. Carroll is careful to describe the moral persuasion abetted by *Philadelphia* as "*one way* in which moral change can be engineered in movies" (2013, 54, my italics). On his view, screen stories can facilitate moral change in various ways: clarificationism is one, and moral persuasion is another.[2] Yet the contrast between these two processes is useful because it offers us an initial grip on the *value* of moral understanding as an epistemic good and on the particular value of screen stories that facilitate moral understanding as distinct from those that merely yield moral knowledge via moral persuasion.

One initial point of distinction is that moral persuasion, as Carroll points out, can be used for good or for ill purposes. Although Carroll offers a case in which moral persuasion yields moral knowledge, he rightly acknowledges that moral persuasion can also lead to morally odious and/or false views (think *Triumph of the Will* [1935]). Clarificationism seems unlike moral persuasion in part because it is plausible that moral understanding involves not only beliefs but *true* beliefs—that it is "factive" (Hills 2009; but see Elgin 2007 for a contrasting view). If moral understanding is indeed factive, then it is easy to see how screen stories that facilitate it differ in epistemic value from screen stories that morally persuade. Of course, moral persuasion *can* yield moral knowledge, but it need not do so as a matter of necessity.

So I am not claiming that the sort of moral persuasion afforded by *Philadelphia* is of no epistemic or moral merit, for it certainly is, if it does, in fact, induce viewers to adopt the true belief that gay people and people with AIDS have the same moral standing as anyone else. But if moral understanding is factive, then clarificationism offers a more epistemically reliable route to moral knowledge than moral persuasion does. To be clear, this is *not* the view, from which I should distance myself, that artworks which aim at moral persuasion are less epistemically valuable because they manipulate the audience's emotions rather than spur the audience's capacity for reasoning. (On the contrary, there are good reasons to think that the emotions can yield epistemic gains *including* understanding [see esp. Elgin 2008], and persuasion typically involves higher-level reasoning as well as the emotions.) The issue, rather, concerns the reliability of the routes to true belief.

Yet, as I suggested above, moral understanding seems to involve more than true belief—more than moral knowledge. If, for the same reason that in the *Philadelphia* case moral understanding is of greater epistemic value than moral knowledge, screen stories which facilitate moral understanding generally have a distinctive epistemic value, then the question is whether those which merely yield moral knowledge do not. So what *is* the particular epistemic value of moral understanding—if there is one?

The Intrinsic Value of Moral Understanding

As I indicated, one initial explanation of why moral understanding might be of greater epistemic value than propositional moral knowledge starts with the observation that, in some cases, understanding involves not only knowledge of a (true) proposition but also grasping the reason why the proposition is true. This idea is developed by Alison Hills, among others (in a different direction by Grimm 2010), who takes this "grasp" of the reasons why to be characteristic of understanding and its value. As she puts it, "when you grasp a relationship between two propositions, you have that relationship under your control. You can manipulate it. You have a set of abilities or know-how relevant to it, which you can exercise if you choose" (2016, 663). One of the upshots of having this set of abilities, which Hills calls "cognitive control," is that one can think about the propositions and their relationship modally. To put it in the terms of the *Philadelphia* example, if one understands the reason why gay men and people with AIDS are not the fitting objects of moral disgust, one will also know that gay men and people with AIDS who do not have the sort of loving families that Andrew Beckett does have the same moral standing as those who do. One will also know, presumably, that gay women are not the fitting objects of moral disgust. One might even come to know, on this basis, that a person's sexual orientation never warrants moral disgust.

If something like this is right, then understanding looks like it might have a distinctive epistemic value in virtue of being a kind of cognitive achievement—and, indeed, might have an additional instrumental value if the sorts of abilities it involves increase the likelihood of one *acting* in the right sort of way. Let me first say something about understanding as a cognitive achievement and how screen stories might facilitate that sort of achievement. It is important to see that there is a close connection between the abilities account of understanding advanced by Hills and the account of the value of understanding in terms of achievement. As Duncan Pritchard succinctly puts it, "Achievements are … successes that are because of ability; that is, where the success in question is primarily creditable to the agent's exercise of the relevant ability" (2014, 318).

What sort or sorts of ability are constitutive of or necessary for understanding? There's no reason to commit to a particular account in this context, though it will be useful to sketch one (plausible) possibility as a reference point. Michael Patrick Lynch, for example, suggests that understanding might be characterized in this way: "A state of some agent plays the understanding-role with regard to some subject when its content concerns dependency relations between propositions or states of affairs relevant to the subject; it is conducive of the agent's ability to offer justified explanations of the relevant subject; and it disposes the agent to make further justified inferences both factual and counterfactual about the subject" (2017, 1999). Usefully, Lynch's account leaves open the details about the psychology of understanding—a topic that we don't need to broach here—yet it identifies understanding with the sorts of abilities that point toward an explanation of its value.

An abilities account of understanding bears a number of similarities to knowing-how. Once again, there are complexities here that are best avoided for the present purpose—namely, the debate about whether understanding is a kind of knowledge, whether knowing-how reduces to propositional knowledge or knowledge-that, and so forth. Complexities aside, understanding seems similar to knowing-how in the sense that both are gradable (admitting of degrees), related to the possession of abilities, and plausibly thought of as particular sorts of achievements. For both understanding and knowing-how, there is plausibly a (context-dependent) threshold for understanding or knowing-how to obtain at all. Beyond that, however, it would seem that one can have anything from minimal understanding or know-how of a subject through to expert understanding or expert know-how of a subject.

And this connects with the idea that understanding and know-how both essentially involve abilities. Understanding or know-how in one domain may require relatively little cognitive effort and may happen quite quickly in a way that an agent does not even consciously apprehend. Nevertheless, some have argued that in many such cases, understanding occurs quickly and easily precisely because the agent is "bringing to bear significant cognitive ability" on the subject at hand (Pritchard 2010, 83). At the other end of the spectrum, it might take years of study and practice for one to understand another language well enough not just to speak fluently but to make jokes, perceive irony, and the like. So, too, with quantum mechanics and various other specific fields of study. In the more cognitively challenging sorts of cases, understanding is dependent upon a temporally extended process that requires an agent's commitment, effort, and, interestingly, possibly even fairly settled dispositions or character traits. Leave that latter idea—about character traits—to the side for a moment.

A number of authors underscore the temporal dimension and cognitive effort often involved in attaining understanding. Stephen R. Grimm, for example, observes that in some cases "understanding is a process that stretches out over time and involves *inquiry*" (2019, 343). Likewise, Pritchard notes that "typically, after all, one gains understanding by undertaking an obstacle-overcoming effort to piece together the relevant pieces of information." The often temporally extended cognitive effort required to gain understanding is another reason to think of understanding as a kind of cognitive achievement, not radically different from the way in which coming to know how to read music constitutes a kind of cognitive achievement (2010, 82–83).

From the premise that understanding is a kind of achievement and the additional premise that achievements are intrinsically (or, if one prefers, finally) valuable, it follows that understanding has final value in virtue of being a particular kind of achievement. This seems like a plausible enough argument, although a full defense of it would require me to say more in support of the second premise (see Pritchard 2010). Rather than doing so, however, I want to shift focus to the question of whether understanding is instrumentally valuable and, if so, how. But before moving on, I want to flag a potential challenge for the prospect of screen stories yielding moral understanding in relation to conceiving of understanding as involving cognitive effort and its value in terms of cognitive achievement.

It's natural to think that the amount of cognitive effort deployed by an agent in the pursuit of understanding is at least partly constitutive of the value of achieving it. There are exceptions, of course. For example, my impatience with formal logic means I have to deploy more cognitive effort to follow any of it, but it doesn't follow that my impatience would thereby make my attainment of understanding formal logic a pro tanto more valuable achievement. So I'm not sure we should even say that cognitive effort and cognitive achievement have a directly proportional relationship. But there will be many cases in which the value of a cognitive achievement is increased in proportion to the amount of cognitive effort an agent needs to deploy.

The challenge is this: screen stories themselves tend to have a fairly short duration. They almost never require, and tend not to promote, the sort of temporally extended process of inquiry or overcoming of obstacles that seem to be partly constitutive of the particular cognitive achievement of understanding. On the contrary, if they afford the sort of moral understanding that, say, Carroll hypothesizes in relation to *A Raisin in the Sun* (1961)—as fostering "recognition that African Americans are persons, like any others, and therefore, should be accorded the kind of equal treatment for persons that such audiences already endorse as a matter of principle" (1998b, 326)—one might worry that, given the relative lack of cognitive effort involved in such a case, the sort of understanding screen stories might afford is rather cheaply bought—that it isn't particularly valuable.[3] There are a few ways one could respond to this challenge. One, of which I am skeptical for reasons described below, is to appeal to the phenomenology of understanding—that is, to point to various contexts in which people experience an "Aha!" moment of "getting it" that *feels* valuable.

A preferable response, which meshes well with the view toward which I work later in the chapter, would be to deny the assumption on which the objection is based—namely, that if audiences grasp the moral understanding offered by screen stories, they do so during or immediately upon the conclusion of a single viewing. On the contrary, a screen story may be valuable insofar as an initial viewing of it may spark an idea, a question, a challenge that a viewer wrestles with during what Peter Kivy calls "the afterlife" of (an aesthetic appreciation of) the film before returning to it again, perhaps a third or fourth time, noticing new details or reinterpreting aspects of the film in a way that is very much in line with a conception of understanding as a temporally extended process of inquiry (1997, 131–134). Of course, this response entails that the moral understanding yielded by screen stories depends on a number of contingent variables. For one thing, it might be that relatively few screen stories offer the challenge or prompt the sort of sustained reflection that seems necessary for understanding to obtain; indeed, this is another reason to think about films of moral persuasion, like *Philadelphia*, as operating rather differently and yielding different, arguably lesser cognitive rewards. For another, only certain viewers will be disposed to take up the challenges offered by screen stories in committed, reflective ways that eventually yield understanding. More on this presently.

The Instrumental Value of Moral Understanding

However, rather than developing a more extensive reply to this potential objection, which I believe can be overcome, I would like now to focus on the other sort of value that understanding might possess, which is instrumental. This is in part because the instrumental value of understanding is less often discussed, perhaps because it seems harder to know how it would be manifested in identifiable, observable ways. I want to develop the idea that the value of moral understanding afforded by screen stories stems from its connection to action. There's a quick and easy way to run this sort of argument, which I want to sketch even though I don't want to commit to it.

Roughly speaking, the argument would begin with the premise that screen stories do, at least sometimes, yield moral understanding. Moral understanding, we saw, necessarily involves (true) beliefs. The next premise, which does the heavy lifting, is controversial: it is the claim that moral judgments and/or beliefs necessarily involve a motivation to act in accordance with them. As Thomas Nagel puts it, "On this view the motivation must be so tied to the truth, or meaning, of ethical statements that when in a particular case someone is (or perhaps merely believes that he is) morally required to do something, it follows that he has a motivation for doing it" (1970, 7). If this claim, known as "motivational internalism," is true, then it follows that, since screen stories can impart or change our moral beliefs, they also motivate us morally.[4] Thus, we could conclude that the moral understanding is instrumentally valuable insofar as it motivates us morally (to do the right thing, for the right reasons—as I explain below), and in turn, screen stories which yield moral understanding are instrumentally valuable because they are the source of the moral understanding that motivates us morally.

However, motivational internalism faces a number of well-known objections—most notably, with regard to the existence of agents who are apparently simply *not* motivated by moral judgments or beliefs because they are amoral, listless or depressed, and the like (e.g., Brink 1986; Svavarsdóttir 1999; Mele 2003, esp. ch. 5; Miller 2008). The debate between "internalists" and "externalists" is a complex one that I cannot review here. I am happy to acknowledge, as externalists urge, that moral motivation is defeasible, and will say a bit more about this presently. The important point for now is just that the argument I am going to advance does not depend for its success on the truth of internalism (even though it is hospitable to moderate versions of it) and is indeed compatible with some forms of externalism (e.g., Shafer-Landau 2003).

Recall that, according to the abilities account, understanding essentially involves particular cognitive abilities, including the ability to successfully give causal explanations, draw inferences, and reason counterfactually about a particular subject. In most contexts, I think, we simply assume, for good reason, that understanding in a certain domain facilitates action in that domain. If, for example, you have a rough understanding of why climate change is happening and what its implications are, it's likely that you act on that understanding, at least sometimes, in at least some aspects of your life. Maybe you use a refillable coffee cup or pack your lunch in a washable container. Maybe you use only public transportation or divest your stock portfolio of fossil fuel companies. What you do will be constrained by various environmental and psychological factors, but it would be very odd if your understanding in this domain had no bearing at all on your actions—or, perhaps more precisely, if it did not even motivate you to act in accordance with it.[5]

One might press this idea further: if you didn't act at *all* in accordance with your understanding, it would seem that your understanding must be very minimal and of relatively little value.[6] The value of understanding the causes and implications of climate change is surely that such understanding will, everything else being equal, tend to manifest itself in action. Talbot Brewer offers a more general statement of this idea: "The real value of understanding seems to lie in the running actualization of that understanding itself, both in one's own life and in the lives of others" (2009, 308). Phrased another way, "understanding *qua* potentiality is valuable because of the intrinsic value of the activities in which it is expressed or actualized" (309). The phrase "understanding *qua* potentiality" points to the fact that what's valuable about understanding is not merely the cognitive achievement of acquiring the abilities that are constitutive of it, but furthermore deploying those abilities.

Shifting focus to the domain of moral understanding, we see a very similar argument in Hills's work. According to Hills, moral understanding is valuable as a means to "reliably doing right," "justifying yourself to others," "virtue," and "morally worthy action" (2009). Let's focus on the first and last of these elements for now. One might, Hills acknowledges, do the morally right thing pretty consistently solely on the basis of, say, moral intuitions or reliable moral testimony. But moral intuitions can lead us astray, and sometimes we find ourselves in situations where we need to act without consulting the testimony of moral experts. For these reasons, Hills claims that moral understanding will more reliably lead us to do right. Hills also notes, with reference to Kant's shopkeeper example, that one can do the right thing for the wrong reasons. If you are a shopkeeper who gives customers the correct change only because your reputation depends on it, you do the right thing yet do not act morally since your action is motivated by self-interest. In contrast, if you give customers the correct change because you are motivated by fairness and respect, you act morally insofar as you do the right thing for the right reasons. The important connection to understanding is that insofar as moral understanding involves a grasp of the reasons why an action is right, it enables one to not only do the right thing but to do the right thing for the right reasons—in Hills's terms, "to perform morally worthy actions"[7] (2009, 113).

Moreover, as I suggested, it would be very odd if one's understanding, including moral understanding, had no motivational force whatsoever. This may sound like a return to motivational internalism, but I think there is an important difference. According to a prominent version of motivational internalism, it is the *moral* part of moral beliefs (or moral judgments) that does the heavy lifting.[8] So, on a strong version of the thesis, one is *always* motivated by moral considerations. In contrast, the view I am sketching here suggests that *understanding* itself (cognitive considerations) motivates in a way that is defeasible. Without wading into the broader debates, we might simply say that this is somehow a feature of our rationality.[9] If one understands the reasons why, say, using ethnic slurs is morally wrong, then there's considerable rational pressure on one not to use ethnic slurs. In contrast, the mere *knowledge* that using ethnic slurs is wrong seems not to exert the same rational force on people or, perhaps, simply doesn't motivate action in the same way in part because it does not essentially involve the sorts of *abilities* that understanding does.

So, on the abilities account of understanding that I have outlined here, understanding plausibly has intrinsic value as a cognitive achievement and instrumental value as a prompt for action. The particular instrumental value of moral understanding derives from the fact that it has the potential to motivate us—at least under certain conditions—not only to (reliably) do the right thing but to do the right thing for the right reasons.

Screen Stories and the Cultivation of Moral Understanding

What, then, does this account of moral understanding and its value lend to our particular concern with screen stories' cultivation of moral understanding? A few things. For one, it may help us address certain challenges to aesthetic cognitivism. A concern about the lack of empirical evidence in support of aesthetic cognitivism has recently been forcefully expressed by Gregory Currie, who points out that "claims about the educative value of narrative are ... essentially claims about the effects of literature on human beings in certain circumstances" (2020, 97). Such claims are empirical and, as such, stand in need of supporting evidence. As he puts it in a pithy sentence, "You can rationally believe that we learn from fictions only if you believe there is evidence that someone has learned from some fiction" (98). If one accepts the general thrust of this challenge, as I think one ought to, then what sort of response is possible on the part of humanists, who cannot themselves carry out the sorts of experiments that might yield empirical evidence—indeed, who might even have worries about what sort of evidence such experiments could even provide?

Clearly, there are some replies that won't meet Currie's challenge on the terms it sets. One of them is introspection or self-report. There's no doubt in *my* mind that my epistemic standing improved—that I came to a better understanding of racism in America—by watching *Do the Right Thing* (1989). But introspection is notoriously unreliable when it comes to such matters, and furthermore, I am hardly in an ideal position to judge whether or not my understanding has improved when the subject matter is something I didn't understand very well to begin with. More generally, there are good reasons to think that understanding is not *transparent*—that it does not have a special "reflective accessibility" (Grimm 2016, 212) which allows us to know, via introspection, whether we truly understand something (Hazlett 2017; Trout 2017). This is because it is more or less obvious that there are all sorts of contexts in which we think we understand things and turn out to be wrong. In any case, one surely ought to avoid being the sort of aesthetic cognitivist who "suggest[s] that their own manifestly civilized values and demeanor are evidence enough for the claim" (Currie 2020, 5).

But if understanding is construed in the right sort of way, we should be able to avoid falling back on claims about reflective accessibility and offer some empirical evidence. Here it is important to see the costs and benefits of glossing aesthetic cognitivism as a thesis about moral understanding rather than moral knowledge. We have already seen that the acquisition of understanding is, in various ways, more demanding than the acquisition of knowledge. In this sense, Currie (2020, 91) is right to point out that "introducing understanding into the picture makes the task of someone who wants to articulate a persuasive picture of learning from literature harder, not easier" (2020, 91).

In another sense, however, running the aesthetic cognitivist argument in terms of understanding does make the job easier. This is because, as I claimed, understanding exerts a kind of rational force that is action-motivating in a way that knowledge does not—or, perhaps, does to a lesser extent. If that's right, the benefit of moral understanding is that it allows us at least to say what sort of empirical evidence is available to the aesthetic cognitivist in contexts when understanding motivates in a way that issues in action: the evidence just is the actions undertaken by those people who have putatively gained understanding from screen stories. Of course, the practical job of collecting such evidence is a complex and difficult matter. But it is important to see that the point of my argument here is to shift Currie's challenge from a conceptual one to a practical one.

Objections and Replies

Practical challenges aside, I want dwell a bit more on the potential problem that, in some cases, moral motivation is defeasible. Let me offer a few personal examples. There is a shot in the film *Loveless* (Zvyagintsev, 2017), that nearly brings me to tears every time I see it. The parents of 12-year-old Alyosha are heading toward a divorce and hold nothing back when they fight. The setup for this particular shot is one such fight that occurs after Alyosha's father, Boris, has arrived home from work late at night. Boris finds his wife, Zhenya, on the couch of the lounge, and asks her if she has given the prospect of divorce more consideration. Ostensibly, Boris is worried about how the divorce will affect Alyosha. "You're the mother," he says. Zhenya looks up from her phone long enough to sip her wine. "I'm so sick of you," she replies. "At his age, he needs his father more . . . although maybe not one like you." They then proceed to bicker over who will have to care for Alyosha: Zhenya suggests boarding school, Boris suggests Zhenya's mother's house. Both are having affairs and neither wants responsibility for Alyosha. The topic shifts: who will be responsible for telling Alyosha about the divorce? They can't even agree on that. "Why not wake him up right now?" Zhenya asks. "I've fucking had it with you," Boris hisses. "Scumbag," Zhenya retorts, as she walks to the bathroom. The camera stays with Boris long enough for us to see him trying to guess the passcode on Zhenya's phone. Then it cuts to her in the bathroom. It pans with her as she heads back to the lounge, but hangs back so that as Zhenya closes the door behind her, we see that Alyosha has been hiding behind the door and heard the whole conversation.

Despite my earlier acknowledgment that understanding is not transparent, I at least *think* that this moment has thrown into sharp relief for me how harmful the witnessing of such parental fights can be for children. My own situation is not actually very close to that of Boris, but I'm quite sure that my children have overheard my wife and me saying things to each other that are very close to what Boris and Zhenya say to each other. In this way, I have felt that my moral understanding of the reasons why it is wrong to fight like this with children in earshot has been clarified, in Carroll's sense, and I have at least resolved to do better. And yet that resolve has not prevented verbal sparring from occurring in my home. So it may be the case that I don't really understand the reasons why such behavior is morally wrong, but if I do, then it seems like we have a case in which understanding does not motivate action in the way that I've claimed.

Here is another example in the same vein: *The Tree of Life* (2011) devotes quite a bit of detailed attention to the relationship between a father, a mother, and their sons. The father clearly loves his family. When his children are born, he is in awe, and their first years are filled with happiness and wonder. But as the children grow up, things change. It is hard to say exactly why. In some sense, the father wants his children to grow up faster than they can. "It takes fierce will to get ahead in this world," he tells them. Of their eldest boy, the mother tells the father, "He's afraid of you. You expect things of him that only an adult could accomplish." The father is easily irritated with the children, taunts and bullies them, and sometimes blows up in fits of rage. In part, this seems to be a symptom of a more general frustration—a frustration with his lot in life and a sadness about not reaching his potential as a person. The father seems to recognize, at times, that he is poisoning his relationship with his children, and yet he seems unable to change his behavior toward them. What moments of joy remain in the children's lives occur when their father is away, but even then, the eldest son struggles with feelings of resentment and bitterness toward his father, feelings that haunt him into adulthood.

With the caveat that understanding is not transparent, I at least think *The Tree of Life* has helped me to understand the way a father's interactions with his children can slowly tear at the fabric of their relationship and even scar them for life. Of course, I already knew that the behavior of physically abusive fathers did this and is morally wrong because of it (and for other reasons). But the particularity of the father and his children in *The Tree of Life*—the emphasis on his love for his sons, the depiction of how their relationship changed over time, the examination of the lingering effects of his demands and bullying behavior—threw into sharp relief for me the various sorts of harms that fathers can inflict on their sons and clarified for me the moral responsibility fathers have to overcome their own frustrations and disappointments so their sons can flourish.

Or so I think. I hope I am a better father than the Brad Pitt character, but much of that character's interactions with his sons resonates with me. The aforementioned scenes from the film remind me of specific moments of my own life. Certainly, I have been told by my own wife that my children are afraid of me and that my expectations of them are too high. And yet I struggle to modulate my behavior as it would seem I should if I have truly gleaned the moral understanding offered by the film. So have I not understood after all, or is moral understanding not as tightly connected with action as I have made out?

For the sake of argument, suppose that I really did gain the moral understanding I think I gained from *Loveless* and *The Tree of Life*. If I did, then the challenge is to defend the connection between understanding and action that I have posited. More generally, the challenge is to articulate the conditions under which audiences might actually come to grasp the moral understanding offered by a particular screen story. Can we say anything general about the sorts of conditions that need to obtain for audiences to gain moral understanding from a film, irrespective of the various ways in which they might be different?

I think the best response here is to insist on the plausibility of the general picture of the *normative* relationship between moral understanding, motivation, and action, while acknowledging that, as a matter of fact, whether moral understanding plays the action-guiding role I've claimed for it will, in any particular context, depend upon a number of contingent variables.[10] I have already mentioned the significance of rationality. Let me now add, as another important variable, character traits and, perhaps, virtues. I follow a widely held view of character traits that understands them to be, roughly speaking, dispositions. More specifically, I think of a character trait in terms outlined by Christian B. Miller as "a disposition to form beliefs and/or desires of a certain sort and (in many cases) to act in a certain way, when in conditions relevant to that disposition" (2013, 6). And, like Miller, I think of moral virtues as particular sorts of character traits: "those good traits of character which are such that, other things being equal ... directly lead to action (whether mentally or bodily) ... that is (typically) a good action and is performed for the appropriate reasons" (24). The distinction between character traits and moral virtues is important both because not all character traits are moral virtues (or moral vices) and because on at least some well-substantiated views, including Miller's, many people commonly have character traits but relatively few people possess virtues.[11]

Assuming something like this account of character traits is correct, there are a number of ways in which character traits and moral understanding interact. First, as I suggested above, it may be the case that even if moral understanding is motivational, it may not lead to action if one does not already have the character traits that would dispose one to act in relevant conditions. Thus, my response to the potential challenge raised by *Loveless* and *The Tree of Life* would be to say that the moral understanding those films afforded me did not lead (has not yet led?) to action on my part because I don't possess the character traits that are necessary to supplement the motivational component of moral understanding. Moreover, it may be the case that someone who lacks relevant character traits—say, sensitivity, compassion, perceptiveness—simply cannot grasp the moral understanding offered by a screen story.

More positively, the attainment of moral understanding in some domain might be thought of as a potential stimulus event or stimulus condition that can trigger one's disposition to be sensitive, perceptive, or compassionate, thus leading to action (Miller 2014, 20–21). Furthermore, it may be the case, as Hills argues, that moral understanding abets the development of good character or virtue. Central to her view is the concept of orientation—a "responsiveness to moral reasons" (2009, 112). According to Hills, "Without moral understanding, you cannot be properly oriented with regard to your moral beliefs: moral understanding is the cognitive, intellectual aspect of correct orientation to moral reasons, and as such it is an essential part of good character" (112).

In light of these considerations, we might think of moral understanding and character traits (that are morally good even if they do not reach the threshold for virtues) as existing in a feedback loop. One needs certain character traits to be in a position to glean moral understanding, yet moral understanding is also essential to the development of good character. One might worry that this is circular. On the contrary, it simply means that moral understanding and character are mutually developed. As Carroll emphasizes in his chapter in this volume, the start of one's moral development plausibly involves a reliance on exemplars and a process of habituation. It may be that one has very little moral understanding as one's character is initially developed via these mechanisms. But at a certain point, one will have the character traits needed to attain at least *some* moral understanding in *some* domain. And then the understanding one does possess feeds into the further development of good character (i.e., a variety of good character traits), perhaps eventually into the development of virtue (see Annas 2011). It is also worth noting, in support of this idea of a feedback loop constituted by moral understanding and character traits, that the two are similar in an important way: they are motivational. Moreover, if a character trait meets the threshold for a virtue, there is an additional connection: moral understanding and virtues are both plausibly thought of as kinds of skills that are often deployed in action (Annas 2011).

What role, then, do screen stories play in this general picture? Following Aristotle, we might emphasize habituation since the development of character or virtue is a process that extends over time. In this sense, it is like moral understanding. We should therefore not expect too much of screen stories. We should acknowledge, as Carroll puts it, that "they are only one force among many converging forces in the process of moral transformation," and that this process will likely involve addressing morally blameworthy views "more than once and along multiple, redundant channels of communication and feeling" (2013, 55). It is important therefore to think of the reflective afterlife of a screen story partly as disposing one to, or issuing in, or involving a *return* to the screen story in a way that facilitates the temporally extended processes of moral understanding and character development.

Conclusion

In closing, I'd like to briefly suggest two potential implications for further work on this topic. First, there is an implication for how we ought to think about the contribution of close analysis of screen stories. There is one sense in which scholars like Currie are right to be wary of inferring the moral understanding a screen story affords via a close analysis of it—not only because of complexities around meaning and interpretation but because the notion of a screen story affording moral understanding needs to be qualified in all the ways suggested above. In particular, it seems right and important to acknowledge that a single encounter with a screen story is fairly unlikely to issue in a particularly rich or valuable moral understanding because that's not how moral understanding is acquired. But perhaps the conclusion to be drawn is not that close analysis is irrelevant. Rather, it might be the case that close analysis illuminates the aspects of a screen story to which we *should* attend, over several viewings, in the sense that it might offer us moral insight or improve our moral understanding.

Second, there is another possibility for responding to Currie's challenge to produce evidence that screen stories do yield moral understanding or moral improvement. Earlier I said that if the focus is moral understanding, we can at least tell the skeptic where the evidence will be in a general sense—i.e., in action. But given the temporally extended nature of moral understanding and its complex interaction with the development of moral character in general, it seems unreasonable to expect that the aesthetic cognitivist should be able to point to a specific action on the part of a viewer in the wake of a screening or expect that an experiment could be designed that offers evidence of a causal link between the viewing of a screen story and a morally relevant action on the part of the viewer. For although a viewing of a screen story may have a causal impact on one's moral understanding or character, which in turn leads to action, the impact is likely to be processional or cumulative, developed over several screenings at different points in the development of one's moral character.[12] Indeed, there seem to be numerous possibilities for distal or diffuse causal connections between a screen story and moral understanding if we accept that sometimes even a single image or line of dialogue (let alone full viewing) might spark many more hours' worth of reflection and conversation. To borrow a phrase from Carroll, this is another aspect of "the power of movies" and their place in our moral lives that we have only begun to understand.

Notes

1. Actually, Carroll first presented the argument slightly earlier in an essay titled "Art, Narrative, and Moral Understanding" (1998a), a book chapter that was subsequently published as a chapter in his *A Philosophy of Mass Art* (1998b). I'm working with the latter source both because Carroll shifts his focus to mass art, including screen stories, and because it gives him more space to expand his argument.

2. I'm grateful to Carroll for elaborating his view for me in oral comments and in personal communication.

3. It is worth mentioning that Carroll's description of moral understanding lines up rather neatly with my earlier discussion about what *Philadelphia* would have needed to do to facilitate moral understanding rather than to merely persuade.

4. Here I am assuming that a cognitive state like a belief is sufficient for motivation in at least some contexts. There is a somewhat technical debate in the literature about whether a belief alone is sufficient to motivate or if it needs to be supplemented by an additional conatative state like a desire. The view that it does—known as the Humean view of motivation—is logically distinct from motivational internalism. As will become clearer in a paragraph or so, I don't accept the Humean view.

5. It is in this way that I depart from the Humean view of motivation. I take it that cognitive states like belief and understanding "may motivate in virtue of [their] own nature and content" (Shafer-Landau 2003, 147), and I would point the reader to Shafer-Landau for a defense since I don't have the space to mount one here.

6. Or that you were irrational—a possibility taken up by Smith (1994) in the context of his defense of motivational internalism.

7. Hills notes that one need not be a Kantian to accept the thrust of the idea of acting for the right reasons. If one prefers, one could think about this idea in Aristotelian terms—e.g., "acting from virtue." See, e.g., Audi (1995).

8. For example, Jesse Prinz (2015, 70) offers an elegant argument for motivational internalism that appeals to the distinctively *moral* nature of moral judgments: "1. Moral judgments consist of emotional attitudes; 2. Emotional attitudes are motivating; 3. Therefore, moral judgments are motivating."

9. See Smith (1994) on the significance of practical rationality to the motivational force of moral judgments.

10. This is Smith's (1994, 1995) strategy for defending motivational internalism. Nevertheless, it seems compatible with various moderate versions of motivational externalism (e.g., Shafer-Landau 2003), and nothing of significance depends, in this context, on adopting one of these labels for the view I describe. See the discussion, to which I am indebted, in Rosati (2016).

11. Perhaps needless to say, there is not enough space to address the "situationist critique" of character traits. Miller (2014, 187–223) offers an extensive rebuttal.

12. I'm grateful to Matthew Cipa for a discussion in which he suggested this idea—or suggested an idea close enough that it prompted this related one. I am indebted to him, Noël

Carroll, Iris Vidmar Jovanović, Panos Paris, Héctor J. Pérez, Carl Plantinga, Malcolm Turvey, René Weber, and Nicholas Wolterstorff for helpful comments on earlier versions of this chapter. I would also like to thank the audiences of the Screen Stories and Moral Understanding seminar and the Cognitive Impact of Serial Television seminar for their productive questions. Whatever flaws or infelicities remain are solely my responsibility.

References

Annas, Julia. 2011. *Intelligent Virtue*. Oxford: Oxford University Press.

Audi, Robert. 1995. "Acting from Virtue." *Mind* 104, no. 415: 449–471.

Baumberger, Christoph. 2013. "Art and Understanding: In Defence of Aesthetic Cognitivism." In *Bilder sehen: Perspektiven der Bildwissenschaft*, edited by Christoph Wagner, Marc Greenlee, Rainer Hammwöhner, Bernd Körber, and Christian Wolff, 41–67. Regensburg: Schnell + Steiner.

Brewer, Talbot. 2009. *The Retrieval of Ethics*. Oxford: Oxford University Press.

Brink, David. 1986. "Externalist Moral Realism." *Southern Journal of Philosophy* 24, Supplement: 23–41.

Carroll, Noël. 1998a. "Art, Narrative, and Moral Understanding." In *Aesthetics and Ethics: Essays at the Intersection*, edited by Jerrold Levinson, 126–160. Cambridge: Cambridge University Press.

Carroll, Noël. 1998b. *A Philosophy of Mass Art*. Oxford: Oxford University Press.

Carroll, Noël. 2013. "Moral Change: Fiction, Film, and Family." In *Cine-Ethics*, edited by Jinhee Choi and Mattias Frey, 43–56. New York: Routledge.

Currie, Gregory. 2020. *Imagining and Knowing: The Shape of Fiction*. Oxford: Oxford University Press.

Elgin, Catherine Z. 1993. "Understanding: Art and Science." *Synthese* 95: 13–28.

Elgin, Catherine Z. 2002. "Art in the Advancement of Understanding." *American Philosophical Quarterly* 39, no. 1: 1–12.

Elgin, Catherine Z. 2007. "Understanding and the Facts." *Philosophical Studies* 132: 33–42.

Elgin, Catherine Z. 2008. "Emotion and Understanding." In *Epistemology and Emotions*, edited by Georg Brun, Ulvi Doguoglu, and Dominique Kuenzle, 33–49. Aldershot: Ashgate.

Gibson, John. 2008. "Cognitivism and the Arts." *Philosophy Compass*, nos. 3–4: 573–589.

Grimm, Stephen R. 2010. "Understanding." In *The Routledge Companion to Epistemology*, edited by Sven Bernecker and Duncan Pritchard, 84–94. New York: Routledge.

Grimm, Stephen R. 2016. "Understanding and Transparency." In *Explaining Understanding: New Perspectives from Epistemology and the Philosophy of Science*, edited by Stephen R. Grimm, Christoph Baumberger, and Sabine Ammon, 212–229. New York: Routledge.

Grimm, Stephen R. 2019. "Understanding as an Intellectual Virtue." In *The Routledge Handbook of Virtue Epistemology*, edited by Heather Battaly, 340–351. New York: Taylor & Francis.

Hazlett, Allan. 2017. "Understanding and Structure." In *Making Sense of the World: New Essays on the Philosophy of Understanding*, edited by Stephen R. Grimm, 135–158. Oxford: Oxford University Press.

Hills, Alison. 2009. "Moral Testimony and Moral Epistemology." *Ethics* 120: 94–127.

Hills, Alison. 2016. "Understanding Why." *Noûs* 50, no. 4: 661–688.

Kivy, Peter. 1997. *Philosophies of Arts: An Essay in Differences*. Cambridge: Cambridge University Press.

Lynch, Michael Patrick. 2018. "Understanding and Coming to Understand." In *Making Sense of the World: New Essays on the Philosophy of Understanding*, edited by Stephen R. Grimm, 194–208. Oxford: Oxford University Press.

Mele, Alfred R. 2003. *Motivation and Agency*. Oxford: Oxford University Press.

Miller, Christian B. 2008. "Motivational Internalism." *Philosophical Studies* 139: 233–255.

Miller, Christian B. 2013. *Moral Character: An Empirical Theory*. Oxford: Oxford University Press.

Miller, Christian B. 2014. *Character and Moral Psychology*. Oxford: Oxford University Press.

Nagel, Thomas. 1970. *The Possibility of Altruism*. Oxford: Oxford University Press.

Nussbaum, Martha C. 1990. *Love's Knowledge: Essays on Philosophy and Literature*. Oxford: Oxford University Press.

Prinz, Jesse. 2015. "An Empirical Case for Motivational Internalism." In *Motivational Internalism*, edited by Gunnar Björnsson, Caj Strandberg, Ragnar Francén Olinder, John Eriksson, and Fredrik Björklund, 61–84. Oxford: Oxford University Press.

Pritchard, Duncan. 2010. "Knowledge and Understanding." In *The Nature and Value of Knowledge: Three Investigations*, by Duncan Pritchard, Alan Millar, and Adrian Haddock, 5–88. Oxford: Oxford University Press.

Pritchard, Duncan. 2014. "Knowledge and Understanding." In *Virtue Epistemology Naturalized: Bridges between Virtue Epistemology and Philosophy of Science*, edited by Abrol Fairweather, 315–327. Synthese Library 366. Cham, Switzerland: Springer.

Rosati, Connie S. 2016. "Moral Motivation." In *The Stanford Encyclopedia of Philosophy* (Winter 2016 edition), edited by Edward N. Zalta. https://plato.stanford.edu/archives/win2016/entries/moral-motivation/.

Shafer-Landau, Russ. 2003. *Moral Realism: A Defense*. Oxford: Oxford University Press.

Smith, Michael. 1994. *The Moral Problem*. Oxford: Blackwell.

Smith, Michael. 1995. "Internalism's Wheel." *Ratio* 8: 277–302.

Svavarsdóttir, Sigrún. 1999. "Moral Cognitivism and Motivation." *Philosophical Review* 108, no. 2: 161–219.

Trout, J. D. 2017. "Understanding and Fluency." In *Making Sense of the World: New Essays on the Philosophy of Understanding*, edited by Stephen R. Grimm, 232–254. Oxford: Oxford University Press.

2
Understanding (Mis)understanding: Sally Be a Lamb

Paul C. Taylor

Obstacles and Obstacles

In 1965, just as the U.S. civil rights movement achieved its greatest successes on the terrain of formal politics, the great religious thinker Howard Thurman (1989) published a book-length reflection on the links between segregation and understanding. The following passage develops an idea near the book's core message: "When a man says, 'I understand,' he may mean something kind, warm, and gracious. But there is an understanding that is cold, hard, minute, and devastating. It is the kind of understanding that one gives to the enemy, or that is derived from an accurate knowledge of another's power to injure" (40).

Thurman describes this cold and devastating understanding as "unsympathetic" and reports that it "is very easily activated into ill will," which makes even people who come into contact with each other "move around as shadows in a world of shadows" (1989, 40–41). This unsympathetic understanding enshrouds social life in societies struggling with the legacies of systematic oppression, like the postsegregation United States, because it results from "contacts without fellowship." It is "understanding of a certain kind, but it is without the healing and reinforcement of personality" (39–40).

I have come unconscionably late to the task of building a relationship to Thurman's work, so I won't pretend to have divined every level of meaning that he mobilizes here. What interests me is his anatomizing critique of understanding and his refusal to assume that inhabitants of fraught ethical contexts actually understand what understanding is and does and requires of us. What interests me beyond the critique and the refusal is his subsequent turn to what he calls "the reinforcement of personality."

In what follows, I will closely follow Thurman's lead. I will distinguish two modes of understanding, insist on some problems with the less familiar one, and recommend a kind of personalist turn in response. The problems will have to do with certain obstacles that we encounter in the search for moral understanding and with our common failure, or refusal, to notice them or to credit the importance of confronting them. That there are obstacles may be obvious. But I want to say that there are obstacles and there are *obstacles*, and we tend not to give ourselves the resources to distinguish the two or, better, to connect them.

Paul C. Taylor, *Understanding (Mis)understanding: Sally Be a Lamb* In: *Screen Stories and Moral Understanding*. Edited by: Carl Plantinga, Oxford University Press. © Oxford University Press 2023.
DOI: 10.1093/oso/9780197665664.003.0003

The obstacles to understanding come in a variety of forms, and confrontations with the obstacles can aspire to a handful of different outcomes. This leaves a moderately complicated possibility space in need of mapping, and I'm tempted to begin by drawing that map. The temptation lessens when I remember that I have no interest in providing the comprehensive account of moral understanding that would make the map most useful. I will, therefore, subordinate the mapmaker's desire for comprehensiveness and precision to a focus—Whose focus? The phenomenologist's? The essayist's?—on particular cases, and perhaps on only one case, depending on how things go. I want to start with the obstacles in action, and then zoom out to see what to say about them.

Introducing *Hamilton*

Lin-Manuel Miranda's *Hamilton* is, in a couple of ways, the exemplary 21st-century cultural sensation. First, there is the postracial-slash-multicultural content of the production itself. It is a hip hop musical, reimagining America's founders as Black and Brown people, as people culturally, demographically, and ideologically continuous with today's striving immigrants and people of color.

Then there's the long, evolving career of the production as a commodified cultural artifact. After the musical opened at the Public Theater in 2015, it quickly moved on to a lauded and lucrative Broadway run, and then to other platforms for cultural production. It spawned an album-length cast recording, a "mixtape" album (of popular musicians performing the songs), a songbook, a crowdsourced annotation project (think a Norton Critical Edition of the lyrics by way of Wikipedia), and an official book of annotations, blessed by Miranda himself.[1]

Most important for my purposes here, the production had three additional outcomes. Ticket prices soared, controversy raged, and a movie version appeared. The soaring ticket prices were a function of Broadway supply and demand: if a show everyone has heard of and wants to see is available only a handful of times a week in a venue with a few hundred seats, the math is the math. A combination of forces like this makes some kind of wider video release nearly inevitable, especially when the demand has been stoked by years of reviews, think pieces, and other content (including the albums and books) circulating among people who, for the most part, will not be able to see the production itself. The production eventually made its way to the screen, premiering on Disney+ on July 3, 2020, just in time for the Independence Day holiday.

Like many people, I have seen *Hamilton* only on Disney+. This shift in platform and idiom matters, not just because it makes the production accessible to more people but also because the screened production is an artifact in its own right. My hope is that this new artifact, and its distance from its cousins in other idioms, can give us a resource for examining the ethical life of the spectator. But more of this anon.

Before thinking about the difference that moving pictures make, I want to think about the controversial features of the narrative, irrespective of idiom. The first and most basic worry involves the question that attaches to any creative engagement with historical figures: Have the artists illuminated the history or distorted it? Many professional historians saw mostly distortion in this case, especially with respect to the production's soft-pedaling (to put it very gently) of Hamilton's relationship to the slavery system.

A second worry follows directly from the first and presses the link between history and politics. Musicologist Philip Gentry puts it this way: "Hamilton has ... become a metonym for a certain kind of liberal identity politics characterized most of all by aspirational optimism tinged with nationalist fervor" (2017, 273). Gentry's gesture at the way liberal desire sanitizes our political history points toward a tension that plays out in the gap between the reactions that two other writers had to the play. Blogger Kendra James praises *Hamilton* for doing "what many history curricula fail to do: allow young people of color to see themselves in history" (2015). The great Ishmael Reed (2015), by contrast, wonders, "Can you imagine Jewish actors in Berlin's theaters taking roles of Goering? Goebbels? Eichmann? Hitler?" (2015).

A third worry, the one that provides our point of entry to the piece itself, comes from a volume of essays by historians reacting to the production. Lyra Monteiro's contribution explores, among other things, what she calls "a damning omission in the show":

[D]espite the proliferation of black and brown bodies onstage, not a single enslaved or free person of color exists as a character in this play. For the space of only a couple of bars, a chorus member assumes the role of Sally Hemings, but is recognizable as such only by those who catch Jefferson's reference to the enslaved woman with whom he had an ongoing sexual relationship. Unless one listens carefully to the lyrics—which do mention slavery a handful of times—one could easily assume that slavery did not exist in this world, and certainly that it was not an important part of the lives and livelihoods of the men who created the nation (2018, 62).

Monteiro locates the concerns about distorting and sanitizing history directly in a particular moment from the production. I find this moment particularly telling.

The Hemings Cameo

As Monteiro notes, Miranda's production makes precisely one reference to Hemings, in the middle of a song about Jefferson's triumphant return to the United States. The sage of Monticello, played as a kind of hip hop dandy by Daveed Diggs, sings the following lines:

> There's a letter on my desk from the president
> Haven't even put my bags down yet
> Sally, be a lamb, darling, won't you open it
> It says the president's assembling a cabinet.

Between the third and fourth lines of this quatrain, a member of the production's ever-present dance chorus momentarily assumes the role of Hemings (or so we're left to assume), dances over to Jefferson with the opened letter and a smile, and then dances away.

To its credit, the production does foreground a critique of slavery and gives Miranda's Hamilton a couple of opportunities to call out the tensions between Jefferson's commitment to liberty and his commitment to slaveholding. To its discredit, though, it also offers this fleeting, playful glimpse of Hemings in a cameo appearance that is—or at least should be, or so I will argue—most unsettling. What are we to make of this?

One thought is that the cameo is consistent with Miranda's limited feeling for his female characters. Hilton Als (2015) makes a great deal of this thought in his *New Yorker* review of the staged musical. I don't know enough about Miranda's other work to press this claim against him generally, but the intersectional gender politics of this particular creative choice will be of some concern here in a moment.

Another thought is that the cameo reveals the project's deeper tensions, or the way its deepest imperatives rely on certain tensions or contradictions in American self-conceptions. *Hamilton* is rooted in a manic desire to desegregate or decolonize our national mythology, as Miranda has for years told anyone who will listen. But the historic personages, the actual persons, who built an actual colonial power are difficult to transpose into the heroes of multicultural myth. (Yes, desegregation, decolonization, and multiculturalism are different. *Hamilton* seems not to know this.)

Alex Nichols makes a point like the one I'm after in a *Buzzfeed* article delightfully titled, "You Should Be Terrified That People Who Like 'Hamilton' Run Our Country" (2016). He explains that the economics and logistics of high-end stage productions are such that only a very small number of very influential people can score a ticket to popular productions, and he notes that the word of mouth on *Hamilton* quickly drew in *very* influential people who saw the production as the embodiment of the Obama era's continued bending of America's moral arc. Critical praise followed, some of it, Nichols notes, delighting in "the novel incongruousness" of seeing Jefferson swagger and drawl in hip hop drag. A sense of incongruity is more apt than the critics realize, he points out, "because the actual Thomas Jefferson *raped slaves.*"

The imperatives of multicultural mythmaking seem to require the Hemings cameo, which in turn implicates the questions of moral understanding that I want to take up. For me, this scene more than any other in the production shows ethics and aesthetics intertwined in a simultaneous failure of craft and ethical sensibility. At a minimum, the ethical and emotional tone of the scene is wrong, inadequate to the gravity of what we now know about Hemings and Jefferson. The tone is so wrong, in fact, that one can't credit what one needs to credit or grant what one needs to grant in order to make the piece work (optimally). This is (not just a spur to reflection on the ethical criticism of art but also) a failure of ethical understanding, in a sense that points toward Thurman's critique (and refusal, and turn).

Perfection, Disunion

Seen from one angle, the ethical misunderstanding at work in *Hamilton* seems to involve an improper orientation to some obvious ethical truths concerning slavery and sexual violence. This is an epistemic failure, involving a disconnect between the propositions we all endorse and the propositions that would capture the ethos of the production. On this approach, the production just got the ethical facts wrong.

Seen from another angle, though, the failure may lie elsewhere. It may lie less in a disconnect between propositions than in the distance between forms of ethical life. On one side we have the ethos of the production and its creators and of some social world they inhabit, an ethos in which women matter less than men and embracing the myth of America is more important than condemning the sexual violence and social death of slavery. On the other side we have the ethos of the community of people who are brought up short by the liberties that *Hamilton* takes with its historical figures and by its willingness to prioritize nationalism over decolonization (where "decolonization" includes calling out and contesting the way racialized sexual violence, among other things, saturates familiar modern political and ideological formations).

On this second approach, the problem of understanding in *Hamilton* is the yawning gap that separates distinct ethical communities. Once critics highlight this gap, spectators have an opportunity to reckon with their relationship(s) to these communities. One might describe this reckoning as a matter of discerning moral truths, but it registers more immediately as a matter of locating oneself in a sociohistorical and ethical context and of grappling with the self that undertakes and results from this effort.

Putting the issue that way, in terms of putting the work of self-creation in a context of community relationships, begins to reveal some baggage that I bring to this project and that I want to make explicit. I approach this topic from the perspective of Deweyan pragmatism, which means a great many things that will not matter much to people outside of philosophy. A better name, one that comes a trifle closer to signaling its meaning plainly, is "democratic perfectionism."[2] (No, that's not much of an improvement. It gets better.)

To be a democratic perfectionist in the sense I have in mind is to foreground at least three key moves. The first move insists on the role of habit in the moral life and on the tight links that connect virtue to the formation and re-formation of habit. The second highlights the contingency of ethical phenomena, their dependence on accidents of history and vulnerability to change, and insists, as a result, on the experimental spirit that seeks to embrace and manage the dynamism of existence, and of the ethical life, instead of fleeing it to search for eternal verities. The third attempts to rec-óncile contingency with normativity, to show that embracing dynamism and change and context needn't hollow out our resources for distinguishing right from wrong and good from bad.

Committing to this mode of perfectionism means in practice that ethical knowledge is a community resource, formed and re-formed in the long-running conversations and debates that define our cultural traditions. It means that we make our ethical judgments against the backdrop of history and culture but also against the backdrop of epistemic responsibility, which rules out the thought that anything goes or that justice is just a compliment we pay to whatever it is we happen to endorse. And it means that the work of the moral life is bound up with the work of creating selves, both in our solitude as we reflect on our own habits and in the cultural institutions, like schools, that we charge with recording and passing on and building shared discursive and epistemic resources around our endorsements.

Three Categories, Four Obstacles

The turn to democratic perfectionism gives me the resources to complete the mapping I mentioned earlier. I began this piece by distinguishing obstacles from *obstacles* in a way that I now want to complicate. To start with, I want to sort the impediments to understanding into three categories: epistemic, sociological, and phenomenological.

The epistemic obstacles are the familiar problems of ignorance and ideology. "Ignorance" refers here to the things we genuinely don't know, while "ideology" refers, a bit too broadly, to the social and cognitive mechanisms that systematically cultivate ignorance. Ignorance is what makes it possible to watch Steve McQueen's *Twelve Years a Slave* and come away with a new, perhaps newly detailed, awareness of the conditions that confronted the enslaved person. Ideology—specifically, white supremacist ideology, or the insinuation of this ideology into U.S. politics and culture, including our school systems and curricula, *and* into our socially given cognitive heuristics and biases—is what makes it possible, or necessary, for a film released in the 21st century, two centuries after the abolition of the transatlantic trade in slaves, to make up for this particular form of ignorance.

Of course, describing the payoff of McQueen's film in epistemic terms is somewhat misleading. After all, one might say, the point of art and of aesthetic experience is not just to transmit knowledge but to engage us more holistically, mobilizing the affects and priming motor function and so on, in addition to presenting new facts and wider perspectives. This is surely right, and it anticipates some questions we'll soon need to ask at the intersection of visual culture studies and sonic studies. First, though, I want to note that it points us to two other kinds of obstacles.

Alongside ignorance and ideology, we might worry about the obstacles of isolation and innocence. "Isolation" refers here, in part, to the sociological conditions of segregation and social closure, the walling off of some kinds of people from other kinds.

There is a considerable and growing body of evidence that social closure has a variety of knock-on effects. For example, it undermines epistemic efficacy by undermining epistemic diversity. (This is why the *Harvard Business Review* points out every now and then that diverse teams produce better outcomes.) Knowledge, whatever else it is, is the fruit of a process; call this "inquiry." Isolation undermines the conditions for effective inquiry by, among other things, protecting potential knowers from the challenges to their existing convictions, challenges that can produce what Peirce called "the irritation of doubt." (Social epistemologist José Medina puts a related point in terms of epistemological resistance and builds a rich and complex view around it.)

In addition to minimizing occasions for inquiry and reducing the urgency of the occasions that arise, isolation has phenomenological implications. This is why the word "isolation" registers differently, and in some ways more effectively, than "segregation." It signals the senses of alienation, exclusion, and the like that tend to accompany social closure.

Isolation has the additional effect of reinforcing the fourth obstacle, innocence. I'm using "innocence" in the way James Baldwin did, to talk not just about the things we don't know but also about the things we don't *want* to know, or about our desire not to know them. The problem of ethical understanding, Baldwin rightly saw, is not just a problem of misinformation, missing information, or systematically organized barriers, including sociological barriers, to gathering information; it is also a problem of will, desire, and affect. It is a phenomenological problem of being invested in the world that our epistemic failures reflect and protect. (This is the spirit in which Robin DiAngelo invites us to talk about white fragility. It is also one reason Medina refers to his intervention as an epistemology of *resistance*, and not an epistemology of, say, countervailing social information signals.)

Ignorance and ideology are importantly epistemic and are (one might say) about complicating the relationships between knowers and propositions. Isolation and innocence are sociological and phenomenological and are (one should say) about complicating relationships between distinct—provisionally distinguishable—ethical communities and between differently ordered and temporally distinct states of the self. I propose to leave the epistemic obstacles to the social epistemologists and critical theorists and focus instead on the phenomenological questions (into which I will subsume as much sociology as is appropriate for this setting, which isn't much). This is where the aesthetic naturally finds its footing and where ethical life in some ways most clearly imposes itself on the practices of filmmaking, criticism, and spectatorship.[3]

The Personal and the Phenomenological

Screen stories are a particularly useful resource for thinking about the more broadly phenomenological forms of ethical misunderstanding. Like all art, these stories decenter explicit avowals and endorsements: they restore arguments about the right and the good to their place alongside the experiences that inform the arguments. They return our attention to affect and immediacy and community, and in so doing help reveal what really matters to us. (They also do more than this, and do this on a particular scale. I'll return to this in the penultimate section.)

We know what matters to the people who terrify Nichols. They will likely dismiss the Hemings cameo as a small gaffe or an artistic necessity. They might point out that Miranda had planned to include a rap battle about slavery—a demo for it appears on the mixtape as "Cabinet Rap Battle #3"—but he cut it from the production so as not to, as he put it later, bring the show to a halt. They might suggest that the same reasoning discouraged him from sacrificing the entire production to the Hemings controversy. With this backstory in place, they might then say that Miranda tried to keep Hemings in view without letting her take over the proceedings, but what he tried didn't work. This is an unfortunate slip in technique but, they will in essence say—"in essence" because what they tend actually to say is nothing—it's not that big a deal.

The problem is that to say these things is surely to move too quickly, both with respect to the ethical issues in play and with respect to the work of artistic creation. If you've seen the production, you may already have noted that it has its share of tragedy. Hamilton's son dies. The family mourns. The show pauses and grows somber. And then the show goes on. The worry about bringing the show to a halt ceases to be a worry when the tragedy is one that *matters*: when the act of violence takes away something that (the production thinks) the spectator is supposed to care about. (Having listened to "Cabinet Rap Battle #3," I suggest that the show seemed likely to grind to a halt less because of the subject than because of the number. But that's a question for people who know more about musical theater than I do.)

Similarly, tragedy is not absent from the musical and cultural idiom that Miranda has so successfully inhabited. Hip hop in its highest forms is precisely about the existential challenge of precariousness in a land of plenty and of plenteous security. It is about these things and about the absurdities that result from managing these things in a society structured in various forms of dominance, beginning with gender and race. The story and the store of cultural resources that made *Hamilton* such a sensation were capacious enough to promote a clearer understanding of what Hemings means for America's mythology. But the production was more invested in making a tragic figure of its main character's mistress than in making anything of Ms. Hemings. (Or of people like her, since, no, the show was not called *Jefferson* or *Hemings*.)

What does it mean that the mania for *Hamilton* survived these considerations, that it did not, in any far-reaching way, even recognize these considerations? I take it to mean that when it comes to these issues, the issues of actual as opposed to cosmetic decolonization, many people simply do not feel the irritation of doubt that triggers the process of ethical inquiry. They are not moved to seek out moral understanding with respect to these issues. They belong to communities whose shared understanding of the moral life allows for the thought that racialized sexual violence and social death are, ultimately, no big deal, not relative, say, to the grand drama of American mythmaking.

Of course, the people who terrify Nichols would likely not assent to the description I've just given of the ethos that informs their fandom. Which is why it's important to insist that the relevant form of understanding here is not a relationship to propositions. We know, *they* know, that rape is wrong, that Hemings was harmed, that Jefferson's status as an icon of liberty and such is forever compromised by his role in this drama. If given the chance to say yea or nay to claims like "Women matter less than men" or "Sustaining American mythology is more important than decolonizing U.S. history," they would probably say nay. (Probably.)

The obvious reason not to be encouraged by this is that humans routinely act in ways that belie our explicit avowals. This is why the study of implicit attitudes has become a thriving industry, along with behavioral science and choice architecture and dual-process theories of cognition and all the rest. Some parts of those industries bear on what I want to say here, but I want to draw out a dimension of this issue that they tend to leave in the background.

The real question that *Hamilton* raises, the real question raised by all invitations to ethical criticism of art, is this: *What matters to you deeply enough to bring you up short? What matters to you so much that you will not, cannot bracket it?* I should add a second question: *What will you do to keep this first question in view?* This second question can take more pointed forms, and probably should. Such as: *How will you keep track of your commitments? What discipline will you institute and practice in order to force yourself to face the (really) real question: What kind of person will I be?*

It is important to insist on the personal dimension of social ethics—the phenomenologically rich, culturally rooted, affectively loaded, *personal* dimension, which is not the same as individual scale—because it is easy to overlook in theory but unavoidable in ethical practice. (Wherever you go, there you are.) For example, our choice architects and libertarian paternalists, in their (not unreasonable) eagerness to sidestep conscious deliberation altogether, inevitably find the level where their spade is turned. Even nudging can't be nudging all the way down; it is supposed to be part of a public policy regime that someone, somewhere has to design and defend and implement with ethical considerations in mind. One can only hope that these someones have been edified and fortified by some personal practice of ethical self-scrutiny.

Similarly, in our eagerness to use film to win more or more ardent converts to the ethical truths that we all accept, we can forget that truth often gives way to solidarity and fragility and rationalization and desire, including the desire for vindication, the desire not to be caught out, the desire not to know. All of which is to say that the path to ethical understanding depends on the work of interpretation, which is a mode of criticism, which must, at some point, involve *self*-criticism, which in ethically loaded contexts must also involve some kind of *social* criticism. This inward turn toward the self—toward the concrete, culturally encumbered self—has unavoidably affective dimensions and carries with it the burden of temporality, of building and monitoring and maintaining and, if one can manage it, *improving* a self over time, in relation to the challenges and opportunities that one's time presents. It is therefore a phenomenological turn, but also a social turn. (Again for the philosophers: it is a turn toward *critical* phenomenology.)

Building an Ethical Practice

Having recommended a personalist, richly self-critical turn in the ethical criticism of artworks and in ethical life more generally, I should say more about what it looks like in practice.

In that spirit, I have to tell you that I enjoy *Hamilton*. I can bracket everything in the production other than the Hemings cameo. And I might simply be bracketing that, since I am, usually, willing just to skip that scene and return to the show. (True, my worries matter enough for me to skip the scene. I also avert my gaze during a couple of the more gruesome moments in *John Wick*, a fact that may shed even more light on my place in all this.)

And now I have to tell you that writing those words in the previous paragraph made me less interested in watching *Hamilton* in the future, and it made the memory of watching it a bit less pleasurable, which means that the act of taking this experience seriously has slightly reoriented me to the prospects for that experience and to the requirements of my moral experience.

And now I have to tell you that I'm going to try the approach that one of my friends has adopted. He is a civil rights historian and scholar of American history more broadly, and so has no interest in reclaiming the American myth. As a result, he is a bitter critic of Miranda's production. But he enjoys the score and has the cast album and mixtape on heavy rotation. Which suggests that seeing, watching people act out, this exercise in historical revisionism—*seeing* the production as opposed to just hearing the music—does important work.

Thinking about the impact of the visual here intrigues me, though I confess I don't yet know what to make of it. Film and stage are more holistically involving idioms, involving more sensory modalities, combining lighting, movement, sound design, choreography, and more into a comprehensive experience; and where the stage can add the kinesthetic dimension of three-dimensional performance, motion pictures present opportunities to do things like focus attention with editing and camera angles. There is a story to tell here about the psychology of human aesthetic appreciation, a story about what happens to us when we watch our fellow humans do things under certain conditions, a story that I trust my friends who study the psychology of aesthetics to fill in if asked. That story, plus white supremacy, helps explain why we can entertain the apocryphal report that Woodrow Wilson described *Birth of a Nation* as "history written in lightning," and it helps explains why Gentry, the musicologist cited earlier, reports that he found the stage performance of *Hamilton* much funnier than the cast album (2017, 23).

All of which makes it important for me to tell you now that the version of Jefferson's offending song that appears on the cast album does have at least one advantage over its cousin in the stage and video productions. (The mixtape doesn't include a version of this song, which makes sense given the tune's odd boogie-woogie style.) Hearing it instead of seeing it removes one particularly distressing element of the Hemings cameo: the Hemings cameo. It is one thing to hear Jefferson summon Hemings and then hear him continue in a way that makes clear that she answered his call. It is another thing entirely to hear the summons and then *see* her spring into action, cheerfully and eagerly. This is not a problem of the visual as such; it may be a problem of choreography as much as anything. But it matters that the video won't let me imagine Hemings being sullen or reluctant or resentful, that it refuses the blanks that Jefferson and Hemings conspired to leave in the record and fills them with a smiling dancer. (I have to ask: Why was the "be a lamb" quatrain even in the song?)

Cinema and theater differ from song and literature, when they want to, in their ability to prescribe certain modes of imagining. They have more resources at their disposal to constrain what appears to the mind's eye. This gives the artist more resources, but also more responsibilities; with more levers to pull, it is important to keep the consequences of all the machinations in view. A line that might read on the page as a safe way to acknowledge Jefferson's moral, um, complexity might, when sung by a preening showman wreathed in bright lights, when answered by an eager dance partner, register quite differently.

The words on the page might have seemed, might *be* safe in part because they preserve the new balance between silence and disclosure that we have recently achieved in relation to Hemings. The old silence pretended she didn't exist, but the new silence, critically confined to a smaller sphere by Annette Gordon-Reed and others, insists on Hemings's existence and on her agency. We now know a fair bit about what she did, much of it, apparently, in the context of an ongoing contest of wills with the man, the American hero, who owned her. But we know very little about what she thought and felt. Accepting what we don't know about her, leaving some silences and shadows in place, while fleshing out and insisting on what we do know feels like a way of honoring the fact that she was her own person, with her own aims and goals. Glibly depicting her in a way that seems to align her aims and goals with those of the slavery system seems dishonorable and irresponsible. Encountering the Hemings cameo on the page or as a song leaves the silences and shadows appropriately undisturbed while nevertheless gesturing at Jefferson's moral failures. Seeing the cameo on the stage or screen recruits Hemings into her own subordination and softens the contradictions between Thomas Jefferson, rapist, and Thomas Jefferson, founder.

I've arrived at the start of a claim about the difference that visuality makes in the experience of the *Hamilton* narrative/enterprise. It will soon become a point about the ethical burdens that attach to the work of making screen stories. But I can't move on without first answering the questions that got me here: What does the personalist turn in ethical criticism look like in action? And what matters to me, matters enough to bring me up short, in the moral universe of *Hamilton*?

About the personalist turn: it looks, at least sometimes, like the previous few paragraphs. It is an iterative, probing inquiry that begins with art criticism and transitions into self-criticism. It asks what one enjoys—that is, what is it that one is enjoying, and what does one enjoy about that thing—and then asks what kind of creature enjoys such things, and whether a creature like that has a place in the world one means to inhabit and in the future that one imagines for oneself.

About what matters to me and what brings me up short: I will probably continue to watch *Hamilton*, not least because my daughter enjoys it, and because the miracle of streaming video means that I can skip the offending scene and skip around to the bits I enjoy the most. The full *Hamilton* production is not lost to me the way it is to my friend or to Ishmael Reed in part because I am not a professional historian or Ishmael Reed, which means, among other things, that playing fast and loose with the founders' relationships to slavery doesn't bother me overmuch. It remains a viable entertainment option also because one learns swiftly in the contemporary media environment to raise bracketing to a fine art, especially when it comes to celebrations of America's myths. Which is to say: I'm happy to eat barbecue on Independence Day like most of the other people I know, even though I also make my kids listen to Frederick Douglass's 4th of July address.

Having made my peace with *Hamilton*, such as it is, or, better put, having made my accommodations with it, I can turn my ethical attention elsewhere. Which brings me, finally, to the difference that the screen makes.

Bounden Duties

With the great power of moving pictures comes great responsibility. If, as noted above, the move to cinema gives the artist more resources to constrain or guide the spectator's imaginings, then, one might think, the artist has more vectors of potential harm to monitor. This creates a burden of craft and of character. Artists who work across media and idioms should attend to the way these crossings change the work, both for the sake of achieving their artistic goals and for the sake of responsibly confronting the ethical challenges that define their cultures. As the debates about the ethical criticism of art remind us and as W. E. B. Du Bois pointed out a century ago, ethical commitments are among the resources and constraints that inform the work of art, irrespective of whether the artist has this in mind. As Du Bois put it, it is the "bounden duty" of the artist to attend to this dimension of the work with care (1986, 1000). I would add that when the art mobilizes ethical resources, implicates ethical controversies and problems, that the artists hadn't considered, there is also a bounden duty to interrogate the self that lacked this foresight or that decided, or assumed, the implications didn't matter.

This leaves me, for now, with two thoughts about film as a possible resource for promoting ethical understanding. I fear that neither will be terribly original. But both are easy to lose sight of if we imagine ethical understanding as something we seek out, in the spirit of clarification or of dramatic rehearsal or whatever, against a backdrop of established ethical truths that we—whoever the "we" turns out to be—all already accept.

The first thought is that there is something to the talk one sometimes hears about teachable moments. Moving pictures are always grist for the mill of vernacular criticism. Moving pictures that take up controversial topics and do so in ways that require critical engagement can occasion and sustain vibrant participatory exercises in the criticism of self and society. It is tempting to think that the authors of problematic fictions are broken beyond repair, irretrievable and irredeemable; we can instead think of them as speaking on our behalf, entering into the public record some recognizable piece of our checkered but shared inheritance that requires our attention. I've argued here that artists and spectators should themselves take moments like this as occasions also for self-interrogation, but that is a matter for individuals in their solitude. What a community does with the object the artist builds from the cultural (ideological, historical) materials we all share is a matter to put at the heart of the conversations and exchanges that define our traditions. Or, better: what overlapping but distinct ethical communities do with their divergent readings of and reactions to the artist's work can be a step on the road toward greater understanding and away from Thurman's contacts without fellowship.

The second thought is that it is important to remember that the distinctiveness of film is, in some ways, as much about the business models and organizational forms as about the nature of the aesthetic medium. The economic context for the stage production—high costs, small consumer base, high barriers to consumer entry—differs from the context that confronts the creative team behind a moving picture. Film is, we used to say, a more democratic medium, which now seems to mean at least two things. It means that more people can see a film, both because the technology allows for the indefinite proliferation of instances and because, as a result, the tickets are cheaper. But it also means that expensive films answer to more people, in the sense that the investors need to appeal to as many people as possible to secure the best return, and as a result are keen not to alienate or challenge any more people than they have to.

This thought about business models and organizational forms supplements our reading of *Hamilton* with a crucial critique of political economy. Artworks are no more separated from the economic context of production than from the desires and aspirations of their creators. It is inappropriate to reduce the work to either of these contexts, but it is instructive to remember the contexts, especially if one means to tell a story not about the work in isolation but about what the artist has done and what we can expect the artwork to do. There is a story to tell about *Hamilton* as an expression of naked artistic ambition and political opportunism: as an artifact that emerges not from the artist's willingness to sacrifice decolonization to mythmaking but to sacrifice whatever needed sacrificing to get both Mike Pence and Barack Obama to attend his show. I won't tell that story because I don't know Miranda and I don't care to study his words and biography closely enough to find out. (The intentional fallacy is not the path of least resistance.) But I'll wave at the possibility of the story because possibilities like this bear on the tasks of prodding the artist toward self-examination and of properly calibrating one's expectations for a work (and for future work from members of the same creative team).

Conclusion

I have been trying to find words for a series of thoughts that have nagged at me since I started thinking about the ethical criticism of art and about the discipline of reading film. Those thoughts nagged at me because much of the work I was encountering seemed to rely on the assumption of a unified ethical community whose wayward members sometimes needed correction. The lines between good and evil, right and wrong were supposed to be bright and clear, and the burden seemed to involve getting people to see more clearly the consequences of views to which they were already committed.

That, to me, has never been the most interesting picture of ethical life. On the picture I see, bright lines simply mark the points at which evolving traditions briefly come to rest, and unified ethical communities often buy their unity at the expense of other communities, communities with whom, as Thurman put it, they have contacts without fellowship. In the grip of a picture like this, Thurman argues that what often passes for shared understanding actually marks a narrow "zone of agreement" that is defined, as Pateman and Mills and others have argued, by foundational agreements to accept that some people matter less than others (2007, 88). (Glaude calls this "the value gap" (2018, 28).) Seen from this angle, from the underside of history, informed by the hidden transcripts of the marginalized, the quest for ethical understanding requires a strenuous regime of self-critique and self-correction and the humility to accept that this discipline can always call our most cherished assumptions into question.

Notes

1. There were, in addition, Chicago and London runs of the musical with different casts, as well as a U.S. national touring production. As of this writing, plans are in place for productions outside the United States as well, starting in London's West End.
2. But first, for the philosophers, and against ecumenicism: in a germinal essay from some years back, Cynthia Freeland (1997) helpfully distinguishes Aristotelian and pragmatist approaches to issues of moral knowledge, using Nussbaum and Putnam as exemplars of the two approaches. I am firmly in the pragmatist camp, but in the wing of it—do camps have wings?—that, like Dewey after his encounters with Frederick Woodbridge, helps itself to all sorts of Aristotelian insights. It also embraces the phenomenological residues of Hegelianism that people like Putnam and Rorty found abhorrent, as well as the third-wave Peircean turn that people like Cheryl Misak and Robert Brandom enact against the normative breeziness of middle-period Rorty. This form of pragmatism is interested all at once in the three key considerations I connect here to perfectionism.

3. For people keeping score at home, here's a stab at mapping the obstacles and categories in the way I (falsely) declared earlier that I wouldn't attempt:

Categories	Obstacles	Taken up in this essay?
Epistemic	Ignorance, ideology	No
Phenomenological	Isolation, innocence	Yes
Sociological	Isolation, innocence	A bit

Works Cited

Als, Hilton. 2015. "Bromance at the Revolution." *New Yorker*, March 9. http://www.newyorker.com/magazine/2015/03/09/boys-in-the-band.

Du Bois, W.E.B. 1986. "Criteria of Negro Art." In *Writings*, edited by Nathan Huggins, 993–1002. New York: Library of America.

Freeland, Cynthia A. 1997. "Art and Moral Knowledge." *Philosophical Topics* 25, no. 1 (Spring): 11–36.

Glaude, Eddie S., Jr. 2016. *Democracy in Black: How Race Still Enslaves the American Soul.* The Crown Publishing Group.

Gentry, Philip. 2017. "Hamilton's Ghosts." *American Music* 35, no. 2 (Summer): 271–280.

James, Kendra. 2015. "Race, Immigration, and Hamilton: The Relevance of Lin-Manuel Miranda's New Musical." *The Toast*, October 1. https://the-toast.net/2015/10/01/race-immigration-and-hamilton/.

Monteiro, Lyra D. 2018. "Race-Conscious Casting and the Erasure of the Black Past in Hamilton." In *Historians on Hamilton: How a Blockbuster Musical Is Restaging America's Past*, edited by Renee C. Romano and Claire Bond Potter, 58–70. New Brunswick, NJ: Rutgers University Press.

Nichols, Alex. 2016. "You Should Be Terrified That People Who Like 'Hamilton' Run Our Country." *Buzzfeed*, July 29. https://www.currentaffairs.org/2016/07/you-should-be-terrified-that-people-who-like-hamilton-run-our-country.

Pateman, Carole, and Charles W. (Charles Wade) Mills. 2007. *Contract and Domination.* Cambridge, UK: Polity.

Reed, Ishmael. 2015. "'Hamilton: The Musical': Black Actors Dress Up Like Slave Traders … and It's Not Halloween," *Counterpunch*, August 21. https://www.counterpunch.org/2015/08/21/hamilton-the-musical-black-actors-dress-up-like-slave-tradersand-its-not-halloween/.

Thurman, Howard. 1989. *The Luminous Darkness: A Personal Interpretation of the Anatomy of Segregation and the Ground of Hope.* Richmond, IN: Friends United Press.

PART II

TRANSFER AND CULTIVATION

3
Phenomenal Experience and Moral Understanding

A Framework for Assessment

Carl Plantinga

What is it like to be a refugee escaping poverty and violence, and in desperate straits? What is it like to gradually go deaf? To play chess with the custodian in the bowels of an aging stone building of an orphanage? To be a young woman working in a profession dominated by men? Many would argue that the narrative arts generally, and the art form I am most interested in here—narrative film—can provide us with a semblance of those experiences.

Perhaps having the sorts of experiences that films offer, under certain conditions, leads to phenomenal knowledge. As Murray Smith writes, "If art can provide us with knowledge, and if it is uniquely or especially well-placed to furnish us with particular kinds of knowledge, then phenomenal knowledge ... must be a frontrunner" (2017, 118). Perhaps I can learn what it actually might be like to go deaf, to suffer the unwelcomed looks of desirous men, or to engage in a violent battle in war.

Yet phenomenal knowledge isn't *all* we are after, at least most of the time. Aesthetic cognitivism is the view that the arts are not valuable solely because they provide pleasure, amusement, and delight, but also because they are sources of knowledge and understanding (Baumberger 2013; Freeland 1997; Graham 2005, 52–75). It does not seem outlandish to argue that films such as *District 9* (2009), *Children of Men* (2006), *Hotel Rwanda* (2004), and *El Norte* (1983) may play a role in developing empathy for and increased understanding of refugees and their plight. Many have argued for the capacity of films to enlarge empathy and moral understanding (Kozloff 2013; Plantinga 2018; Sinnerbrink 2016; Stadler 2014). What I claim in this chapter is that the *phenomenal experiences* provided by films can, under certain conditions, lead to phenomenal knowledge about the actual world, and that this can lead to further sorts of knowledge and understanding—perhaps even a deeper moral understanding.

In the interest of space I will remain ecumenical about just what moral understanding is, though I further discuss this below. It could be the development of our ability "to perceive the world from multiple perspectives," what Hannah Meretoja calls "perspective awareness" and "perspective-sensitivity" (2018, 4). It could be that fiction, as Keith Oatley argues, "enlarges empathy in the context of a hundreds-year

Carl Plantinga, *Phenomenal Experience and Moral Understanding* In: *Screen Stories and Moral Understanding.*
Edited by: Carl Plantinga, Oxford University Press. © Oxford University Press 2023.
DOI: 10.1093/oso/9780197665664.003.0004

old march toward equality and humane treatment of others" (2011, 167). It could be, as Martha Nussbaum (1990) claims, that fictions can embody ethical commitments and lead to a certain ethical conception that is highlighted by the form of the narrative.

Worth noting is that most conceptions of the ethical benefits of fiction in some way involve empathy and the capacity of fictions to enlarge our understanding of the people around us. Also worth noting is that all of the sources mentioned in the previous paragraph focus on literature rather than screen stories. But is there something that screen stories have to offer in these regards that is strikingly different from what literature offers? If there is something different, it is likely the sorts of phenomenal experiences that screen stories can afford. We would not want to claim that literature offers *no* phenomenal experiences to readers; that would clearly be false. But what we can say is that screen stories have particular and powerful ways of representing and eliciting phenomenal experience that are worth examining.

This chapter describes four methods by which screen stories provide remarkable phenomenal experiences. It then examines some conditions under which these experiences can be said to lead to phenomenal knowledge and moral understanding of the world beyond the screen. The hypotheses and claims I make are far from settled; nothing here is the last word. Indeed, nearly every important concept dealt with here can be contested, and there is obviously much we do not yet know about both the mysterious workings of screen stories on the human mind and the cultural contexts in which minds operate. The question of whether and how screen stories *in particular* can increase moral understanding is an important one; the purpose of this chapter is to offer a plausible framework to carry the discussion forward.

Phenomenal Experience in Screen Stories

It is highly plausible that screen stories enact embodied cognition and what Vittorio Gallese and Michele Guerra (2020) call "liberated embodied simulation" much differently than literature. Embodied cognition is an expansive research program that focuses on the relationship of the human body to cognitive activities. Gallese and Guerra's research into the neuroscience of film is one strain of that research program. They propose as a "new perceptual model" *embodied simulation*, a basic functioning mechanism of the brain-body system in primates. Embodied simulation applies both to our interactions with the real world and to screen narratives. Embodied simulation activates sensorimotor and visceromotor maps in the brain of the observer and can, they say, "facilitate the construction of a direct and non-linguistic relationship with space, objects, and the actions, emotions, and sensations of others." Moreover, such simulation is "strongly involved in generating human imaginative abilities" (xix).

In what Gallese and Guerra call *liberated embodied simulation*, which occurs when we watch narrative films, the viewer still experiences simulation, but without certain of its more concerning real world implications. To put this in layman's terms, seeing or hearing human actions on the screen activates the brain in ways that are free of many of the fears and anxieties of our interactions with the actual world, thus stimulating the imagination and, arguably, enlarging understanding (Smith 1997, 413).

The kinds of phenomenal experiences that are represented and simulated in various artistic media are varied and diverse. Screen stories offer such experiences in four primary ways: (1) illustrative representation, (2) looking and being looked at, (3) phenomenal aspects of social cognition, and (4) audiovisual metaphors.

Illustrative Representation

Philosopher James O. Young, in his discussion of art and knowledge, claims that the arts feature what he calls "illustrative representation" (2001, 23–64). In illustrative representation, a work of art represents by a similarity between some aspects of the experience of the representation and the experience of the object represented. Thus a painting represents by illustration when it presents, for example, a picture of a stroll in the park in autumn that is similar to what a stroll in the park in autumn might look like. A piece of music represents sadness when the experience of the music is similar to the experience of actual sadness. A work of literature may depict conversation that may replicate the rhythms and cadences of actual conversation. Thus when a work of art *illustrates* something, it does so in large part by offering an experience that is similar to the experience of the object represented.

Young's theory is too complex to examine in depth here. Three things should be noted, however, lest this simple summary misleadingly make the theory seem naïve. First, Young does not deny that artistic convention plays a role in illustrative representation. Second, Young notes that the similarity condition characteristic of illustrative representation need not be absolute. Obviously, the experience of a two-dimensional photograph differs from that of a three-dimensional scene in important ways. Yet the experience of the photograph may in some regards be similar to the experience of the scene. In both, for example, one may be see the same colors, or in both one might have the sensation of eyes peering toward the observer. It is only in virtue of relevant similarities that a photograph can be said to illustratively represent a three-dimensional scene. Third, this discussion, due to space constraints, elides a discussion of whether sound or image recordings are reproductions of or else representations of the actual sounds or images recorded. For the purposes of this chapter, we can consider them to be representations that preserve some of the sonic or visual characteristics of the represented sonic or visual environment.

What is it like to suddenly go deaf? To have Locked-in Syndrome? To be high on heroin? To have landed on Omaha Beach as an American soldier in France during the Normandy landings of World War II? Arguably, *The Sound of Metal* (2020), *The Diving Bell and the Butterfly* (2007), *Trainspotting* (1996), *and Saving Private Ryan* (1998) are able to provide a semblance of what it is like to have these experiences. They do this with myriad filmic techniques, depending on the film in question.

Take *The Sound of Metal* as an example. The film follows a heavy metal drummer as he loses his hearing, and director Darius Marder and sound designer Nicolas Becker work hard to provide the audience with a semblance of that experience. Mikado Murphy (2020), writing in the *New York Times*, provides an excellent overview of the film's phenomenological qualities and includes links to salient clips from the film.

People who experience deafness do not experience total silence. They sometimes hear muffled sounds, low-frequency vibrations, and other tones, as does Ruben (Riz Ahmed) in *The Sound of Metal*. Since film narratives occur in time, they can represent gradual or sudden hearing loss. In the film, as Ruben loses his hearing, the transition from "normal" hearing to his partial deafness can be played out in real time. When Ruben gets cochlear implants, he experiences another transition as he regains some of his hearing. The sounds he hears are initially distorted and unrecognizable, and he is told that the implants basically trick his brain into thinking he is hearing sound.

So far we have discussed two tools that are used to create the phenomenal experience of going deaf: sound recording and the manipulation of the soundtrack, and second, the shots and scenes in which Ruben experiences (and we hear) the gradual or abrupt changes in his hearing. Many other techniques are important in communicating Ruben's phenomenal experience. We see reaction shots of Ruben as he responds to changes in his hearing, and the face of his partner, Lou (Olivia Cooke), as she struggles to comprehend Ruben's condition. And sound editing provides quick transitions from the sound Ruben hears to that experienced by those with normal hearing, and back again. It is the storytelling, cinematography, editing, acting, and sound design that convey this phenomenal experience, and not any single expressive tool used in isolation.

Film critic and theorist V. F. Perkins has written that no scene in a film is reduceable to the "verbal concepts" which its actions suggest (1972, 75). It does not convey purely propositional knowledge, but rather, as Perkins notes, favors "the communication of vision and experience" (75). Scientists, philosophers, and theorists have noted that the cinema mimics human consciousness itself in the throes of diverse sorts of experiences. As I write in *Moving Viewers*, a film can represent "not just a mental universe (of perception and cognition), but ... the phenomenological contours of conscious experience" (Plantinga 2009, 43–44).

So far this discussion seemingly implies that phenomenal knowledge is firmly tethered to empathy and "in one's shoes" experiences. But phenomenal knowledge need not be restricted to any single character or to subjective representation "from the inside." The celebrated second scene of Steven Spielberg's *Saving Private Ryan*, a 24-minute depiction of the Allied invasion of Normandy and landing on Omaha Beach during World War II, is restricted to no single soldier's perspective. It pivots between subjective and objective perspectives on the battle but manages to represent the phenomenological qualities of the experience with unparalleled power.

To represent the battle, the filmmakers show us the sights and sounds we would expect, but also employ innovative stylistic techniques to provide new perspectives on the experience. For example, the landing is amphibious, and the filmmakers provide alternating perspectives from both underwater and above water, with the concomitant changes in sound quality from below and above. The cameras were altered to provide a staccato feel to the movements of the soldiers, conveying the confusion of the battle. As the scene progresses, we periodically come back to the perspective of Captain Thomas Miller (Tom Hanks), who is apparently suffering from "shell shock." During these moments the roaring cacophony of war is replaced with muffled low tones to suggest an interior experience incapable of taking in the horrific world outside. Spielberg decided not to storyboard the scene in advance, instead opting for a kind of chaotic progression of shots designed to mimic the anarchy and disorientation of the battle.

Seeing this scene could help some to understand what battle is like phenomenologically, and such an understanding can contribute to the viewer's empathy for anyone who has experienced it. Yet it isn't solely about empathy. The scene, arguably, also helps viewers to understand the violence and chaos of war itself, and thus can figure into the moral stance toward war that is merited by its very nature.

Looking and Being Looked At

Film and cultural theory have long been interested in the political and sociomoral implications of what is now commonly called "the gaze." The gaze refers to the way that seeing and point of view are instantiated in a film, from the perspective of producers, viewers, or the characters within the fiction. What is shown, and how is it meant to be looked at and responded to? In addressing these questions, the point-of-view structure has been shown to have important political and moral implications. Laura Mulvey, in her canonical article "Visual Pleasure and the Narrative Cinema," identified the male gaze as it was instantiated in classical Hollywood cinema, arguing that such films were designed for a heterosexual male spectator and featured women primarily as passive objects of voyeuristic desire (1975). Since Mulvey, the idea of the gaze has been elaborated on from many perspectives, for example, bell hooks's identification of the "oppositional gaze" of the Black female viewer (1992).

"Gaze theory" points to the centrality of point of view, looking, and being looked at in visual storytelling. One of the primary tools of the filmmaker in constructing point of view is the point-of-view structure: a shot of the character looking (often in close-up), followed by a shot of what the character sees (the point-of-view shot), followed by a reaction shot. The importance of the point-of-view structure in screen storytelling is not easy to exaggerate. While a literary narrative may describe what a character is thinking or feeling, a film will most often show us what a character is thinking and feeling by the use of sequences of point-of-view structures. The viewer sees the character looking, what the character sees, and the character's response. Within its narrative context, this reveals what the character is attending to and what she thinks and feels about it. As Per Persson notes in his discussion of the psychology of point-of-view editing, the structure depends on the viewer's "deictic gaze ability," or in other words, the ability to follow and learn from other people's gazes (2003, 66–70. The point-of-view structure, along with the close-up of the human face, are primary ways that screen stories provide striking phenomenal experiences that can strongly impact moral understanding.

In *The Silence of the Lambs*, Clarice Starling (Jodie Foster) is in training to become an FBI agent. She is an ingenue who has been given the monumental and dangerous task of obtaining information from Hannibal Lecter (Anthony Hopkins) to assist in the identification of a serial killer. As a young woman in an overwhelmingly patri-archal situation, Clarice is the object of countless looks and intense visual scrutiny from those around her: Hannibal himself and other inmates, other FBI trainees, FBI agents, and just about any other men she comes into contact with. Clarice's reactions are also central to the film. She needs to put on a professional face, but her discomfort and distress are often very apparent, clearly displayed through numerous close-ups of Foster's expressive face (Plantinga 2015).

The point-of-view structure, together with other techniques, is also a remark-able way to represent differences in perspective nonverbally. In Episode 9 of the fourth season of *The Crown* (2020), Prince Charles (Josh O'Connor) and Lady Diana (Emma Corrin) attend a gala performance at the Royal Opera House in honor of the prince's 37th birthday. During the performance of various scenes from classical operas, we see by reaction shots that Charles is visibly moved. Diana, who appears to be distracted, excuses herself. Then, to Charles's surprise, she appears on stage with a ballet dancer, performing to Billy Joel's "Uptown Girl." The scene's point-of-view structure demonstrates the prince's growing discomfort with what he is seeing in a series of reaction shots. Diana, on the other hand, considers this to be a magnificent surprise birthday gift to her husband. She had secretly been practicing the dance for weeks; her face is radiant as she performs. The audience cheers her madly, further exacerbating Charles's anger as the attention is once again being drawn to her rather than to him.

The point-of-view structure draws our attention to the diverging ways that Charles and Diana understand this performance. To further demonstrate Charles's alienation from what he sees, as the camera rests on him, the diegetic sound is submerged be-neath discordant musical notes that drown out the sound of the performance, signaling Charles's upset. In close-up we see him beginning to breathe heavily. Later, in the car on their way home, he angrily calls her performance a "grotesque, mortifying display." We don't read about the diverging perspectives, and not until after the performance do the characters verbally express them. During the performance scene, we see and hear social and artistic signs of them that make these diverging perspectives readily apparent.

The portrayal of human perspective through looks and close-ups is arguably a key way in which narrative can increase moral understanding. Moral cognition certainly requires that we understand how others see the world—their experiences, motiv-ations, intentions, and influences. It is not merely sorting through what the charac-ters see and do that can lead to moral reflection and understanding, but also sorting through how they *understand* what they see and do.

Phenomenal Aspects of Theory of Mind

If we can learn to understand other people better, presumably this is a cognitive achievement that could increase moral understanding. Knowing why people behave and think in various ways in situations with diverse moral demands is arguably a central facet of moral reflection. To understand how a character exemplifies moral virtue, for example, one must first understand the character's motivations and intentions. To understand how a character falls short of virtue, one must first understand the nature and implications of that falling short.

The virtual exercise of social cognitive skills and knowledge is not solely a feature of screen stories, of course. Lisa Zunshine has argued that the exercise of "mind reading" or "Theory of Mind," which she describes as "the evolved cognitive adaptation that makes us see behavior as caused by underlying mental states," is a prominent feature of our engagement of many genres of popular culture and the arts, including novels, theater, movies, reality TV, mockumentaries, photography, stand-up comedy, and painting (2012, 2). Psychologist James Cutting argues that the recent predominance of visual culture has made us more facile in visual cognition, and that this, together with our access to stories in general, has left us "better primed to understand protagonists and their panoply of difficulties than were our great grandparents and those before them" (2021, 137). The exercise of social cognitive skills extends beyond mind reading per se, as it would include the interpretation of context in social interaction. Yet mind reading is a central feature of social cognition nonetheless.

How does screen storytelling engage mind reading and social cognition differently? When we watch stories on screens, we consistently ascribe to characters mental and bodily states based not only on verbal description or on dialogue alone but also on what we see and hear: facial expression, posture, gesture, vocal intonation, interactive movement, and numerous other social cues. Filmmakers have many tools to highlight and draw the viewer's attention to all of these through point-of-view editing, close-ups, camera movements, framing, blocking, sound manipulation and mixing, and various other means of emphasis through editing, such as sudden and surprising juxtapositions of elements. Elsewhere I have argued that the close-up of the human face engages mind reading on the part of the audience (Plantinga 2015), as does what I call the "scene of empathy" (Plantinga 1999). And Cutting (2021, 168–184) has argued that the reaction shot, for similar reasons, is the most important shot in popular cinema.

Here the relationship between the director and the actor is vital. In acting the role of a character, do actors draw from natural expression when portraying, for example, anger or disgust, or are acting styles idiosyncratic or perhaps wholly conventional? The answer most likely lies somewhere in between these choices. Clearly the way that Jack Nicholson is able to raise his eyebrows is particular to Jack Nicholson's remarkable face. Yet this does not show that his raised eyebrows necessarily mean something different from the raised eyebrows of other humans in similar contexts, or of other actors working in similar performance styles. Nicholson's peculiar face may lend a special force to expressions that we nonetheless understand as conventional and/or natural.

In the case of theatrical filmmaking, it has often been said that the running time of a traditional film prohibited films from examining character and social cognition at the deep levels of the novel. A 90-minute movie has the narrative length, in relation to number of events represented, of a short story more than a novel. It isn't that shorter narratives can't lead to moral learning, necessarily. The parable of the Good Samaritan, arguably, can bring home the basic nature of altruism as well as the lengthiest and most complex narrative. And a traditional-length film such as *M* (1931), as James Harold notes in his book *Dangerous Art: On Moral Criticism of Artworks*, may successfully illustrate the ethically complex nature of guilt and punishment (2020, 81).

But complexity and length, as in the streamed drama, may facilitate moral learning in a different way, as viewers virtually interact with a cast of characters with whom they become utterly familiar and whom they see in a variety of social environments and situations. The extended time frame of serial dramas such as *Mad Men* (2007–2015, 92 total episodes), *Borgen* (2010–2013, 30 episodes), and *Breaking Bad* (2008–2013, 62 episodes) have arguably enabled visual storytellers to approach novelistic complexity together with the visual and auditory signs of social cognition that are characteristic of stories on screens. Various scholars have noted that the extended storylines of streamed narratives provide many opportunities for viewers to engage with the complex mental states of characters in social situations (Blanchet and Bruun Vaage 2012; Mittel 2015).

A series like *Mad Men* essentially consists of people talking to each other: negotiating, warning, seducing, enticing, ordering, entertaining, boasting, informing, and cajoling. The characters do it before our eyes and ears, demonstrating the degree to which social cognition is played out in material contexts and is manifested in looks and glances, postures and poses, gestures and vocal intonations. As Jason Gendler argues, this series "excels at creating psychologically rich situations, routinely prompting viewers to make rich and rewarding inferences about character interiority" (2016, 40).

Audiovisual Metaphor

What I have covered so far—illustrative representation, looking and human perspectives, and the sensory nature of social cognition and theory of mind—rest on the particular way that screen stories engage "hot" cognition, that is, embodied cognition. Another particularly powerful means of doing so is the use of audiovisual, embodied metaphors. Cognitive linguist George Lakoff and philosopher Mark Johnson (1980) claim that the metaphors we use, heavily dependent on embodied perceptual experience, are key to how we make sense of the world. Cognitive metaphors function by referring to one idea (the source domain) in terms of another, related idea (the target domain).

The audiovisual metaphors used in screen stories are peculiar in how closely tied they can be to natural perception, due to the fact that the one "idea" compared with another (for purposes of illumination or illustration) is an actual visual image and/or physical sound (Forceville and Urios-Aparisis 2009; Grodal 1997; Fahlenbrach 2010). Thus we could also call these multimodal or cross-modal metaphors. Media scholar Charles Forceville uses the final scene of Stanley Kubrick's *Dr. Strangelove* (1964) to illustrate.

Unbeknownst to the intrepid pilots of an American military jet carrying atomic bombs, their order to drop their payload has been rescinded, but a malfunction in their communications equipment, together with security measures with unintended catastrophic consequences, means that they are unaware of the orders to stand down. In this scene, the crafty crewmembers manage to release their payload, but Major Kong ends up riding the bomb as though it were a kind of bucking bronco, befitting his cowboy persona. The audiovisual metaphor here blends and compares various ideas: Kong's joy in having successfully performed his duty against significant odds, the exhilaration of riding a bomb as though it were a bucking bronco, and the expected outcome that the dropping of this bomb may result in World War III. The ironic contrast between the perspective of Major Kong and that of the viewer is a chasm, and this chasm is brought home not only symbolically but also in sharply physical ways that depend on what we see (the image displayed) and what we hear (Kong's cheering wildly). This is a moral perspective that illustrates the possibility of radically different interpretations of an event and illustrates it in ways that are powerfully sensory.

For another example, in *The Silence of the Lambs*, Clarice gets on an elevator with several other FBI trainees, all of whom are men, and all of whom wear red shirts (while she is dressed in blues and grays and thus stands out as different, as a potential outsider). The two men in front look at her, while she looks up at the elevator ceiling, clearly uncomfortable. She stands out by the framing, as she is placed in the middle of the frame, surrounded by the men, standing out due to her smaller size, the colors of her clothes, her posture and stance, and the stares of each of the two men to her left and right (Plantinga 2015).

The image itself is an audiovisual metaphor for being, and feeling to be, conspicuously different, and is an excellent device to bring home Clarice's experience in a patriarchal environment. A linguistic metaphor with similar meaning, "standing out like a sore thumb," also has a bodily force as it suggests what it feels like to have a sore thumb, and we may be able to access this feeling through memory. But audiovisual metaphors have a more direct relationship to the body, as they provide an actual visual or audio perception. Such audiovisual metaphors can also be presented as sounds or as combinations of elements, including sound and image.

Knowledge and Moral Understanding

Suppose that we accept the proposition that screen stories, under some conditions, can provide not just a phenomenological experience but also phenomenological *knowledge* of what it is like to have a kind of experience. Suppose further that such knowledge can contribute to moral understanding. We then want to know: What are those conditions? How can we tell the difference between phenomenological experiences that are mystifying and misleading, and those that impart knowledge?

This determination would be a two-step process, requiring that we establish that a scene or film offers a phenomenological experience that (1) leads to phenomenal knowledge (what something sounds, looks, and/or feels like, for example) and (2) contributes to moral understanding. It may be easier to win agreement on what constitutes phenomenal knowledge than on what constitutes moral understanding. There is likely to be more agreement, for example, about what the situation of a refugee in dire straits looks or sounds like than on whether said refugee ought to be welcomed in crossing a national border to obtain a better life. People obviously disagree about moral issues, and thus will disagree about what constitutes a moral understanding of those issues. At the outset, then, we need to admit that whether a scene or film contributes to moral understanding depends in part on the perspective of the person who makes that determination. The fact that there is disagreement about what moral understanding constitutes, however, should not dissuade us from pursuing the conditions under which such agreement may be obtained in principle. After all, most of us believe that moral understanding *can* be obtained, despite disagreements about its nature.

Directed Realism and Patterns of Salience

Let us first take up the relationship between phenomenal experience and knowledge. How can the phenomenal experience of a scene lead to phenomenal knowledge? A simple answer to that question might appeal to the ontological realism of a film scene. By "ontological realism," I mean a certain kind of relationship between a film or scene and the actual world (Plantinga 2021, 20–28). A scene that is ontologically realistic conforms with or is like what it represents in salient respects. Thus we might say that a scene may contribute to phenomenological knowledge just in case the experience it provides in representing a situation or condition is, objectively speaking, similar in relevant ways to the experience of the actual situation or condition. Rafe McGregor argues that certain narratives, what he calls "exemplary narratives," can impart "lucid phenomenal knowledge," or in other words, a knowledge of what something is like, or what it might be like to "live though" an experience. Such an exemplary narrative "reenacts" an experiential structure that overlaps and resembles the experience that it represents (2015, 330).

Yet an appeal to ontological realism is not by itself a sufficient criterial requirement for phenomenal knowledge. One might ask *to what degree* ontological realism must be at work for a series such as *Mad Men* to have the capacity to teach us about the visual and aural cues of social cognition. One could similarly ask this question about my claims regarding phenomenological knowledge and human perspectives as represented though point-of-view structures in *The Silence of the Lambs*. Must the ontological realism in these cases be absolute, total, and comprehensive?

I would answer this question partly by saying that for a screen story to have value in moral learning, there must be some degree of ontological or objective realism, some contact with the world we actually live in. It is not the case, however, that maximum realism leads to maximum learning, as though there is a simple one-to-one correspondence here. It could be that stylized, exaggerated, or idealized behaviors, characters, and interactions may highlight moral truths more clearly and effectively than the complexities and ambiguities of the real world. Thought experiments such as the famous trolley problem are simple in their construction and perform whatever intuitive work they *do* perform despite the unlikeliness that such a scenario would ever occur in the actual world. It could be that the nature of racism, homophobia, adultery, narcissism, or kindness, in some cases and contexts, is best illustrated by the sort of hypercoherent or "erotetic" narrative that Nöel Carroll finds to be characteristic of the movies (1996, 78–93).

I will return to the notion of realism below. At this point I introduce the notion of *patterns of salience*. A film scene is never simply an imitation of any actual experience. A scene is designed and formed—or in other words, directed by the filmmakers, in many cases for maximum clarity, in other cases to create the *frisson* of ambiguity, or for diverse other purposes. Yet in any case, it is the patterns of salience by which the representation is organized that also contribute to phenomenal knowledge. These patterns come in many forms in film narrative, from editing structures (including point of view) and the production design of a scene to the narrative itself. In writing of lucid phenomenal knowledge, McGregor (2015) acknowledges this point, holding that it is only *exemplary* narratives that have the potential to provide such knowledge. He defines an exemplary narrative as one that "represents (1) one or more agents and (2) two or more events that are (3) causally connected, (4) thematically unified, and (5) conclude" (328).

The sort of narrative that can lead to phenomenal knowledge would require what I will call *directed realism*. One could also call it "focused" or "modeled" realism. A scene that features directed realism will be focused on exhibiting not all features of an experience, but the *salient* features of an experience. It will offer an experiential structure that resembles the experience it represents in key regards, yet makes no attempt to replicate that experience exactly. Take *The Sound of Metal* as an example. In representing Ruben's loss of hearing, the film condenses his experiences of hearing loss, which occur over a matter of months, into a film of two hours. This is hardly an exact replication of Ruben's experience; how could it be? Yet it is arguably realistic in that it provides a sense of what hearing loss is like by picking out and highlighting key moments and experiences that Ruben has while suffering the consequences.

As mentioned, Carroll (1996) argues that films can be hypercoherent in that through editing, framing, and other devices, they can guide the attention of the viewer in ways much more efficient and streamlined than in natural perception (see also Carroll 2003, 10–58). Such streamlined coherence, however, is not necessarily misleading with regard to phenomenal knowledge. In fact, it could be used to draw the viewer's attention to the salient elements of a scene such that the viewer's knowledge is enhanced and extraneous detail omitted. This well-formed, or hypercoherent, version of directed realism is not the only sort possible; various forms of ambiguity and self-referentiality, in other contexts, could arguably promote phenomenal knowledge as well.

The main point is that the phenomenal experiences provided by films are not unformed representations of phenomenal experience. They may feature elements that are conventional. They may feature patterns of salience that are characteristic of directed realism. They may provide a semblance of an experience within the context of patterns and forms designed to highlight its salient features. *The Sound of Metal* does not merely provide random sonic experiences of someone going deaf, but patterns them in a carefully crafted, temporally structured narrative designed to highlight the phenomenal experience of increasing deafness. *The Silence of the Lambs*, similarly, uses patterns of editing to suggest Clarice's perspective as she navigates the dangerous criminal investigation that is her mission. And *Mad Men* features blocking, production design, and character interactions in patterns designed to cue insights into the minds of individual characters, and into the workings of group dynamics and social cognition generally. A scene of directed realism, then, is a *model of experience*. In cognitive terms, it incorporates both bottom-up phenomenal experiences and top-down patterns of salience, the cognitive frameworks that enable us to make sense of our experiences.

Not all models of experience are equally capable of offering phenomenal knowledge, of course. Not all patterns of salience will lead to phenomenal knowledge. Some may, in fact, mislead us. What I have offered thus far is a clearer path to assessing the success of a scene or entire film in providing such knowledge. The assessment of particular screen stories will have to be made on a case-by-case basis.

A Qualifying Ethical Project

Once we have determined that a phenomenal experience may lead to knowledge, the next step is to gauge the success of this knowledge in contributing to moral understanding. I follow the lead of other scholars in taking understanding to be a more significant epistemic achievement than knowledge. Though here I can only nod to this literature, an understanding of an issue or problem assists us in the development of models, in the asking of salient questions, in "understanding why," in grasping connections, in categorization, and in improving cognitive abilities (Baumberger 2013; Hills 2016). A *moral* understanding of an action or situation would comprehend the

moral implications of human behavior in contexts that can be fraught with ambiguities and contradictions. How do the demands of loyalty to a friend measure up to the
demands of justice, once one discovers that the friend has committed a serious crime?
How do the circumstances of refugees and immigrants relate to the moral obligations
of a wealthy country to take them in and care for them? One of the chief traditional
concerns of narrative, broadly speaking, is to engage the moral imagination in ways
that can exercise just this sort of understanding (see Nannicelli in this volume).

For a screen story to employ phenomenal knowledge in the service of moral understanding, it must have what I will simply call a *qualifying ethical project*, that is, a
project that generates phenomenal knowledge for the purpose of examining a moral
theme in an ethically responsible way. What constitutes a qualifying ethical project
depends in part on how one conceives of the possible effects of viewing various sorts
of screen stories. While this issue obviously deserves a much longer and deeper discussion, I will say that in this regard I side with Sarah Kozloff (2013), who advocates
for the benefits of what she calls a "cinema of engagement" over alternatives such
as (1) cine-Brechtianism, with its emphasis on reflexivity and distanciation; (2) the
cinema of irony, providing "a wink between the filmmaker and the audience at the expense of the characters"; and (3) postmodern cinema, which she calls "without hope
or people" and "unmoored from Enlightenment faith in reason, knowledge, and social progress" 2013, 8, 11). A cinema of engagement recognizes the central importance of character engagement, empathy, and emotional response in engaging the
viewer's moral imagination.

What constitutes a qualifying ethical project *also* depends on the particular ethical and political principles to which one appeals. Thus it is doubtful that there can
be an objective measure of such a project. While some may find Spike Lee's films *Do
the Right Thing* (1989) and *BlacKkKlansman* (2018) to be exemplary ethical projects
in their examination of racism, others may not. It is for this reason that Kozloff advocates that anyone writing about ethics or politics in screen stories ought to identify
their ethical/political perspective.

Despite possible disagreements, any determination of the nature of a qualifying
ethical project will at least need to identify the ethical and moral principles or problems it illuminates. Thus one could argue that *Mad Men* may provide understanding
of the moral implications of decision-making in the context of group dynamics; it
may lead to an understanding of the moral complexity of common situations. *The
Sound of Metal* may lead to understanding and empathy for those experiencing deafness or other disabilities. *The Silence of the Lambs* may similarly lead to an understanding of the experience of women in patriarchal environments.

The means by which films can employ phenomenal experience in the service of
moral understanding has been a significant direction of research recently. One thinks,
for example, of Jane Stadler's (2014) examination of "cinema's compassionate gaze" in
her treatment of *The Diving Bell and the Butterfly* (2007), Robert Sinnerbrink's (2016)
considerations of the ethical implications of marital conflict in *A Separation* (2011),
or Kozloff's (2013, 29) insistence that it is our engagement with films such as *The*

Insider (1999), including both empathy and emotional response, that leads to their capacity to teach us and perhaps lead to a change in "hearts, minds, and laws." The list could go on substantially.

Conclusion

The purpose of this chapter is to establish a plausible analytic framework to gauge whether the phenomenal experiences offered by screen stories can be said to promote both phenomenal knowledge and moral understanding. I describe four major means by which films provide phenomenal experiences to increase knowledge both of what something is like and what it means for a character: through illustrative representation, the representation of looks and looking, the representation of visual and sonic cues to social cognition, and audiovisual metaphors. I go on to argue that adducing whether these phenomenal experiences lead to phenomenal knowledge requires that we understand the patterns of salience and directed realism through which filmmakers put such experiences into a context and elicit various forms of top-down cognition. Finally, I claim that for such knowledge to lead to moral understanding, it must be employed in the context of a qualifying ethical project.

As I write in the introduction, this framework is not meant to settle this enormously complex issue but rather to provide a good ground for further discussion. Let the debate continue.

Acknowledgments

Thanks to Roy Anker, Noël Carroll, Eileen John, Héctor Peréz, Malcolm Turvey, Nicholas Wolterstorff, and participants in the Screen Stories and Moral Understanding symposium for their comments on earlier versions of this chapter.

Works Cited

Baumberger, Christoph. 2013. "Art and Understanding: In Defense of Aesthetic Cognitivism." In *Bilder sehen: Perspektiven der Bildwissenschaft*, edited by Mark Greenlee, Rainer Hammwöhner, Christoph Wagner, and Christian Wolff, 41–67. Regensburg: Schnell & Steiner.

Blanchet, Robert, and Margrethe Bruun Vaage. 2012. "Don, Peggy, and Other Fictional Friends? Engaging with Characters in Television Series." *Projections* 6, no. 2: 18–41. https://doi.10.3167/proj.2012.060203.

Carroll, Nöel. 1996. *Theorizing the Moving Image*. Cambridge: Cambridge University Press.

Carroll, Nöel. 2003. *Engaging the Moving Image*. New Haven, CT: Yale University Press.

Cutting, James. 2021. *Movies on Our Minds: The Evolution of Cinematic Engagement*. New York: Oxford University Press.

Fahlenbrach, Kathrin. 2010. *Audiovisuelle Metaphern: Zur Körper- und Affectästhetik in Film und Fehrnsehen*. Marburg: Schüren.

Forceville, Charles, and Eduardo Urios-Aparisis. 2009. *Multi-Modal Metaphor*. Berlin: Mouton de Gruyter.

Freeland, Cynthia. 1997. "Art and Moral Knowledge." *Philosophical Topics* 25, no. 1: 11–35.

Gallese, Vittorio, and Michele Guerra. 2020. *The Empathic Screen: Cinema and Neuroscience*. Oxford: Oxford University Press.

Gendler, Jason. 2016. "The Rich Inferential World of Mad Men: Serialized Television and Character Interiority." *Projections* 10, no. 1: 39-62. https://doi.org/10.3167/proj.2016.100.107.

Graham, Gordon. 2005. *Philosophy of the Arts*. 3rd ed. London: Routledge.

Grodal, Torben. 1997. *Moving Pictures: A New Theory of Film Genres, Feelings, and Cognition*. Oxford: Clarendon Press.

Harold, James. 2020. *Dangerous Art: On Moral Criticism of Artworks*. New York: Oxford University Press.

Hills, Alison. 2016. "Understanding Why." *Noûs* 50, no. 4: 661–688.

hooks, bell. 1992. *Black Looks: Race and Representation*. Boston: South End Press.

Kozloff, Sarah. 2013. "Empathy and the Cinema of Engagement: Reevaluating the Politics of Film." *Projections: The Journal for Movies and Mind* 7, no. 2: 1–40.

Lakoff, George, and Mark Johnson. 1980. *Metaphors We Live By*. Chicago: University of Chicago Press.

McGregor, Rafe. 2015. "Narrative Representation and Phenomenological Knowledge." *Australasian Journal of Philosophy* 94, no. 2: 327–342.

Meretoja, Hannah. 2018. *The Ethics of Storytelling: Hermeneutics, History, and the Possible*. Oxford: Oxford University Press.

Mittell, Jason. 2015. *Complex TV: The Poetics of Contemporary Television Storytelling*. New York: New York University Press.

Mulvey, Laura. 1975. "Visual Pleasure and Narrative Cinema." *Screen* 16, no. 3: 6–18.

Murphy, Mikado. 2020. "What Hearing Loss Feels Like in 'Sound of Metal.'" *New York Times*, December 4. https://www.nytimes.com/2020/12/04/movies/sound-of-metal-hearing-loss.html.

Nussbaum, Martha. 1990. *Love's Knowledge: Essays on Philosophy and Literature*. New York: Oxford University Press.

Oatley, Keith. 2011. *Such Stuff as Dreams: The Psychology of Fiction*. Malden, MA: Wiley-Blackwell.

Perkins, V. F. 1972. *Film as Art: Understanding and Judging Movies*. Harmondsworth: Penguin Books.

Persson, Per. 2003. *Understanding Cinema: A Psychological Theory of Moving Imagery*. Cambridge: Cambridge University Press.

Plantinga, Carl. 1999. "The Scene of Empathy and the Human Face in Film." In *Passionate Views: Film, Cognition, and Emotion*, edited by Carl Plantinga and Greg M. Smith, 239–255. Baltimore, MD: Johns Hopkins University Press.

Plantinga, Carl. 2009. *Moving Viewers: American Film and the Spectator's Experience*. Berkeley: University of California Press.

Plantinga, Carl. 2015. "Facing Others: Close-ups of Faces in Narrative Film and in *The Silence of the Lambs*." In *The Oxford Handbook of Cognitive Cultural Studies*, edited by Lisa Zunshine, 291–312. Oxford: Oxford University Press.

Plantinga, Carl. 2018. *Screen Stories: Emotion and the Ethics of Engagement*. New York: Oxford University Press.

Plantinga, Carl. 2021. *Alternative Realities*. New Brunswick, NJ: Rutgers University Press.

Sinnerbrink, Robert. 2016. *Cinematic Ethics: Exploring Ethical Experience through Film.* London: Routledge.

Sinnerbrink, Robert. 2019. *Terrence Malick: Filmmaker and Philosopher.* London: Bloomsbury Academic.

Smith, Murray. 2017. *Film, Art, and the Third Culture: A Naturalized Aesthetics of Film.* Oxford: Oxford University Press.

Stadler, Jane. 2014. "Cinema's Compassionate Gaze: Empathy, Affect, and Aesthetics in *The Diving Bell and the Butterfly.*" In *Cine-Ethics: Ethical Dimensions of Film Theory, Practice, and Spectatorship*, edited by Jinhee Choi and Mattias Frey, 79–95. New York: Routledge.

Young, James O. 2001. *Art and Knowledge.* London: Routledge.

Zunshine, Lisa. 2012. *Getting Inside Your Head: What Cognitive Science Can Teach Us about Popular Culture.* Baltimore, MD: Johns Hopkins University Press.

4

Moral Cultivation

The Slow, Subtle, Small Effects of Filmic Narrative on Moral Understanding

Helena Bilandzic

Stories are permeated with lessons about adequate and inadequate behavior, constituting a narrative morality of human coexistence (Bilandzic 2018; Bilandzic, Hastall, and Sukalla 2017). Filmic narrative in television, the cinema, streaming services, and video platforms on the internet are popular sources of such moral messages. Although television is gradually being replaced as a "primary storyteller" (Morgan, Shanahan, and Signorielli 2009, 41) by streaming services like Netflix, Hulu, and Disney+, it is still filmic narrative that remains important for audiences, delivering similar content through different platforms (Morgan, Shanahan, and Signorielli 2015). Often it is serial narratives that capture the attention of audiences; plots and characters are developed over multiple episodes, increasing the complexity, richness, and appeal of both (Schlütz 2016). The availability of episodes independently of broadcasting time enables audiences to binge on the suspenseful stories for several hours in one session and have intense exposures across several days or weeks (Castro et al. 2021). This also means that people spend a considerable amount of time with the moral fabric of filmic narrative: audiences vicariously experience morally relevant situations; they are outraged by unfairness to the protagonist, feel the need for revenge, and are moved by altruistic actions.

While moral development is a lifelong process and primarily shaped by real-life socialization instances such as parents and peers (Kohlberg 1981), media narratives can contribute to that development through constant, repeated, and intensive exposures. Filmic narratives do not simply provide an educational message on morality; they also equip their audience with vivid examples of characters and actions and express moral judgment implicitly though storylines and emotions, which makes the moral messages both "invisible" and influential.

Corresponding to the long-term, cumulative nature of moral development through socialization instances, it stands to reason that media influence is equally long term and cumulative. Cultivation analysis investigates such long-term processes in which media messages influence and stabilize views of the audience (Busselle and Van den Bulck 2019). Adapting the approach to morality, I define moral cultivation as the long-term, cumulative shaping of the audience's perceptions, expectations, and

Helena Bilandzic, *Moral Cultivation* In: *Screen Stories and Moral Understanding*. Edited by: Carl Plantinga, Oxford University Press. © Oxford University Press 2023. DOI: 10.1093/oso/9780197665664.003.0005 thinking about good and bad behavior, which emerges as a result of repeated exposures to similar moral patterns in media stories.

In this chapter, I will review theoretical approaches and empirical results of studies that fall under this definition of moral cultivation, with a specific focus on the role of narrative experiences in this process.

Cultivation and Morality

The cultivation approach is in many ways suitable and useful to be applied for moral effects of media. First, while cultivation was not primarily concerned with morality, some of the descriptions of the theory contained references to morality. For example, an early account by its founder, George Gerbner, states with regard to the tight and supportive connection between societal power relations and television, "The rules of the games and the morality of its goals can best be demonstrated by the dramatic stories of their symbolic violations. The intended lessons are generally effective and the social order is only rarely and peripherally threatened" (Gerbner and Gross 1976, 177). Stories "about what to do" (Gerbner et al. 1978, 178) are also references to the moral question about right and wrong behavior (Gerbner et al. 1978).

Second, although filmic narrative comes in many shapes and variations, at a deeper level we often find similar moral messages that confirm an existing moral order. Gerbner et al. (2002, 44) state for such common lessons in television content, "Programs that seem to be intended for very different market segments are cut from the same mold; when surface-level differences are wiped away, what remains are often surprisingly similar and complementary visions of life and society, consistent ideologies, and stable accounts of the 'facts' of life." For example, the moral value "fairness" may be demonstrated in a crime story in which the criminal is found and put in jail, or a drama in which betrayal among friends leads to unhappiness for the betrayer.

Third, as is true for cultivation in general, filmic narrative reflects commonsense morality of our everyday world; it is not something apart from our lives that can be pinpointed as an external and singular influence. Rather, morality in stories often confirms moral standards that are also valid in the actual world (for an overview, see Bilandzic 2018). In this way, moral effects function in a similar way as cultivation: we see moral standards reflected in stories, expand our moral understanding, and turn back to stories with a somewhat modified mindset. This stresses that fact that media effects regarding morality do not find a tabula rasa in their audience but more or less differentiated moral views that may change the way moral content is processed and experienced. Thus, it makes sense to assume that there is an interaction of effects and voluntary exposures, gradually evolving over time.

Polysemy, the potential of a text to have multiple meanings, has always been an issue in cultivation. Gerbner et all (18 million) acknowledge the problem of individual interpretation, but at the same time emphasize the "enduring, resilient, and residual core" of the "massive flows of messages over long periods of time," which imply preferred readings and a stable common understanding of the message (2002, 48).

The problem of polysemy is exacerbated in moral cultivation. First, morality can be located in different places of a narrative. It can be a single norm violation, for example, a lie or an insult which does not have consequences for the plot. It can also be the central conflict that defines narrative progression, for example, when a film starts with the protagonist being betrayed by her best friend and the plot is defined by this norm violation. Or, rather than manifesting in norm violations, morality can emerge from *confirmations* of moral norms, for example, when one character is helping another.

Second, polysemy exists not only on the level of a single message. Cultivation does not work with single narratives, but with a series of narratives that have similar properties regarding their moral message. This means that the moral message need not be determined only within a narrative but can develop across a series of narratives. In addition to the aggregation of the moral message to a pattern that makes sense, we also need to determine the units in which these patterns exist; for example, is the correct boundary a genre, a show, or filmic narrative in general? Certainly it is a challenge to find labels for genres that audiences recognize and understand in the same way as the researcher (Bilandzic and Busselle 2012). There are two ways to tackle this problem. One is to conduct content analyses that parallel the message system analysis in cultivation (Busselle and Van den Bulck 2019) for morality (Bilandzic, Hastall, and Sukalla 2017; Daalmans, Hijmans, and Wester 2017). Another (possibly additional) way is to validate an analysis of the moral content by asking audiences what they think a typical moral message of a genre is. For example, Potter presents a study on the perception of general lessons or "primary values" of television content, which can be regarded as a preparatory study for a cultivation analysis (1990). Potter found that the notion "Good wins over evil" was considered an important theme in television content; the more people regularly watched prime-time soaps and daytime soaps, the more they identified this value as an important one in television. Conversely, watching sitcoms, action-adventures, and cartoons lowered the perception as important. Then the perception "Truth always wins out; honesty is best policy" as an important TV theme was increased with prime-time and daytime soap exposure, and the perception "Evil wins over good" being an important TV lesson was strengthened by prime-time soap exposure and lowered by sitcom exposure.

Similarly, Bilandzic, Schnell, and Sukalla (2019) conducted a validation study for moral content in genre series as preparation for a cultivation study. They investigated "idealistic moral expectations"—"a person's belief that the world, essentially, functions in a morally acceptable way" (605)—and used three idealistic moral expectations: the just world belief (a moral pattern of crime drama), doctors' professional altruism (a moral pattern of medical drama), and tolerance of otherness (a moral pattern of sitcoms). To validate the idealistic moral expectations, Bilandzic, Schnell, and Sukalla created three short descriptions for each of the beliefs and asked respondents how typical each of the descriptions were for the three genres. Confirming the "genre lessons," respondents found the respective idealistic moral expectations most typical for the correct genre.

We can conclude that a simple content analysis may not be enough to determine the relevant media lessons for moral cultivation. The "double polysemy" of moral cultivation (on the level of a single message and on the level of a whole genre or other larger units) certainly requires some additional effort to determine a genre's, a program's, or a film's moral message.

Types of Moral Cultivation Outcomes

Cultivation outcomes are roughly divided into first-order judgments (e.g., frequencies of events such as murders or proportions of demographic groups such as women) and second-order judgments, such as fear of crime or mistrust of people (Hawkins and Pingree 1990).

This distinction is useful for moral cultivation, but it is not sufficient. Therefore, this chapter suggests a new way to structure existing research on long-term moral effects and will do so by using concepts from moral psychology. This will help to identify similar research without being distracted by different labels. Five outcomes of moral cultivation can be identified: (1) estimates of norm violations, (2) moral values and intuition, (3) moral reasoning, (4) moral judgment of actions and people, and (5) moral sensitivity (see Figure 4.1). The following sections will explain these types

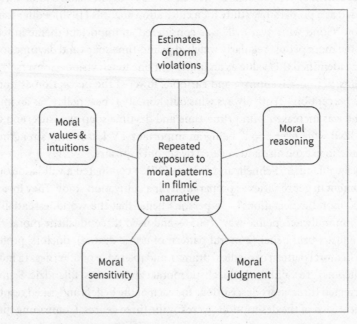

Figure 4.1 Types of Moral Cultivation Outcomes

of moral cultivation outcomes, present examples of research for each of them, and highlight the role of narrative experience in these effects.

Estimates of Norm Violations

Parallel to the first-order estimates in traditional cultivation, an indicator of moral cultivation is whether viewers overestimate the prevalence of norm violations that appear frequently in media. This is the one of the few domains of moral cultivation in which we can find results from traditional cultivation studies. While many first-order effects were investigated in cultivation, many did not touch upon moral issues (like gender distribution, occupational roles, divorce rates). However, one domain that was important from the start does represent a norm violation: estimates of crime. In an early study, Gerbner and Gross (1976) found that heavy television viewers over-estimated their own chances of being involved in violence compared to light viewers. However, this study did not differentiate between genres, using television exposure as a whole, which may contain narrative *and* nonnarrative programs. Other studies explored the relationships between crime estimates and a semantically related genre. For example, Hawkins and Pingree (1981) used a composite index for an estimate of violence in society among children; the index included estimates of the respondent being involved in some kind of violence, the percentage of Australian men who work in law enforcement, the percentage of murders being committed among strangers, and the prevalence of violent crimes. They found a positive relationship with viewing crime adventure shows. But research is inconsistent here—other studies found no effects (O'Keefe 1984) or negative effects of genre viewing and crime estimates (Potter and Chang 1990). In an attempt to systematically investigate the perception of norm violations across different genres, Bilandzic and Schnell (2019) conducted a cross-sectional survey of 520 German adults (for details on the methods, see Bilandzic, Schnell, and Sukalla 2019); they collected data on genre viewing for crime drama, medical drama, and comedy as well as estimates on norm violations in each of the genres (crime: estimates of murder, burglaries, and assault; medical drama: violations of professional rules, eliminating professional competition through collusion, care-lessness, and disregarding the will of others; comedy: jokes at the expense of others, insults and provocations, carelessness, and mocking other people's weaknesses). They also included a scale for narrative engageability (Bilandzic et al. 2019), the propen-sity to become intensely and emotionally engaged in a story, expecting that regular immersed viewing experiences would strengthen the cultivation effect. Narrative engageability encompasses four dimensions: (1) "Propensity for Presence" describes how much people feel present in that narrative (rather than the actual) world when they watch or read a narrative; (2) "Emotional Engageability" refers to the extent that people let themselves be emotionally affected by a story and its characters; (3) "Propensity for Suspense/Curiosity" refers to the processing the representation of events, suggesting that the viewer not only understands events but also has the

Table 4.1 Regression Analysis for Genre Viewing and Narrative Engageability Predicting Estimates of Norm Violations Typical for Crime Drama, Medical Drama, and Comedy

	Estimates of Norm Violations Typical for …		
	Crime Drama	Medical Drama	Comedy
Crime viewing	.02	—	—
Medical drama viewing	—	−.005	—
Comedy viewing	—	—	.05
Narrative engageability	.05	.11*	.11*
Model summary	$R^2 = .00$, $F = .61$ n.s.	$R^2 = .01$, $F = 3.1$*	$R^2 = .02$, $F = 4.3$*

Note: n = 520. Values represent standardized regression coefficients. *p < .05; **p < .01; ***p < .001.
Source: Bilandzic and Schnell (2019).

impression of being in the middle of the events and is keen on learning how the plot is resolved; (4) "Ease of Accepting Unrealism" expresses that viewers, to some extent, are able to tolerate violations of realism and process the story even if it does not correspond to the actual world (Bilandzic et al. 2019). The assumption is that repeated exposures while highly engaged increase the effect of narratives, as the exposures happen with more elaboration and less critical scrutiny (Bilandzic et al. 2019). Bilandzic and Schnell (2019) found no effects of genre viewing on the estimates of norm violations. However, narrative engageability was positively related to estimates of norm violations regarding medical drama and comedy, but not crime viewing (see Table 4.1). The more people have the propensity to be engaged in narratives, the more norm violations related to medical drama and comedy they perceive.

Nonetheless, the patterns found in empirical research are less than conclusive. There is no strong evidence to indicate that viewing a specific genre increases a viewer's perceptions of related norm violations. Still, first evidence from the study by Bilandzic and Schnell (2019) shows that narrative engageability increases, albeit slightly, the perception of norm violations in medical drama and comedy. This may point to interesting yet unexplored effects of intense viewing, suggesting that mere exposure matters less than the quality and intensity of exposure.

Moral Values

In general, a value is commonly defined as "an enduring belief that a specific mode of conduct or end-state of existence is personally or socially preferable to an opposite or converse mode of conduct or end-state of existence" (Rokeach 1973, 5). Moral values are a subset and can be defined as "beliefs about what is good and evil behavior within the individual's control, bearing on relations to self, to others, to God, and to the natural and animal world," for example, respect for life, respect for property, honest communication, and respect for religion (Scott 2000, 510).

There are some early examples of values in cultivation research. Gerbner et al. (1980, 17) used a measure for cultivation that can be considered an indicator of moral values that prevail in society: the mean world index captures the "degree to which respondents agree that most people are just looking out for themselves, that you can't be too careful in dealing with people, and that most people would take advantage of you if they got a chance." They found a positive relationship between TV viewing and the mean world index: the more people watched television, the more they agreed with the mean world index. This can be considered an assessment of how others in society act according to common moral values.

Other studies have focused on the values that audience members themselves hold. For example, Morgan, Leggett, and Shanahan (1999) found that heavy television viewing lowered endorsement of traditional values and increased acceptance of single parenthood. This study, however, did not differentiate between narrative and nonnarrative elements in television consumption—it was simply overall television viewing that served as an independent variable. Another example exploring long-term cultivation effects on values is a study by Appel (2008) that found a positive relationship of watching fiction on television with the notion that the world is a just place (belief in a just world).

Bilandzic, Schnell, and Sukalla (2019) investigated cultivation effects of typical moral messages in the popular television genres of crime drama, medical drama, and sitcom. For each of these, they identified a prevalent moral theme from existing literature that is able to generate expectations about the moral functioning of the real world, the "idealistic moral expectations," which describe the belief that the world functions in a morally acceptable way. Crime drama as a genre in which a crime threatens the social order by creating injustice, but in the end presents how order is reinstated and justice served, is expected to generate just world beliefs (the belief that the world is a just place). Medical drama featuring plot lines around medical doctors working hard for their patients is expected to cultivate the belief that doctors prioritize the welfare of their patients and display professional altruism. Finally, sitcoms foreground friendships and relationships and often draw humor from the characters' idiosyncratic, surprising, and at times odd behaviors. As described in detail above, these idealistic moral expectations were validated in a pretest to ensure that the beliefs are congruent with viewer perceptions of moral genre stereotypes. Contrary to cultivation expectations, viewing the three genres did not correlate with any of the idealistic moral expectations. However, the study also collected data on trait narrative engageability—the individual propensity to become deeply engaged in narratives. Results show that all three idealistic moral expectations positively correlate with narrative engageability. The more people become cognitively and emotionally engaged in narratives on a regular basis, the more they expect the world to function according to the moral genre stereotypes.

Closest to the general nature of (moral) values are approaches based on the Social Intuitionist Approach, which states that moral judgment is triggered by quick, spontaneous moral intuitions; more deliberate moral reasoning, in this approach, is activated only afterward, when needed, and happens much more slowly (Haidt 2001; Haidt and Joseph 2008). For moral intuitions, people do not consciously weigh evidence or deliberate; they are defined as "the sudden appearance in consciousness of a moral judgment, including an affective valence (good-bad, like-dislike), without any conscious awareness of having gone through steps of search, weighing evidence, or inferring a conclusion" (Haidt 2001, 818). The Social Intuitionist Approach identifies five sets of moral concerns, which together form the moral foundations of human morality: harm/care (protecting the young and vulnerable, having compassion, and acting with kindness), fairness/reciprocity (being fair, honest, and trustworthy), in-group/loyalty (averting threats from one's ingroup, being loyal and patriotic, accepting sacrifices for the group), authority/respect (showing obedience and deference to authority, respecting people higher up in the hierarchy), and purity/sanctity (exhibiting temperance, chastity, piety, and cleanliness) (Haidt and Joseph 2008, 382). This basic idea was adapted by Tamborini (2011, 2012) in his Model of Intuitive Morality and Exemplars (MIME) to explain how morality and media exposure interact. Viewers observe exemplars in narratives, that is characters and actions that either adhere to a moral domain or violate it; this will activate one or more moral intuitions, lead to certain short-term outcomes (such as automatic appraisals of characters or events, decisions to continue or end exposure). For the long term, repeated exposure to exemplars that make certain moral domains salient will lead to chronic accessibility of these domains, making them more influential for social judgments, even outside the viewing situation (Tamborini 2012). The long-term component of the MIME connects the approach to the long-term nature of cultivation processes. A study by Eden et al. (2014) specifically tests the long-term component of the MIME and explores changes in the accessibility of moral domains through repeated exposure to a soap opera. Respondents received eight weeks of prolonged exposure to a soap opera; moral domain salience was measured before and after exposure. While the measures for salience of the moral domains did not increase after eight weeks of exposure, the authors observed that they remained constant in the experimental group, and dropped in the control group with no exposure. The authors argue that the "natural" process includes a positivity bias in the salience measures that fades over time; in the experimental group, fading was prevented by exposure.

Moral Reasoning

The first two types of cultivation effects, estimation of norm violations and moral values, both imply a straightforward, consistent relationship between media content and beliefs held by the viewers: the more people watch television, the more consistent the relationship should get, because viewers are exposed to either more instances of violations of norms or more instances of moral values. These two types describe how people think the moral texture of the world is and what is important and what is not important. The type described in this section—moral reasoning—is on a more abstract level and concerns the way people *justify* moral decisions (rather than actually make the decisions). Moral reasoning is based on moral schemas as "general knowledge structures used in social cooperation" that essentially represent different ways to justify moral decisions (Narvaez and Bock 2022, 302). The moral schemas help the decider navigate the moral decision, for example, by directing attention, filling in missing information, or connecting different stimuli; schemas make processing relevant information more efficient (Narvaez and Bock 2002). While moral schemas are developed by experiences in actual social interaction, they can also be influenced by symbolic and vicarious experiences from media.

Rather than looking at moral reasoning as developmental stages, as Kohlberg (1981) did, the "neo-Kohlbergian approach" distinguishes between three moral reasoning schemas that—combined—can characterize the unique style of a person's moral decision-making and that are more flexible and subject to situational experiences and influences (Rest et al. 2000). (1) The *personal interest schema* puts forward the needs, wants, and fears of the individual, for example, when a person eats the last cookie in the house because they anticipate how good it will taste. (2) The *maintaining norms schema* emphasizes the importance of rules and regulations; moral decisions are made to respect those rules. For example, a driver does not park their car in a tow-away zone because they know it is forbidden and they will receive a fine for doing so. (3) The most sophisticated moral schema is the *postconventional schema*. Rather than strictly following rules, the guiding principles are shared ideals. But these are open to negotiation and rational scrutiny. For example, while lying is a norm violation, a person may come to the decision to tell their friend that their home-cooked meal is very good, even if tastes like day-old cardboard.

Considering that personal interest, norms, and more differentiated moral deliberations are differently represented in plots of filmic narrative, it makes sense to assume that one's viewing repertoire matters for how we justify moral decisions. Schnell and Bilandzic (2017) tested the relationship between exposure to three genres of television series (crime drama, medical drama, and sitcoms) and agreement to moral schemas. In a prolonged exposure design, participants received around five hours of series from one genre per week over the course of four weeks. After four weeks, moral reasoning was measured with an adaption of the Defining Issues Test (Rest et al. 1999) for each of the three genres: respondents received six scenarios containing moral dilemmas that might typically be encountered in each of the genres. The example in Table 4.2 shows the vignette of the moral dilemma for medical drama.

After reading the vignette, respondents had to decide what the main character should do; after that, they rated 12 statements, four of which represented one type of reasoning schema (Table 4.3). Finally, the respondents had to rank the four most important considerations, from 1 to 4. One score for each reasoning schema was computed.

Table 4.2 Vignette of the Moral Dilemma for Medical Drama

A patient is suffering from a rare disease, for which currently no treatment is available. In the coming months, the patient will gradually grow weaker and finally die. His doctor learns from a colleague that a new, possibly helpful medication will go into clinical trials soon. When the doctor looks into the requirements for the test, he finds that his patient would be a great fit and might benefit immensely from the medication. However, sometime in the past his patient confided in him that he had a drug addiction 10 years ago, but has been clean for several years now. The doctor knows that this information will lead to his patient being automatically excluded from the trial.

Should the doctor keep this information for himself and recommend his patient for the clinical trial?

yes no can't decide

Source: Schnell and Bilandzic (2017).

Table 4.3 Ratings for Moral Schemas

Now we will show you some considerations which may be relevant for your decision. Please place yourself into the position of the doctor and indicate for every consideration, how important it would be for you (scale from 1 "not at all important" to 7 "very important").

Personal interest

1. Whether the patient will be grateful if he is cured by the medication.
2. Whether it will be an advantage for your career if your patient is one of the first people to be cured by the medication.
3. Whether it is more important to cure the patient than what society thinks of you.
4. Whether you are truly only acting to help the patient.

Maintaining norms

1. Whether clinical trials make any sense if doctors lie for their patients.
2. Whether you are obligated to be truthful to the developers of the medication.
3. Whether you have to respect the developers' rules about the clinical trial.
4. Whether you are breaking confidentiality if you are talking about the drug past of the patient.

Postconventional

1. Whether it is more important to heal a single ill person than to have a scientifically sound test for the medication before it is introduced to the market.
2. Whether the public does have a right to have only medication available, which has been tested in a correct medical trial.
3. Whether any doctor is obligated to help his patient at any cost.
4. Whether it isn't more important to save a life than to follow protocol.

Source: Schnell and Bilandzic (2017).

The study showed that exposure to crime drama did not have any effect on the moral reasoning schema. As for medical drama, exposure strengthened the maintaining norms schema, but weakened postconventional thinking. And comedy exposure strengthened postconventional thinking. Again, narrative engageability was included in the study in an attempt to assess the role of intensive viewing.

And indeed, narrative engageability proved once again to be a good predictor of morality: engageability showed a negative relationship with the maintaining norms schema and a positive relationship with postconventional thinking. Thus, independently of actual exposure, people who engaged in narratives on a regular basis had more sophisticated moral schemas.

Moral reasoning refers to the way people justify their moral decisions. On a more abstract level, there are two phenomena that are indicative of ongoing moral reasoning: moral reflection and moral rumination. Rather than detailing the criteria for moral judgment, moral reflection and rumination inform about the extent of moral thinking.

The concept of "moral reflection" specifies that viewers engage in thoughts and discussions about moral topics from television (Krijnen and Verboord 2016). For this construct, people were asked to state how often they think or talk during or after watching television about topics such as "people should always keep their promises" or "how real friends should treat each other." For a related construct, "moral orientation," people were asked to indicate whether they start thinking about the consequences of behavior after watching television programs. Results of this study show that segments of the audience who consume information as well as those who consume fiction/entertainment also tend to engage in moral reflection to a greater extent; the same is true for moral orientation (Krijnen and Verboord 2016).

Moral rumination is defined as the individual involvement with a moral issue contained in a narrative (Eden et al. 2017). While theirs is not a cultivation or a long-term study, Eden et al. present one of the few studies that tap into deliberative moral activity: they measured moral rumination with an open-ended question that asked participants why they agree or disagree with a choice made by the protagonist. The answers were coded for moral rumination, or more specifically, for the complexity of moral argumentation, from "none" to "complex." This may be a worthwhile construct for long-term cultivation processes as well.

Moral Judgment

Moral judgment, according to Narvaez and Rest is the "decision which of the possible actions is most moral" (1995, 386). In a slight variation, as the moral evaluation of narrative characters and actions, we encounter moral judgment quite frequently in media entertainment research, for example, in affective disposition theory, which explains the liking of characters and subsequent enjoyment of media narratives (Raney 2003, 2004). However, this paradigm is not suitable for long-term effects because it is always tied to specific media characters and actions during the reception of a film.

However, it is conceivable that long-term exposure, in which viewers "rehearse" moral reactions and emotions in many individual exposures, has an influence on other moral judgments outside of the narrative world. An interesting study by Tamborini et al. (2010) addressed this question and explored how prolonged exposure to soap opera affected character dispositions as well as real-world moral judgments. The length of exposure was varied in the experiment: participants watched from 0 to 7 weeks of a soap opera; all participants watched week 8, which served as the basis for evaluating moral aspects of the characters of the very same show. Seventeen scenarios of real-world moral dilemmas on common antisocial behaviors in soap operas were used, involving topics such as cheating, invasion of privacy, abuse/addiction, pilfering, medical issues, reckless behavior, abuse of power, and lying about one's past. For each of these, respondents had to assess to what extent they found the behavior of the character in the scenario ethical. Results show that the longer exposure went on, the more good characters were perceived as more virtuous, while bad characters were perceived as even less virtuous, indicating a polarization effect with increasing length of show exposure. Moral judgments on the real-world scenarios were shifted toward social convention with increasing exposure.

Moral Sensitivity

So far, we have discussed the ability of filmic narrative to change the frequency with which we think norm violations happen (estimates of norm violations), to change what we think are important guidelines of action (moral values), the standards we use for evaluating other people and actions (moral judgment), and the way we justify our actions (moral reasoning). All these processes require some sort of understanding that a social situation is morally relevant. This ability to detect moral content and moral implications of a social situation is called "moral sensitivity" (Narvaez and Rest 1995; Rest 1986). While recognizing moral issues in a given situation does not guarantee morally balanced actions (You and Bebeau 2013; Sadler 2004), not recognizing the moral relevance may have (detrimental) consequences for moral decision-making, reasoning, and actions (Sparks and Hunt 1998; Jordan 2007; Christen and Katsarov 2016).

Narratives offer the kind of symbolic environment that presents an ideal "playground" or "laboratory" (Hakemulder 2000) that allows viewers to witness moral situations and observe reactions of characters in these moral situations. In this sense, they offer the "narrative imagination" necessary to experience and understand morally relevant actions and emotions (Nussbaum 1997). Repeated, frequent exposures to televised narratives with their high density of presentations regarding values and norms, justifications and punishments of norm violations, as well as explicit or implicit moral lessons (Bilandzic, Hastall, and Sukalla 2017; Daalmans, Hijmans, and

Wester 2014, 2017) should provide such an everyday, casual, and unobtrusive moral classroom.

Whereas the basic idea is plausible and evident, there is surprisingly little empirical evidence for narrative effects on moral sensitivity. One example is the study by Glover, Garmon, and Hull (2011), who had participants rate the presence of 10 moral messages in a one-hour episode of a fictional teen drama. This construct is not called moral sensitivity but "recognition"; nonetheless, it can count as an example of moral sensitivity as it corresponds to the definition outlined above. Examples for moral messages are forgiveness, kindness, healthy anger, deception, prejudice, and threat. The study found that negative moral messages were more likely to be recognized by people who had higher moral expertise (i.e., more sophisticated moral reasoning schemas). How much TV respondents usually watched did not affect the ability to recognize moral messages.

Possibly the amount of television viewing is less important than the amount spent with *stories*. Bilandzic and Schnell (2018) addressed this issue and explored the effects of long-term exposure to several fictional genres on moral sensitivity. Two different measures of moral sensitivity were used. In the first study, participants watched an episode of the series *Grey's Anatomy*. Afterward they listed their thoughts about the series and the actions of the characters. The answers were coded for the presence of moral considerations; coding was based on the Moral Foundations Questionnaire (Graham et al. 2011). In the second study, rather than being asked to identify moral issues in the television content itself, respondents were presented with vignettes depicting a morally charged situation about issues related to one of the three genres. After reading the vignettes, participants listed their thoughts elicited by the vignette and were asked to give a possible resolution of the issue. These answers were again coded for the presence of moral considerations with the same coding system as in study 1; see an example of the vignette relating to topics of the sitcom in Table 4.4.

Results for study 1 show that habitual exposure to fictional series in television increased the sensitivity for moral issues in an episode of *Grey's Anatomy*. Both studies 1 and 2 provided evidence that people who have a higher propensity to be regularly engaged in stories (narrative engageability) also recognized more moral issues, that is, showed a higher moral sensitivity.

Conclusions

Filmic narratives provide a symbolic environment rich in morally relevant situations, norm violations, moral dilemmas, and more or less moral characters; they function as moral "training material" for viewers, helping them build moral capacity and capability for real-life situations.

The three S's of moral cultivation—small, slow, subtle—make the empirical approach relatively difficult. The effect of narratives on moral understanding is small, because our real-world reference groups remain our main and dominant moral

Table 4.4 Sample Vignette to Measure Moral Sensitivity

Vignette Pickup Artists (Sitcom)

The term "pickup artist" describes men who consider themselves part of the "seduction community," which is most prevalent in the United States. Their aim is to develop and practice techniques, which are geared toward meeting women and eventually seducing them. By now there is an industrial complex behind this phenomenon, which offers videos, books, websites, and seminars, which are meant to teach men to establish sexual contact with women. The providers understand themselves as offering a kind of dating advice for men, whereas this type of advice is usually geared toward women, notably in women's magazines.

The movement takes its theoretical roots from evolutionary psychology, which claims that women are biologically predisposed to prefer certain types of men and ignore others. Members of the seduction community try to improve their success rate by occupying themselves with (controversial) psychological concepts and trying to improve their social skills and physical attractiveness. While members usually claim that personal development is at the center of the movement, the general public often criticizes that the movement reduces contacts between men and women to mere conquests, that women are objectified, and that relationships are not based on seduction techniques but on empathy and true genuine interest.

Questions:

What do you think about the text you just read? Please describe your thoughts and impressions.

Do you think the aims of the pickup movement are sensible? Please justify your answer and write down some reasons for or against the pickup movement.

Source: Bilandzic and Schnell (2018).

forces. Morals are permanently negotiated in actual social interactions. Media dependency is smaller than in other fields of cultivation. Accordingly, we cannot expect large media effects. And effects are slow. To compete against real-world moral socialization, the narrative influence needs to be as constant and persistent as the real world itself. Single exposures are unlikely to dramatically overhaul a lifetime of socialization; rather, shifts in moral understanding evoked by media narratives will be cumulative and slow. Effects are also subtle. It will be impossible to evoke drastic shifts in the audience's morality, first and foremost because commercial filmic narrative will always to a good extent represent mainstream morality. Shifts will be subtle, most reasonably even "just" reinforcements of what we perceive in the real world.

The long-term perspective, while complicating the clarity of the moral message, is nonetheless deeply ingrained in the patterns of contemporary media usage of films and series. Widespread streaming technology makes a multitude of high-quality filmic narratives available at any time, at a viewing rate determined by the viewer alone. Character development is extended over multiple episodes, and plots evolve in a granularity that used to be the prerogative of written fiction. In these circumstances, moral issues get more space and attention and are used to make the shows more interesting, for example, with well-prepared and differentiated moral dilemmas or morally ambiguous characters.

Approaches presented in this chapter show that processes happening during exposure may be responsible for the emergence of long-term moral effects. (For an overview of the mechanisms of moral cultivation, see Figure 4.2.) First, moral schemas are repeatedly activated by similar moral patterns in filmic narrative content. This builds and refines moral schemas—possibly sophisticated ones such as the postconventional reasoning schema. Repeated activation increases the accessibility and salience of a moral schema or a moral value; repeated exposures lead to chronic accessibility, which then make moral issues more accessible and influential for real-life interactions. Second, moral judgments are rehearsed in a way that is consistent with the narrative. For example, lying may be disapproved of by other characters and thus serve the audience as a cue for negative moral judgment. Third, with repeated exposures to similar moral patterns, viewers will build and expand a repertoire for moral action; this is a prediction consistent with social cognitive theory, which assumes that people build up action repertoires from symbolic representations of social situations, with characters serving as role models (Bandura 2001). Viewers observe rewards and punishments of morally relevant actions and form an impression about how successful an action is in the narrative and will be in real life. Stories provide space in which moral issues are negotiated: audiences witness virtuous and immoral behavior, reactions from other characters condemning immoral behavior, and also justifications for not adhering to a moral norm. Every social situation bears moral implications, and in narratives, both are condensed. Often there is conflict between what is allowed (e.g., by law or social convention) and what should be done—which is essentially a moral dilemma and involves elements of moral reasoning (e.g., the negotiation between maintaining norms and postconventional thinking). By understanding and

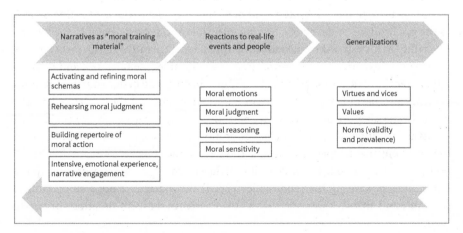

Figure 4.2 Overview of the Mechanisms of Moral Cultivation

processing a multitude of stories, people are able to extend their experience of moral judgment and deliberation.

Finally, and most important, it seems to matter for moral cultivation how people perceive and experience the narrative: intensive, emotional, and vivid experiences—in transportation or narrative engagement mode—make the narrative resemble real-life experiences. Viewers in an intensive viewing mode rehearse moral capabilities *as if* they were experiencing a social situation in real life. Empathy is an important part of the emotional processes of narrative engagement—and it connects narratives and morality. Several studies have shown that fiction reading is positively related to empathy. For example, a meta-analysis by Mumper and Gerrig (2017) found that reading narrative fiction significantly correlates with dispositional empathy across a number of studies. Similarly, a meta-analysis by Dodell-Feder and Tamir (2018) concluded that reading fiction (compared to nonfiction) has a significant positive effect on social-cognitive skills. For long-term reading there is also some evidence that empathy and reading are related, but the evidence is a bit weaker; Lenhart, Dangel, and Richter (2020) found positive relationships between lifetime book reading and empathy (but that effect disappeared after including control variables).

There is also evidence that empathy and narrative engageability are related: the scale for narrative engageability is positively related to trait empathy, and even more strongly for the emotional dimension of narrative engageability (Bilandzic et al. 2019). Lenhart, Dangel, and Richter (2020) also found consistently positive relationships for transportability (a similar construct as narrative engageability) and all dimensions of empathy.

At the same time, narrative engageability is also related to exposure to narrative series (Bilandzic, Schnell, and Sukalla 2019). Thus, both narrative engageability *and* empathy are related to exposure to narrative fiction. These relationships point to a reinforcing process of capability and gratification: in order to understand stories, we need to be able to understand the motivations, goals, and intentions of characters. If we understand the inner world of a character, their course of action as well as the implications of the action become plausible and more relevant to the viewer. Engaging in this way with a narrative (i.e., perceiving narrative engagement) makes the narrative experience more rewarding and enjoyable (see Bilandzic and Busselle 2011; Green, Brock, and Kaufman 2004). Thus, people with better empathic abilities are drawn to narratives and find them enjoyable because of the narrative engagement they enable. At the same time, narrative engagement makes the social situations and the inner world of the characters more accessible to viewers. They expand the occasions that people can rehearse their empathic abilities; like exercise for the body, narratives provide training for moral development. This is consistent with the notion put forward by Mar and Oatley (2008) that narratives are a simulation of social life and enable readers or viewers to experience different situations in a vivid manner.

Lessons that viewers take away from narratives as "moral training material" can affect their reactions to people and events in real life. Viewers can apply the moral emotions they rehearsed during exposure, for example, contempt, anger, gratitude, admiration, to situations in their lives that present similar triggers as in the narrative world. Their moral judgment, moral reasoning, and moral sensitivity can be altered by constant and repeated exposures. These reactions may condense into more generalized conceptions of virtue and vice, values and norms, or change and stabilize existing moral systems. This process is described as a force from narratives to real-world morality, but of course we are not dealing with linear progressions from medium to real life. Rather, real-life morality has an impact on how we process and perceive narratives, thus establishing an ever-evolving interaction of the narrative and the actual world (see Figure 4.2).

Another crucial issue for moral cultivation concerns the relationship of short-term, large effects and long-term, small effects. The overall effect of repeated exposures likely consists of both types—the dramatic and sudden shift caused by one exposure only (dubbed the "drench effect" by Greenberg 1988) and the small, cumulative effects of multiple exposures ("drip-drip"). Direct relationships between exposure and moral outcomes often do not emerge, but our overview shows that positive relationships between narrative engageability and moral outcomes are consistent across different moral outcomes (Bilandzic, Schnell, and Sukalla 2019; Schnell and Bilandzic 2017). This is an ambiguous result: it allows the interpretation that exposure effects do not cumulate in a linear fashion, but that a few exposures in high-engagement mode suffice. An alternative explanation may be that cumulative effects arise from narratives of very different genres that were not captured by the exposure measure.

Narrative engagement is a process that happens while watching a filmic narrative. In the next step, people apply their "trained moral compass" in real-life situations, exhibiting the moral emotions rehearsed during exposure, and judging, reasoning, and detecting moral issues with their narratively sharpened moral abilities in social situations in real life. This may generalize into building up ideals of characters (i.e., virtue and vice), and of actions (norms and values).

The close connection between narratives, narrative engagement, and morality is as evident as it is (still) puzzling. Ultimately, the notion of cultivation that being exposed to more cultural indicators—or in our case, more moral indicators—makes viewers more moral may be a possibility, but certainly not the only one. If moral media narratives are a moral training ground, their influence may be more complicated: different moralities can be tried on, experienced, accepted, but also rejected if they do not suit. Terms like "'moral playground' or a 'moral sandbox' in which viewers can safely try out and practice different responses to social situations" (Eden et al. 2017, 144) or "moral laboratory" (Hakemulder 2000) underline this playful function of narratives. Future research and theorizing will need to reconcile such very different perspectives and differentiate narratives, situations, individuals, and groups that facilitate one effect or the other.

Works Cited

Appel, M. 2008. "Fictional Narratives Cultivate Just-World Beliefs." *Journal of Communication* 58: 62–83. https://doi.org/10.1111/j.1460-2466.2007.00374.x.

Bandura, A. 2001. "Social Cognitive Theory of Mass Communication." *Media Psychology* 3, no. 3: 265–299. https://doi.org/10.1207/s1532785xmep0303_03.

Bilandzic, H. 2018. "Morality in Entertainment." In *Communication and Media Ethics.* Vol. 26 of *Series Handbooks of Communication Science,* edited by P. Plaisance, 329–346. Boston: de Gruyter Mouton.

Bilandzic, H., and R. W. Busselle. 2011. "Enjoyment of Films as a Function of Narrative Experience, Perceived Realism and Transportability." *Communications: European Journal of Communication Research* 36, no. 1: 29–50. https://doi.org/10.1515/comm.2011.002.

Bilandzic, H., and R. W. Busselle. 2012. "A Narrative Perspective on Genre-Specific Cultivation." In *Living with Television Now: Advances in Cultivation Theory and Research,* edited by M. Michael, J. Shanahan and N. Signorielli, 261–285. New York: Peter Lang.

Bilandzic, H., M. R. Hastall, and F. Sukalla. 2017. "The Morality of Television Genres: Norm Violations and Their Narrative Context in Four Popular Genres of Serial Fiction." *Journal of Mass Media Ethics* 32, no. 2: 99–117. https://doi.org/10.1080/23736992.2017.1294488.

Bilandzic, H., and C. Schnell. 2018. "Media Narratives and Moral Sensitivity: Empirical Evidence from Two Studies." Paper presented at the ECREA conference, Lugano, Switzerland.

Bilandzic, H., and C. Schnell. 2019. "The Perception of Genre-Specific Norm Violations across Three Different Genres (Comedy, Medical Drama, Crime)." Unpublished data set.

Bilandzic, H., C. Schnell, and F. Sukalla. 2019. "The Cultivation of Idealistic Moral Expectations: The Role of Television Exposure and Narrative Engageability." *Mass Communication and Society* 22, no. 5: 604–630. https://doi.org/10.1080/15205 436.2019.1606247.

Bilandzic, H., F. Sukalla, C. Schnell, M. R. Hastall, and R. W. Busselle. 2019. "The Narrative Engageability Scale: A Multidimensional Trait Measure for the Propensity to Become Engaged in a Story." *International Journal of Communication* 13: 801–832.

Busselle, R. W., and J. Van den Bulck. 2019. "Cultivation Theory, Media, Stories, Processes, and Reality." In *Media Effects: Advances in Theory and Research,* edited by M. B. Oliver, A. A. Raney and J. Bryant, 69–82. New York: Routledge.

Castro, D., J. M. Rigby, D. Cabral, and V. Nisi. 2021. "The Binge-Watcher's Journey: Investigating Motivations, Contexts, and Affective States Surrounding Netflix Viewing." *Convergence: The International Journal of Research into New Media Technologies* 27, no. 1: 3–20. https://doi.org/10.1177/1354856519890856.

Christen, M., and J. Katsarov. 2016. "Moral Sensitivity as a Precondition of Moral Distress." *American Journal of Bioethics* 16, no. 12: 19–21. https://doi.org/10.1080/15265 161.2016.1239787.

Daalmans, S., E. Hijmans, and F. Wester. 2014. "'One Night of Prime Time': An Explorative Study of Morality in One Night of Prime Time Television." *Journal of Mass Media Ethics* 29: 184–199. https://doi.org/10.1080/08900523.2014.918498.

Daalmans, S., E. Hijmans, and F. Wester. 2017. "From Good to Bad and Everything in Between: An Analysis of Genre Differences in the Representation of Moral Nature." *Journal of Mass Media Ethics* 32, no. 1: 28–44. https://doi.org/10.1080/23736992.2016.1258992.

Dodell-Feder, D., and D. I. Tamir. 2018. "Fiction Reading Has a Small Positive Impact on Social Cognition: A Meta-analysis." *Journal of Experimental Psychology—General* 147, no. 11: 1713–1727. https://doi.org/10.1037/xge0000395.

Eden, A., S. Daalmans, M. Van Ommen, and A. Weljers. 2017. "Melfi's Choice: Morally Conflicted Content Leads to Moral Rumination in Viewers." *Journal of Mass Media Ethics* 32, no. 3: 142–153. https://doi.org/10.1080/23736992.2017.1329019.

Eden, A., R. Tamborini, M. Grizzard, R. Lewis, R. Weber, and S. Prabhu. 2014. "Repeated Exposure to Narrative Entertainment and the Salience of Moral Intuitions." *Journal of Communication* 64, no. 3: 501–520. https://doi.org/10.1111/jcom.12098.

Gerbner, G., and L. Gross. 1976. "Living with Television: The Violence Profile." *Journal of Communication* 26: 173–199.

Gerbner, G., L. Gross, M. Jackson-Beeck, S. Jeffries-Foy, and N. Signorielli. 1978. "Cultural Indicators: The Violence Profile no. 9." *Journal of Communication* 28: 176–207.

Gerbner, G., L. Gross, M. Morgan, and N. Signorielli. 1980. "The Mainstreaming of America—Violence Profile No 11." *Journal of Communication* 30, no. 3: 10–29.

Gerbner, G., L. Gross, M. Morgan, N. Signorielli, and J. Shanahan. 2002. "Growing Up with Television: Cultivation Processes." In *Media Effects: Advances in Theory and Research*, edited by J. Bryant and D. Zillmann, 43–67. Mahwah, New Jersey: Lawrence Erlbaum.

Glover, R. J., L. C. Garmon, and D. M. Hull. 2011. "Media's Moral Messages: Assessing Perceptions of Moral Content in Television Programming." *Journal of Moral Education* 40, no. 1: 89–104. https://doi.org/10.1080/03057240.2011.541773.

Graham, J., B. A. Nosek, J. Haidt, R. Iyer, S. Koleva, and P. H. Ditto. 2011. "Mapping the Moral Domain." *Journal of Personality and Social Psychology* 101, no. 2: 366–385. https://doi.org/10.1037/a0021847.

Green, M. C., T. C. Brock, and G. F. Kaufman. 2004. "Understanding Media Enjoyment: The Role of Transportation into Narrative Worlds." *Communication Theory* 14, no. 4: 311–327. https://doi.org/10.1111/j.1468-2885.2004.tb00317.x.

Greenberg, B. S. 1988. "Some Uncommon Television Images and the Drench Hypothesis." In *Applied Social Psychology Annual*, Vol. 8: *Television as a Social Issue*, edited by S. Oskamp, 88–102. Newbury Park, CA: Sage.

Haidt, J. 2001. "The Emotional Dog and Its Rational Tail: A Social Intuitionist Approach to Moral Judgment." *Psychological Review* 108: 814–834.

Haidt, J., and C. Joseph. 2008. "The Moral Mind: How Five Sets of Innate Intuitions Guide the Development of Many Culture-Specific Virtues, and Perhaps Even Modules." In *The Innate Mind*. Vol. 3: *Foundations and the Future (Evolution and Cognition)*, edited by P. Carruthers, S. Laurence and S. Stich, 367–392. New York: Oxford University Press.

Hakemulder, F. 2000. *The Moral Laboratory: Experiments Examining the Effects of Reading Literature on Social Perception and Moral Self-Concept*. Amsterdam: Benjamins.

Hawkins, R., and S. Pingree. 1981. "Uniform Messages and Habitual Viewing: Unnecessary Assumptions in Social Reality Effects." *Human Communication Research* 7, no. 4: 291–301.

Hawkins, R., and S. Pingree. 1990. "Divergent Psychological Processes in Constructing Social Reality from Mass Media Content." In *Cultivation Analysis: New Directions in Media Effects Research*, edited by N. Signorielli and M. Morgan, 35–50. Newbury Park, CA: Sage.

Jordan, J. 2007. "Taking the First Step toward a Moral Action: A Review of Moral Sensitivity Measurement across Domains." *Journal of Genetic Psychology* 168, no. 3: 323–359. https://doi.org/10.3200/gntp.168.3.323-360.

Kohlberg, L. 1981. *The Philosophy of Moral Development: Moral Stages and the Idea of Justice*. Vol. 1 of *Essays on Moral Development*. San Francisco, CA: Harper and Row.

Krijnen, T., and M. Verboord. 2016. "TV Genres' Moral Value: The Moral Reflection of Segmented TV Audiences." *Social Science Journal* 53, no. 4: 417–426. https://doi.org/10.1016/j.soscij.2016.04.004.

Lenhart, J., J. Dangel, and T. Richter. 2020. "The Relationship between Lifetime Book Reading and Empathy in Adolescents: Examining Transportability as a Moderator." *Psychology of*

Aesthetics, Creativity, and the Arts 16, no. 4: 679–693. Advance online publication. https://doi.org/10.1037/aca0000341.

Mar, R. A., and K. Oatley. 2008. "The Function of Fiction Is the Abstraction and Simulation of Social Experience." *Perspectives on Psychological Science* 3, no. 3: 173–192. https://doi.org/10.1111/j.1745-6924.2008.00073.x.

Morgan, M., S. Leggett, and J. Shanahan. 1999. "Television and Family Values: Was Dan Quayle Right?" *Mass Communication and Society* 2, nos. 1–2: 47–63. https://doi.org/10.1080/15205436.1999.9677861.

Morgan, M., J. Shanahan, and N. Signorielli. 2009. "Growing Up with Television: Cultivation Processes." In *Media Effects*, edited by J. Bryant and M. B. Oliver, 34–49. Los Angeles: LEA.

Morgan, M., J. Shanahan, and N. Signorielli. 2015. "Yesterday's New Cultivation, Tomorrow." *Mass Communication and Society* 18, no. 5: 674–699. https://doi.org/10.1080/15205436.2015.1072725.

Mumper, M. L., and R. J. Gerrig. 2017. "Leisure Reading and Social Cognition: A Meta-analysis." *Psychology of Aesthetics Creativity and the Arts* 11, no. 1: 109–120. https://doi.org/10.1037/aca0000089.

Narvaez, D., and T. Bock. 2002. "Moral Schemas and Tacit Judgement or How the Defining Issues Test Is Supported by Cognitive Science." *Journal of Moral Education* 31, no. 3: 297–314. https://doi.org/10.1080/0305724022000008124.

Narvaez, D., and J. Rest. 1995. "The Four Components of Acting Morally." In *Moral Behavior and Moral Development: An Introduction*, edited by W. Kurtines and J. Gewirtz, 385–400. New York: McGraw-Hill.

Nussbaum, M. C. 1997. *Cultivating Humanity: A Classical Defense of Reform in Liberal Education*. Cambridge, MA: Harvard University Press.

O'Keefe, G. J. 1984. "Public Views on Crime: Television Exposure and Media Credibility." In *Communication Yearbook 8*, edited by R. N. Bostrom and B. H. Westley, 514–536. Beverly Hills, CA: Sage.

Potter, W. J. 1990. "Adolescents' Perceptions of the Primary Values of Television Programming." *Journalism Quarterly* 67, no. 4: 843–851. https://doi.org/10.1177/107769909006700439.

Potter, W. J., and I. C. Chang. 1990. "Television Exposure Measures and the Cultivation Hypothesis." *Journal of Broadcasting and Electronic Media* 34, no. 3: 313–333.

Raney, A. A. 2003. "Disposition-Based Theories of Enjoyment." In *Communication and Emotion: Essays in Honor of Dolf Zillmann*, edited by Jennings Bryant, David Roskos-Ewoldsen, and Joanne Cantor, 61–84. New York, NY: Lawrence Erlbaum.

Raney, A. A. 2004. "Expanding Disposition Theory: Reconsidering Character Liking, Moral Evaluations, and Enjoyment." *Communication Theory* 14, no. 4: 348–369. https://doi.org/10.1111/j.1468-2885.2004.tb00319.x.

Rest, J. 1986. *Moral Development: Advances in Research and Theory*. New York: Praeger.

Rest, J., D. Narvaez, S. J. Thoma, and M. J. Bebeau. 1999. "DIT2: Devising and Testing a Revised Instrument of Moral Judgment." *Journal of Educational Psychology* 91, no. 4: 644–659. https://doi.org/10.1037//0022-0663.91.4.644.

Rest, J., D. Narvaez, S. Thoma, and M. Bebeau. 2000. "A Neo-Kohlbergian Approach to Morality Research." *Journal of Moral Education* 29, no. 4: 381–395. https://doi.org/10.1080/713679390.

Rokeach, M. 1973. *The Nature of Human Values*. New York: Free Press.

Sadler, T. D. 2004. "Moral Sensitivity and Its Contribution to the Resolution of Socio-scientific Issues." *Journal of Moral Education* 33: 339–358. https://doi.org/10.1080/0305724042000733091.

Schlütz, Daniela M. 2016. "Contemporary Quality TV: The Entertainment Experience of Complex Serial Narratives." *Annals of the International Communication Association* 40, no. 1: 95–124. https://doi.org/10.1080/23808985.2015.11735257.

Schnell, Cornelia, and Helena K. Bilandzic. 2017. "Television Stories and the Cultivation of Moral Reasoning: The Role of Genre Exposure and Narrative Engageability." *Journal of Media Ethics* 32, no. 4: 202–220. https://doi.org/10.1080/23736992.2017.1371022.

Scott, Elizabeth D. 2000. "Moral Values: Situationally Defined Individual Differences." *Business Ethics Quarterly* 10, no. 2: 497–520. https://doi.org/10.2307/3857888.

Sparks, J. R., and S. D. Hunt. 1998. "Marketing Researcher Ethical Sensitivity: Conceptualization, Measurement, and Exploratory Investigation." *Journal of Marketing* 62, no. 2: 92–109. https://doi.org/10.2307/1252163.

Tamborini, R. 2011. "Moral Intuition and Media Entertainment" *Journal of Media Psychology: Theories, Methods, and Applications* 23: 39–45.

Tamborini, R. 2012. "A Model of Intuitive Morality and Exemplars." In *Media and the Moral Mind*, edited by R. Tamborini, 43–74. Electronic Media Research Series. Abingdon: Routledge.

Tamborini, R., R. Weber, A. Eden, N. D. Bowman, and M. Grizzard. 2010. "Repeated Exposure to Daytime Soap Opera and Shifts in Moral Judgment toward Social Convention." *Journal of Broadcasting & Electronic Media* 54, no. 4: 621–640. https://doi.org/Pii 93124896410.1080/08838151.2010.519806.

You, D., and M. Bebeau. 2013. "The Independence of James Rest's Components of Morality: Evidence from a Professional Ethics Curriculum Study." *Ethics and Education* 8, no. 3: 202–216. https://doi.org/10.1080/17449642.2013.846059.

5

Moral Conflict, Screen Stories, and Narrative Appeal

René Weber and Frederic R. Hopp

Moral conflict—violating particular moral norms in order to uphold others (Tamborini 2011, 2012)—is a central principle permeating human culture and history. Manifested in early philosophical discussions between Plato and Socrates on the relative priority of repaying one's debts over protecting others from harm, notions of moral conflict have since influenced myriad aspects of modern life, from debates on climate change (Feinberg and Willer 2013) to autonomous decision-making during moral dilemmas (Awad et al. 2018). Notably, moral conflicts have also been an instrumental tool for ancient and contemporary storytellers; in Aeschylus's *Agamemnon*, for example, the protagonist has to decide between saving his daughter or sending his Greek troops to Troy, whereas in Spielberg's *Schindler's List*, saving the life of persecuted Jews during Nazi Germany conflicts with following orders of the authorities and risking one's life. As famous author and story consultant Robert McKee formulates it, "You can't have complexity of character necessary to sustain eighty, ninety, hundred hours of storytelling without moral contradiction.... There's various kinds of inner conflicts, but the most compelling are moral conflicts of course" (2017).

Echoing McKee, narrative psychologists have long recognized that moral conflicts undergird all appealing narrations (László 2008), elevating "the strength of any exciting character and story.... [W]ithout [conflict], characters don't have drive, desire, or desperation.... [T]here is no story, just words" (Ballon 2014, 49–51). Likewise, narratology has distinguished external and internal moral conflicts, the former describing a character's goals and resistance from the environment (including interactions with other characters) and the latter occurring within a character and involving their internal needs. (For an overview, see Szilas, Estupiñán, and Richle 2018.) Moral conflict has also been related to the moral values of characters and to the ethical dimension of the story as a whole (Altman 2008; McKee 2017; Truby 2008). Findings from media psychology suggest that stories featuring moral conflict are processed and appraised in a slower, more rational fashion and elicit cognitions associated with deeper and meaningful insights into life (Tamborini 2011, 2012; Tamborini and Weber 2020). Indeed, moral conflict is frequently regarded as an especially salient component of compelling narrative that can foster moral understanding (Knop-Huelss, Rieger, and

René Weber and Frederic R. Hopp, *Moral Conflict, Screen Stories, and Narrative Appeal* In: *Screen Stories and Moral Understanding*. Edited by: Carl Plantinga, Oxford University Press. © Oxford University Press 2023.
DOI: 10.1093/oso/9780197665664.003.0006

Schneider 2019; Lewis, Tamborini, and Weber 2014; Lewis et al. 2019; Tamborini 2012; Weber et al. 2008).

But what exactly is it about moral conflicts that audiences of screen stories find compelling? Why are some types of moral conflict avoided and disliked by certain groups of audiences, yet lead to shared moral understanding and appreciation among others? And how can scholars, storytellers, and decision-makers identify and understand the moral conflict patterns that permeate narratives, despite the latent, contextual nature of moral information? In this chapter, we seek to provide answers to these questions. We begin with a review of ongoing research addressing how moral conflict in screen stories relates to moral understanding and affective responses among audiences. Subsequently, we elaborate on recent methodological advancements for identifying and quantifying latent moral conflict in narratives. We then introduce a novel framework for analyzing the composition and impact of morally relevant stories, highlighting how storytellers and decision-makers in the film industry can bridge moral divides and assist in promoting shared moral understanding. We conclude with an overview of future research trajectories operating at the exciting intersection of narratology, communication research, and moral psychology.

On Moral Conflict and Audience Responses

Traditionally, moral conflict has been defined as conflict between moral requirements. Moral requirements are moral reasons for adopting an alternative, justified solution. When these requirements conflict, and if neither requirement clearly overrides the other (i.e., is "stronger overall in some morally relevant way"; Sinnott-Armstrong 1988, 20), a moral dilemma arises. The Model of Intuitive Morality and Exemplars (MIME; Tamborini 2011, 2012; Tamborini and Weber 2020) provides a theoretical framework for understanding how individuals' moral sensitivities, the evaluation of moral conflict expressed in screen stories, and content producers' emphasis on particular moral concerns are intertwined in a dynamic, reciprocal influence process. To derive a conceptual understanding of moral intuitions, the core of the MIME draws on theorizing from moral foundations theory (MFT; Graham et al. 2013). MFT suggests that there are five culturally universal moral foundations that guide morally relevant behaviors: (1) care/harm (an intuitive concern for the suffering of others); (2) fairness/cheating (an intuitive preference for reciprocity and justice); (3) loyalty/betrayal (an intuitive concern for the common good and bias against outsiders); (4) authority/subversion (an intuitive deference to dominance hierarchies); and (5) sanctity/degradation (an intuitive concern for purity, broadly defined, including pathogen avoidance). Although these moral foundations are argued to be innate, that is, organized in advance of experience, it is suggested that nature provides only a first draft of the moral mind (Haidt and Joseph 2007), which experience and socialization subsequently shape and edit. To date, research has identified various factors that influence individuals' moral understanding and shape their moral foundation salience—the degree to which particular moral foundations are valued over others. These factors span, among others, political socialization (Graham, Haidt, and Nosek 2009) or historical pathogen prevalence (Van Leeuwen et al. 2012). Notably, recent research has highlighted that even short-term exposure to morally relevant screen stories can shape audiences' moral value system (Eden et al. 2014; Tamborini et al. 2010).

Relating Screen Story Appeal, Selective Exposure, and Moral Values

The MIME contends that moral foundation salience exerts a direct influence on how morally relevant narratives, including morally conflicted storylines, are evaluated. In order to explain this process, the MIME combines logic from affective disposition theory (Zillman and Cantor 1977; Weber et al. 2008), selective exposure theory (Bryant and Davies 2006; Festinger 1957), and exemplification theory (Zillmann 2002), positing that receivers of narratives act as "untiring moral monitors" (Zillman and Cantor 1977; but see Raney 2004) who continually evaluate whether characters' morally relevant behaviors satisfy their distinct moral expectations. During this process, it is argued, receivers develop affective dispositions (e.g., like or dislike) toward characters. In general, characters whose actions align with the moral salience profile of audiences are liked, whereas characters who violate audiences' moral attitudes and expectations are disliked (Zillman and Cantor 1977; Grizzard et al. 2019; but see Krakowiak and Oliver 2012). In turn, the selection of narratives and their appeal is modulated by the degree to which liked characters are rewarded and disliked characters are punished (Tamborini et al. 2013). Based on this logic, the selective exposure to narratives and their evaluation becomes a function of the interactions between audiences' moral foundation salience, the degree to which story characters' actions uphold or violate moral foundations, and whether these characters are being rewarded or punished (Weber et al. 2008).

Notably, narrative scenarios where prototypical characters (e.g., heroes and villains) completely uphold or violate moral standards recruit little cognitive effort to be morally understood and evaluated. Indeed, stories wherein characters' actions clearly violate or uphold a viewer's moral standards result in fast, intuitive moral judgments (Lewis, Tamborini, and Weber 2014). In contrast, when characters are confronted with moral conflicts and dilemmas, where certain moral norms can be upheld only by violating others, determining the appropriate moral course of action is more opaque. As a result, audiences have to engage in a slower, more rational moral judgment process to evaluate the righteousness of the witnessed behavior (Lewis, Tamborini, and Weber 2014; Greene et al. 2004). During this evaluative process, narrative consumers act as "moral lawyers" (Haidt 2001) who compare the observed moral conflict against their own moral salience system to reason whether immoral means justify certain moral ends.

To provide a concrete example, imagine the following scenario (adapted from Lewis, Tamborini, and Weber 2014):

> Enemy soldiers have taken over Ava's village and are killing all civilians. Ava and some townspeople are hiding in a cellar when she hears soldiers. Her baby begins to cry loudly. She covers his mouth to block the sound. If she removes her hand the soldiers will find and kill her child and everyone else.

This scenario provides a classic example of a within-foundation conflict (Hopp, Fisher, and Weber 2020), as the main protagonist has to decide whether she suffocates her baby (harm) to save others (care). If the protagonist suffocates the baby to save the group, audience members have to decide whether killing a baby justifies the saving of other lives. If the moral transgression is perceived as warranted and in line with one's moral compass, the story outcome will be perceived as more appealing, whereas the outcome will be less enjoyable if suffocating the baby to save others is not perceived as a justified behavior.

Now, imagine a different scenario:

> Oliver and Joey are good friends who both attend the same introductory lecture in their first year of college. During finals week, both desperately want to attend the on-going parties. Oliver decides to avoid the parties and study, while Joey has fun at the parties. On the day of the final, Oliver witnesses that Joey is cheating on the test. If he calls out Joey, Joey will receive an F on his test.

In this scenario, we observe a between-foundations conflict, as the main protagonist has to decide whether to call out a cheater (fairness) who decided to party while he was studying, even if the cheater is his good friend (betrayal). Should Oliver proceed and call out Joey, a person whose fairness/cheating salience is higher than their concern for loyalty/betrayal will come to enjoy this story ending more, whereas someone who values loyalty/betrayal over fairness/cheating will find this outcome less appealing.

While these scenarios highlight the basic mechanisms undergirding moral conflicts, the full nuances and complexity of moral dilemmas cannot be explicated in detail here. (For a more detailed overview and explication, see Sinnott-Armstrong 1988.) In addition, our taxonomy of within- and between-foundations conflict reflects a first endeavor to formally define and conceptualize the types of moral conflict that may exist within the realm of storytelling and shape story appeal. Hence, much remains to be learned about additional moral conflict scenarios that permeate screen stories, how audiences make sense of these dilemmas, and how exposure and engagement with moral conflict modulates moral understanding.

Moral Conflict and Moral Understanding

In the parlance of entertainment theory, confronting narrative consumers with moral conflicts elicits the experience of *appreciation*, an audience response characterized as thought-provoking, moving, and meaningful (Oliver and Bartsch 2009). Analogously, evaluating a morally conflicted situation recruits various cognitive processes associated with perspective-taking and mentalizing. Among other things, audiences have to take into account a character's mental state (Young and Saxe 2009), personality (Inbar, Pizarro, and Cushman 2012; Uhlmann, Pizarro, and Diermeier 2015), intention (Schaich Borg et al. 2006), and context (Schein 2020). Taken together, we contend that the elicitation of these mentalizing processes via moral conflicts in screen stories is an important catalyzer for moral understanding. First, by illuminating a wide array of moral standards in different contexts and from different viewpoints, narrative consumers may come to realize under which circumstances moral transgressions may be permissible (or forbidden) if they yield a valued moral outcome. Second, vicariously observing the struggles of morally conflicted characters (e.g., Walter White in the U.S. TV show *Breaking Bad*) over longer time frames may lead audiences to empathize with similar individuals in the real world (Rohm, Hopp, and Smit 2021). Third, acquiring moral understanding from real-life interactions is comparatively risky, difficult, and rare. However, embedding moral conflicts into the "narrative mode" (Bruner 1987) may be an effective, wide-reaching shortcut to easily transmit moral norms and foster moral understanding (Bandura 2004; Raney 2003; see also Green et al. 2002; Aristotle's *Poetics*). Indeed, exposure to screen stories featuring moral conflict has been shown to be an important vector for moral learning, promoting honesty (Lee et al. 2014) and empathy (Dodell-Feder and Tamir 2018), reducing intergroup prejudice (Paluck and Green 2009), fostering deeper knowledge (Knop-Huelss, Rieger, and Schneider 2019), and shifting moral judgment toward social convention (Tamborini et al. 2010).

In view of these considerations, engagement with narratives that are rich in moral conflict may be explained as a "map exercise" (Schwab 2004) that allows viewers to continually develop and update their moral understanding. Supporting this notion, we add that screen stories featuring moral conflict are "attended to, valued, preserved, and transmitted because the mind detects that such bundles of representations have a powerfully organizing effect on our neurocognitive adaptations, even though the representations are not literally true" (Tooby and Cosmides 2001, 21). Taken together, embedding moral conflict in screen stories may not only elevate the strength of a particular plot or character, but may indeed lead audiences to gain a better sense of and appreciation for life's moral dilemmas, thereby fostering a more enhanced and nuanced understanding of morality.

Extracting Moral Conflicts from Screen Stories

Despite the previously discussed relevance of moral conflict for storytelling and moral understanding, large-scale and methodical empirical assessments of the kinds of moral conflict that permeate human narratives remain few, with only a handful of studies simulating agent-based moral conflicts in digital interactive storytelling (Battaglino and Damiano 2014). This lack of knowledge has not only limited the ability of artists, scholars, and decision-makers in the film industry to develop an inventory of moral conflict in narratives at scale, but it also stymies further research synergizing moral conflict, narrative appeal, and moral understanding.

Naturally, detecting and identifying moral conflict in screen stories necessitates the ability to identify general moral information in narratives. However, attempts to reliably and validly extract moral information from textual stories have been challenged by the latent, context-dependent nature of moral information, people's fast, intuitive response to moral cues, and differences across individuals' moral salience system. (For a recent discussion, see Hopp and Weber, 2021a, 2021b.) In fact, across a series of six studies that focused on manually detecting moral foundations in text narratives, we demonstrated that traditional, deliberate content analysis[1] protocols fail to capture the intuitive nature of moral judgments, whereas an intuitive text highlighting technique that treats moral foundations as the products of fast, spontaneous intuitions led to higher interrater agreement and a higher validity of extracted moral foundations (Weber et al. 2018). In addition, we showed that a large crowd of coders who learned only the basic premises of MFT outperformed the reliability and validity of moral foundation codings produced by a few coders who were extensively trained in MFT. Building on this knowledge, we utilized a crowdsourced content annotation procedure to develop an extended Moral Foundations Dictionary (eMFD; Hopp et al. 2021) that is able to computationally capture moral information from large textual corpora. The eMFD contains word lists in which each word is assigned a vector of five probabilities, denoting the likelihood that this word belongs to any one of the five moral foundations. These probabilities were derived from over 60,000 content annotations and have been shown to improve the detection of moral foundations compared to extant, automated moral foundation classification procedures. The eMFD can be easily applied with the open-source research tool eMFDscore[2] to extract the representation of moral foundations from text-based documents.

In view of these findings, the extraction and detection of morally relevant information in textual narratives has witnessed significant advancements over the past few years. Importantly, this progress has directly informed novel techniques for detecting moral conflicts in screen stories. In a recent study, we introduced a procedure that can detect and evaluate moral conflict in screenplays (Hopp, Fisher, and Weber 2020).

This approach theorizes moral conflict as a set of hypotheses about the moral content and social network structure of narratives. Specifically, we assumed that moral conflict is likely to arise when characters from opposing groups, communities, or factions collide. Notably, screenwriters frequently describe different communities of characters in alteration, thereby constructing simultaneously evolving storylines (Weng, Chu, and Wu 2007). Thus, as a story progresses, communities of characters come into focus as particular characters more frequently interact with each other. Based on this rationale and in line with narrative theory (Altman 2008; Booker 2014), we predicted that narrative events in which characters from different communities collide highlight discrepancies across characters' group-based, moral motivations and thereby presage moral conflict (Tamborini and Weber 2020). In order to test this hypothesis, we put forth two advancements.

First, we derived formal definitions for different types of moral conflict. As per our previous definition and outlined scenarios, we operationalized moral conflict as a situation in which one foundation (or perhaps more than one) is violated in order to uphold the same foundation or other foundations (Tamborini 2011, 2012). As a reminder, we contend that moral conflict can occur in two ways: within-foundation conflict describes scenarios in which the same foundation is simultaneously upheld and violated, whereas between-foundations conflict occurs in contexts where some moral foundations are upheld while others are violated. Additionally, the degree of moral conflict can be expressed as a function of the magnitude to which a foundation is upheld and violated and the polarity (i.e., difference) of simultaneously upholding and violating a foundation.[3] While magnitude signals the general moral relevance of a particular event (e.g., killing has a stronger moral relevance than hitting), polarity denotes the degree to which conflicting moral requirements are incomparable, such that one moral requirement cannot override another (and multiple moral requirements cannot override each other) as "neither is stronger than, weaker than, or equal in strength to the other" (Sinnott-Armstrong 1988, 58; see also Tamborini 2012). Second, to detect scenes where characters from different moral communities collide, we applied tools from natural language processing and social network analysis to translate screenplays into social character networks. The extraction of moral communities from these networks is then based on computations that partition the social character network into communities that maximize the density of links between characters of the same community compared to links between different communities. Compellingly, applying this procedure on a total of 894 movie scripts encompassing 82,195 scenes, our findings demonstrated that scenes in which characters from different communities co-occur are characterized by higher levels of moralized language (as indexed per the eMFD) and moral conflict compared to scenes in which characters from the same moral community are co-present. These findings suggest that screenplay writers use moral conflict to highlight discrepancies between different groups of characters and their moral motivations (Tamborini and Weber 2020), a finding that is supported by the attentional capture of moral cues (Gantman and Van Bavel 2015), which assist audiences in directing their attention toward important plot points. An interesting question for future investigation is whether characters in screenplays are more homogeneous in their moral language use *within* communities and more heterogeneous in moral language use *between* communities, and, crucially, whether this within-/between-group ratio increases during scenes where group identity becomes hypersalient. If confirmed, this would suggest that moral language and moral understanding in screenplays may primarily serve as an artistic tool for fostering group polarization and group conflict.

What's Next? A Look into the Future of Moral Storytelling

In the previous sections, we outlined past and ongoing research for developing a better understanding of how moral conflict embedded in screen stories affects audiences, and how latent representation of moral information and conflict patterns may be extracted from textual corpora. To catalyze and foster a flourishing future for studying moral storytelling, we call for a more formalized, methodical, and scalable approach to studying moral representations in narratives. With this motivation in mind, over the past few years our group has been developing an online research platform: the Moral Narrative Analyzer, or MoNA (https://mona.mnl.ucsb.edu/; Weber et al. 2018; Weber, Hopp, and Fisher 2020). MoNA's vision is to provide a forum and research platform for extracting the latent moral signatures of narratives, how these moral signatures interact with character and group relations, and how these interactions predict the appeal, impact, and performance of narratives in diverse audiences. In addition, MoNA allows for the automatic detection of character attributes such as gender, ethnicity/race, and story centrality, as well as for capturing the visual representation of characters (e.g., close-ups, viewing angle, motion) via computer-vision algorithms. With this information it is possible, for instance, to address important diversity, equity, and inclusion questions in screenplays from a moral understanding perspective (Smith et al. 2020). For example, do moral violations and specific moral conflict patterns interact with race/ethnicity? Are characters from underrepresented groups less central in character networks compared to whites? Are minorities and/or women shown on screen in visually less dominant positions (looked down on, in motion away from the viewer, in the periphery of the screen, etc.)? And ultimately, how do these character attributes and representations interact with the moral framing of characters and subsequently shape the perceptions of women and underrepresented groups from a moral understanding perspective? In view of recent critiques that highlight historical shortcomings in diversity, equity, and inclusion across the Hollywood industry (e.g., the #OscarsSoWhite movement; see Ugwu 2020), addressing these questions is timely and of great social importance. At the same time, researchers, inclusion advocates, and screen story writers must be aware that analytic models linking a story's diversity, equity, and inclusion index with underlying moral conflict patterns capitalize on past data that may inherit implicit biases toward underrepresented groups. Thus, to avoid reinforcing and perpetuating these biases in future models and analyses, structural changes in the creation (e.g., story centrality of characters from underrepresented groups, production budget, etc.) and distribution (e.g., marketing) of screen stories are necessary to level the movie industry's playing field (Smith et al. 2020), ultimately leading to fair and inclusive, data-driven decisions (Crawford 2021).

Predicting Movie Performance from Moral Values and Conflict in Movie Scripts

If moral conflict lies at the center of appealing stories, as argued previously, then moral conflict embedded in screenplays should be among the predictors of movies' large-scale performance as indexed by box-office sales and critical evaluations by movie experts. Generally, movie performance is contingent upon a host of decisions during postproduction, including, but not limited to, release date, production costs, content rating, advertising budget, and cast. Although undoubtedly relevant for stakeholders in the film industry, these factors primarily reflect decisions made after a film has already been selected for production. Decision-makers in the film industry face an even more critical decision during the "green-lighting" process: "choos[ing] among thousands of scripts to decide which ones to turn into movies" (Eliashberg et al. 2007, 881). Green-lighting is slow and labor-intensive, relying largely on guesswork by "experts" (many of whom are film students), resulting from subjective ratings and individual intuitions (Eliashberg et al. 2007). Because screenplay green-lighting is a complex, dynamic, and multidimensional process, it follows that no single concept provides an overarching explanation as to why screenplay readers, studio officials, and audiences prefer particular narrative structures over others. Yet among the plethora of phenomena that explain the appeal of a storyline, we have argued that moral intuitions and moral conflict embedded in screenplays have consistently been shown to exert a robust influence on story evaluation processes (Tamborini et al. 2011, 2012; Weber et al. 2008). Hence, in a preliminary study (Hopp, Fisher, and Weber 2020), we examined how latent moral cues and moral conflict patterns in movies' screenplays predict performance-related variables, including audience engagement and box-office sales. Our initial analyses demonstrated substantial contributions of our moral content and narrative structure predictors, and this above and beyond production budget and the numbers of theaters in which a movie was presented. These findings certainly motivate us, and hopefully other research groups, to further refine our moral content and narrative structure predictors and to investigate the complex interactions between moral content, narrative structure, character attributes, genre, and production value metrics. At the same time, we must emphasize that our current procedure of extracting moral content and conflict in screenplays and relating these to a movie's performance does not reflect how audiences view movies "in the wild." Movie viewing and evaluation naturally is a more complex process that dynamically evolves over time. Thus, to capture a more nuanced understanding of how people respond to and evaluate moral conflict in screen stories, we are planning to employ continuous response measurements (Biocca et al. 1993) in order to measure movie evaluation in a more naturalist, dynamic fashion.

Beyond Moral Foundations Theory

While MFT has served as the main theoretical framework to identify moral information in screen stories, it is not the sole approach to defining what people understand as "moral." In particular, a recently emerging framework roots morality in notions of cooperation (Curry, Chesters, and Van Lissa 2019). According to this theory of Morality as Cooperation (MaC), morality is a collection of cooperative rules that help us get along, work together, resolve conflicts, and promote the common good. The basic idea of this MaC approach is that humans are social animals who have lived together in groups for millions of years; during this time, we faced (and continue to face) a range of different problems of—or opportunities for—cooperation, for mutually beneficial social interaction. And we have evolved and invented a range of solutions to those problems—ways of unlocking the enormous benefits that cooperation provides. These solutions come in many different shapes and sizes. Some are social instincts, the legacy of evolution. Some are more recent cultural innovations—norms, customs, and laws. Together, these biological and cultural mechanisms motivate us to cooperate, and they provide the criteria by which we evaluate the behavior of others. It is precisely this collection of cooperative traits—these instincts, intuitions, and institutions—that philosophers and others have called "morality."

There are many types of cooperation, and so the theory of MaC leads us to expect many types of morality. So far, the theory has identified seven distinct types of cooperation: (1) the allocation of resources to kin; (2) coordination to mutual advantage; (3) social exchange; and conflict resolution through contests featuring (4) hawkish displays of dominance and (5) dove-ish displays of submission; (6) division of disputed resources; and (7) recognition of possession. And the theory has shown how each of these types of cooperation explains a corresponding type of morality: (1) family values, (2) group loyalty, (3) reciprocity, (4) heroism, (5) deference, (6) fairness, and (7) property rights.

In addition, MaC conceptualizes morality as a combinatorial system in which simple moral *elements* combine to create complex moral *molecules,* much like a finite number of elements in the periodic table combine to produce a large number of complex chemical molecules (Curry et al. 2022). For instance, the seven types of morality can be combined in multiple ways representing themes that are frequently represented in popular literature, such as fraternity, blood revenge, family pride, filial piety, gavelkind, primogeniture, friendship, patriotism, tribute, diplomacy, common ownership, honor, confession, turn-taking, restitution, modesty, mercy, munificence, arbitration, mendicancy, and queuing. Taken together, we contend that the MaC framework provides a refreshing, promising perspective on how moral conflicts can be conceptualized and identified in more detailed ways than MFT would allow.

Conclusion

In this chapter, we highlighted the central role of moral conflict in screen stories for shaping audiences' selective exposure, narrative appeal, and moral understanding. As ongoing and past research demonstrates, the question of how moral conflict is processed, appreciated, and understood by audiences remains a vibrant research area within moral philosophy, media psychology, and communication science. At the same time, we discussed the nuisances associated with the scalable, reliable, and valid extraction of moral conflict from screen stories and illustrated current solutions for mitigating and addressing these challenges. In the ensuing years, we envision that a more formalized, methodical, and scalable approach for examining moral conflict in screen stories will yield unprecedented insights into the relationship between moral conflict and story performance; how the representation of historically underrepresented and marginalized groups in morally relevant screen stories can contribute to greater moral understanding among audiences; and how novel theoretical conceptualizations of morality will lead to the development of new hypotheses about the moral content, selection, and processing of screen stories. We realize that our quantitative, "big data" approach to moral storytelling and conflict, which emphasizes standardization, methodical exploration, and accurate, falsifiable predictions, may seem overly simplistic and reductionist for scholars with a different epistemological background and focus, especially when it comes to highly contextual phenomena such as moral reasoning and moral conflict. Nonetheless, we hope that our approach and perspective, combined with fair statistical modeling and machine learning techniques (Crawford 2021), can make an innovative contribution to elucidating the complexity of moral storytelling across different kinds of stories, time, cultures, and contexts. We believe that the future of studying moral storytelling is bright and offers a welcoming home for a wide range of interdisciplinary scholarship.

Notes

1. Content analysis is a social scientific technique for the methodical study of communication artifacts. All content analyses include the systematic assignment of content codings to specified units of communication artifacts. The process of assigning codes to content units follows a priori specified rules and is called "coding." Usually, coding is done by a small number of specifically trained content coders. For more information, please see Krippendorff (2003).
2. For more detail, see https://github.com/medianeuroscience/emfdscore.
3. For a more detailed, mathematical formulation, see Hopp, Fisher, and Weber (2020).

Works Cited

Altman, Rick. 2008. *A Theory of Narrative*. New York: Columbia University Press.

Awad, Edmond, Sohan Dsouza, Richard Kim, Jonathan Schulz, Joseph Henrich, Azim Shariff, Jean-François Bonnefon, and Iyad Rahwan. 2018. "The Moral Machine Experiment." *Nature* 563: 59–64. https://doi.org/10.1038/s41586-018-0637-6.

Ballon, Rachel. 2014. *Blueprint for Screenwriting: A Complete Writer's Guide to Story Structure and Character Development*. New York: Routledge.

Bandura, A. 2004. "Selective Exercise of Moral Agency." In *Nurturing Morality*, edited by T. A. Thorkildsen and H. J. Walberg, 37–57. New York: Kluwer Academic/Plenum Publishers.

Battaglino, Cristina, and Rossana Damiano. 2014. "A Character Model with Moral Emotions: Preliminary Evaluation." In *2014 Workshop on Computational Models of Narrative*, edited by Mark A. Finlayson, Jan Christoph Meister, and Emile G. Bruneau, vol. 41, 24–41. Dagstuhl: Schloss Dagstuhl-Leibniz-Zentrum fuer Informatik.

Biocca, Frank, David Prabu, and Mark West. 1993. "Continuous Response Measurement (CRM): A Computerized Tool for Research on the Cognitive Processing of Media Messages." In *Measuring Psychological Responses to Media Messages*, edited by Annie Lang, 15–65. New York: Routledge.

Booker, Christopher. 2014. *The Seven Basic Plots: Why We Tell Stories*. London: Continuum.

Bruner, Jerome. 1987. *Actual Minds, Possible Worlds*. Cambridge, MA: Harvard University Press.

Bryant, J., and Davies, J. 2006. "Selective Exposure Processes." In *Psychology of Entertainment*, edited by J. Bryant and P. Vorderer, 19–33. Mahwah, NJ: Lawrence Erlbaum.

Crawford, Kate. 2021. *The Atlas of AI*. New Haven, CT: Yale University Press.

Curry, Oliver Scott, Mark Alfano, Mark Brandt, and Christine Pelican. 2022. "Moral Molecules: Morality as a Combinatorial System." *Review of Philosophy and Psychology* 13: 1039–1058.

Curry, Oliver Scott, Matthew Jones Chesters, and Caspar J. Van Lissa. 2019. "Mapping Morality with a Compass: Testing the Theory of 'Morality-as-Cooperation' with a New Questionnaire." *Journal of Research in Personality* 78: 106–124.

Dodell-Feder, David, and Diana I. Tamir. 2018. "Fiction Reading Has a Small Positive Impact on Social Cognition: A Meta-analysis." *Journal of Experimental Psychology: General* 147, no. 11: 1713–1727. https://doi.org/10.1037/xge0000395.

Eden, Allison, Ron Tamborini, Matthew Grizzard, Robert Lewis, Rene Weber, and Sujay Prabhu. 2014. "Repeated Exposure to Narrative Entertainment and the Salience of Moral Intuitions." *Journal of Communication* 64, no. 3: 501–520. https://doi.org/10.1111/jcom.12098.

Eliashberg, Johoshua, Sam K. Hui, and Z. John Zhang. 2007. "From Story Line to Box Office: A New Approach to Green-Lighting Movie Scripts." *Management Science* 53, no. 6: iv–1031.

Feinberg, Matthew, and Robb Willer. 2013. "The Moral Roots of Environmental Attitudes." *Psychological Science* 24, no. 1: 56–62. https://doi.org/10.1177/0956797612449177.

Festinger, Leon. 1957. *A Theory of Cognitive Dissonance*. Stanford, CA: Stanford University Press.

Gantman, Ana P., and Jay J. Van Bavel. 2015. "Moral Perception." *Trends in Cognitive Sciences* 19, no. 11: 631–633. https://doi.org/10.1016/j.tics.2015.08.004.

Graham, Jesse, Jonathan Haidt, Sena Koleva, Matt Motyl, Ravi Iyer, Sean P. Wojcik, and Peter H. Ditto. 2013. "Chapter Two–Moral Foundations Theory: The Pragmatic Validity of Moral Pluralism." *Advances in Experimental Social Psychology*, vol. 47, 55–130. https://doi.org/10.1016/B978-0-12-407236-7.00002-4.

Graham, Jesse, Jonathan Haidt, and Brian A. Nosek. 2009. "Liberals and Conservatives Rely on Different Sets of Moral Foundations." *Journal of Personality and Social Psychology* 96, no. 5: 1029–1046. https://doi.org/10.1037/a0015141.

Greene, Joshua D., Leigh E. Nystrom, Andrew D. Engell, John M. Darley, and Jonathan D. Cohen. 2004. "The Neural Bases of Cognitive Conflict and Control in Moral Judgment." *Neuron* 44, no. 2: 389–400. https://doi.org/10.1016/j.neuron.2004.09.027.

Green, Melanie C., Jeffrey J. Strange, and Timothy C. Brock, eds. 2002. *Narrative Impact: Social and Cognitive Foundations.* New York: Psychology Press.

Grizzard, Matthew, Jialing Huang, Changhyun Ahn, Kaitlin Fitzgerald, C. Joseph Francemone, and Jess Walton. 2019. "The Gordian Knot of Disposition Theory." *Journal of Media Psychology* 32, no. 2: 100–105. https://doi.org/10.1027/1864-1105/a000257.

Haidt, Jonathan. 2001. "The Emotional Dog and Its Rational Tail: A Social Intuitionist Approach to Moral Judgment." *Psychological Review* 108, no. 4: 814–834. https://doi.org/10.1037/0033-295x.108.4.814.

Haidt, Jonathan, and Craig Joseph. 2007. "The Moral Mind: How Five Sets of Innate Intuitions Guide the Development of Many Culture-Specific Virtues, and Perhaps Even Modules." In *The Innate Mind*, vol. 3: *Foundations and the Future*, edited by Peter Carruthers, Stephen Laurence, and Stephen Stich, 367–392. Oxford Scholarship Online. https://doi.org/10.1093/acprof:oso/9780195332834.003.0019.

Hopp, Frederic R., Jacob T. Fisher, Devin Cornell, Richard Huskey, and René Weber. 2021. "The extended Moral Foundations Dictionary (eMFD): Development and Applications of a Crowd-Sourced Approach to Extracting Moral Intuitions from Text." *Behavior Research Methods* 53, no. 1: 232–246. https://doi.org/10.3758/s13428-020-01433-0.

Hopp, Frederic René, Jacob Taylor Fisher, and René Weber. 2020. "A Graph-Learning Approach for Detecting Moral Conflict in Movie Scripts." *Computational Approaches to Media Entertainment Research* 8, no. 3: 164–179. https://doi.org/10.17645/mac.v8i3.3155.

Hopp, Frederic René, and René Weber. 2021a. "Reflections on Extracting Moral Foundations from Media Content." *Communication Monographs* 88, no. 3: 371–379. https://doi.org/10.1080/03637751.2021.1963513.

Hopp, Frederic René, and René Weber. 2021b. "Rejoinder: How Methodological Decisions Impact the Validity of Moral Content Analyses." *Communication Monographs* 88, no. 3: 389–393. https://doi.org/10.1080/03637751.2021.1963517.

Inbar, Yoel, David A. Pizarro, and Fiery Cushman. 2012. "Benefiting from Misfortune: When Harmless Actions Are Judged to Be Morally Blameworthy." *Personality and Social Psychology Bulletin* 38, no. 1: 52–62. https://doi.org/10.1177/0146167211430232.

Knop-Huelss, Katharina, Diana Rieger, and Frank M. Schneider. 2019. "Thinking about Right and Wrong: Examining the Effect of Moral Conflict on Entertainment Experiences, and Knowledge." *Media Psychology* 23, no. 5: 625–650. https://doi.org/10.1080/15213269.2019.1623697.

Krakowiak, K. Maja, and Mary Beth Oliver. 2012. "When Good Characters Do Bad Things: Examining the Effect of Moral Ambiguity on Enjoyment." *Journal of Communication* 62, no. 1: 117–135. https://doi.org/10.1111/j.1460-2466.2011.01618.x.

Krippendorff, K. 2003. *Content Analysis: An Introduction to Its Methodology.* 2nd ed. Thousand Oaks, CA: Sage.

László, János. 2008. *The Science of Stories: An Introduction to Narrative Psychology.* New York: Routledge.

Lee, Kang, Victoria Talwar, Anjanie McCarthy, Ilana Ross, Angela Evans, and Cindy Arruda. 2014. "Can Classic Moral Stories Promote Honesty in Children?" *Psychological Science* 25, no. 8: 1630–1636. https://doi.org/10.1177/0956797614536401.

Lewis, Robert Joel, Matthew N. Grizzard, Jin-A. Choi, and Pei Ling Wang. 2019. "Are Enjoyment and Appreciation Both Yardsticks of Popularity?" *Journal of Media Psychology: Theories, Methods, and Applications* 31, no. 2: 55–64. https://doi.org/10.1027/1864-1105/a000219.

Lewis, Robert J., Ron Tamborini, and René Weber. 2014. "Testing a Dual-Process Model of Media Enjoyment and Appreciation." *Journal of Communication* 64, no. 3: 397–416. https://doi.org/10.1111/jcom.12101.

McKee, Robert. 1997. *Story: Substance, Structure, Style and the Principles of Screenwriting.* Kent, U.K.: Methuen, HarperCollins e-books.

McKee, Robert. 2017. "You Need Moral Conflict to Create Compelling Characters: Robert McKee on London Real." Video, 6:43. LondonReal TV Story podcast, May 19. https://www.youtube.com/watch?v=3nM2Tz-EkrI.

Oliver, Mary Beth, and Anne Bartsch. 2009. "Appreciation as Audience Response: Exploring Entertainment Gratifications beyond Hedonism." *Human Communication Research* 36, no. 1: 53–81. https://doi.org/10.1111/j.1468-2958.2009.01368.x.

Paluck, Elizabeth Levy, and Donald P. Green. 2009. "Prejudice Reduction: What Works? A Review and Assessment of Research and Practice." *Annual Review of Psychology* 60: 339–367. https://doi.org/10.1146/annurev.psych.60.110707.163607.

Raney, Arthur A. 2003. "Disposition-Based Theories of Enjoyment." In *Communication and Emotion*, edited by J. Bryant, J. Cantor, and D. Ewoldsen, 69–92. New York: Routledge.

Raney, Arthur A. 2004. "Expanding Disposition Theory: Reconsidering Character Liking, Moral Evaluations, and Enjoyment." *Communication Theory* 14, no. 4: 348–369. https://doi.org/10.1111/j.1468-2885.2004.tb00319.x.

Rohm, Sonja, Frederic Hopp, and Edith Smit. 2021. "Exposure to Serial Audiovisual Narratives Increases Empathy via Vicarious Interactions." *Media Psychology* 25, no. 1: 106–127. https://doi.org/10.1080/15213269.2021.1879654.

Schaich Borg, Jana, Catherine Hynes, John Van Horn, Scott Grafton, and Walter Sinnott-Armstrong. 2006. "Consequences, Action, and Intention as Factors in Moral Judgments: An fMRI Investigation." *Journal of Cognitive Neuroscience* 18, no. 5: 803–817. https://doi.org/10.1162/jocn.2006.18.5.803.

Schein, Chelsea. 2020. "The Importance of Context in Moral Judgments." *Perspectives on Psychological Science* 15, no. 2: 207–215. https://doi.org/10.1177%2F1745691620904083.

Schwab, Frank. 2004. *Evolution and Emotion: Evolutionary Perspectives in Emotion Research and Applied Psychology.* Stuttgart: Kohlhammer Verlag.

Sinnott-Armstrong, Walter. 1988. *Moral Dilemmas.* Oxford: Basil Blackwell.

Smith, Stacy L., Rene Weber, Marc Choueiti, Katherine Pieper, Ariana Case, Kevin Yao, and Carmen Lee. 2020. "The Ticket to Inclusion: Gender and Race/Ethnicity of Leads and Financial Performance across 1,200 Popular Films." Los Angeles, CA: University of Southern California, Annenberg School for Communication and Journalism. https://assets.uscannenberg.org/docs/aii-2020-02-05-ticket-to-inclusion.pdf.

Szilas, Nicolas, Sergio Estupiñán, and Urs Richle. 2018. "Automatic Detection of Conflicts in Complex Narrative Structures." In *11th International Conference on Interactive Digital Storytelling, ICIDS 2018*, edited by R. Rouse, H. Koenitz, and M. Haahr, 415–427. Dublin, Ireland. https://doi.org/10.1007/978-3-030-04028-4_49.

Tamborini, Ron. 2011. "Moral Intuition and Media Entertainment." *Journal of Media Psychology: Theories, Methods, and Applications* 23, no. 1: 39–45. https://doi.org/10.1027/1864-1105/a000031.

Tamborini, Ron. 2012. "A Model of Intuitive Morality and Exemplars." In *Media and the Moral Mind*, edited by Ron Tamborini, 453–474. New York: Routledge.

Tamborini, Ron, Allison Eden, Nicholas David Bowman, Matthew Grizzard, René Weber, and Robert Joel Lewis. 2013. "Predicting Media Appeal from Instinctive Moral Values."

Mass Communication & Society 16, no. 3: 325–346. https://doi.org/10.1080/15205 436.2012.703285.

Tamborini, Ron, and René Weber. 2020. "Advancing the Model of Intuitive Morality and Exemplars." In *The Handbook of Communication Science and Biology*, edited by K. Floyd and R. Weber, 456–469. New York: Routledge.

Tamborini, Ron, René Weber, Allison Eden, Nicholas David Bowman, and Matthew Grizzard. 2010. "Repeated Exposure to Daytime Soap Opera and Shifts in Moral Judgment toward Social Convention." *Journal of Broadcasting & Electronic Media* 54, no. 4: 621–640. https://doi.org/10.1080/08838151.2010.519806.

Tooby, John, and Leda Cosmides. 2001. "Does Beauty Build Adapted Minds? Toward an Evolutionary Theory of Aesthetics, Fiction, and the Arts." *SubStance* 30, nos. 1–2: 6–27. https://doi.org/10.2307/3685502.

Truby, John. 2008. *The Anatomy of Story: 22 Steps to Become a Storyteller*. New York: Farrar, Straus and Giroux.

Ugwu, Reggie. 2020. "The Hashtag That Changed the Oscars: An Oral History." *New York Times*, September 9. https://www.nytimes.com/2020/02/06/movies/oscarssowhite-hist ory.html.

Uhlmann, Eric Luis, David A. Pizarro, and Daniel Diermeier. 2015. "A Person-Centered Approach to Moral Judgment." *Perspectives on Psychological Science: A Journal of the Association for Psychological Science* 10, no. 1: 72–81. https://doi.org/10.1177/174569161 4556679.

Van Leeuwen, Florian, Justin H. Park, Bryan L. Koenig, and Jesse Graham. 2012. "Regional Variation in Pathogen Prevalence Predicts Endorsement of Group-Focused Moral Concerns." *Evolution and Human Behavior* 33, no. 5: 429–437. https://doi.org/10.1016/j.evolhumbehav.2011.12.005.

Weber, Rene, Frederic René Hopp, and Jacob Fisher. 2020. "The Moral Narrative Analyzer (MoNA): A Platform for Extracting Moral Emotions and Conflict from Messages at Scale." In *Neuromarketing: Yearbook 2020*, edited by F. V. Zandvoort, 50–51. Utrecht, Netherlands: Neuromarketing Science & Business Association.

Weber, René, J. Michael Mangus, Richard Huskey, Frederic R. Hopp, Ori Amir, Reid Swanson, Andrew Gordon, Peter Khooshabeh, Lindsay Hahn, and Ron Tamborini. 2018. "Extracting Latent Moral Information from Text Narratives: Relevance, Challenges, and Solutions." *Communication Methods and Measures* 12, nos. 2–3: 119–139.

Weber, Rene, Ron Tamborini, Hye Eun Lee, and Horst Stipp. 2008. "Soap Opera Exposure and Enjoyment: A Longitudinal Test of Disposition Theory." *Media Psychology* 11, no. 4: 462–487. https://doi.org/10.1080/15213260802509993.

Weng, Chung-Yi, Wei-Ta Chu, and Ja-Ling Wu. 2007. "Movie Analysis Based on Roles' Social Network." In *2007 IEEE International Conference on Multimedia and Expo*, 1403–1406. http://doi.org/10.1109/ICME.2007.4284922.

Young, Liane, and Rebecca Saxe. 2009. "An fMRI Investigation of Spontaneous Mental State Inference for Moral Judgment." *Journal of Cognitive Neuroscience* 21, no. 7: 1396–1405. https://doi.org/10.1162/jocn.2009.21137.

Zillmann, Dolf. 2002. "Exemplification Theory of Media Influence." In *Media Effects: Advances in Theory and Research*. 2nd ed., edited by Jennings Bryant and Dolf Zillmann, 19–41. New York: Routledge.

Zillman, Dolf, and Joanne R. Cantor. 1977. "Affective Responses to the Emotions of a Protagonist." *Journal of Experimental Social Psychology* 13, no. 2: 155–165. https://doi.org/10.1016/S0022-1031(77)80008-5

6

How Screen Stories Can Contribute to the Formation of Just Persons

Nicholas Wolterstorff

In this essay I will focus on just one aspect of morality: justice. And the question I will be asking is not how screen stories can foster moral *understanding* with respect to justice but how they can foster moral *formation*. A person's moral formation, as I understand it, includes their moral understanding, but more as well. Though most of what I have to say applies both to documentaries and to fiction films, it will simplify the discussion if we focus on the latter. And sometimes I will speak of fiction in general, prose and film.[1]

Moral Formation

Let me begin with some brief remarks about moral understanding. Understanding is not to be identified with knowledge. An excellent discussion of the nature and importance of understanding, in the context of engagement with works of art, is Christoph Baumberger's (2011) essay "Art and Understanding: In Defence of Aesthetic Cognitivism."[2] Baumberger identifies three related but distinct phenomena that are called "understanding": "We can distinguish between understanding as a cognitive faculty in an inclusive sense consisting of a collection of abilities, understanding as the process of using such abilities in our inquiries, and understanding as what the cognitive process achieves" (3). Employing the last of these three meanings, he says, "[Understanding] more aptly captures what we consider a cognitive achievement in science, philosophy, and everyday life. Some knowledge is no cognitive achievement; some cognitive achievements do not constitute knowledge, others go beyond it" (3).

Baumberger's elaboration of the various ways in which understanding is not to be identified with knowledge is rich and perceptive. Let me, ever so briefly, mention a few of the points he makes. "Cognitive progress," he notes, "may be made by developing categories that impose an order on a domain appropriate to our cognitive goals" (4). So too, "cognitive progress may be made by developing adequate three-dimensional models, drawing accurate maps and producing apt diagrams" (4). And again, "cognitive progress may be made by asking new questions, clarifying the questions we are trying to answer or replacing misguided questions by better ones" (5).

Nicholas Wolterstorff, *How Screen Stories Can Contribute to the Formation of Just Persons* In: *Screen Stories and Moral Understanding*. Edited by: Carl Plantinga, Oxford University Press. © Oxford University Press 2023.
DOI: 10.1093/oso/9780197665664.003.0007

Baumberger notes that we speak both of understanding *something* and of understanding *that so-and-so.* To use his examples: "[W]e say that Sophie understands the history of the Soviet Union or that Paul understands thermodynamics," and "[W]e say that Sophie understands *that* the Soviet Union collapsed or that Paul understands *that* heat cannot spontaneously flow from a colder location to a hotter location" (2–3). He calls the former "objectual understanding" and the latter, "propositional understanding."

Moral understanding is a species of objectual understanding. Its object is *the moral domain*—alternatively described, *the moral order.* Or more precisely, some aspects of the moral domain. In the next section I offer a brief analysis of the justice dimension of the moral domain. The analysis—assuming it to be accurate—will constitute an example of moral understanding.

A person's moral formation includes more than moral understanding. It also includes the practice of making moral *discernments,* that is, the practice of discerning the moral significance of actions and situations that one encounters, and of types of actions and situations—discerning, for example, that this sort of action is demeaning and hence unjust. Moral understanding is something one has or possesses; discerning the moral significance of individual actions and situations, and of types of actions and situations, is something one does.

Whereas most human beings have some degree of moral understanding, it's the business of moral philosophers to develop and articulate moral understanding. A person might be a very good moral philosopher, however, but quite inept at discerning the moral significance of actual situations and actions and of types of situations and actions. We say he has "poor judgment."[3] Having a well-developed moral understanding is distinct from being well-developed in one's practice of moral discernment.

In addition to possessing moral understanding and engaging in the practice of making moral discernments, a person's moral formation includes the capacity and disposition to respond emotionally in appropriate ways to what one discerns to be the moral significance of actions and situations.

Last, one might have a well-developed understanding of justice, be well-developed in one's practice of discerning instances of justice and injustice, and be disposed to respond emotionally in appropriate ways to perceived instances of justice and injustice, while nonetheless, in certain situations, not being disposed, or being only weakly disposed, to do what one discerns to be just or to come to the aid of those one discerns to be victims of injustice. Instead of doing what one discerns to be just, one yields to the temptation to give priority to one's own comfort; instead of trying to get those who are perpetrating injustice to stop doing what they are doing, one is immobilized by fear of what might happen to one if one got involved. What's lacking in such cases is moral *commitment.* Obviously this too is a component of a person's moral formation.

To summarize: a person's moral formation, as I understand it, has the following components, related but distinct: moral understanding, the practice of making moral discernments, being disposed to respond emotionally in appropriate ways to what one discerns to be the moral significance of actions and situations, and moral commitment. Screen stories can foster all of these. Our question is, how do they do that, when they do? How do screen stories foster just action, and active opposition to injustice, on the part of certain viewers on certain occasions?

Justice

To address our question, I must briefly present the lineaments of my understanding of justice. Begin by noting that there are two fundamentally different types of justice—a point noted already by Aristotle. A variety of terms have been used for these two types; let me call them *first-order* justice and *second-order* justice.

First-order justice consists of agents treating each other justly in their ordinary interactions with each other: teachers and students treating each other justly, banks and lenders, and so on. Second-order justice consists of just responses to violations of first-order justice. It takes many forms, including fines, reprimands, incarceration, restitution.

Many people, when they hear the word "justice," think primarily, if not exclusively, of second-order justice; they think of police, court proceedings, prisons, and the like. Second-order justice is, obviously, of fundamental importance—not only for its own sake but because, given our human propensity for wrongdoing, first-order justice cannot flourish without the support of a just and effective system of second-order justice. First-order justice is structurally basic, however, in that there would be no second-order justice and injustice if there were no first-order justice and injustice.

Given this structural connection between the two types of justice, only if one understands first-order justice and injustice can one understand second-order. For that reason, I will focus my attention in what follows on first-order justice.

When Justinian became head of the Roman Empire in 527 CE, he commissioned a compilation and organization of everything that was of value in Roman law up to that time. The compendium, called the *Digest*, became foundational for law in the West. It opened with a definition of "justice" that came from the Roman jurist Ulpian (170–223 CE). Justice, said Ulpian, "is a steady and enduring will to render to each their *ius suum ius cuique tribuere*" (my translation, n.p.). The usage in Ulpian's time of the Latin term *ius* does not map precisely onto the usage of any term in present-day English. Translators use a range of terms to capture Ulpian's thought: to be just is to render to each person what is their due, their right, what is theirs by right, what they have a right to, what is owed them, what they have a rightful claim to, what they are entitled to. It's the virtue of justice, *being just*, that Ulpian is defining. Justice is present in society insofar as its members exercise this virtue.

I know of no writer who explicitly contests Ulpian's understanding of justice. There are some who pay no attention to it; there are some who hold that we should talk not of rights but of responsibilities. But I know of no one who explicitly contests Ulpian's thought that justice has to do with what is due one, with what one has a right to. It is the case, however, is that there is a good deal of disagreement as to what accounts for our having the rights we do have.

All parties agree that we have some of our rights because of some speech-act directed toward us, such as a promise, that others come attached to some official position that we occupy, and that others have been conferred on us by some social practice or law. My right to a monthly Social Security check from the U.S. government is an example of this last. Rights conferred by social practice or law have traditionally been called *positive* rights; rights of the former two sorts have no common name. Let me call rights of all three sorts *conferred* rights.

By no means are all rights conferred, however; and of those that are conferred, we would have some of them even if they had not been conferred—for example, the right not to be tortured as a means of punishment. We have some of our rights just by virtue of being the sort of creature that we are and standing in the sorts of relations in which we do stand.

Begin with the fact that that to which one has a right is always a good in one's life, a life-good, never a life-evil. I do not have a right to someone's breaking my leg, *period*. In case I am in a car accident, I would have a right to someone's breaking my leg if that was necessary for extricating me from the wreckage. But then it is to that complex good, of which breaking my leg is a component, that I have a right.

A life-good to which one has a right is, or implies, a way of being treated. That is not always evident on the face of things. My purchase of a ticket gives me the right to a seat on the plane, and that, obviously, is not a way of being treated! However, what's implied by my right to a seat on the plane is that I have a right to the airline officials *permitting* me to take a seat on the plane, and that is a way of being treated.

Though that to which one has a right always is, or implies, some life-good of being treated a certain way, the converse is not the case: there are many ways of being treated that would be a good in one's life to which one does not have a right. A whimsical example that I have offered in some of my writings is this: it would be a great good in my life if the Rijksmuseum in Amsterdam gave me Rembrandt's great painting *The Jewish Bride* to hang on my living room wall, along with a substantial security force to guard against theft and damage. But I do not have a right to the life-good of their treating me that way; I am not wronged by their not giving me Rembrandt's painting.

So what accounts for the fact that one has a nonconferred right to some ways of being treated that would be a good in one's life, whereas to other such ways of being treated one does not have a right? It's my view, shared by many, and explicit in the UN rights documents, that nonconferred rights are grounded in the excellence of the rights-bearer—their goodness, their worth, their dignity, their praiseworthiness. I have a right to the life-good of being treated a certain way just in case, were I not treated that way, I would be treated in a way that does not befit my worth, my dignity, my praiseworthiness. The philosopher Jean Hampton puts it well: a person wrongs another, treats them as they have a right not to be treated, "if and only if (while acting as a responsible agent) she treats him in a way that is objectively . . . demeaning, that is, disrespectful of [that person's] worth" (Murphy and Hampton 1988, 52).

Two fundamental facts about human beings are that we all have excellence in certain respects and to certain degrees, and that there are ways of treating us that show due respect for some excellence that we possess and ways of treating us that do not show due respect. Nonconferred rights are what respect for excellence requires. If a student in a class I am teaching has done top-notch work, then they have a right to my treating them with due respect for the praiseworthiness they have acquired from having done top-notch work. The conventional way of showing such respect in the American academic system is giving the student an A. The student has a right to my giving her an A. If I fail to do so, I have wronged her.

At the heart of how screen stories serve the cause of justice is that they enhance our practice of discerning when someone is treated with due respect for their worth, their excellence, their praiseworthiness, and when they are not treated with due respect.

Some Caveats

We are nearly ready to address our question: How can fictional screen stories foster moral formation with respect to justice? However, a number of caveats are in order before we set out. A fictional screen story may foster moral formation with respect to justice in some viewers but not in others. Or the moral formation it fosters in some viewers may differ significantly from that which it fosters in others. Or it may foster a viewer's moral formation only after repeated viewings. Or it may foster a viewer's moral formation subsequent to the viewing, when they reflect on what they saw. Or it may foster some dimensions of a viewer's moral formation but not other dimensions—may foster, say, their moral discernment, understanding, and emotional reactions but not their moral commitment. Or it may have a morally corrupting influence on some viewers. In short, the moral formation effected by fictional screen stories is very much *viewer- and occasion-specific.*

The fact that fictional screen stories are viewer- and occasion-specific points to a number of beckoning lines of inquiry. What, in general, accounts for the fact that a film fosters moral formation in some viewers and not in others? What accounts for the fact that it fosters a different formation in some viewers from that which it fosters in others? And so on. I will have a bit to say on some of these matters. But the main question I will be addressing is this: When a fictional film story does foster the moral formation of a viewer with respect to justice, how does it do that? How does it work?

Currie's Transmission Theory

In the literature on how fiction influences the everyday lives of viewers and readers, the model most commonly employed is the *transference model.*[4] Recall Aristotle's suggestion concerning the difference between history and fiction: history, he says, deals with particulars; fiction, with types.[5] The transference model explains the influence of fiction on life by postulating that a transference takes place from a person's engagement with types in a fictional world to their employing those same modes of engagement on instances of those types in the actual world. Readers of *War and Peace*, for example, form beliefs about Russian characters in the world of the novel and then believe those same things about the actual world of the 1800s. That is transference.

The main question that proponents of the transference model have to address is: Why does transference take place, when it does? Why is it that beliefs, discernments, and emotions that have as their objects types in the fictional world sometimes subsequently have as their objects instances of those types in the actual world?

Gregory Currie (2020), in the chapter titled "Fiction, Truth, and the Transmission of Belief" of his book *Imagining and Knowing: The Shape of Fiction*, addresses this question and introduces what I will call the *transmission theory* as an explanation of why, for many cases of transference, it takes place.

Fictions, says Currie, are invitations to imagine, not assertions: "The puzzle is how this invitation to imagine should make it reasonable to acquire [certain] beliefs"[6] (2020, 150). "How is it that, having recognized that some particular proposition P is true-in-the-story, such a reader is sometimes able to conclude that P is also true? One simple way," Currie says, "is to consider P and judge it to be true on the grounds that it coheres well with what else one believes" (160). Another way is to ask whether the author believed P and, if one concludes they did, to believe P because the author believed P. The belief gets *transmitted* from author to reader. These are the cases that interest Currie. "There are processes of plausible inference available to suitably prepared readers which enable them to infer from 'P is true-in-the-fiction' to 'P is true,' for some propositions P and some fictions. A complete taxonomy of such inferences would be hard to provide. I describe here one inferential pattern I take to be common and important and where the ascription of serious beliefs to the author plays a key role" (158).

Currie's explanation of how fictions can function as "conduits between authorial opinion and our own" (172) has three major components. First, "fictional works are ... especially rich sources of clues as to the mental states of their makers" (169). In particular, they are *expressive* of authorial beliefs. "A work of fiction may be expressive of the author's beliefs in two ways: it may be expressive of them because the author uses the work as a means to indicate or suggest that she has the belief, in which case the author expresses her belief through the work; [or] it may provide unintended evidence that the author has the belief, in which case the work is *merely* expressive of the belief" (162).

Second, readers of fiction make the judgment that certain features of the work are expressive of the author's beliefs; they judge them to be "evidence" of beliefs the author has. "We take up the invitation to imagine [the work's] contents but in the process we may recognize among those contents propositions the author believes" (166). "Readers take the way the work is written to indicate something about the author's serious beliefs" (157).

These inferences give us cognizance of propositions the author believes. Why do we, in some cases, join the author in believing those things? Why does transmission of beliefs from author to reader take place? The clue, for Currie, is *the assumption of authorial reliability:* "When readers learn from fictions by taking on the beliefs of authors expressed in their works, they often do so because they treat the author as a reliable believer" (169). Currie notes that, when they do this, the fiction is functioning much like testimony and our reception of testimony (163). In testimonial situations, one party asserts something and the other party, assuming the first party to be reliable, believes what they assert on the basis of their asserting it. In fiction, on Curry's view, the reader judges the work to be expressive of the author's beliefs and then, assuming the author to be reliable, adopts those beliefs on the basis of the work's being expressive of them.

Currie devotes a separate section in his chapter to evaluative beliefs. Oddly, the all but acknowledged upshot of the chapter is that the transmission theory has next to no application to evaluative beliefs. "Fictions," he says, "can be powerful vehicles for the expression of evaluative perspectives and their capacity to make us vividly and imaginatively aware of such perspectives can be considered a contribution to understanding" (181). But "unlike the ... purely factual beliefs one might learn from fiction, [evaluative] propositions are typically controversial or at least not widely agreed to, even by experts (assuming there is expertise in the relevant area)" (165). "To the extent that the [authorial] beliefs ... have an evaluative component reliability is likely to be lacking: many such beliefs are inherently unreliable in that we find no convergence of opinion about their truth values, mistakes are hard to identify and anyway not strongly sanctioned" (181).

But if we don't take authors of fiction to be reliable with respect to the evaluative propositions of which we judge their works to be expressive, why then do we come to hold evaluative beliefs concerning the actual world upon reading or viewing a fictional work—as we often do? Currie gives no answer to this question.

Incidentally, applying the transmission theory to film is complicated. Suppose we grant that films can be expressive of beliefs. Whose beliefs? The beliefs of the director? The beliefs of the author of the screenplay? Some imagined blend of the two?[7]

Fiction Evokes Moral Discernments

Let me henceforth speak of *moral* rather than *evaluative* beliefs and discernments. If Currie's transmission theory of transference does not explain how fiction in general, and fictional film stories in particular, sometimes foster moral formation, how is such formation to be explained?

I think Currie is correct in his claim that belief in the reliability of the author or filmmaker has little to do with the impact of fiction on the moral lives of readers and viewers. There is, of course, the phenomenon of regarding someone as *having more wisdom than oneself* on certain matters of morality; one accepts what they say *on their authority.* If someone whom one regards as having more wisdom than oneself on certain matters of morality expresses beliefs on such matters in a work of fiction, if one discerns that they are doing that, and if, consequently, one adopts those beliefs, then their moral reliability is being assumed. That's how the parables of Jesus work for a good many readers of the New Testament gospels. But this is the exception rather than the rule for how fictions foster the moral lives of readers and viewers.

The reason the assumption of the moral reliability of author or filmmaker plays relatively little role in how fictions shape our moral lives is not, however, the reason Currie gives, namely, that moral convictions are controversial, that it's hard to identify mistakes, and so on. The reason is that creators of fiction typically invite us to imagine actions and situations that evoke *our own* capacities for moral discernment. On occasion, the narrator of a fiction, or a character within a fictional world, declares that the situation depicted is just or unjust. But such declarations seldom function as something readers or viewers accept on authority. We don't respond, "Okay, I'll take your word for it. You're in the know, I'm not."

Toward the end of the film *Twelve Years a Slave,* a white man, Bass (Brad Pitt), befriends Solomon (Chiwetel Ejiofor) and declares that the situation in which Solomon finds himself is unjust. The function of this declaration is not to inform us, the viewers, that Solomon's situation is unjust; we discerned that long before. Its function is to gain Solomon's confidence that Bass is a white man he can trust.

Tolstoy had firsthand knowledge of the habits and practices of Russians in the 1800s. You and I do not have that sort of access to those facts, nor do we have the sort of access to those facts that some historians have. So if we accept the propositions on such matters of which *War and Peace* is expressive, it's because we regard Tolstoy's access to those facts as superior to ours. With morality, it's different. Our mode of access to the moral significance of actions and situations is the same as Tolstoy's; I've been calling it "discernment." We resemble Tolstoy in possessing the capacity for moral discernment. Moral discernment resembles mathematical discernment in this respect. Teachers of mathematics don't ask students to accept what they say on their authority; they aim to get students to "see" for themselves. Film directors, and creators of fiction generally, intend and expect that we ourselves, readers and viewers, will discern the moral significance of the actions and situations they depict.

Typically they intend not that their readers or viewers will discern *some moral significance or other* in the actions and situations depicted but that they will discern *a particular* moral significance; they employ the techniques available to authors and directors of film to evoke *that particular* discernment. They engage in what Noël Carroll (2020) has called *criterial prefocusing.* They focus our attention on the aspect of the situation that they want us to notice.

Sometimes they fail in their attempt to get us to see the moral significance of the situation as they intend us to see it. A given viewer may discern no moral significance in a certain action or situation, or may discern a different significance from that which the creator of the fiction intended.

There are, of course, wide variations among us in our skill at exercising our capacity for moral discernment. Whether because of nature or nurture, some are better at this than others; in general, adults are better than children. And we are all susceptible to blockages of various sorts: our personal histories, our social positions, our political convictions hinder us in discerning the moral significance of certain types of actions and situations.

Early in this section I remarked that the reliability of the creator of a fiction has little to do with the impact of the fiction on the moral lives of readers and viewers, and I went on to explain why that is. The reliability of the creator is not entirely irrelevant, however. If I bring to my reading or viewing the conviction that the author or filmmaker is morally corrupt, I will be resistant to discerning the moral significance which they intend that I discern; I will perceive the author or filmmaker as trying to manipulate me, and I will resist. Conversely, if I admire the author or filmmaker, I may more readily "go along."

But now it begins to look as if fiction has no effect on the moral formation of readers and viewers. We bring with us to our reading and viewing of fiction our capacity for moral discernment. And not only do we bring with us that general capacity. We bring with us our particular way of exercising that capacity—along with our particular moral understanding and our particular way of responding emotionally to our discernments. It's essential to our engagement with fiction that we do so. Reading or viewing fiction does not create these in us. We bring them with us to our reading and viewing. So what's new?

Carroll's Clarificationism

Let me briefly interrupt my line of thought to address Carroll's argument that, because we do and must bring with us to our reading or viewing of narratives our moral beliefs and emotional dispositions, narratives cannot induce genuinely new beliefs or genuinely new emotional responses in readers and viewers. In the chapter "Mass Art and Morality" in *A Philosophy of Mass Art* Carroll writes:

> A successful narrative is built so that its anticipated audience can understand it, and in order to understand a narrative successfully, an audience will have to mobilize its knowledge and emotions, moral and otherwise, in the process of filling in the story. This means that to understand a narrative successfully, we must use many of the same beliefs and emotions ... that we use to navigate everyday human events for the purpose of filling in and getting the point of stories. In this sense, it is not the case ... that the narrative teaches us something brand new, but rather it activates the knowledge and emotions, moral and otherwise, that we already possess[8] (1998, 324).

He continues, "[I]f this account is correct, and if we suppose additionally that learning is a matter of the acquisition of interesting, non-trivial propositions, hitherto unknown, and of freshly minted emotions, then ... there is no moral learning of this sort" (325). There is, however, another, less "restrictive ... sense of learning" that narrative artworks can produce: "The narrative artwork can become an occasion for us to deepen our understanding of what we know and feel.... A narrative can become an opportunity for us to deepen our grasp of the moral knowledge and emotions already at our command" (325).

What Carroll here calls "deepening" our understanding of what we already know and feel he elsewhere calls "clarifying" our understanding. He calls his theory *clarificationism*. I understand his thought to be that reading and viewing narratives can induce in us a better cognitive grasp of the moral beliefs and emotional dispositions that we bring with us to our reading or viewing, and that this is a form of learning. Sometimes that "better grasp" seems to me aptly described as *deepening*; sometimes it is better described as *clarifying*. In any case, what our reading or viewing of narratives cannot do is cause us to believe "non-trivial propositions, hitherto unknown," or to experience "freshly minted emotions." It cannot "teach us something brand new."

Carroll's conclusion does not follow from his premise. It's true that to understand a narrative we must bring with us to our reading or viewing a certain body of beliefs, including moral beliefs, and the disposition to feel certain emotions. I would add that we must also bring with us the ability to discern the moral significance of the types of actions and situations presented by the fiction. However, from the fact that we must bring these with us it does not follow that our reading or viewing does not induce us to make genuinely new discernments, form genuinely new beliefs, and experience genuinely new emotional responses.

Suppose that I bring to my reading or viewing of a narrative the belief that charity is a noble thing, especially when it comes at considerable cost to oneself. Not only do I believe this; I have acted on it. I have actively supported, with time and money, a number of charitable organizations.

The narrative depicts a case of well-intentioned charity that its recipients find demeaning. I have never before noticed that charity can be demeaning, and so, of course, I have never felt empathy with the victims of demeaning charity nor indignation at the perpetrators. But the narrative depicts the charity in such a way that the demeaning stares me in the face. I clearly discern it, I feel empathy with the victims and indignation at the perpetrators, and I now hold the belief that, when dispensing charity, one must see to it that one does not do so in such a way as to demean the recipients.

I am now a changed person. There, in my reading or viewing chair, I have done the "brand new" thing of discerning that a recipient of charity was being demeaned, I have had the "brand new" experience of feeling empathy and indignation in response to a discernment of that sort, and I have formed the "brand new" belief that one must be alert to the fact that charity can be demeaning. Given these changes in my moral formation, it's more likely than it was before that there will also be something "brand new" in my engagement with actions and situations in the actual world. It's more likely than it was before that I will discern demeaning where I never saw it before, and more likely that I will feel empathy and indignation when I never felt it before. If that does happen, transference has taken place.

Fiction Can Foster Moral Formation by *Enhancement and Transference*

Fundamental to how film stories can foster moral formation is a phenomenon that I will call "enhancement." Transfer is also important. But if there were no enhancement of one's discernments, understanding, and emotions, there would be no transference of those.

We bring to our viewing of a film not just the general capacity for making moral discernments but a *particular way of employing* that capacity—not just moral understanding in general but a *particular* moral understanding, and not just the general disposition to experience emotions but a *particular complex* of such dispositions. As my example in the preceding section suggests, these may all be flawed or deficient in one way or another. Fundamental to how film stories can foster the moral formation of viewers is by undoing and diminishing such flaws and deficiencies. Such undoing and diminishing is what I call "enhancement." Enhancement of one's practice of making moral discernments is basic. Enhancement of one's moral understanding comes along with enhancement of one's discernments; enhancement of one's complex of emotional dispositions tends to do so as well.

Let me identify a few of the ways in which fiction can produce enhancement.

1. Before I viewed *Twelve Years a Slave* I knew that kidnapping and slavery were wrong, and I thought I had a rather good idea of what slavery in the U.S. South was like, gained from reading a number of histories and novels, in particular *Uncle Tom's Cabin*.[9] Yet, viewing *Twelve Years* was, for me, both profoundly illuminating and deeply moving. It was not just a repetition of what I already knew and felt.[10]

How so? What was the nature of the film's impact on me? It made me discern more acutely than previously the injustice of that particular form of slavery. It did that by inviting and enabling me to imagine more vividly than previously, and in more detail, what such slavery was like, with the result that my emotional reaction was also more intense. I now squirmed with Solomon when he tried to break loose from his kidnapper's shackles. I now winced with each crack of the whip on his back and with each crack of the whip on the back of the young slave girl Patsey (Lupita Nyong'o). When reading *Uncle Tom's Cabin* I had not imagined as vividly and in such detail what Tom was going through as I now imagined what Solomon was going through, with the result that my emotional response to the book was also less intense. Though reading the novel was, for me, an emotional experience, I had not squirmed when Tom was whipped.

And more than discerning more acutely the moral significance of southern U.S. slavery by more vividly and in more detail imagining what it was like, I imagined *what it felt like* to experience what Solomon experienced.[11] I think it is the peculiar power of fiction to enable us to imagine what the inner experience is like of a certain type of person in a certain type of situation, and it seems to me that film is undoubtedly even more powerful than prose fiction in this respect.[12] It's more powerful because, unlike prose fiction, we are presented not just with words but with the language of the body, of the face, and of the inflections of the voice. It's remarkable how often, in *Twelve Years*, we get close-ups of Solomon's face. From his face, we imagine how he felt. And from his bearing, we learn that he never lost his sense of self-worth; he was never broken.[13]

I think we can take a step further and say that we don't just *imagine* how such a person feels in such a situation; we *know* how they feel. It's objectual knowledge rather than propositional. Knowing what a toothache feels like is a different form of knowledge from knowing a number of propositions about teeth and aches.

Here is perhaps a good place to make the point that my response to the episodes in *Twelve Years* was, like everyone's response, not some generically human response but what is nowadays often called, in film studies, a *situated* response. Those whose social and cultural situation is different from mine would respond differently. My situation is that of a senior white middle-class American male. Someone whose situation is that of a young Black male in American society would likely respond differently. How to describe that difference? It's not for me to say. But my guess is that the response of a good many of them would be tinged, as mine was not, by memories of the fear and anger they felt when interacting with white police officers.

When I spoke, above, about the language of the body, of the face, and of the inflections of the voice, I was thinking about the discussion by the 18th-century Scots philosopher Thomas Reid about what he called "natural signs." Natural signs, Reid wrote, "are features of the face, gestures of the body, and modulations of the voice, the variety of which is suited to the variety of things signified by them. Nature hath established a real connection between these signs, and the thoughts and dispositions of the mind which are signified by them" (1970, 235).

It was Reid's view that though our ability to interpret these natural signs is, in part, the result of learning, the learning presupposes our ability to do so "by the constitution of our nature, by a kind of natural perception similar to the perceptions of sense" (1969, 638). Reid writes, "When I see the features of an expressive face, I see only figure and colour variously modified. But by the constitution of my nature, the visible object brings along with it the [grasp] of a certain passion or sentiment in the mind of the person" (638).[14]

Let me bring this point to a conclusion. Screen stories can cause us to discern more acutely than we did before the moral significance of situations familiar to us. They do this, in good measure, by inviting and enabling us to imagine vividly and in detail what such a situation is like, especially what it *felt like* or *feels like* to be such a person in such a situation. Right there, when viewing certain films, one's exercise of the capacity for moral discernment may be enhanced and, along with it, one's moral understanding and one's emotional life.

When I leave the world of the film and return to the actual world, then, if all goes well, I will find myself making discernments, applying my understanding, and experiencing emotions in these newly enhanced ways. That would be transference, and that would be an additional contribution to my moral formation. But the enhancement I experienced when viewing the film was already a positive development in my moral formation. Wholly apart from whether transference of discernment, understanding, and emotions subsequently takes place, my moral formation was fostered by what I experienced when watching *Twelve Years a Slave*.

2. Screen stories can also foster the moral formation of viewers by depicting a type of situation familiar to us in such a way that we, for the first time, discern its moral significance. Perhaps one's moral analysis of certain situations has been simplistic; fiction may open one's eyes to overlooked complexities. One may never have noticed how often what is intended as an act of kindness is perceived by its percipient as condescension. Reading the description, in Richard Wright's *Native Son,* of how Biggar bridles at the condescension he perceives in the "kindness" of his white friends may open one's eyes.

When this sort of thing happens during a film screening, the exercise of one's capacity for moral discernment has been enhanced and, along with it, one's moral understanding and one's emotional life. That is already a positive contribution to one's moral formation. But if, when one exits the world of the film and reenters the actual world, one discerns the moral significance of instances of that same type in this enhanced way and applies one's newly enhanced understanding and experiences new emotions, transference has occurred; that is an additional contribution to one's moral formation.

3. It may be that one did not *overlook* morally significant aspects of familiar situations but *resisted* acknowledging them—resisted, for example, acknowledging the injustice of situations of certain sorts. One may have acknowledged that the suffering experienced by certain human beings was caused by human action or inaction, not by some natural calamity, but told oneself that it's not a case of injustice because there's nothing to be done about it, or because to change it would only make matters worse, or because it's their own fault that they are suffering as they are, or because those who are suffering are not fully human. They don't suffer the way "we" do.

Fiction has the power of overcoming such sources of resistance in at least some readers and some viewers. There cannot have been many readers of *Grapes of Wrath* who emerged from reading the novel still believing that the plight of the Okies was unavoidable, or that it was their own fault. There cannot have been many readers of *Uncle Tom's Cabin* who continued to believe that Tom did not suffer the way "we" do, nor can there be many viewers of *Twelve Years a Slave* who leave the theater believing that Solomon did not suffer the way "we" do.

When one's resistance to acknowledging the injustice of situations of certain sorts has been overcome by reading a novel or viewing a film, the exercise of one's moral discernment has been enhanced and, along with it, one's moral understanding and the range of one's emotional dispositions—enhanced in the film viewing. That represents a change for the good in one's moral formation. If, subsequently, one no longer resists acknowledging the injustice of such situations in the actual world, transference has taken place. And that constitutes an additional contribution to one's moral formation.

I have distinguished three ways in which film stories can enhance a person's exercise of their capacity for moral discernment, along with their moral understanding and their dispositions to experience emotions: film stories can cause a person to discern more acutely than they did previously the moral significance of familiar types of actions and situations; they can cause a person to discern for the first time certain aspects of the moral significance of familiar types of actions and situations; and they can overcome a person's resistance to discerning the moral significance of familiar types of actions and situations. And, of course, fiction may enhance a person's moral formation by depicting a type of situation unfamiliar to them whose moral significance they discern, a type of situation they have never previously come across.[15]

An important point that I will have to forgo exploring is the role of background music in film. Among the many things background music does, it can intensify our emotional reactions to what we are seeing. Might that intensification of emotional reactions intensify, in turn, the acuity of our discernment of the moral significance of the actions and situations presented? If so, that would be a sort of feedback.[16]

In closing this section of our discussion, let me note that, as well as fostering our moral formation by presenting us with situations whose moral significance we newly discern, fiction can also do so by presenting us with situations whose moral significance remains unclear or ambiguous. We are baffled. A superb example of the point is *The Thin Red Line*. Rather than evoking discernment in us, the film raises questions. We may put those questions out of mind, or we may find ourselves compelled to reflect on them. If our reflections go well and culminate in enhanced discernment and understanding, our moral formation has been advanced.

And let's not forget that a work of fiction may have a damaging, rather than an enhancing, effect on the moral formation of some readers or viewers, possibly on all. How that works is an important topic in its own right.

How Fiction Can Foster Moral Commitment

Up to this point in my discussion of how screen stories can foster moral formation I have said nothing about the fostering of moral commitment; I have focused exclusively on moral discernment, moral understanding, and morally relevant emotions. It's time to turn to the fostering of commitment. Fiction in general, and screen stories in particular, have the power of fostering moral commitment by enhancement plus the workings of what I will call "quasi-transference."

Some people act justly or oppose injustice out of a sense of duty. Some do so because they believe that God asks this of them. Others, schooled along the lines of virtue theory, do so because they think that is what a good person does. Some do so because of the modeling effect: psychologists have shown that we are disposed to model our actions after those of persons whom we respect or admire. And many of those committed to opposing certain forms of injustice are motivated by feelings of empathy with the victims and/or feelings of indignation toward the perpetrators.

Fictions in general, and screen stories in particular, have the power to evoke in a reader or viewer any of these motivations to act justly or oppose injustice. The injustice depicted in a film sometimes evokes in certain viewers the strong conviction that they are duty-bound to actively oppose injustice of that sort in the actual world. So, too, for the other motivations mentioned.[17]

It is my impression, however, that when it's not so much a commitment to acting justly that is evoked but a commitment to oppose injustice, almost always an important aspect of how fictions in general do this, and film stories in particular, is that they evoke in a reader or viewer an emotional engagement with those perceived to be the victims and/or the perpetrators of unjust actions and situations depicted in the fiction. Prominent among these emotions are empathy and indignation. Empathy *with* the perceived victims: the reader or viewer feels demeaned *with* the victims, grief *with* them, apprehension *with* them, horror *with* them, relief *with* them, joy and elation *with* them. Indignation *at* the perceived perpetrators: the reader or viewer feels anger *at* the perpetrators, disgust *at* them, revulsion *at* them, horror *at* their deeds.[18] As mentioned above, watching *Twelve Years a Slave* was, for me, an intensely emotional experience: I experienced intense feelings of empathy with the slaves, especially, of course, Solomon, and intense feelings of indignation at the kidnappers and the slaveholders.[19]

People obviously differ in the intensity of their emotional engagement with fiction. Some, like myself, need a handkerchief at hand when watching *Twelve Years a Slave*; others are moved but watch dry-eyed. Only those few who are incapable of empathy or indignation—the sociopaths among us—are unmoved. I cannot imagine what the experience of reading novels or watching films is like for them.

I assume that if, when watching a film, one discerns more acutely than one did previously in the actual world the injustice of a certain type of action or situation, then it's likely that one will also feel more intensely the emotions of empathy and indignation. The greater intensity of the emotions comes along with the greater acuity of the discernment.[20]

Suppose, now, that when viewing a film I discern more acutely than previously the injustice of a type of situation with which I am familiar in the actual world, and consequently also feel more intensely the relevant emotions of empathy and indignation. Those heightened emotions might then evoke in me a commitment to working to oppose injustice of a similar sort in the actual world—or, in case I already had that commitment, might strengthen that commitment. So too if the injustice depicted in a film is of a sort unfamiliar to me but which I now believe to be present in the actual world: the feelings of empathy and indignation stirred up in me by viewing the film might evoke in me a commitment to working to oppose injustice of a similar sort in the actual world.

Note well: my feelings of empathy and indignation do not evoke in me a commitment to work to oppose the injustice depicted in the film. Though I discern that Solomon, in the fictional world of *Twelve Years a Slave*, was treated with gross indignity and injustice, and though I feel intense empathy with him and intense indignation at the slaveholders, I do not commit myself to working to liberate Solomon. Because I can't do that; only someone in the world of the film could do that. My commitment—evoked in me then and there by the empathy and indignation I experience while watching the film—is a commitment to working to oppose injustice of a similar sort *in the actual world*.

It is for his reason that I call the workings "quasi-transference." If all goes well, transference of a certain sort does take place: the moral commitment evoked in me while watching the film goes with me when I leave the theater and return to my life in the actual world. But this is not the phenomenon that I (and others) call "transference." True transference consists of the transference of certain modes of engagement with types in the world of a fiction to engagement by those same modes with instances of those types in the actual world. Whereas I have moral discernments, beliefs, and emotions that can be transferred from fictional actions and situations to actions and situations in the actual world, I do not have moral *commitments* with respect to entities in the fictional world that can be transferred to entities in the actual world.

It is *enhancement* plus *quasi-transference* that accounts for a screen story evoking in a viewer a new or strengthened abiding commitment to seek justice and oppose injustice. The complex of moral commitments that the viewer brought to the viewing has been *enhanced*; if all goes well, that enhancement accompanies the viewer in the transition from fiction to life.

I spoke of the injustice depicted in a film evoking in a viewer a commitment to working to oppose injustice of "a similar sort" in the actual world. What should be noted is that there is no such thing as *the* similar sort. Some injustices in the actual world will be similar in certain respects to the injustice depicted; others will be similar in other respects; yet others will be similar in yet other respects. This has the implication that the same film may well evoke significantly different moral commitments in different viewers, each of these commitments being a commitment to work to oppose a sort of injustice n the actual world similar to that in the world of the film. Here, especially, the *situatedness* of viewers is relevant. *Twelve Years a Slave* will evoke different moral commitments in differently situated viewers.

Sad to say, it's possible for a person to discern acutely the injustice of the actions and situations depicted in a film, and to experience intense feelings of empathy with the victims and indignation at the perpetrators, without those feelings evoking moral commitment. Doing what one knows to be unjust is often irresistibly tempting: money, power, and prestige beckon. Working to oppose injustice is often frightening: it's likely to be conflictual, who knows with what consequences to one's life, limbs, and liberty? Or one has other priorities. Or one is overcome by inertia. Do films have the power of eliminating such blockages to commitment? Sometimes, for some persons, yes; for others, no.

In Conclusion

In bringing my discussion to a close, let me highlight a central feature of my analysis. Every reader of *War and Peace* believes that many Russians in the world of the novel speak French. Something else has to happen for transference of this belief to take place—for readers of the novel to believe that, in the actual world, a good many Russians in the 1800s spoke French. Currie's transmission theory postulates that this "something else" is the reader's belief that the novel is expressive of the writer's belief that, in the Russia of his day, a good many Russians spoke French, plus the reader's belief that the writer was reliable on this matter.

I have not addressed the question of the plausibility of Currie's transmission theory for our belief of such contingent factual propositions as that many 19th century Russians spoke French; I have argued only that the theory has little application to moral beliefs.

"Facts" about Russia in the world of *War and Peace* may or may not be facts about Russia in the actual world of the time. That's why one's believing that something is a "fact" about Russia in the novel is not sufficient for believing that it was a fact about Russia in the actual world. Something has to be added.

Moral beliefs are different. If I discern that such-and-such is the moral significance of a type of situation depicted in a film, and if I form the corresponding belief that that is its significance, then I perforce believe that such-and-such is also the moral significance of instances of that type in the actual world. Nothing, such as belief in the reliability of the filmmaker, has to be added. It would be irrational to believe that such-and-such is the moral significance of a certain type of situation in the world of the film but that it might not be the moral significance of instances of that type in the actual world.[21]

And if one's discernment and understanding of the moral significance of episodes in the film is an *enhancement* of the discernments and understanding that one brings to one's viewing, then what one experiences when watching the film is itself a change for the better in one's moral formation. One's moral formation has been fostered.

Discerning the moral significance of a certain type of situation in a fictional world is, obviously, a distinct act from discerning the moral significance of an instance of that type in the actual world. So if one first discerns the moral significance of a certain type of situation in a fictional world and then, subsequently, discerns the same moral significance in instances of that type in the actual world, *transference* has occurred. And that too is a change for the better in one's moral formation. But one's moral formation was already changed for the better there in the theater, by enhancement.

Treating someone justly consists, at its core, of treating them with due respect for their worth, their dignity, their praiseworthiness. In order for fiction to foster just action and active opposition to injustice, readers and viewers must bring with them to their reading and viewing the capacity for discerning when persons have been treated with due respect and when they have been treated, instead, with disrespect. At the core of the power of fiction to contribute to the formation of just persons is its power to enhance our exercise of that capacity. Enhancement of our understanding of justice and injustice, and enhancement of appropriate emotional responses, flow from the enhancement of our discernings, as does, if all goes well, enhancement of our commitment to do and seek justice.

Notes

1. I thank Terence Cuneo and Carl Plantinga for incisive comments on an early draft of this essay. And I thank those who participated in the virtual seminar, Screen Stories and Moral Understanding (January 16, 2021), for their many perceptive comments on the penultimate draft.
2. See also the fine essay in this present collection by Ted Nannicelli, "Clarifying Moral Understanding."
3. If one discerns that a certain action or situation has such-and-such moral significance, then, normally, one will also *judge* that it has that significance. I think that, for our purposes, nothing will be lost if we subsequently make no mention of such judgments.
4. I myself employed this model in my *Art Rethought* (Wolterstorff 2015).
5. In my *Works and Worlds of Art* (Wolterstorff 1981) I developed the theory that the ontological status of fictional entities is that of types; it did not occur to me at the time that this was Aristotle's view.
6. Currie focuses exclusively on beliefs; he mentions emotions only by the way, and discernments not at all. And the only form of fiction to which he makes reference is literary fiction.
7. Berys Gaut (2010) has a long and insightful discussion of the problems raised by collective authorship in film in the chapter titled "Cinematic Authorship" of his book *A Philosophy of Cinematic Art*. I thank Carl Plantinga for this reference.
8. This is no longer Carroll's position. I introduce it here because it is a lucid statement of an objection to the line that I am developing. For Carroll's current position, see his 2020 essay, "Literature, the Emotions, and Learning." The essay develops the thesis that literature can not only reinforce "existing emotional tendencies but can also change social sentiment," and it offers an account of how such "moral education" works.
9. In chapter 14 of my *Art Rethought* (Wolterstorff 2015) I explore at length the merit of *Uncle Tom's Cabin* as a work of social protest art.
10. I thank Carl Plantinga for refreshing my faded memory of *Twelve Years* by giving me a private viewing of the film while I was working on this essay.
11. I did not find myself imagining the feelings of the slave owners; I observed them and what they did from the outside, as it were. This may point to some general truth.
12. Perhaps here is the place to note that *Twelve Years* is a quasi-documentary or docufiction, based on the story told by Solomon Northop, a real person, about what happened to him. But the film necessarily fleshes out the story well beyond what Northop wrote.
13. Plantinga (1999) is a superb analysis of how films enable us to grasp the emotion of characters in the film by the ways in which they present the faces of those characters.
14. Plantinga (1999, 242) cites recent empirical studies of what Reid called "natural signs." These studies confirm Reid's view that we have an innate ability to read these natural signs.

15. In the virtual seminar Screen Stories and Moral Understanding, Mary Beth Oliver made the important point that a good deal of the gratification film viewers experience is the gratification of finding their moral discernments, understanding, and emotional responses enhanced.

16. Carl Plantinga called my attention to this point about the function of music in film.

17. In their contributions to this volume, Allison Eden and Mathew Grizzard and Noël Carroll explore the modeling effect on viewers of characters in films.

18. Notice the contrast of prepositions: we feel empathy *with* a person, indignation *at* or *toward* a person.

19. I mentioned that Plantinga (1999) presents an excellent analysis of how the ways in which films depict the faces of characters enable us to grasp their emotions. That essay offers an equally fine analysis of the conditions under which grasping their emotions evokes empathy. He offers a helpful description of empathy: "Empathy consists of a capacity or disposition to know, to feel, and to respond congruently to what another is feeling, and the process of doing so" (245).

20. But recall that in the previous section I floated the possibility that increasing the intensity of viewers' emotional reactions to actions and situations in films by background music, by angles and lengths of shots, and so on might in turn increase the acuity of their discernment of the injustice of those actions or situations.

21. Of course, they have to be instances of the type that possess its morally relevant features.

Works Cited

Baumberger, Christoph. 2011. "Art and Understanding: In Defence of Aesthetic Cognitivism." In *Bilder Sehen: Perspectiven der Bildwissenschaft*, edited by C. Wagner, M. Greenlee, R. Hammwöhner, and C. Wolff, 1–24.. Regensberg: Schnell & Seiner.

Carroll, Noël. 1998. *A Philosophy of Mass Art*. Oxford: Clarendon Press.

Carroll, Noël. 2020. "Literature, the Emotions, and Learning." *Philosophy and Literature* 44, no. 1 (April): 1–18.

Currie, Gregory. 2020. *Imagining and Knowing: The Shape of Fiction*. Oxford: Oxford University Press.

Gaut, Berys. 2010. *A Philosophy of Cinematic Art*. Cambridge: Cambridge University Press.

Murphy, Jeffrie, and Jean Hampton. 1988. *Forgiveness and Mercy*. Cambridge: Cambridge University Press.

Plantinga, Carl. 1999. "The Scene of Empathy and the Human Face on Film." In *Passionate Views: Film, Cognition, and Emotion*, edited by Carl Plantinga and Greg M. Smith, 239–255. Baltimore, MD: Johns Hopkins University Press.

Reid, Thomas. 1969. *Essays on the Intellectual Powers of Man*. Cambridge MA: MIT Press.

Reid, Thomas. 1970. *Inquiry into the Human Mind*. Edited by Timothy Duggan. Chicago: University of Chicago Press.

Wolterstorff, Nicholas. 1981. *Works and Worlds of Art*. Oxford: Oxford University Press.

Wolterstorff, Nicholas. 2015. *Art Rethought*. Oxford: Oxford University Press.

PART III
AFFECT

7
Affect and Moral Understanding

Robert Sinnerbrink

What is the relationship between affect and moral understanding?[1] Much recent work in philosophical film theory has focused on emotion in narrative cinema and explored the links between emotional engagement and moral understanding (Carroll 2010; Cooper 2006; Choi and Frey 2014; Downing and Saxton 2010; Grønstad 2016; Jones and Vice 2011; Plantinga 2009a, 2009b, 2010, 2018; Shaw 2012; Sinnerbrink 2016; Stadler 2008). Theories of emotional engagement (e.g., Murray Smith's 1995 account of the "structure of sympathy") analyze the related aspects of what an earlier generation of film theorists called "identification." (See Gaut 2010, 252–262 for a nuanced defense of identification.) Focusing on audiovisual strategies generating varieties of perceptual alignment, emotional engagement, and moral allegiance, such theories foreground the key role of emotional engagement in fostering sympathetic (or antipathetic) engagement with characters coupled with prosocial (versus antisocial) forms of moral evaluation (see Carroll 2010; Plantinga 2010). At the same time, such theories highlight the manner in which affective and emotional responses to cinema—encompassing engagement with characters as well as aesthetic responses to movement, color, form, sound, music, and duration—are also linked with moral evaluation and ethical understanding (see Plantinga 2018).

Within such discussions, however, the role of affect is often subsumed into that of emotion, which is understandable given the close relations between affect and emotion in understanding narrative film. Nonetheless, there are important differences in the role of affective responses in eliciting, directing, and sustaining emotional engagement along with sympathetic, as well as antipathetic, forms of moral evaluation. In this chapter, I shall explore some of these important differences, analyzing the distinctions between prevailing accounts of affect within different theoretical approaches and examining the relationship between affect and emotion in our engagement with narrative cinema. I turn then to the relationship between affect, emotion, and moral understanding in response to cinema, examining the manner in which affect typically primes and sustains emotional engagement, which is essential to prompting conventional forms of moral evaluation that can consolidate, or sometimes reconfigure, important aspects of our moral understanding. At the same time, we can also describe affect in an impersonal sense, as a mode of aesthetic expression using film form, and even as an "unconscious" form of bodily response that can influence conscious moral perception and judgment. This more aesthetic and ethical perspective

Robert Sinnerbrink, *Affect and Moral Understanding* In: *Screen Stories and Moral Understanding*. Edited by: Carl Plantinga, Oxford University Press. © Oxford University Press 2023. DOI: 10.1093/oso/9780197665664.003.0008 on affect can contribute to our understanding of how particular cinematic sequences can generate complex and sometimes conflicted affective and ethical responses. For not all films align affect, emotion, and (prosocial) moral attitudes in harmonious ways; some disrupt or undermine this alignment in ways that force moral reflection or ethical revision of our affective, aesthetic, and emotional responses to characters, actions, or narrative situations. This "moral-cognitive dissonance" effect, as I shall discuss, can prompt us to question or review our habitual or routine forms of emotional engagement and moral evaluation of film in ways that can deepen and revise moral understanding. I conclude my discussion with an analysis of a key sequence from Michael Haneke's *Amour* (2012)—a film much praised for its morally confronting but thought-provoking presentation of dementia and euthanasia—as an example of how disrupting the alignment between affective-emotional and moral-cognitive responses, using an affectively dissonant mode of presentation, can deepen our moral understanding of ambiguous ethical situations.

Conventional (Exoteric) versus Unconventional (Esoteric) Senses of Affect

There is little doubt that "affect" has become one of the most pervasive and popular topics in film theory, but one that remains obscure, ambiguous, or subject to variable interpretations (see Plantinga 2009a). Given the common conflation of "affect," "emotion," "feeling," and "mood" in ordinary language, the proliferation of diverse strands of affect theory within film studies might seem peculiar or confusing when viewed from outside the discipline. It does start to make sense, however, when one contextualizes the rise of affect theory. Indeed, there is now a whole subfield of film theory that draws on what is often called "affect theory,"[2] which in these contexts refers to the theoretical focus on the primacy of affect in our complex experience of and engagement with cinema. When cognitivist film theorists talk of affect, for example, it generally refers to somatic or bodily forms of feeling, that is, all manner of sensuous and corporeal, felt but involuntary or even "automatic" responses to audiovisual images (Plantinga 2009a; Stadler 2014). These include bodily feeling, physical sensation, muscular tension, somatic excitation, audiomotor entrainment, as well as much discussed phenomena such as affective mimicry or "emotional contagion," and so on (see Coplan 2006). As psychological studies suggest, bodily feelings are "non-specific and somewhat ambiguous" (see Dutton and Aaron 1974; Schachter and Singer 1962; Zillmann 1983).[3] Matthew Grizzard points out that the same bodily feeling can be interpreted differently, "as fear or excitement," for example, "due to cognitive labelling," which suggests that the ambiguity of affect can affect our understanding of situations as well as moral evaluation. Call this the conventional or "exoteric" view of affect understood as bodily feeling (2021).

Another approach to affect, common among Continental film theorists and film philosophers, refers to more obscure aspects or unconventional accounts of affect than the subjective experience of bodily feeling. Drawing on theoretical perspectives as diverse as those of Spinoza, Sylvan Tomkins, Freud, Gilles Deleuze, Alberto Damasio, Brian Massumi, Eve Kosofsky Sedgwick, Teresa Brennan, and many others, affect theory in this Continental approach posits a range of phenomena pertaining to affect that have subjective, aesthetic, even ethical dimensions. These include unconscious affects, nonintentional affects, transformative or intensive affects ("flashes of mental or somatic activity") that can have hedonic, revelatory, or intuitional qualities (Figlerowicz 2012, 4). Some accounts refer to "autonomous" affects that subsist without a subject, or which can have aesthetic and "ethical" qualities independent of the human beings affected by them (see Brennan 2004; Brinkema 2014; Massumi 2002; Shaviro 2010). This conception detaches affect from the domain of consciously felt experience, emphasizing its impersonal and "unconscious" aspects, but also posits its independent aesthetic and ethical qualities, in ways that do not readily correspond to the conventional understanding of affect. Call this the unconventional or "esoteric" view of affect, where affects need not be anchored within a viewing subject, nor attributed to a body (whether human or filmic), but can subsist as quasi-independent entities manifesting according to particular kinds of aesthetic form.

Given that both schools of philosophical film theory use the same term, however, it is not surprising that much confusion has arisen concerning how to theorize affect and its relation to both aesthetic and moral experience in cinema. To take one example, consider Julian Hanich's remarks in his review of Eugenie Brinkema's *The Forms of the Affects*, a book he describes as one of "remarkably frustrating brilliance":

> Initially drawing on Deleuze's notion of affect, Brinkema ultimately aims to go beyond the French philosopher and his followers in film and media theory like Steven Shaviro, Brian Massumi, or Lisa Cartwright. She believes that these scholars still cling too much to *bodies* affected by affects: "Affect, as I theorize it here, has fully shed the subject, but my argument goes a step further and also loses for affects the body and bodies. This book regards any individual affect as a self-folding exteriority that manifests in, as, and with textual form" ([Brinkema 2014], 25). Affects do not need an experiencing subject—there are forms and there are affects, and the affects *have* forms just as much as they *inhere* in forms. (Hanich 2015, 113–114)

As Hanich notes, Brinkema's unconventional approach to the "forms of the affects" can be compared with other aesthetic theories of affect expressed in aesthetic form, such as Susan K. Langer's 1953 work, *Feeling and Form*. In the latter, Hanich remarks, "there is a *similarity* between the dynamics of an art form and the dynamics of emotional life," analogies between feelings and aesthetic patterns or forms, but this does not mean that there is an identification of specific emotions or affective states and specific formal sequences as we find in Brinkema's work (2015, 114). Hanich is pointing here, I suggest, to the two senses of affect identified above: the conventional (exoteric) sense of affect as bodily feeling and the unconventional (esoteric) sense of affect as autonomous expression of form. The difficulty arises when these two senses are conflated or run together (where a theorist at times refers to affect as bodily feeling and at other times to affect as nonsubjective, expressive form), or when one sense of affect is given precedence without acknowledging the role of the other (as Brinkema does in rejecting the conventional sense of affect altogether). Given these two distinct, even conflicting approaches to affect, examining the role of affect in cinema, particularly with reference to moral understanding—a topic only occasionally mentioned in Continental approaches—quickly becomes confused and confusing.

The confusion is compounded if we turn to the contrast between conceptions of "moral understanding" prevalent in analytic-cognitivist philosophy of film and those within Continental strains of film theory. In the latter, the term "moral understanding" rarely appears, but there is frequent reference to "ethics" in relation to affect (see, e.g., Boljkovac 2013; Cooper 2006; Grønstad 2016; Kendall 2012). What's the difference, one might ask, given the relative equivalence of these terms within philosophy? As Carl Plantinga remarks, in such approaches the term "morality" (and cognate terms like "moral understanding") is eschewed in favor of "ethics" presumably because of infelicitous connotations relating to 19th-century "moralism" or unwanted associations with universalist conceptions of morality (2018; Kantian, for example). Within these contexts, "ethics," I would add, is considered less prescriptive and more practical, contextualist, or agential in orientation than universalist accounts of "morality" (Aristotelian ethics, for example). For many theorists, especially those influenced by Deleuze, it also carries felicitous connotations evoking the Spinozist conception of "ethics" grounded in the power of bodies to act or be affected within the monistic, dynamic, relational whole of Nature (see Deleuze 1988).

There is further hesitation, in these approaches, over the term "understanding" (as in "moral understanding"). For "moral understanding" introduces the cognitive, reflective, and normative dimensions of emotional engagement that some theorists are quick to reject or dismiss. (The term "affect" is ubiquitous in Deleuzian film theory which avoids any references to "emotion"; see Boljkovac 2013; Del Rio 2012.) Why this hesitation? I would suggest it is because references to emotional engagement as conducive to moral understanding—via notions of sympathy, empathy, or perspective-taking, for example—refer to a "moral subject" or rational agent capable of affective-emotional and cognitive-reflective responses to given social situations (whether fictional characters within a narrative situation or film spectators within a viewing context). This is precisely the view of the morally autonomous "humanist subject," however, that is questioned, criticized, or rejected in certain Continental strains of film theory or film philosophy (see Sinnerbrink this volume and 2019).

In keeping with the downplaying of the exoteric sense of affect (bodily feeling) and valorizing of its esoteric sense (unconscious, nonintentional, nonrational, nonsubjective, or expressive states), the cognitive and normative dimensions of moral understanding are likewise downplayed or ignored. Instead, we find a valorizing of an "affective ethics" of bodily intensities or impersonal transformative experience that bypasses more cognitively oriented or normatively framed modes of moral understanding (Boljkovac 2013; Shaviro 2010; Marks 2000). According to these approaches, moral understanding, as elicited via cinema, is not anchored within a moral subject or rational agent. Rather, certain kinds of cinematic experience, which elicit "affect" in this unconventional esoteric sense, have the potential to alter our perception, orientation, and experience. These affective encounters can also provide material for speculative theorization concerning the emancipatory sensuous and affective capacities of the body, the possibility of a "decentred subjectivity," articulating a posthumanistic ethics, a deconstructive critique of the "false universalism" of the (white, male, heterosexual, Eurocentric) humanist subject, an acknowledgment of the "alterity" of "the Other," and much else besides.

Once again, the difference between approaches focusing on the conventional versus unconventional (exoteric versus esoteric) senses of "affect" becomes apparent. Analytic-cognitive approaches to affect and emotional engagement focus on establishing the processes involved in cinema spectatorship that might be conducive to the cultivation of moral understanding (e.g., the role of sympathy and/or empathy in engaging with screen stories). Moral understanding, on this approach, in the cognitive sense refers to a rational awareness of the moral-practical significance of our beliefs or shared practices. This understanding can be developed and enhanced through experiential and reflective means, and typically involves forms of imaginative projection and practical reasoning (see, e.g., Carroll 2010; Gaut 2010; Nannicelli and Taberham 2014; Moss-Wellington 2019; Plantinga 2018; Smith 2017). In contrast, theorization on (esoteric) affect within Continental strains of film theory/film philosophy is focused on ethically transformative critical engagement with conventional norms and practices defining subjectivity—including gendered and racialized forms of subjectivity—that are to be questioned, deconstructed, or transformed (see, e.g., Barker 2009; Boljkovac 2013; Brinkema 2014; Del Rio 2012; Koivunen 2015; Marks 2000). Despite some overlap, there is a clear contrast between analytic-cognitivist approaches to affect, which share much with ordinary cognitive experience, and Continental film-philosophical approaches, which emphasize how affect might challenge or transform ordinary cognitive and social experience, even subjectivity itself.

Despite the potential for confusion or misunderstanding, however, I would contend that both approaches to affect—the exoteric sense of bodily feeling and the esoteric sense of nonsubjective intensity and expressive form—have something important to offer our understanding of the relationship between affect and moral understanding (or transformative ethical experience). In what follows, I shall focus largely on the conventional (exoteric) sense of affect, referring to varieties of bodily feeling, which also encompass emotional responses, and examine the role of affect and emotion in cultivating moral understanding. I shall also refer, however, to the esoteric sense of affect and the role it might play in more complex forms of cinematic experience that involve what I am calling "moral-cognitive dissonance." For the most part, I focus on the priming role played by affective responses in eliciting and sustaining emotional engagement as well as the "cognitive biasing" effect of affective responses in relation to moral evaluation. As I shall discuss, affect plays a key role in priming us for emotional engagement—particularly in cases of sympathetic and empathetic engagement—and thus for favorable as well as unfavorable, prosocial as well as antisocial, forms of moral response. There are cases in cinema, however, where affective response does not align with moral evaluation, where sympathetic engagement with a character clashes with the revelation of their duplicity, amorality, or morally disturbing behavior. Such cases of cinematic experience often involve affect in the esoteric sense—or the interplay between exoteric and esoteric senses of affect in complex configurations—in order to create a moral-cognitive dissonance effect that can also serve an important ethical purpose, prompting us to reflect upon or revise our moral judgments based upon underlying affective-emotional sympathies and antipathies.

In these cases, I shall consider how the esoteric (nonsubjective, aesthetic, formal-expressive) senses of affect can also play a role in accounting for the aesthetically and morally disorienting effects that such films can generate in viewers. This moral-cognitive dissonance effect is evident in a powerful sequence in Haneke's *Amour* (the mercy killing scene), where our initially sympathetic affective emotional engagement with a character clashes with the aesthetically distanced yet affectively charged manner in which the film presents his crucial action. Such cases suggest the need for a later critical moral revision of initial affective-emotional evaluation, which adds depth and complexity to our moral understanding of action within ethically ambiguous situations. One could suggest, further, that it is the clash or conflict between exoteric and esoteric forms of affect that makes such sequences—as in Haneke's *Amour*—not only aesthetically complex and morally ambiguous but also likely to prompt critical reflection in response to these aesthetically expressed forms of moral-cognitive dissonance.

Affect and Emotion

Affect and emotion are among the most familiar, yet complex, of experiential phenomena. To paraphrase Christian Metz, an emotion is hard to explain because it is so easy to understand. On the one hand, we readily understand emotions in everyday experience and in ordinary language; they are in many ways constitutive features of our personal identity and ability to engage in social interactions. On the other, the theorization of emotions involves a complex and confusing array of approaches focusing on different levels of explanation and diverse aspects of affective and emotional experience (see Sinnerbrink 2011, 73–77). Most theorists agree, however, that emotions include a *physiological* aspect (changes in autonomous physiological processes), a *psychological* aspect, an *affective* or *feeling* aspect, a *sensory-motor* or *action-oriented* aspect, and an *evaluative* or *cognitive* aspect (de Sousa 1987; Goldie 2002; Plantinga 2009b). When I am angry I experience physiological changes in my body (accelerated heartbeat, muscle tension, adrenaline flow), in my psychological state (increased aggression or a desire to "act out"), in my affective state (feeling tense, a sense of agitated arousal), linked with a rapid cognitive appraisal, judgment, or evaluation of my situation (a belief that I have been wronged, a construal of the other's behavior as posing a threat). My anger has an object, which serves as the reason for my getting angry (a reckless driver swerving in front of me), and it enables me to evaluate my situation promptly and act accordingly (to take evasive action). Emotions condense these affective, bodily, and cognitive responses in a manner that enables the rapid evaluation of my situation and the taking of appropriate action depending on how I respond to having the particular emotional responses that I do in a given situation (I can refrain from action or respond spontaneously, with deliberation and reserve, etc.).

Analyzing emotions from a phenomenological and cognitivist perspective reveals a number of constitutive elements (see Sinnerbrink 2016, 87–89). To list the most salient: (1) Emotions are *temporal and episodic*: they unfold in time, have a definite duration, and are generally transient phenomena. (2) They arise and develop according to *feedback from our bodies and from our environment*: our emotional life, as Plantinga (2009b, 60) observes, "occurs in streams that continuously evolve in response to everchanging construals, actions and action tendencies, bodily states, and feelings," any of which can serve as feedback to modify our subsequent emotional responses. (3) Emotions are *intimately related to narratives*; they can be triggered by acquired "paradigm scenarios" (de Sousa 1987), namely, socially recognized, familiar, or characteristic patterns of feelings, actions, and reactions, organized in narrative terms, that occur in specific situations leading to a "learned" emotional response. My emotional state is thus shaped by the kind of narrative meaning through which I make sense of my identity and describe my emotions to others, usually through shared narrative schemata within familiar social contexts. (4) Emotions *vary in duration and intensity*, waxing and waning over time, varying in affective amplitude. (5) Emotions are often *mixed or ambiguous*: primary emotions (anger, fear, disgust, happiness, sadness, and surprise) are often discrete and identifiable, yet emotions usually occur in complex affective clusters or overlapping combinations that can be difficult to distinguish or define. Plantinga mentions, for example, the simultaneous horror and fascination felt in response to "a monster in a horror film," a complex of emotional responses that combines contrary affective valences (negative and positive) and conflicting action tendencies (repulsion and attraction). Think of the German term *Schadenfreude* (malicious pleasure in the misfortune of another) or the Japanese *arigata meiwaku* (when one is the recipient of an unwanted favor or unwelcome kindness which makes one feel both obliged to and secretly resentful of the giver). (6) Emotions are distinct from moods, which are more global, encompassing, diffuse, and "world-disclosing" (Heidegger), which orient us toward things and others in particular practical and attitudinal ways ("cognitive biasing"). To be more precise, emotions have *intentional objects* (fear of a speeding car, of losing one's job, of getting cancer), whereas moods tend to lack a definite intentional object, so can be "free-floating" affective states oriented toward our existential "being-in-the-world" in general (Heidegger). From a hermeneutic point of view, emotions can be understood in terms of *reasons* (I was angry with you because of what you did to me), whereas moods have more dispersed *causes* (physical fatigue, environmental factors, physiological changes, the aesthetic qualities of my surroundings, existential feelings, etc.). Nonetheless, moods and emotions remain intimately related, moods priming us for particular emotions, and particular emotions being enhanced or diminished by background moods. (7) Emotions can be further "primed" or "cued" according to discrete environmental factors, background mood, mental outlook, and ongoing emotional dynamics. Finally, (8) we can have propensities toward certain emotional responses ("character traits") that make up an *emotional disposition* (someone prone to anger, someone habitually cheerful, someone consistently calm and measured, someone who enjoys risk and thrills, someone who tends toward feeling fear or anxiety) as opposed to emotions as occurrent states (a flash of anger, a sense of joy). These general features of emotions all come into place during our aesthetic experience of cinema, which can be described, in Ed Tan's nice phrase, as an "emotion machine" (1995). Cinema possesses the power to engage us emotionally through audiovisual means, bringing into play perceptual, corporeal, affective, physical, psychological, cognitive, and, at a broader social contextual level, cultural, historical, political, and ideological factors.

Definitions of emotion are legion. Peter Goldie (2002) points out, however, there are two aspects that any definition of emotion should capture, namely the *affective* or feeling aspect and the *cognitive* or appraisal aspect. Although emotions involve and express feelings, they are also linked to, or expressive of, appraisals that have a cognitive dimension (sometimes involving definite beliefs or propositional attitudes, for example, but also including nonpropositional forms of affective appraisals). At the same time, emotions are complex phenomena that comprise a number of overlapping elements, both affective and cognitive. Following Robert C. Roberts, Plantinga defines emotional responses as *concern-based construals* that are at once cognitive, relational, intentional, and embodied (2009b, 55–56). Robert Solomon (2003) defines then as *cognitive judgments* that work through feeling more than reasoning. Goldie describes the intentionality of emotions as a phenomenological "feeling towards" that expresses both a concern and a potential for action, without necessarily being "intellectual" or "cognitive" in the narrower sense of these terms (2002). Contra common criticisms of cognitivist theory, this view of emotions as affective-cognitive forms of judgment or construal does not imply the banishment of unconscious processes from our cognitive experience. On the contrary, Plantinga points to the crucial role of the "cognitive unconscious" in our engagement with others and the world; consciousness requires unconscious cognitive operations and "automatic" affective responses to various stimuli in order to facilitate our successful emotional and practical engagement with our environment (2009b, 50). Affective responses (bodily feelings, sensations, corporeal states) often occur in ways that are involuntary or below the threshold of conscious intention, yet they orient and qualify emotional responses and prime our bodies to take appropriate action depending on our emotional-cognitive appraisal of a situation. Affects and emotions thus provide a cognitive-evaluative, sensory-motor way of responding rapidly and adroitly to complex social situations within our culturally diverse life-worlds.

Affect, Emotion, and Moral Evaluation

How are affect and emotion related to moral evaluation? Noël Carroll (2010) and Carl Plantinga (2010) have theorized the important role of the moral emotions as a means of normative appraisal—the elicitation of pro- and contra-attitudes toward different characters—in our response to narrative film. The emotional "power of movies," according to Carroll, is explained in large part by their capacity to activate moral emotions and recruit them in the service of sympathetic or antipathetic character engagement. Emotions provide rapid evaluations of situations and individuals in relation to our practical interests and normative concerns. Since emotions can be elicited by imaginings, narrative film, by making situational elements more salient and articulating character and action in structured ways, is particularly suited to the elicitation of emotional appraisals of characters, thereby guiding viewer responses toward sympathetic or antipathetic engagement. Carroll (2010), for example, identifies the manner in which cinema *prefocuses* our emotive responses according to given criteria (values, cues, norms, or scripts) by using specific cinematic devices to direct and modulate our affective and emotional responses. Variable framing, "the alteration of what is made visually salient to the viewer," is the most common device and involves three processes: scaling (making the object of attention larger in the visual field), indexing (pointing the camera toward the object), and bracketing (placing the object within a frame that excludes what is irrelevant) (6). Cinema also uses sound effects, music, lighting, camera angles, shot duration and cutting rhythms, visual patterning, and performance cues to elicit and enhance the emotional uptake of a scene by the audience.

In the case of moral emotions, our evaluation or appraisal of a character or situation involves normative construals linked with pro- or con-attitudes toward the character based on our perception or understanding of his or her relevant cares, concerns, or interests (Carroll 2010). Harm and welfare, justice and injustice, the "ethics of community" or need for social bonding and interpersonal relationships are widely cross-culturally shared, socially familiar areas of emotional-moral evaluation that provide powerful ways of eliciting sympathetic and antipathetic responses from movie viewers. As Carroll argues, movies typically divide characters into emotionally engaging, morally admirable protagonists and emotionally repellent, morally detestable protagonists: "what bonds us to the protagonists affectively is sympathy which emotional attachment is secured primarily by moral considerations and that, contrariwise, what engenders antipathy towards the villains is their discernible moral failings" (15). Moviemakers thereby appeal to the moral sentiments of audiences, our sense of moral approval or disapproval, by presenting "heroes" and "villains" in an emotionally appealing or repelling, morally admirable or repellent light, highlighting their virtues or vices. These visual "rhetorical" strategies serve to forge a moral consensus by eliciting sympathetic or antipathetic responses, and modulating them according to the dramatic demands of narrative and the filmmakers' intentions. In this sense, Carroll concludes, the elicitation of moral emotions via sympathetic and anti-pathetic response to characters is essential to the successful emotional uptake of the narrative. Far from being a trivial distraction or "acme of moral decadence," "movies and morals belong together," relying as they do on the solicitation of moral senti-ments and the emotional evaluation of character and situation (19).

Plantinga too focuses on the capacity of narrative film to elicit "sympathies, antip-athies, allegiances," and other emotional-moral responses as central to its aesthetic success and "moral and ideological impact" (2010, 34). Contra Smith, however, Plantinga argues that, while moral approval or disapproval comes into play in the case of what Smith calls "allegiance" with a character, "other sorts of responses to fictional characters have less to do with moral judgment" (2018, 193). One can like a char-acter, find him or her appealing, for a variety of nonmoral reasons (attractiveness, humor, style, acting persona, etc.) that are independent of one's moral evaluation (ap-proval or disapproval) of that character. Plantinga (2010) also develops a typology of responses, from strong allegiance or antipathy to milder forms of approval and disapproval, including indifference, in order to account for the range of emotionally engaged responses elicited by narrative film. This means that movies are also capable of rhetorically manipulating spectator judgments in ways that accord with various cognitive biases well known from the psychological literature on the subject—an im-portant aspect of their rhetorical power and ideological influence.

Different kinds of narrative cinema do not always elicit sympathetic and antipa-thetic responses to characters in the same ways. As Plantinga points out, popular films or "sympathetic narratives" are generally intended to elicit "clear allegiances and oppositions" with what Carroll calls protagonists and antagonists (2010, 35). Complex dramas, such as network narratives (like Altman's *Short Cuts* or Inárrittu's *Babel*), tend to discourage clear-cut allegiances (approvals or disapprovals) and work more with ambiguous sympathies and antipathies, often prompting shifts in spectator "allegiances or oppositions" as the narrative unfolds (35). Sympathetic narratives, whether clear or ambiguous, all tend to encourage "close" involvement or engagement with characters and use a variety of devices and techniques to elicit strong forms of emotional-moral evaluation (narrative structuring, character focus, casting, clear demarcation between engaging, virtuous characters and those that are not, use of close-ups, dialogue, music, lighting, etc.). By contrast, what Plantinga calls "distanced narratives" (in modernist or art cinema) tend to eschew "closeness" in favor of a distanced, detached, or ironic stance, one that "discourages sympathetic at-tachment to character" (36). His analysis focuses, however, on sympathetic narratives and the manner in which different kinds of emotional engagement can be elicited, from mild to strong, with the rhetorical power to influence spectators' moral judg-ments. For these reasons, film theory has long been critical of the medium's poten-tial for moral-ideological manipulation, offering various critical theories to account for these effects, while certain filmic traditions have developed that block or atten-uate close emotional engagement in favor of more distanced, reflexive, or ambiguous forms of narrative presentation.

Carroll's and Plantinga's approaches both center on *sympathetic* narratives, namely those that solicit strong forms of emotional engagement with correspondingly unambiguous forms of moral allegiance. It is clear that emotional engagement is closely linked with moral allegiance, even though these do not always correspond with each other. We can have sympathetic forms of engagement with characters that are not moral or are amoral (sympathizing with *Breaking Bad*'s Walter White [Bryan Cranston] as he tries to keep his criminal drug activities hidden from his family, or with Cersei Lannister's [Lena Headey] attempts in *Game of Thrones* to hold political power despite her ruthless cruelty toward her enemies).[4] We can also have forms of moral allegiance that are not accompanied by (positive) emotional engagement. Plantinga's example here is Larry Gopnik (Michael Stuhlbarg), a "nice" but nervy middle-aged college professor in the Coen Brothers' film *A Serious Man* (2009), whose personal and professional life falls apart and who faces his many problems "with passivity and confusion" yet elicits sympathy while not being particularly likeable—presumably, the film's point (2010, 42). Indeed, we can like characters for all sorts of reasons without being committed to a particular kind of moral allegiance toward them. At the same time, as Plantinga (2010, 46ff.) points out, this leaves open the possibility of manipulating moral judgment, given our propensity to confuse moral and nonmoral judgments, as evinced by the prevalence of various cognitive biases (see Haidt 2001; Appiah 2008).[5] Think, for example, of cases of an appealing or attractive character being given the benefit of the moral doubt, claiming our sympathies or approval despite their immoral or amoral behavior, with all sorts of post hoc justifications being used to reconcile these conflicting affective-emotional and moral-cognitive responses.[6]

Nonetheless, for both Carroll and Plantinga, emotional engagement with movies plays an important role in prompting viewers toward sympathetic and antipathetic responses, which in turn tends to favor certain forms of moral approval or disapproval of characters and actions. The relationship between emotional response and moral evaluation (within sympathetic narratives) is typically coherent and synergistic. It involves the affective/emotional priming of spectators toward certain intended or preferred forms of moral approval/disapproval, relying heavily on familiar emotion scripts, paradigm scenarios, cognitive biases, and the like. We might call this the emotional engagement/moral allegiance model of spectator response common to many popular movies (Plantinga's sympathetic narratives); it is a model that assumes a typical coherence or synergy between emotional response and moral evaluation, which amounts to an aesthetic confirmation of "what we already know" from a normative perspective. As I discuss below, however, not all ethical experience in narrative film works this way, nor do all forms of narrative cinema adhere to the emotional response/moral allegiance model (Plantinga's "distanced narratives," for example). It is important to stress that both Plantinga and Carroll refer primarily to popular narrative film/screen stories (movies), which they distinguish from the distanced narratives more typical of "art cinema" (2010, 36). In the latter, we find less synergy or coherence and more dissonance or uncertainty about the relationship between emotional engagement and moral allegiance (indeed, where emotional engagement may be diminished and moral allegiance compromised).[7] As we shall see, this makes *Amour* an ideal case study to examine the ways in which moral-cognitive dissonance can work with emotional estrangement to complexify the relationship between affect and moral understanding.

Emotional Estrangement and Moral-Cognitive Dissonance

Although emotional engagement is typically discussed as involving sympathetic (or antipathetic) responses, many films modulate or complicate emotional engagement via the solicitation of emotional estrangement (ambivalence, lack of context, opacity of motivation, clashing emotional and evaluative responses that resist reconciliation or unification; see Sinnerbrink 2016, 135–136, 147–149). Such affective and emotional disruption, in turn, can complicate or interrupt the assumed alignment or consonance between emotional engagement and moral evaluation, generating what I call "moral-cognitive dissonance" (inconsistent emotional and evaluative responses that resist alignment, synthesis, or consilience). *Emotional estrangement* (rather than simply emotional engagement) can be defined as the working through of conflicting or ambivalent forms of emotional response and the conflicting forms of critical reflection to which such experience often gives rise. It is not just a matter of sympathy and/or empathy with characters in particular situations but the solicitation of strains of antipathy and/or ambivalence that do not readily yield to rapid judgments and hence force spectators into more complex forms of critical reflection. *Moral-cognitive dissonance* (rather than unified, aligned, or harmonious emotional-cognitive understanding) encompasses varieties of ambivalent moral-cognitive responses solicited by a film, responses which complicate more straightforward forms of moral allegiance, soliciting critical reflection on our emotional responses, moral intuitions, and ethical attitudes. We are confronted not only by incompatible beliefs or attitudes but by conflicting moral-ethical forms of evaluation and responsiveness that thwart straightforward moralizing judgments.

Both approaches open up a range of possible spectator responses, from rejection, hostility, confusion, and imaginative resistance on the one hand, to the critical questioning, reflection, and cognitive reframing of thoughts, beliefs, and evaluations on the other. Such films, what Plantinga (2010) describes as "distanced narratives," evoke a movement from affect/emotion to concept/reflection (and back again) in a feedback look that modulates during the course of the narrative, forcing the viewer to reframe his or her responses in light of his or her experience of emotional estrangement and moral-cognitive dissonance. These aesthetic strategies prompt an ethical experience of uncertainty and questioning, of critical reflection and reevaluation of what we have seen. It may also be where the more "esoteric" forms or conceptions of affect (as discussed earlier), with their particular aesthetic and ethical dimensions, come into play, encouraging both a challenging and transformative aesthetic response and a disruption of routine moral evaluations. Such experiences, I suggest, have the potential to enhance our receptivity to complexity, particularity, and ambiguity in moral situations and to develop our capacity for more complex forms of ethical experience. As an example of this kind of distanced narrative, let us consider a crucial scene from Haneke's *Amour* (2012).

Emotional Estrangement and Moral-Cognitive Dissonance in *Amour*

Hailed as Haneke's masterpiece and greeted with critical acclaim, *Amour* generated strong and varied responses. A love story focusing on a cultivated, octogenarian couple, the film opens with a powerful depiction of an old woman's dead body laid out in burial rite position and decorated with flowers. From this shocking prologue, the story of music teacher Anne (Emmanuelle Riva) and her husband Georges (Jean-Louis Trintignant) unfolds with an exacting and tragic rigor, as they confront the realities of illness, incapacitation, and death. The film's most dramatic and controversial moment is the depiction of Georges's unexpected mercy killing of his ailing wife, smothering her with a pillow after alleviating her distress by telling her a story from his childhood. The film ends with an ambiguous presentation of the dead Anne, now washing dishes in the kitchen, rousing Georges from his bed and leading him out of their apartment into an unknown realm.

It is clear from the start that Anne's death will be the central event, narrative focus, and moral question defining the film. Indeed, for many critics *Amour* is a film dealing explicitly with euthanasia, offering, as Thomas Wartenberg (2017) claims, a powerful cinematic argument in its favor. At the same time, it has been criticized for precisely the same reasons, namely, for offering, as one critic put it, an "advert for euthanasia" with "dangerous social fallacies at its core" (Gullette 2014). The film depicts, in minute detail, the escalating demands and difficulties Georges faces in caring for Anne, who has refused hospital treatment and is losing mobility, speech, and responsiveness as her condition deteriorates following a number of debilitating strokes. This process of decline culminates in the climactic but unexpected sequence of Georges's mercy killing of Anne.

By this stage, she has been confined to bed, calling out "Mal, mal" in what may either be an inchoate expression of pain and sorrow or an involuntary vocalization devoid of meaning. Georges comes to her aid, calming her down by stroking her hand and telling her a story from his childhood. While at summer camp as a boy, he tells her, he was punished for refusing his dinner by being made to wait three hours before he could leave the table. He then came down with a fever (diphtheria) and was admitted to the hospital, where his beloved mother, who finally visits, was unable to reach or comfort him because she remained confined behind a glass partition. The story is personal and poignant and has the desired effect of calming Anne. It is at this moment, when his story has concluded and Anne has relaxed, that Georges reaches over the bed for a pillow and smothers her. Her struggles and contortions, as Georges lays his full weight on the pillow, are awful to witness. It is not a painless, quiet, or dignified death, but a visceral struggle to kill an old woman.

In contrast with some critics' claims that Georges's act of killing is an act of love, the manner in which her death is shown—preceded by a scene showing Georges slapping her, and following his story about refusal, suffering, and separation—suggests that his spontaneous act of mercy is also marked by ambiguity and ambivalence. It may be a case of euthanasia, an opportunistic mercy killing, but it does not appear premeditated or carefully prepared (unlike his ritualized laying out of Anne's corpse). This is not to deny that Georges's act is a mercy killing, but the impulsive manner in which he performs—and the manner in which it is presented cinematically—suggests a mixture of motivations (even underlying aggression). This may also be coupled with the sense that, as he sees it, mercy killing is the only viable solution to their situation. (As Georges explains bluntly to his daughter Eva [Isabelle Huppert], "How will it go? It will go steadily downhill for a while, then it will be over.") In short, the sympathetic portrayal of Georges as a devoted husband and thoughtful carer is disrupted by the brutal and visceral manner of Anne's killing and by the suggestion that he has refused all offers of help, and so can see no other solution to their tragic situation.

This captures the sequence of events in narrative terms, but how does the film express these particular affective states—thereby eliciting affective responses—via cinematic means? Here it is worth reflecting on the difference between literal narrative description of the event and the affective presentation or pervasive mood evoked and expressed by this sequence. Typically, as I have argued, these align or cohere, but sometimes they can clash or be in tension with each other. Like Haneke's other works, Amour excels in heightening these kinds of affective dissonances (presenting violent, disturbing content or situations, for example, in a flat, precise, affectively distanced manner). In this sense, drawing on my earlier discussion, we could say that it combines both conventional and unconventional or exoteric and esoteric senses of affect, which may help explain the polarized, ambivalent, or conflicting responses often noted in relation to the death scene.

Consider the cinematic expression of affect in the aesthetic presentation of the scene itself. The sequence is filmed using one static long take, a medium-long shot focusing on the two bodies framed in profile, Anne in bed and Georges seated next to her. It features naturalistic but subdued lighting, with drab monochromatic color tones, devoid of contrasts, an ordinary, unobtrusive mise-en-scene (messy bedroom with all the medical accoutrements of care plainly visible), an audio track comprising nothing more than the sounds of physical struggle. It is a coolly distanced presentation of violent corporeal suffering and distress. If we describe it in terms of a standard or exoteric sense of affective response, we can underline the conflicting character of our visceral responses to the sight of physical struggle clashing with our more intellectual appraisals of the "moral" justification of the act within its context. If we focus on a nonstandard/esoteric sense of affect, however, we can articulate more concretely the "mood" of the sequence. How its aesthetic mode of presentation itself expresses or conveys a distanced but visceral form of conflict without sentimentality, rationalization, or qualification, or how the expression of ambiguous or conflicting affects in the audiovisual "form" of the sequence contributes to the unsettling and dissonant effect of the scene. The impersonal nature of the affective expression, coupled with the intensely physical/visceral qualities of the struggle—and the "unconscious" manner in which such affective expression can influence conscious moral appraisals of the depicted situation—all contribute to the strikingly disturbing and disorienting character of this sequence. Focusing on the expressive features of the sequence, I suggest, helps us to understand why this sequence generates such ambivalent and "undecidable" moral evaluations and emotional responses. The esoteric sense of affect captures more fully the ambiguous aesthetic dimensions of this scene than if we focused simply on narrative descriptions of the action and events and the (conventional or exoteric) elicitations of affect that these typically generate. Indeed, it might help explain why this scene—not to mention this film and others like it—tend to generate such polarized, ambivalent, and ambiguous responses in viewers and critics alike.

This is one instance of moral-cognitive dissonance in *Amour*, one of many such instances in the film: a situation where our affective response, reflective understanding, and moral evaluation of what we are seeing generate an attitudinal conflict. This conflict is heightened by the fact that Georges's act of mercy killing is presented in an aesthetically distanced yet visceral manner. The sequence is not only affectively charged in the conventional sense but expresses cinematically an affective ambivalence—combining distance and intimacy, concern and violence—in ways that are both impersonal and aesthetically expressive (affect expressed in the aesthetic features of the scene itself). Georges is a loving, caring husband, calming Anne when she is distressed, telling her a touching story from his childhood, who then brutally smothers her with a pillow, forcing his entire weight upon her delicate frame, overpowering her physical struggles, in what appears to be a spontaneous act. He then leaves the apartment and later carefully prepares cut flowers and a special dress for the laying-out of his wife's corpse. The act of euthanasia is presented, on the one hand, as an ethically intelligible action (even a moral obligation to preserve the dignity of a loved one, according to Wartenberg) yet, on the other, is depicted with an affective tonality that is viscerally violent, conveyed impersonally via the aesthetic features of the sequence itself. The killing itself seems spontaneous, unpremeditated, and impulsive, yet it is violent, protracted, and painful, confronting us with the awful reality of a mortal struggle between husband and wife. This sequence thereby thwarts the expectation of moral allegiance with Georges thanks to the manner in which his action is depicted: a relentless, detached long take that commences with gentle intimacy and concludes with a violent struggle to the death. This is a powerful, affectively charged sequence where the conventional (exoteric) affects suggesting care, distress, and confusion are themselves ambiguously expressed in the (esoteric) affective aesthetic features of the scene. The film thereby presents Georges's act of mercy killing in a cinematic style that heightens the ambiguity of that action. Here the tension between conventional affective responses and the ambivalent affective charge of the scene itself contributes to the sense of emotional and moral confusion, the cognitive and affective moral dissonance that renders aesthetic evaluation and moral judgment of this scene so difficult.

This dissonance between affective/cognitive and moral evaluative dimensions makes it challenging to define the meaning of Georges's mercy killing of Anne. Indeed, it is hard to decide whether it expresses, unequivocally, either a defense or a critique of euthanasia. On the one hand, it can be construed as the difficult but merciful act of love on the part of a devoted partner desperate to preserve his beloved's dignity; on the other, as an impulsive violent response to a situation perceived as untenable thanks to Georges's refusal to accept help or consider other options. In short, the film offers an ethically powerful experience of moral-cognitive dissonance that forces us to think, to reevaluate what we have seen, inviting but also questioning our immediate judgments concerning the moral significance of the characters' actions. This conflicted process of both soliciting openness and confronting us with violence, cultivating a sensitivity to context and pressing our moral convictions, inviting both a provocation and a suspension of moralizing judgment, is an example of what I call cinematic ethics. *Amour* evokes a profoundly unsettling, ambivalent form of ethical experience—an emotional estrangement generated by ambivalent forms of affective expression—that demands a considered, thoughtful response. It is a film that questions settled attitudes toward euthanasia, and it does so by eliciting an experience of emotional estrangement and moral-cognitive dissonance that lasts well after the movie's end.

In this manner, cinema can offer us a way of exercising our moral imaginations through affective involvement and critical reflection. Cinematic narrative has the power to elicit both sympathetic and antipathetic responses, linking affective responsiveness and emotional engagement with moral evaluation. The ethical experience afforded by *Amour* engages us in affectively ambiguous ways, thereby soliciting varying and even conflicting forms of moral evaluation. Thanks to the variable, sometimes conflicting relationship between affective engagement and moral evaluation, complex cinematic narratives can exercise and challenge our moral imaginations, prompting critical reflection on our ability to perceive, interpret, and understand moral situations. Indeed, films such as *Amour* prompt us to move from what we feel and what we think we already know to what we should try harder to understand.

Notes

1. I would like to thank Anne Eaton and Matthew Grizzard for their excellent commentaries on an earlier draft of this paper delivered at the Screen Stories and Moral Understanding Seminar, April 17, 2021. My thanks to Carl Plantinga, Malcolm Turvey, Wyatt Moss-Wellington, and Noël Carroll for their helpful comments and questions on my presentation, and Carl Plantinga, Garrett Strpko, and John Rhym for further feedback on my draft.

2. Although not always explicitly referencing Tomkins's (1997, 33–74) famous psychological account of affect as variation in bodily intensities.

3. According to Zillmann's excitation-transfer theory of emotion, given the variable temporal duration of (fast) cognitive versus (slow) physiological processes, cognitive labeling can refer to the affective backwash of earlier physiological responses, resulting in ambiguous or variable identification of affective states. Zillmann's (2006) recent work on "how plot elements elicit differential emotions and how pacing elements can lead to the enhancement of emotional responses," according to Grizzard (2021), suggests important avenues for further research regarding the relationship between narrative/aesthetic features of film and affective-emotional responses as well as the study of morally ambiguous characters (see also Grizzard 2020).

4. Anne Eaton (2021, 1–2) points out that *Breaking Bad* offers a case quite different from that of *Amour*. *Breaking Bad* generates allegiance for a character we are also supposed to find morally depraved; when we desire that Walt and Jesse continue their criminal drug activities, "we find ourselves being made to want things that we are simultaneously supposed to know are deeply wrong." *Amour*, by contrast, is supposed to show the moral ambiguity of euthanasia and encourages ambivalent responses to the act of mercy killing. The important difference here, for Eaton, is between "ambivalence about a deeply complex character or a situation ... and allegiance on the basis of morally unworthy traits."

5. Haidt (2001) argues that psychological evidence favors the view that moral judgments are typically subsequent to, and supportive of, affective-emotional responses. Moral reasoning is more like a "lawyer" making a case based on emotive responses than a "judge" rationally searching for the truth. Appiah (2008) refers to three demonstrable phenomena (framing effects, order effects, and priming) as examples of how moral intuitions and evaluations are influenced by nonmoral factors (how a problem or situation or decision is framed; the order in which options are presented; various unconscious "triggers," e.g., hypnotic priming).

6. Plantinga's (2010, 44–46) example is Brad Pitt's wild and romantic character Tristan in *Legends of the Fall* (2004), who remains a fan favorite, even a role model, despite his violence toward others and self-serving, wanton ways. Many of the characters in Tarantino films— Lieutenant Aldo "The Apache" Raine (Brad Pitt) in *Inglorious Basterds* and Jules Winnfeld (Samuel L. Jackson) in *Pulp Fiction*—would also be good examples.

7. Carroll (2009, 7–9) makes just this point in his introduction to Eaton's excellent volume of essays on Almodóvar's *Talk to Her*, citing it as an example of "philosophy *through* the motion picture." See also Eaton's (2009) discussion of Almodóvar's "Immoralism." I discuss this film along similar lines as a case of "moral melodrama" in Sinnerbrink (2016, 125–136).

Works Cited

Appiah, Kwame Anthony. 2008. *Experiments in Ethics*. Cambridge, MA: Harvard University Press.

Barker, Jennifer M. 2009. *The Tactile Eye: Touch and the Cinematic Experience*. Berkeley: University of California Press.

Boljkovac, Nadine. 2013. *Untimely Affects: Gilles Deleuze and an Ethics of Cinema*. Edinburgh: Edinburgh University Press.

Brennan, Teresa. 2004. *The Transmission of Affect*. Ithaca, NY: Cornell University Press.

Brinkema, Eugenie. 2014. *The Forms of the Affects*. Durham, NC: Duke University Press.

Carroll, Noël. 2009. "Talk to Them: An Introduction." In *Talk to Her: Philosophers on Film*, edited by A. W. Eaton, 1–10. London: Routledge.

Carroll, Noël. 2010. "Movies, the Moral Emotions, and Sympathy." *Midwest Studies in Philosophy* 34: 1–19.

Choi, Jinhee, and Mattias Frey, eds. 2014. *Cine-Ethics: Ethical Dimensions of Film Theory, Practice, and Spectatorship*. Abingdon: Routledge.

Cooper, Sarah. 2006. *Selfless Cinema? Ethics and French Documentary*. London: Legenda.

Coplan, Amy. 2006. "Catching Characters' Emotions: Emotional Contagion Responses to Narrative Fiction Film." *Film Studies: An International Review* 8: 26–38.

Deleuze, Gilles. 1988. *Spinoza: Practical Philosophy*. Translated by Robert Hurley. San Francisco, CA: City Lights Books.

Del Rio, Elena. 2012. *Deleuze and the Cinemas of Performance: Powers of Affection*. Edinburgh: Edinburgh University Press.

de Sousa, Ronald. 1987. *The Rationality of Emotion*. Cambridge MA: MIT Press.

Downing, Lisa, and Libby Saxton. 2010. *Film and Ethics: Foreclosed Encounters*. Abingdon: Routledge.

Dutton, D. G., and A. P. Aaron. 1974. "Some Evidence for Heightened Sexual Attraction under Conditions of High Anxiety." *Journal of Personality and Social Psychology* 30, no. 4: 510–517.

Eaton, A. W. 2009. "Almodóvar's Immoralism." In *Talk to Her: Philosophers on Film*, edited by A. W. Eaton, 11–26. London: Routledge.

Eaton, A. W. 2021. "Comments on Robert Sinnerbrink's 'Affect and Moral Understanding.'" Paper presented at Screen Stories and Moral Understanding Seminar (online), April 17.

Figlerowicz, Marta. 2012. "Affect Theory Dossier: An Introduction." *Qui Parle* 20, no. 2: 3–18.

Gaut, Berys. 2010. *A Philosophy of Cinematic Art*. Cambridge: Cambridge University Press.

Goldie, Peter. 2002. *The Emotions: A Philosophical Investigation*. Oxford: Oxford University Press.

Grizzard, Matthew. 2021. "Grizzard's Response to Sinnerbrink." Paper presented at Screen Stories and Moral Understanding Seminar (online), April 17. Grand Rapids, Michigan.

Grizzard, Matthew, C. J. Francemore, K. Fitzgerald, J. Huang, and C. Ahn. 2020. "Interdependence of Narrative Characters: Implications for Media Theories." *Journal of Communication* 70, no. 2: 274–301.

Grønstad, Asbjørn. 2016. *Film and the Ethical Imagination*. London: Palgrave Macmillan.

Gullette, Mary M. 2014. "Euthanasia as a Caregiving Fantasy in the Era of the New Longevity." *Age, Culture, Humanities: An Interdisciplinary Journal,* 1: 211–219. http://ageculturehum anities.org/WP/euthanasia-as-a-caregiving-fantasy-in-the-era-of-the-new-longevity/\

Haidt, Jonathan. 2001. "The Emotional Dog and Its Rational Tail: A Social Intuitionist Approach to Moral Judgment." *Psychological Review* 108: 814–834.

Hanich, Julian. 2015. Review of *The Forms of the Affects*, by Eugenie Brinkema. *Projections: The Journal for Movies and Mind* 9, no. 1: 112–117.

Jones, Ward E., and Samantha Vice, eds. 2011. *Ethics at the Cinema*. Oxford: Oxford University Press.

Kendall, Tina. 2012. "Cinematic Affect and the Ethics of Waste." *New Cinemas: Journal of Contemporary Film* 10, no. 1: 45–46.

Koivunen, Anu. 2015. "The Promise of Touch: Turns to Affect in Feminist Film Theory." In *Feminisms: Diversity, Difference and Multiplicity in Contemporary Film Cultures*, edited by Laura Mulvey and Anna Backman Rogers, 97–110. Amsterdam: University of Amsterdam Press.

Marks, Laura U. 2000. *The Skin of the Film: Intercultural Cinema, Embodiment, and the Senses*. Durham, NC: Duke University Press.

Massumi, Brian. 2002. *Parables for the Virtual*. Durham, NC: Duke University Press.

Moss-Wellington, Wyatt. 2019. *Narrative Humanism: Kindness and Complexity in Fiction and Film*. Edinburgh: Edinburgh University Press.

Nannicelli, Ted, and Paul Taberham, eds. 2014. *Cognitive Media Theory*. London: Routledge.

Plantinga, Carl. 2009a. "Affect and Emotion." In *The Routledge Companion to Philosophy and Film*, edited by Paisley Livingston and Carl Plantinga, 86–96. London: Routledge.

Plantinga, Carl. 2009b. *Moving Viewers: American Film and the Spectator's Experience*. Berkeley: University of California Press.

Plantinga, Carl. 2010. "'I Followed the Rules, and They All Loved You More': Moral Judgment and Attitudes towards Fictional Characters in Film." *Midwest Studies in Philosophy* 34: 34–51.

Plantinga, Carl. 2018. *Screen Stories: Emotion and the Ethical Experience*. Oxford: Oxford University Press.

Schachter, S., and J. Singer. 1962. "Cognitive, Social, and Physiological Determinants of Emotional State." *Psychological Review* 69, no. 5: 379–399.

Shaviro, Steven. 2010. *Post-Cinematic Affect*. Winchester UK/Washington US: John Hunt Publishing/Zero Books.

Shaw, Dan. 2012. *Morality and the Movies: Reading Ethics through Film*. London: Continuum.

Sinnerbrink, Robert. 2011. *New Philosophies of Film: Thinking Images*. London: Continuum.

Sinnerbrink, Robert. 2016. *Cinematic Ethics: Exploring Ethical Experience through Film*. London: Routledge.

Sinnerbrink, Robert. 2019. "Poststructuralism and Film." In *The Palgrave Handbook of the Philosophy of Film and Motion Pictures*, edited by Noël Carroll, Laura T. Di Summa-Knoop, and Shawn Loht, 441–465. New York: Palgrave Macmillan.

Smith, Murray. 1995. *Engaging Characters: Fiction, Emotion, and the Cinema*. Oxford: Oxford University Press.

Smith, Murray. 2017. *Film, Art, and the Third Culture*. Oxford: Oxford University Press.

Solomon, Robert C. 2003. "Emotions, Thoughts, and Feeling: What Is a 'Cognitive Theory' of the Emotions and Does It Neglect Affectivity?" *Royal Institute of Philosophy*, supplement 52: 1–18.

Stadler, Jane. 2008. *Pulling Focus: Intersubjective Experience, Narrative Film, and Ethics*. New York: Continuum.

Stadler, Jane. 2014. "Film and Affect." In *The Routledge Encyclopedia of Film Theory*, edited by Edward Branigan and Warren Buckland, 1–6. London: Routledge.

Tan, Ed. S. 1995. *Emotion and the Structure of Narrative Film: Cinema as an Emotion Machine*. Mahwah, NJ: Lawrence Erlbaum.

Tomkins, Silvan. 1997. "What Are Affects?" In *Shame and Her Sisters: A Silvan Tomkins Reader*, edited by Eve Kosofsky Sedgwick, 33–74. Durham, NC: Duke University Press.

Wartenberg, Thomas. 2017. "'Not Time's Fool': Marriage as an Ethical Relationship in Michael Haneke's *Amour*." In *Film as Philosophy*, edited by Bernd Herzogenrath, 286–305. Minneapolis: University of Minnesota Press.

Zillmann, D. 1983. "Transfer of Excitation in Emotional Behavior." In *Social Psychophysiology: A Sourcebook*, edited by J. T. Cacioppo and R. E. Petty, 215–240. New York: Guilford Press.

Zillmann, D. 2006. "Dramaturgy for Emotions from Fictional Narration." In *Psychology of Entertainment*, edited by J. Bryant and P. Vorderer, 215–238. Mahwah, NJ: Erlbaum.

8
Morality and Media

The Role of Elevation/Inspiration

Mary Beth Oliver

Issues of morality have played an important role in many foundational theories of media psychology. For example, disposition theory argues that viewers' like or dislike of media characters reflects their evaluations of the characters' morality, with "just" resolutions (e.g., the "good" character prevails) resulting in heightened enjoyment (Zillmann and Cantor 1977; Zillmann and Bryant 1986). Subsequent extensions of disposition theory also address moral concerns, arguing that, in some instances, characters may be understood as protagonists even before the narrative fully begins, with viewers' then demonstrating greater latitude for moral transgressions that the character may perform (Raney 2004).

In addition to theorizing about viewer enjoyment and character perception, perhaps the largest share of research from media psychology has situated questions of morality in terms of the effects on viewers' attitudes, beliefs, and behaviors. Further, this research has typically examined harmful outcomes such as increased aggression and heightened stereotyping (e.g., Anderson and Bushman 2002; Mastro 2009). Additionally, research from a cultivation perspective suggests that prolonged, cumulative exposure to recurrent themes in media (e.g., violent crime) leads viewers to perceive the world in ways that are consistent with these themes (e.g., most individuals are selfish or dangerous; Gerbner et al. 2002; Gerbner and Gross 1976).

With this background in mind, this chapter focuses on more recent scholarship that has also grappled with questions of morality, though generally from a more optimistic perspective. Specifically, research in *positive* media psychology has increased dramatically over the past decade, with researchers examining the myriad ways that media consumption can be harnessed for purposes of social good (Raney et al. 2021). Although a variety of approaches have been employed, in general this research often focuses on the role that emotion plays in eliciting outcomes that imply heightened moral understanding and/or moral motivations (e.g., wanting to help others, recognizing interconnectedness with others). Importantly, however, to my knowledge, scholars in media psychology have yet to specifically assess moral understanding, meaning that there are large gaps in the literature that require our careful consideration. Consequently, this chapter provides an overview of existing research in this area, and then turns to the many questions and challenges that arise from this body of

Mary Beth Oliver, *Morality and Media* In: *Screen Stories and Moral Understanding*. Edited by: Carl Plantinga,
Oxford University Press. © Oxford University Press 2023. DOI: 10.1093/oso/9780197665664.003.0009

work. I begin by briefly touching on how scholars in this area typically situate moral concerns in models of positive media psychology.

Overview of Scholarship in Positive Media Psychology

In many respects, research trends in positive media psychology can be understood as a reaction to foundational theories of entertainment research and the assumptions that they made about the audience's motivations for media consumption. In particular, disposition theories, with their emphasis on enjoyment (Zillmann and Bryant 1986), and mood management theory, with its emphasis on hedonic motivations (Zillmann 2000), presented paradoxes not only for why sad or somber entertainment is frequently consumed but also for why it appears to be particularly valued. In discussing why "enjoyment" as audience response may not aptly describe viewers' responses to such fare, Oliver and Bartsch (2011) proposed that the word "appreciation" may be a more appropriate descriptor of the gratifications associated with consuming entertainment that explores both the joys and tragedies of the human condition, as well as entertainment that frequently focuses on human virtue, such as courage, kindness, and compassion.

The suggestion that human virtue may play a role in viewers' feelings of appreciation then led scholars to turn their attention to the emotions associated with witnessing portrayals of moral virtue. In particular, Oliver, Hartmann, and Woolley (2012) employed Haidt's (2003) and Algoe and Haidt's (2009) concept of elevation as a way of explaining the feelings of being touched, moved, or inspired by dramatic entertainment that frequently focuses on questions concerning the human condition. Briefly, elevation is conceptualized as an other-praising, moral emotion that occurs when witnessing exemplary portrayals of moral virtue such as deep generosity, gratitude, or kindness. This emotion, also characterized as an example of a self-transcendent emotion (along with other emotions such as awe and gratitude), is often associated with mixed affect, physiological responses such as tears or a warmth in the chest, and with prosocial motivations such as wanting to be a better person, heightened altruism, and perceived connectedness with others.

Given the positive outcomes associated with the experience of elevation, scholars saw an opportunity for using media exposure as a means for eliciting elevation or inspiration and, hence, for enhancing social good. In other words, scholars began to examine how media portrayals of moral virtue may heighten feelings of elevation, such feelings then leading to a host of prosocial outcomes. Since the early days of such research, support for this general hypothesis has been obtained across a wide range of media platforms and for a variety of prosocial indicators. For example, scholars have employed full-length films (Oliver et al. 2021), short videos (Slater, Oliver, and Appel 2019), political speeches (Ellithorpe, Huang, and Oliver 2019), newspaper articles (Aquino, McFerran, and Laven 2011), and social media (Krämer et al. 2017) in their studies of elevating media. Likewise, prosocial outcomes have included heightened feelings of connection with diverse groups (Oliver et al. 2015), reductions in stereo-typing and stigmatization (Bartsch et al. 2018), altruism (Schnall, Roper, and Fessler 2010), charitability (Freeman, Aquino, and McFerran 2009), and increased information seeking (Bartsch et al. 2018).

In sum, the existing and growing body of work in positive media psychology has demonstrated that media portrayals of moral virtue appear to give rise to the emotion of elevation (or related self-transcendent emotions), with elevation leading to height-ened indications of moral behaviors that reflect values such as compassion, love, and giving. Although this research is promising, there remain many questions and chal-lenges. In the next section I overview many of the conceptual questions that await our further study, and following this, I discuss the challenges that may arise when trying to use "positive" media for prosocial ends.

Conceptual Questions in Positive Media Psychology

The typical way that media psychologists have, thus far, studied prosocial media and its effects is in experimental contexts. Consequently, in a typical experiment, partici-pants will be exposed to some media stimulus (e.g., a video, a commercial), they will rate their perceptions of the media (e.g., moving, touching, uplifting) and/or their emotional responses (e.g., moved, emotional, compassionate), and finally some out-come will be assessed (e.g., prosocial motivations). The running interpretation of such experiments is causal in nature: moving video → elevation/self-transcendent emotions → prosocial outcomes. Questions of morality are generally thought to op-erate both in terms of the message itself (i.e., portrayals of moral virtue) and in terms of the ultimate outcomes (i.e., virtuous attitudes/behaviors/motivations). However, alternative interpretations are possible, including the causal direction, the impor-tance of moderators, and the fundamental nature of the outcomes observed.

Does "Inspiring" Media Result in Moral Understanding?

Perhaps one of the most pressing questions in this body of research is whether or not exposure to uplifting, positive, or inspiring media results in greater moral under-standing. In general, the answer to this question is unknown. Insofar as moral un-derstanding goes beyond moral knowledge, it seems quite a leap of faith to think that exposure to a single media offering would result in enhanced moral understanding. However, to the extent that the development moral understanding is a gradual pro-cess of acquiring knowledge of actions that are laudable or contemptible, of hav-ing the capability of synthesizing this knowledge in a more holistic moral schema, and of engaging new experiences and perspectives through this cognitive lens, even exposure to a brief media offering may contribute to at least *part* of the development of heightened levels of moral understanding.

For example, similar to the classic Heinz dilemma, one popular video frequently employed in experimental studies is a Thai commercial that features the story of a generous restaurant owner who gives food to needy people, including a young boy caught shoplifting medicine for his mother. Thirty years later, the owner collapses in the restaurant and is rushed to the hospital. His desperate daughter cannot afford his treatment and is despondent. However, the young boy from years ago has become a doctor, remembers the generosity of the owner, and leaves the hospital bill for the daughter with a note that the fees had been paid thirty years earlier (https://www.yout ube.com/watch?v=XADBJjiAO_0). An examination of the user comments leaves little doubt that many people find the video elevating: "One of the most beautiful and moving videos on YouTube. It brought me to tears"; "Gave me goosebumps"; and "I wept but I also smiled."

But can we see evidence that this video resulted in moral understanding? The answer to this question awaits our further investigation; to the best of my knowledge, moral understanding has not been specifically operationalized in experimental positive-psychology research. Nevertheless, existing data and user comments imply that viewers may have experienced an enhancement of moral understanding, evidenced in their summaries of the "takeaway" message: "Giving is not only to help people in need, but to fulfill our empty heart and make the world we live in more beautiful" and "The good you put out into the world always finds a way of coming back to you." Further, the common finding in extant research that elevation experiences motivate prosocial behavior provides additional support for the notion that they do more than provide only moral knowledge. For example, if a person sees a moving portrayal of a former child soldier becoming an attorney for refugees (https://www.youtube.com/watch?v=buA3tsGnp2s), they may report wanting to be a better person, to show love or to better understand childhood trauma. In other words, people's motivations after experiencing elevation appear to go beyond mere desires to imitate; they also imply the internalization of a larger understanding of human virtue. However, before concluding that uplifting or elevating media can result in heightened moral understanding, a host of additional questions and critiques remain.

Is Moral Understanding a Trait or a State?

Many of the essays in this volume argue for the distinction between moral knowledge and moral understanding, the latter referring to the capabilities to understand the "why" questions of moral propositions, to apply this capability to new or unique situations, and to balance and modify one's moral judgments when they seem to conflict. If we adopt this (and related) conceptualizations, then moral understanding seems to function as a trait—a capability and a tendency to engage, critique, and apply moral knowledge. However, traits are generally dispositions that are long-lasting and not readily changed by single events. Hence, within the field of media psychology, scholars rarely assess the effects of media on traits such as personality. The exception, perhaps, would be cultivation research that conceptualizes effects as the result of long-term, cumulative exposure (Gerbner 1998).

If we treat moral understanding as a trait, then it seems reasonable that any effects of inspiring media would likely be the result of long-term exposure and that the effects would be long-lasting or enduring. Unfortunately, assessing cumulative exposure is a difficult task for many experimental scholars; it may be frequently *measured* by researchers, but it is infrequently manipulated in ways that allow for causal inference. With this in mind, though, there are some emerging research findings that are consistent with the argument that inspiring media may hold the promise of contributing to long-term changes. First, in terms of exposure, a national survey in the United States found that 63% of individuals reported being inspired by media messages at least a few times a week (Janicke-Bowles et al. 2019). A diversity of media platforms was named, the most common being music (90%) and film (86%), but also online videos (63%) and news (77%) (Raney et al. 2018). These results suggest that long-term and cumulative viewing of inspiring media is possible—at least among some segments of the population. Further, a recent field experiment of long-term exposure to inspiring viral videos assigned participants to view videos every day for 7 days, for 10 days, or for 12 days over the course of a month (Erickson et al. 2018). Consistent with cross-sectional experiments, people who viewed the inspiring videos reported higher levels of elevation immediately after viewing. In addition, though, positive affect, greater feelings of affiliation with others, and feelings of elevation had a sustained impact as well. Because none of the exposures lasted longer than a month, these authors concluded, "Our results cannot speak to long-term character change ... but suggest reasons to test elevation as a component of interventions to shape character" (652; see also Nabi and Prestin 2020; Neubaum, Krämer, and Alt 2020).

Although emerging research suggests that long-term changes in moral understanding may be *possible*, most of the research in positive media psychology treats elevation and related self-transcendent emotions as states. From this perspective, any effects on moral understanding may arguably be merely (or typically) fleeting. Yet even from this perspective, even more transient affective responses may give rise to heightened moral understanding. For example, elevation as a state likely includes both affective and cognitive elements (e.g., I am moved or touched by a character's virtue and I recognize the importance of generosity). In this example, the feelings or affective part of the audience's response likely do not linger much beyond the viewing experience itself, but the cognitions that arise from the experience may become a more stable part of the schema or lens through which moral judgments are applied.

Additionally, even if the experience of elevation itself is somewhat brief, research on the importance of individual differences in the selection of moving entertainment and in the experience of elevation imply that even brief affective responses are associated with more enduring traits that may reflect longer-term impacts on moral understanding. For example, in an earlier study of entertainment preferences, individual differences such as higher levels of need for cognition (Cacioppo, Petty, and Kao 1984), empathy (Davis 1983), and searching for meaning in life (Steger et al. 2006) were predictive of preferences for eudaimonic (e.g., meaningful) films more so than for hedonic films (Oliver and Raney 2011). Likewise, in a selective exposure study in which participants could select and view a series of short videos in a streaming-like format, higher levels of empathy were associated with more frequent selection and longer viewing times of inspiring videos in contrast to humorous or informational videos (Oliver et al. 2017). In addition to predicting a preference for inspiring fare, other individual differences appear to heighten affective responses. For example, individuals who score high on measures of moral identity tend to report higher levels of elevation (Aquino, McFerran, and Laven 2011). Likewise, Diessner et al. coined the phrase "engagement with beauty" to refer to a trait associated with the tendency to experience elevation, noting the trait-state distinction: "Elevation is an emotional state; engagement with moral beauty, on the other hand, is the disposition to experience elevation" (2013, 141).

In discussing whether or not moral understanding is a state or a trait, I would like to point out that it need not be considered one or the other. For example, moral understanding may play an important role in getting viewers to the screen and in heightening the likelihood of elevation-like responses. These responses, in turn, may ultimately lead to greater insight into questions of moral value and the intricacies of moral considerations. If this interpretation is correct, inspiring media and the moral understanding that it elicits may ultimately reflect an upward spiral (see Pohling and Diessner 2016), with the effects of media feeding into moral understanding, and moral understanding then leading to a greater likelihood of selecting and responding to uplifting and morally complex media.

What Role Does Emotion Play?

My discussion of the trait-state distinction is partially driven by the question of whether there are long-term, enduring effects of media on moral understanding (suggesting it becomes a trait or disposition). Additionally, though, this question arises because media psychologists have tended to see elevation or self-transcendent emotion as the driver of moral outcomes that follow. Because emotions (in comparison to moods, for example) are generally thought to be relatively short-lived (Nabi 2009), moral understanding may be short-lived as well. However, if we separate elevation from moral understanding, one question that arises concerns the specific function and causal direction between the two concepts.

The running conceptualizations of the relationship between emotion- and morality-related outcomes (e.g., enhanced altruism) is that the emotion (elicited by some initial stimulus such as a film) causes the outcomes. Perhaps part of the reason for this conceptualization is the typical way that these variables are assessed. Because emotion is thought to be fleeting, experimentalists often assess emotions immediately after viewing and before some other stimulus or activity may disrupt the affective state. Thus, the temporal order in which the variables are assessed implies that the affect comes prior to the additional outcomes assessed, but this temporal order may be an artifact of the methodologies employed.

One interpretation of the assumed causal order is that affective states such as elevation *do* heighten outcomes such moral motivations and perhaps moral understanding. One rationale for this argument rests on some evidence that the experience of this emotion elicits greater cognitive processing and reflection (Bartsch, Kalch, and Oliver 2014). Insofar as reflection signifies grappling with complex issues, such reflection may, ultimately, result in moral learning, thereby ultimately contributing to moral understanding. Likewise, a host of studies have reported that feelings of elevation have a variety of physiological manifestations, including an increase in circulating levels of oxytocin—a hormone and neurotransmitter. Oxytocin is associated with numerous behavioral manifestations, but it is perhaps most commonly associated with human bonding, helping behavior, compassion, and lactation and birth (Saturn 2017; Silvers and Haidt 2008). Hence, viewing and emotionally responding to media portrayals that elicit elevation may play a role in heightening the salience of human connection and, perhaps, clarifying our social and moral connectedness.

An alternative interpretation is that feelings of elevation occur either simultaneously with moral understanding or subsequent to moral understanding. In the latter case, the argument is essentially that moral understanding causes us to feel inspired, moved, or related self-transcendent feelings. Although there are not, to my knowledge, studies of this specific hypothesis, related literatures speak to its plausibility. In particular, research on the experience of "aha" moments describe these experiences as "the sudden appearance of a solution through insight" and as associated with positive affect (Topolinski and Reber 2010, 402). Although "aha" moments have typically been associated with problem-solving activities, additional scholarship has shown that they can also occur in activities such as coming to a sudden understanding of humor (Canestrari et al. 2018). Whereas moral understanding may normally require considerable time and cognitive deliberation, my anecdotal familiarity with short videos frequently employed as stimulus materials leads me to note that many of these videos present the moral "lesson" at the very end of the video. As an example, one video that has been employed in many studies of media and elevation features a young girl who rummages through her mother's cosmetic bag, finds scissors, and proceeds to hack off her hair (https://www.youtube.com/watch?v=7YPwfDBT-QQ). Until the end of the video, viewers may feel confusion, curiosity, or even fear that she may hurt herself, but the ending reveals she is cutting her hair to give to a young friend who is undergoing cancer treatment. These types of "aha" sentimental videos, though sometimes campy and sometimes clickbait (e.g., "Grab a tissue before watching this video!"), nevertheless routinely activate self-reported elevation and heightened moral motivations. My argument that they elicit "aha" moments related to insight into morality clearly awaits empirical investigation, though it is consistent with recent theorizing in media psychology concerning the importance of emotional *shifts* in viewers' responses to media messages (Nabi and Green 2014).

Challenges in Positive Media Psychology

Thus far I have provided an overview of research in positive media psychology and have presented a number of conceptual questions regarding how inspiring media portrayals may (or may not) lead to heightened moral understanding. In this section, I present a series of challenges that researchers may face when attempting to utilize uplifting media for purposes of social good, including moral understanding.

When "Uplifting" Media Fail to Inspire

Even if we could accept the idea that self-transcendent affect can lead to heightened moral motivations and understanding, it is evident that not all media that is intended to be inspiring elicits self-transcendent emotions, nor do all viewers have the same reaction. I previously discussed traits such as moral identity that appear to boost emotional responding, but research has also examined traits that predict a lack of responding or that even elicit more negative evaluations. For example, Appel, Slater, and Oliver (2018) showed respondents either a short video that was meaningful or one that was simply informative or engaging but not particularly meaningful. For many users, the meaningful video was successful in eliciting self-transcendent emotions, though for people who scored high on measures of the "dark triad" (narcissism, Machiavellianism, and psychopathy; see Jonason and Webster 2010), the videos were perceived as corny, inauthentic, and manipulative.

In addition to individual traits that may serve to dampen emotional responses, the actual or assumed source of the message or motivation for its creation may diminish positive reactions. For example, many media messages are driven by commercial interests and employ emotional tactics to elicit "warmth" to persuade their audiences (Aaker, Stayman, and Hagerty 1986). Although this approach may be effective in many instances, it can also backfire, particularly when the product being sold appears to devalue, trivialize, or co-opt deeply important issues. For example, Pepsi's advertisement that alluded to a Black Lives Matter march was pulled after one day when viewers responded with outrage. (Victor 2017; see https://www.youtube.com/watch?v=j9x15lR9VIg). Likewise, a Super Bowl commercial for Ram trucks using a voice-over of Dr. Martin Luther King created a wave of backlash on social media platforms (Maheshwari 2018; see https://www.youtube.com/watch?v=tVz1xa7S4Q4).

Finally, I note that at times, the content of the media messages (and perhaps their source) may intersect with characteristics of the viewer to either heighten or dampen elevating affect and any moral understanding that may follow. For example, research has reported that individuals who favored Hillary Clinton in the 2016 U.S. election were more moved by an inspiring political ad for Clinton than for Donald Trump, whereas the opposite was true for Trump supporters (Seibt et al. 2019). Likewise, media stories of Colin Kaepernick kneeling at a U.S. football game to heighten awareness of and to protest police brutality toward African Americans may inspire many viewers but may elicit disgust or moral outrage among others. Similarly, media coverage of protests in support of the U.S. Second Amendment to the Constitution (i.e., the right to own firearms) likely inspires some on the political right but disgusts (if not horrifies) many on the left. These latter two examples illustrate that what may be "moral" (and therefore inspiring) appears to depend on the "eye of the beholder." Therefore, I will take up this issue in more detail.

Is Moral Understanding Necessarily Morally Good?

The concept of moral understanding seems to imply that individuals have the knowledge and capacity to perceive questions of morality and, in grappling with their intricacies, arrive at the "right" or "good" conclusion or perception. Much of the research in positive media psychology makes these assumptions as well—self-transcendent emotions are thought to lead us away from egoistic concerns and to place an emphasis on the importance of others and our interconnectedness (Yaden et al. 2017; Oliver et al. 2018). However, research in moral psychology illustrates wide variance in how individuals weigh and apply moral considerations. For example, Jonathan Haidt (2001) has argued that people frequently place different emphases on moral considerations when evaluating something as right or wrong, and that such evaluations are often driven by intuition rather than reasoning. Among conservatives, moral considerations focused on purity, loyalty to ingroup, and authority are most salient, whereas liberals place a greater emphasis on fairness and care. Further, the objects of moral concern (e.g., compassion) tend to be broader among liberals than among conservatives, with liberals reporting greater compassion for all of humanity, nature, and even the universe (Waytz et al. 2019).

These differences in moral intuitions and moral concerns have implications for how media may inspire moral understanding and the attitudes and behaviors that may follow. For example, many examples of "inspiring" stories may ultimately serve to reaffirm attitudes that are based in questionable, unsavory, immoral, or racist assumptions. White savior films such as *The Blind Side* and *The Help* are seen as inspiring by many people, and many user reviews on the Internet Movie Data Base characterize them as "heartwarming, inspiring, and memorable," as featuring "incredibly good, strong and brave people," and of serving as "an uplifting reminder of how compassion, courage, empathy and honesty have helped change the world." Likewise, *Fox News*' "Good News" section is populated with "inspiring" stories featuring the unquestioning praise of the military, the police, and of white kindness to African Americans (see https://www.foxnews.com/category/good-news). For example, one story featured on this platform is about a high school football team in Texas that carried American flags onto the field to honor police officers and the military (https://www.foxnews.com/sports/texas-high-school-football-flags). Based on user comments, it seems clear that this story (as did many others) elicited some type of elevation among many users (e.g., "I teared up watching this fine example of patriotism"; "That was beautiful! Sitting here at my computer in tears").

It is evident that these types of media offerings are perceived as morally beautiful by some people and that they elicit the types of emotional responses that have been examined among scholars in positive media psychology. At the same time, however, it is also clear that they are antithetical to the types of prosocial outcomes that media psychologists have hoped for. Although scholarship into the "dark side" of inspiring media is just beginning to gain research attention (Frischlich, Hahn, and Rieger 2021), initial research into this area shows some troubling signs. For example, in a recent content-analytic study of Islamic extremist posts on Instagram, Frischlich (2020) found that inspiring portrayals (e.g., vastness, human connection, moral virtue) were also commonly featured. Likewise, recent experimental research found that the meaningful emotions elicited by "inspiring" right-wing online propaganda were a better predictor of wanting to engage with the author and of sharing the materials than were humorous emotions elicited by comedic propaganda (Frischlich et al. 2021).

In questioning whether or not moral understanding implies moral virtue, it seems reasonable to suggest that it does, despite these seemingly disparate examples. Inspiration involving violence, racism, or extremism may be characterized as *lacking* moral understanding. However, it is important to acknowledge that many individuals who are inspired by these messages likely believe that their responses and resultant actions are morally laudable. As a result, in moving forward with attempts to employ media-induced elevation as a means for enhancing social good, it is important to be mindful of how such emotions can be exploited by entities that have alternative, more sinister motivations.

Concluding Thoughts

The field of media psychology has shown increasing interest in exploring the positive role that media may play in increasing compassion, connectedness, and social justice. Although existing and emerging research suggests that media may play this role, numerous questions remain. Some of these questions are conceptual in nature, and others point to large holes in our understanding, including whether or not inspiring messages necessarily lead to noble or virtuous outcomes. Moving forward, research in this area will benefit from examining the limits and boundary conditions of when media can truly lead to heightened moral understanding and to enable viewers to reach their higher, better selves.

Works Cited

Aaker, David A., Douglas M. Stayman, and Michael R. Hagerty. 1986. "Warmth in Advertising: Measurement, Impact, and Sequence Effects." *Journal of Consumer Research* 12, no. 1: 365–381. doi:10.1086/208524.

Algoe, Sara B., and Jonathan Haidt. 2009. "Witnessing Excellence in Action: The 'Other-Praising' Emotions of Elevation, Gratitude, and Admiration." *Journal of Positive Psychology* 4, no. 2: 105–127. doi:10.1080/17439760802650519.

Anderson, Craig A., and Brad J. Bushman. 2002. "Human Aggression." *Annual Review of Psychology* 53: 27–51. doi:10.1146/annurev.psych.53.100901.135231.

Appel, Markus, Michael D. Slater, and Mary Beth Oliver. 2018. "Repelled by Virtue? The Dark Triad and Eudaimonic Narratives." *Media Psychology* 22, no. 5: 769–794. doi:10.1080/15213269.2018.1523014.

Aquino, Karl, Brent McFerran, and Marjorie Laven. 2011. "Moral Identity and the Experience of Moral Elevation in Response to Acts of Uncommon Goodness." *Journal of Personality and Social Psychology* 100, no. 4: 703–718. doi:10.1037/a0022540.

Bartsch, Anne, Anja Kalch, and Mary Beth Oliver. 2014. "Moved to Think: The Role of Emotional Media Experiences in Stimulating Reflective Thoughts." *Journal of Media Psychology: Theories, Methods, and Applications* 26, no. 3: 125–140. doi:http://dx.doi.org/10.1027/1864-1105/a000118.

Bartsch, Anne, Mary Beth Oliver, Cordula Nitsch, and Sebastian Scherr. 2018. "Inspired by the Paralympics: Effects of Empathy on Audience Interest in Para-sports and on the Destigmatization of Persons with Disabilities." *Communication Research* 45, no. 4: 525–553. doi:10.1177/0093650215626984.

Cacioppo, John T., Richard E. Petty, and Chuan Feng Kao. 1984. "The Efficient Assessment of Need for Cognition." *Journal of Personality Assessment* 48: 306–307. doi:10.1207/s15327752jpa4803_13.

Canestrari, Carla, Erika Branchini, Ivana Bianchi, Ugo Savardi, and Roberto Burro. 2018. "Pleasures of the Mind: What Makes Jokes and Insight Problems Enjoyable." *Frontiers in Psychology* 8: 21. doi:10.3389/fpsyg.2017.02297.

Davis, Mark H. 1983. "Measuring Individual Differences in Empathy: Evidence for a Multidimensional Approach." *Journal of Personality and Social Psychology* 44: 113–126. doi:10.1037//0022-3514.44.1.113.

Diessner, Rhett, Ravi Iyer, Meghan M Smith, and Jonathan Haidt. 2013. "Who Engages with Moral Beauty?" *Journal of Moral Education* 42, no. 2: 139–163. doi:10.1080/03057240.2013.785941.

Ellithorpe, Morgan E., Yan Huang, and Mary Beth Oliver. 2019. "Reach across the Aisle: Elevation from Political Messages Predicts Increased Positivity toward Politics, Political Participation, and the Opposite Political Party." *Journal of Communication* 69, no. 3: 249–272. doi:10.1093/joc/jqz011.

Erickson, Thane M., Adam P. McGuire, Gina M. Scarsella, Tara A. Crouch, Jamie A. Lewis, A. P. Eisenlorh, and Rasha J. Muresan. 2018. "Viral Videos and Virtue: Moral Elevation Inductions Shift Affect and Interpersonal Goals in Daily Life." *Journal of Positive Psychology* 13, no. 6: 643–654. doi:10.1080/17439760.2017.1365163.

Freeman, Dan, Karl Aquino, and Brent McFerran. 2009. "Overcoming Beneficiary Race as an Impediment to Charitable Donations: Social Dominance Orientation, the Experience of Moral Elevation, and Donation Behavior." *Personality and Social Psychology Bulletin* 35, no. 1: 72–84. doi:10.1177/0146167208325415.

Frischlich, Lena. 2020. "#Dark Inspiration: Eudaimonic Entertainment in Extremist Instagram Posts." *New Media & Society* 23, no. 3: 554–577. doi: 10.1177/1461444819899625.

Frischlich, Lena, Lindsay Hahn, and Diana Rieger. 2021. "The Promises and Pitfalls of Inspirational Media: What Do We Know, and Where Do We Go from Here?" *Media and Communication* 9, no. 2: 162–166. doi:10.17645/mac.v9i2.4271.

Frischlich, Lena, Johanna Klapproth, Tobias Kleineidamm, and Tim Schatto-Eckrodt. 2021. "Entertained by Extremists: Staging and Effects of Eduaimonic Instagram Propaganda." Paper presented at International Communication Association, Denver, CO (virtual), May.

Gerbner, George. 1998. "Cultivation Analysis: An Overview." *Mass Communication & Society* 1: 175–194. doi:10.1080/15205436.1998.9677855.

Gerbner, George, and Larry Gross. 1976. "The Scary World of TV's Heavy Viewer." *Psychology Today* 9, no. 11: 41–45.

Gerbner, George, Larry Gross, Michael Morgan, Nancy Signorielli, and James Shanahan. 2002. "Growing Up with Television: Cultivation Processes." In *Media Effects: Advances in Theory and Research*, edited by Jennings Bryant and Dolf Zillmann, 43–67. Mahwah, NJ: Lawrence Erlbaum.

Haidt, Jonathan. 2001. "The Emotional Dog and Its Rational Tail: A Social Intuitionist Approach to Moral Judgment." *Psychological Review* 108, no. 4: 814–834. doi:10.1037//0033-295x.108.4.814.

Haidt, Jonathan. 2003. "Elevation and the Positive Psychology of Morality." In *Flourishing: Positive Psychology and the Life Well-Lived*, edited by Corey L. M. Keyes and Jonathan Haidt, 275–289. Washington, DC: American Psychological Association.

Janicke-Bowles, Sophie H., Arthur A. Raney, Mary Beth Oliver, Katherine R. Dale, Robert P. Jones, and Daniel Cox. 2019. "Exploring the Spirit in U.S. Audiences: The Role of the Virtue of Transcendence in Inspiring Media Consumption." *Journalism & Mass Communication Quarterly* 98, no. 2: 428–450. doi:10.1177/1077699019894927.

Jonason, Peter K., and Gregory D. Webster. 2010. "The Dirty Dozen: A Concise Measure of the Dark Triad." *Psychological Assessment* 22, no. 2: 420–432. doi:10.1037/a0019265.

Krämer, Nicole, Sabrina C. Eimler, German Neubaum, Stephan Winter, Leonie Rösner, and Mary Beth Oliver. 2017. "Broadcasting One World: How Watching Online Videos Can Elicit Elevation and Reduce Stereotypes." *New Media & Society* 19, no. 9: 1349–1368. doi:10.1177/1461444816639963.

Maheshwari, Sapna. 2018. "Ram Trucks Commercial with Martin Luther King Jr. Sermon Is Criticized." *New York Times*, February 5. https://www.nytimes.com/2018/02/05/business/media/mlk-commercial-ram-dodge.html.

Mastro, Dana L. 2009. "Racial/Ethnic Stereotyping and the Media." In *The Sage Handbook of Media Processes and Effects*, edited by Robin L. Nabi and Mary Beth Oliver, 377–392. Newbury Park, CA: Sage.

Nabi, Robin L. 2009. "Emotions and Media Effects." In *The Sage Handbook of Media Processes and Effects*, edited by Robin L. Nabi and Mary Beth Oliver, 205–222. Thousand Oaks, CA: Sage.

Nabi, Robin L., and Melanie C. Green. 2014. "The Role of a Narrative's Emotional Flow in Promoting Persuasive Outcomes." *Media Psychology* 18, no. 2: 137–162. doi:10.1080/15213269.2014.912585.

Nabi, Robin, and Abby Prestin. 2020. "Media Prescriptions: Exploring the Therapeutic Effects of Entertainment Media on Stress Relief, Illness Symptoms, and Goal Attainment." *Journal of Communication* 70, no. 2: 145–170. doi:10.1093/joc/jqaa001.

Neubaum, German, Nicole C. Krämer, and Katharina Alt. 2020. "Psychological Effects of Repeated Exposure to Elevating Entertainment: An Experiment over the Period of 6 Weeks." *Psychology of Popular Media* 9, no. 2: 194–207. doi:10.1037/ppm0000235.

Oliver, Mary Beth, and Anne Bartsch. 2011. "Appreciation of Entertainment: The Importance of Meaningfulness via Virtue and Wisdom." *Journal of Media Psychology: Theories, Methods, and Applications* 23, no. 1: 29–33. doi:10.1027/1864-1105/a000029.

Oliver, M. B., A. Ferchaud, E. Bailey, C. Yang, Y. Huang, R. Wang, P. Diddi, A. R. Raney, S. H. Janicke, and K. Dale. 2017. "Predictors of Selection of Inspiring Media and the Resultant Prosocial Outcomes." Paper presented at annual conference of the National Communication Association, Dallas, TX, November.

Oliver, Mary Beth, Tilo Hartmann, and Julia K. Woolley. 2012. "Elevation in Response to Entertainment Portrayals of Moral Virtue." *Human Communication Research* 38: 360–378. doi:10.1111/j.1468-2958.2012.01427.x.

Oliver, Mary Beth, Keunyeong Kim, Jennifer Hoewe, Mun-Young Chung, Erin Ash, Julia K. Woolley, and Drew D. Shade. 2015. "Media-Induced Elevation as a Means of Enhancing Feelings of Intergroup Connectedness." *Journal of Social Issues* 71, no. 1: 106–122. doi:10.1111/josi.12099.

Oliver, Mary Beth, Jessica G Myrick, Jin Chen, Johanna Blomster, and Arthur A Raney. 2021. "Won't You Be My Neighbor: Longitudinal Effects of an Inspiring Documentary." Paper presented at International Communication Association, Denver, CO (virtual), May.

Oliver, Mary Beth, and Arthur A. Raney. 2011. "Entertainment as Pleasurable and Meaningful: Identifying Hedonic and Eudaimonic Motivations for Entertainment Consumption." *Journal of Communication* 61, no. 5: 984–1004. doi:10.1111/j.1460-2466.2011.01585.x.

Oliver, Mary Beth, Arthur A. Raney, Michael D. Slater, Markus Appel, Tilo Hartmann, Anne Bartsch, Frank M. Schneider, Sophie H. Janicke-Bowles, Nicole Krämer, Marie-Louise Mares, Peter Vorderer, Diana Rieger, Katherine R. Dale, and Enny Das. 2018. "Self-Transcendent Media Experiences: Taking Meaningful Media to a Higher Level." *Journal of Communication* 68, no. 2: 380–389. doi:10.1093/joc/jqx020.

Pohling, Rico, and Rhett Diessner. 2016. "Moral Elevation and Moral Beauty: A Review of the Empirical Literature." *Review of General Psychology* 20, no. 4: 412–425. doi:10.1037/gpr0000089.

Raney, Arthur A. 2004. "Expanding Disposition Theory: Reconsidering Character Liking, Moral Evaluations, and Enjoyment." *Communication Theory* 14: 348–369. doi:10.1093/ct/14.4.348.

Raney, Arthur A., Sophie H. Janicke, Mary Beth Oliver, Katherine R. Dale, Robert P. Jones, and Daniel Cox. 2018. "Profiling the Audience for Self-Transcendent Media: A National Survey." *Mass Communication and Society* 21: 296–319. doi:10.1080/15205436.2017.1413195.

Raney, Arthur A., Sophie H. Janicke-Bowles, Mary Beth Oliver, and Katherine Dale. 2021. *Introduction to Positive Media Psychology.* New York: Routledge.

Saturn, Sarina Rodrigues. 2017. "Two Factors That Fuel Compassion: The Oxytocin System and the Social Experience of Moral Elevation." In *Oxford Handbook of Compassion Science*, edited by Emma M. Seppälä, E. Simon-Thomas, S. L. Brown, Monica C. Worline, C. Daryl Cameron and James R. Doty, 121–132. Oxford: Oxford University Press.

Schnall, Simone, Jean Roper, and Daniel M. T. Fessler. 2010. "Elevation Leads to Altruistic Behavior." *Psychological Science* 21, no. 3: 315–320. doi:10.1177/0956797609359882.

Seibt, B., T. W. Schubert, J. H. Zickfeld, and A. P. Fiske. 2019. "Touching the Base: Heart-Warming Ads from the 2016 U.S. Election Moved Viewers to Partisan Tears." *Cognition & Emotion* 33: 197–212. doi:10.1080/02699931.2018.1441128.

Silvers, J. A., and J. Haidt. 2008. "Moral Elevation Can Induce Nursing." *Emotion* 8: 291–295. doi:10.1037/1528-3542.8.2.291.

Slater, Michael D., Mary Beth Oliver, and Markus Appel. 2019. "Poignancy and Mediated Wisdom of Experience: Narrative Impacts on Willingness to Accept Delayed Rewards." *Communication Research* 46, no. 3: 333–354. doi:10.1177/0093650215623838.

Steger, Michael F., Patricia Frazier, Shigehiro Oishi, and Matthew Kaler. 2006. "The Meaning in Life Questionnaire: Assessing the Presence of and Search for Meaning in Life." *Journal of Counseling Psychology* 53: 80–93. doi:10.1037/0022-0167.53.1.80.

Topolinski, Sascha, and Rolf Reber. 2010. "Gaining Insight into the 'Aha' Experience." *Current Directions in Psychological Science* 19, no. 6: 402–405. doi:10.1177/0963721410388803.

Victor, Daniel. 2017. "Pepsi Pulls Ad Accused of Trivializing Black Lives Matter." *New York Times*, April 5. https://www.nytimes.com/2017/04/05/business/kendall-jen ner-pepsi-ad.html.

Waytz, Adam, Ravi Iyer, Liane Young, Jonathan Haidt, and Jesse Graham. 2019. "Ideological Differences in the Expanse of the Moral Circle." *Nature Communications* 10: 12. doi:10.1038/ s41467-019-12227-0.

Yaden, David Bryce, Jonathan Haidt, Ralph W. Hood, David R. Vago, and Andrew B. Newberg. 2017. "The Varieties of Self-Transcendent Experience." *Review of General Psychology* 21, no. 2: 143–160. doi:10.1037/gpr0000102.

Zillmann, Dolf. 2000. "Mood Management in the Context of Selective Exposure Theory." In *Communication Yearbook*, edited by Michael E. Roloff, 103–123. Thousand Oaks, CA: Sage.

Zillmann, Dolf, and Jennings Bryant. 1986. "Exploring the Entertainment Experience." In *Perspectives on Media Effects*, edited by J. Bryant and D. Zillmann, 303–324. Hillsdale, NJ: Lawrence Erlbaum.

Zillmann, Dolf, and Joanne R. Cantor. 1977. "Affective Responses to the Emotions of a Protagonist." *Journal of Experimental Social Psychology* 13: 155–165. doi:10.1037/ 0022-3514.35.8.587.

PART IV

CHARACTER ENGAGEMENT

9

Media Characters and Moral Understanding

Perspectives from Media Psychology

Allison Eden and Matthew Grizzard

Humans are fascinated by characters. We laugh and cry along with these fictional others. Larger-than-life screen villains and heroes, like Darth Vader, Indiana Jones, Frodo, and more, can have lasting emotional impact on viewers. Sometimes characters present a viewpoint or perspective so original, so compelling, or so persuasive that viewers change their perspective of the world based on their experience with that fictional persona. When this occurs in a domain of human values or ethics, this process can be considered as developing *moral understanding*. While previous theory and research has examined the ability of narratives to spark moral understanding, this research has generally considered narratives in a holistic manner with little attention paid to the specific role characters play in this process, or it has been situated in either psychological or philosophical studies of narrative and literature.

We outline how the experience of moral understanding in response to engagement with media characters is understood from our home discipline of media psychology. Media psychology is broadly situated within the communication discipline and takes an individualist, empirical, deductive approach to understanding the appeal and selection of media, as well as resultant effects on viewers and users of mediated communication forms. We present an overview of research on narrative characters and moral understanding from media psychology.

We begin by describing how characters serve as *moral exemplars* for viewers. When we describe characters as moral exemplars, we mean they are specific instantiations of traits, attitudes, and preferences, which serve to generalize to broader categories of behavior (e.g., Zillmann 1999; Tamborini 2011). These moral exemplars can affect viewers' morals through several mechanisms; first, by serving as models for behavior, thought, and action (Bandura 2001a) and through the consequences that follow these actions. Individuals may view characters as "tutors, motivators, inhibitors, disinhibitors, social prompters, emotion arousers, and shapers of values and conceptions of reality" (283). Second, characters can serve as objects of social comparisons for viewers, illustrating both aspirational and despicable behaviors (Festinger 1954). Finally, characters may serve as a relevant reference group by which normative perceptions

Allison Eden and Matthew Grizzard, *Media Characters and Moral Understanding* In: *Screen Stories and Moral Understanding*. Edited by: Carl Plantinga, Oxford University Press. © Oxford University Press 2023.
DOI: 10.1093/oso/9780197665664.003.0010

can be shifted or changed via increased social exposure to particular beliefs and behaviors (Mead et al. 2014).

Not all characters, however, will serve as moral exemplars. Instead, viewers selectively attend to and differentially respond to some characters over others. We term this attention and response mechanism character engagement, which is similar to how Moyer-Gusé 2008, defined involvement with characters, as "an overarching category that can refer to a variety of ways in which individuals respond to story characters" (Moyer-Gusé 2008, 409). There are specific psychological processes of character engagement which have been studied in past work, including person perception processes, disposition theory (liking and moral evaluation), identification or side-taking, wishful identification, similarity and social identity, and parasocial interaction and relationships. These mechanisms may be moderated by specific use of narrative features, including editorial techniques such as point of view, perspective-taking, music, time on screen, and centrality to narrative conflict, as well as character change or consistency in the face of conflict.

Therefore, we begin with a discussion of psychological processes of character engagement, and then move to a discussion of how characters may serve as moral exemplars. We touch on narrative features and schema which may make characters more or less engaging as moral exemplars. We close by summarizing the total effect of these mechanisms on moral understanding in viewers.

Mechanisms of Character Engagement

Mechanisms of character engagement have been extremely popular *outcome* variables for media scholars interested in how viewers respond to fictional or mediated narratives (see Moyer-Gusé 2008). In this section, we outline findings from media psychological studies on several mechanisms of character engagement, including morality and liking, person perception, identification and wishful identification, similarity and homophily, and parasocial interaction and relationships.

Morality and Liking

Understanding perceptions and responses to character morality has been central to understanding media enjoyment (Raney 2017), mainly due to the moral sanction theory of delight and repugnance (MSTDR; Zillmann 2000). MSTDR states that viewers act as "untiring moral monitors," continually judging whether or not characters meet their moral standards. Characters whom viewers judge as morally correct are liked, and those judged to be immoral are disliked (Zillmann 2000). Liking, in the sense of MSTDR, means a positive evaluation or disposition toward the character. Liking and morality are so intertwined in narrative that disentangling the effects of morality and liking is nearly impossible (see Grizzard et al. 2019). Much media psychological research on character liking has therefore focused on character morality, for example, creating taxonomies of "good" and "bad" behaviors and appearances that help viewers distinguish and attribute intentionality to media characters such as heroes, villains, and those in between (Hoffner and Cantor 1991).

Storylines that reward these liked and moral characters for their actions result in greater enjoyment for the viewer, as the viewer's own moral standards are vicariously upheld and justified. In this way, narratives which feature just endings—that is, reward for moral characters and punishment for immoral characters—may reinforce or strengthen moral values for viewers. Tamborini et al. (2010) found support for this process in their study on prolonged exposure to soap operas, linking the perceived justness of outcomes for characters to the strengthening of conventional moral judgments in viewers. Punishment of moral transgression is a particularly relevant exemplar for transmitting moral norms. Early work by Zillmann and Bryant demonstrated that punishment that is too extreme can reduce enjoyment derived from witnessing a villain receive his just deserts. Moreover, sympathy with the villain can increase as the viewer begins to consider him an additional victim. Recent work on this topic has linked responses to equitable retribution with changes in intuitive moral processing (Grizzard et al. 2019).

Person Perception and Schema

Other work has focused on clearly observable physical traits that lead to quick person perception and categorization (Hoffner and Cantor 1991; Raney 2004) and the role of character schema in disposition formation (Grizzard et al. 2018). Raney (2004) argued that viewers do not enter into narratives as "blank slates"; rather, they carry expectations about characters and character behaviors into a narrative based on past experience with similar characters. Thus, a viewer's moral judgments may be biased before observing a specific character's behavior. Similarly, Sanders's (2010) character impression formation model suggests viewers initially categorize a media character based on existing schema. If that categorization is confirmed, judgments will reflect category-based impressions. If disconfirmed, the viewer will seek additional information about the character's attributes to try to reconcile the discrepancy. This is consistent with past research on schemas/stereotypes which suggests that judgments of others can be influenced by observable characteristics and past experience.

Grizzard et al. (2018) argue that prototypically consistent characters may be categorized more quickly than inconsistent characters. Therefore, the extent to which characters behave in prototypical fashion could make them easier to categorize and more salient as moral exemplars than conflicted characters. Some support for this idea is found in the work of Kinsella, Ritchie, and Igou (2015), who were able to pinpoint common features of a heroic prototype via real-world moral exemplars, and studies by Eden et al. (2017) and Daalmans, Hijmans, and Wester (2017), which examined prototypical features of media characters along a moral continuum from good to evil. Morally ambiguous characters had greater variance in characterization than clear-cut heroes or villains. Recent work by Joyce, Harwood, and Springer suggests there is a "sweet spot" of exemplar typicality wherein characters are most efficacious at enacting attitude and belief change (2020).

Identification and Perspective

Identification is the process of temporarily taking on the role of a character, such that the viewer imagines being that character and replaces his identity with the identity and role of the character (Cohen 2001). Identification involves four dimensions: empathic (sharing feelings with the character), cognitive (sharing the character's perspective), motivational (internalizing the character's goals), and absorption (losing one's self-awareness during exposure; Cohen 2001). Oatley and Duncan (1994, p. 69) states that through identification, the reader adopts the character's goals and plans, and then simulates events that happen to the character and experiences emotions in consonance with the success or failure of these imagined plans (see also Zillmann 2000).

Several scholars have proposed the idea that identification is a mechanism through which narratives can persuade viewers to adopt story-consistent beliefs and change attitudes (Green 2006; Slater and Rouner 2002). Yet it is difficult to disentangle identification from other, similar processes. Indeed, some scholars (Carroll, this volume; Zillmann 1994) argue strenuously against the construct for this reason. For example, many of the effects linked to identification can be explained more parsimoniously through similarity, liking, or sympathetic spectatorship (see Cupchik 1997 for a reconciliation), by empathy (Zillmann 1994), or by admiration (Carroll, this volume). That said, identification with characters enjoys considerable research attention in media psychology. De Graaf et al. (2012) found that identification with protagonists could override preexisting attitude similarity, shifting attitudes in the direction of the character with whom readers identified. The key mechanism in De Graaf et al. was perspective-taking, which refers to the physical and psychological point of perception which is presented in a story (Bal 1997, 143). Therefore, via perspective shifts, narratives may promote more or less identification with characters, which can subsequently affect attitude (and potentially moral) change.

Wishful Identification

When describing identification, it is important not to confuse it with the related but separate notion of wishful identification. In the wishful identification process, viewers form a desire to be like the performers they are watching (Hoffner 1996; Hoffner and Cantor 1991). The early study of potential determinants of wishful identification focused on character attributes. Reviewing more recent studies, Hoffner and

Buchanan (2005) described several character attributes that have been linked to wishful identification, for example, success (see also Bandura 2001b; Hoffner and Cantor 1991), intelligence (see Hoffner 1996), physical attractiveness (see Hoffner 1996), aggressiveness (see Hoffner and Buchanan 2005), and humor (see Hoffner 1996). Importantly, unlike identification, wishful identification is only about aspiration and does not seem to include a desire to be different from the characters.

Admiration and other expressions of affection by characters in a narrative can also have an influence on the wishful identification with those characters. When such feelings of admiration are expressed, they can serve as reinforcement that influences viewers' desires to take over the behaviors of the character who receives this admiration (Carroll, this volume). This desire to be like, or behave in ways similar to, the character may immediately arise in the exposure situation, but may also extend far beyond the instant of watching a film. Admired characters may function as an example or role model for future actions and may thus trigger imitation of attitudes and behavior.

Similarity (Homophily) and Social Identity

Similarity is an important mechanism which may underpin character perceptions such as liking, identification, and wishful identification. Similarity, however, is only tangentially related to liking and does not include the perspective-taking of identification nor the aspirational element of wishful identification. Instead, similarity is best conceptualized as homophily between viewer and character, which may support these other processes. For example, support for the notion of similarity underlying wishful identification can be seen in studies of gender similarity and wishful identification (e.g., Hoffner and Buchanan 2005; Hoffner 1996), although similarity has also been examined in terms of demographic characteristics such as race and age as well as cultural proximity (Trepte 2008). There are important limits to the relationships between similarity and wishful identification that warrant mention. Aspirational desires by definition require some discrepancy between the self and the target of aspiration. Thus, similarity in this context might best be understood as similarity between one's own aspirational self and the target character.

Realism

In addition to ethics and aesthetics (which were covered under morality and person perception), Konijn and Hoorn (2005) suggest that a character's perceived realism (epistemics) may play a role in involvement with the characters. Although in our own work (Eden et al. 2015, 2017; Grizzard et al. 2020) we have not found significant differences in realism on perceptions of character morality, the role of characters as comparison points for real-world experiences has been extensively engaged by others (e.g., Bilandzic 2006; Busselle and Bilandzic 2008; van Ommen et al. 2016).

Parasocial Interaction and Parasocial Relationships

Parasocial interaction is "a media user's reaction to a media performer such that the media user perceives the performer as an intimate conversational partner" (Dibble, Hartmann, and Rosaen 2016, 21). Parasocial interactions are triggered by media performers and characters. These interactions can be magnified if performers acknowledge the presence of the audience in some fashion, adopt an informal, conversational style, and directly (bodily and verbally) address the audience. In terms of moral understanding, recent work suggests that characters directly addressing the audience can increase identification and feelings of complicity with an immoral character (Oliver et al. 2019). In contrast to parasocial interaction, which may be brief or confined to a particular scene or episode, parasocial relationships are the more enduring socioemotional bonds that a media user may form with a mediated performer (Horton and Wohl 1956) and can transcend the viewing experience to resemble a short- or long-term involvement with the performer. These relationships are similar to real-life relationships in a number of ways and may result in users treating media characters as a friend or trusted other (Moyer-Gusé 2008).

Character Agency and Growth

Books on dramatic writing (e.g., Egri 1972; Weijers 2014) postulate the idea that every main character needs contradictions and moral doubts in order to be able to propel the story. "Contradictions within a character and around him, create conflict and decisions" (Egri 1972, 65). Eventually the character will change as she or he attempts to solve this conflict: "Of necessity he must change, and alter his attitude toward life" (61). In other words, characters react to circumstances and happenings, but the way the story progresses (or not) is due to characters and their responses to the world around them.

Similarly, Weijers states, "The main character propels the story forward because s/he is confronted with a problem that requires a response. The character is put in a (moral) predicament, acts according to his/her specific character traits and as a result, the plot develops and the character changes" (2014, 71). These processes were examined by Kleemans et al. (2017) in an analysis of the main protagonists of *Léon the Professional* and *American Psycho*. These two films both feature morally troubling protagonists, but the different choices each protagonist makes in the two stories leads to completely differential involvement from audiences. The upward moral trajectory (from immoral to moral) of Léon causes audiences to engage more with the character. The unchanging morality of the main character in *American Psycho* does not allow for similar viewer engagement. Thus, the extent to which a narrative allows a character to change (or refuse to change) seems particularly important for how a narrative will develop moral understanding in its viewers.

Character Networks

The relationships between characters and their centrality to narrative action have been a topic of recent interest for computational social network researchers. This type of analysis allows for theoretical advancement in understanding characters as embedded in social networks within narratives. For example, computational analysis of movie scripts by Hopp, Fisher, and Weber (2020) found that network structures among characters could accurately identify specific characters, the extent to which characters were central or peripheral to character groups (e.g., the Rebel Alliance versus the Empire in *Star Wars*), as well as the extent to which moral conflict between the characters was present in a scene. Given that conflict is central to the ability of narrative to shift moral salience in viewers, accurately identifying which characters are in conflict, and over what type of moral concern, is vital to understanding effects of characters on viewer morality.

In a different perspective on character networks, Grizzard et al. (2020) posited that character networks were central to understanding character perceptions and character engagement in their *character interdependence hypothesis*. By incorporating balance theory logic with affective disposition theory, Grizzard et al. suggested that the relationships that exist between characters (e.g., whether characters are rivals or friends) will bias viewers' engagement with characters in predictable ways. For example, if viewers have previously developed positive feelings toward a character, a new character who serves as a rival to this character will be intuitively disliked, while a new character who serves as a friend will be intuitively liked. This perspective argues that viewers' dispositions and engagement with characters is as much a function of the author's intentions as the viewers' responses (Grizzard et al. 2020) and that character foils and the general structure of a character network may be important to study to understand the role of characters in moral understanding.

Summary

In this overview, we limited ourselves to the elements of character engagement most strongly associated with subsequent attitude change in viewers (see Moyer-Gusé and Dale 2017). This is not meant to be an exhaustive list but rather touches on the most relevant ways in which characters may engage viewer attention and instigate moral understanding. For example, Plantinga (2010) has examined and formed a typology of sympathies, antipathies, and allegiances toward characters, which we do not touch on here. There is copious work on characters as psychological archetypes (Jung [1875] 2012). However, we have focused here on the most commonly used character variables linked to characters forming strong impressions in viewers' minds. We turn now to how and when characters may be used as moral exemplars, and how that can affect viewers' moral understandings.

Characters as Moral Exemplars

To understand the role of characters as moral exemplars it is relevant to understand how humans make sense of and perceive and categorize people in their environment. Exemplars are concrete instantiations (or examples) of a specific category of persons or trait behaviors (Zillmann 1999). Exemplar models suggest that people use mental representation of individual instances to build a "library" of existing exemplars, which with new stimuli may be compared. In order to function as an exemplar, characters must share primary, defining attributes with other exemplars of that category (Zillmann 2002).These models may be updated with each new instantiation of a similar exemplar (e.g., the Batman movies, with their multiple representations of the titular character.) Exemplar updating is particularly likely when new information is highly emotional or arousing (an *event of consequence*, as Zillmann states).

Perhaps the clearest application of exemplification to media and morality can be found in the Model of Intuitive Morality and Exemplars (MIME; Tamborini 2011). The MIME is a heuristic framework that explains how exposure to media can affect cultural values and attitudes over both short- and long-term processes (Eden et al. 2021) by emphasizing the importance of moral domains and narrative cues. It specifically describes the behavior of heroes and villains as strong exemplars which can influence subsequent audience domain salience. For example, in a longitudinal test of the MIME over eight weeks of soap opera exposure, Eden et al. (2014b) found that the behavior of the villain was related to subsequent shifts in moral domain salience. When the villain violated care, fairness, and purity, it seemed to make these domains more important for rendering moral judgments in viewers (when compared with a control group who did not watch the show). However, no such relationships were found for the hero character. Therefore, we now turn to understanding how and when characters may facilitate moral change via exemplification processes.

Modeling Moral Behavior

Bandura (2001b) suggested that characters in mass media can serve as models for the observational learning component of his social cognitive theory. Bandura has suggested that people are able to extract generic features from social exemplars, which can be then composited into more general rules for behaviors, and these rules will then generate new behaviors. When describing this process in a mediated environment, Bandura called this process the *social construction of reality*. He described and documented how models in media can shift individuals' beliefs and norms in his social cognitive theory of mass communication. As Bandura states, modeling influences can act as "tutors, motivators, inhibitors, disinhibitors, social prompters, emotion arousers, and shapers of values and conceptions of reality" (283). If we consider media characters as models, among the most important attributes are the consequences of character (model) actions and attributes of those characters. For example, Bandura suggests that showing "prestigeful," "popular," "wholesome, handsome, fun-loving," and "erotic" models (283) receiving social rewards and benefits can increase behavioral change in the direction of the modeled behavior. By modeling benefits of new belief and behavior adoption, characters are able to serve as models who exemplify and legitimize new practices, as well as directly encouraging viewers to adopt them (e.g., via advertising).

Additionally, Bandura (2001b) suggests that by negotiating these new ideas interpersonally—for example, seeing a new behavior modeled on television, and then asking your family and friends what they think of the behavior—media can serve as an instigator for change across behavioral, attitudinal, and moral dimensions. He models this change after diffusion practices and suggests that due to the far reach of media, diffusion of new morals may spread more quickly via mass communication models than interpersonal communication. He explains that "a single model can transmit new ways of thinking and behaving simultaneously to countless people in widely dispersed locales" (271). These models will influence people to the extent that viewers attend to media models, retain the information conveyed, are able to reproduce the behavior or attitude, and are motivated to do so via incentive motivators (e.g., direct incentives, vicarious incentives, or self-incentives, i.e., feeling good about oneself).

Evidence in support of characters serving as moral models in this fashion comes from the health communication literature in particular, which examines the extent to which viewing risky smoking, drinking, or sexual behavior as socially rewarded (e.g., cool) can be associated with changes in those behaviors in viewers. In terms of moral (versus behavioral) modeling, Tamborini et al. (2010) combined social cognitive theory with disposition theory to examine the role of character liking and outcomes on moral judgment over prolonged exposure to a soap opera. Over the course of exposure to the narrative, perceptions of narrative outcomes as righteous for characters influenced trends toward more socially conventional judgments in viewers. In this way, Tamborini et al. illustrated the ability of media models to shift moral attitudes and norms through sustained media exposure, consistent with predictions from Bandura.

Inspiring Change via Comparison

Another way characters may shift moral understanding in viewers is by their use as a comparison standard for viewers (Festinger 1954; Sherif and Hovland 1961). By comparing oneself or one's standards to those of a narrative character, one might shift toward or away from the character. The urge to be either more like (assimilate) or more different from (contrast) characters has been examined closely by Tsay-Vogel and Krakowiak (2019), who find that assimilative and contrastive motivations in regard to media characters depend on viewers' own perception of morality (whether virtues or vices were made salient) and the behavior of the character.

The use of assimilative exemplars has been strongest in the moral education literature. In this area of study, moral exemplars are thought to affect behavior by demonstrating possible actions and inspiring moral behaviors in others. As an example of this type of research, van de Ven, Archer, and Engelen (2019) presented subjects with a story featuring a positive moral exemplar (e.g., someone donating a kidney) and measured how elevated participants felt after reading. Findings indicated that admiration of the main character led to greater inspiration to donate to a similar cause. Similarly, Immordino-Yang and Sylvan (2010) found that participants exposed to stories about virtuous acts were likely to mention the desire to be a better person and perform virtuous acts themselves.

Central to the ability of moral exemplars to inspire moral behavior is their demonstration of *moral excellence* (Algoe and Haidt 2009), which is thought to trigger admiration, elevation, and inspiration, as well as the desire to emulate the observed behavior. Broadly, by serving as an inspirational exemplar, characters may inspire a desire to emulate behavior via positive emotions in viewers. However, morally excellent characters may also induce a contrast effect in viewers, wherein viewers decide it is impossible to reach extremes of behavior and act in a contrasting fashion instead (see Dijksterhuis et al. 1998, Study 3). This can work for both extremely moral and extremely immoral characters. Returning to the study by Eden et al. (2014a) discussed above, viewers seemed to view the behaviors of the villain as an example of "what not to do" and kept their own moral standards high in response to her behavior.

On the other hand, even negative moral exemplars (e.g., violence and harm) and the emotions elicited by their depiction can lead to aspirational desires. Two examples are of particular note. Grizzard et al. (2017) found that the level of anger and disgust felt in response to a morally heinous act (a mass execution conducted by ISIS) led to a greater desire to live a more meaningful life. Importantly, the graphicness of the depiction was the driving factor of these effects. Bartsch and colleagues (2010) have found positive relationships between meaning seeking and horror narratives. These effects suggest that both villains and heroes are likely to be sources of contrast and assimilation, respectively, and may drive further moral deliberation in viewers.

Characters as (Mere) Social Exposure

A third way that characters may influence viewer perceptions of morality is by making specific behaviors or attitudes seem more common or accepted simply by portraying them more often on screen. This is akin to the repeated exposure to similar messages across all media exposure, as described in moral cultivation (Bilandzic, this volume). Repeated exposure to messages with similar moral judgment processes or characters (e.g., archetypes) can alter viewers' perceptions of social norms, defined as the perceived ubiquity of behaviors (or approval of behaviors) of a referent group (Lapinski and Rimal 2005).

Individuals learn about group norms via observation and communication from a referent group of important others. Characters may increase the *social exposure* to specific moral messages, and thereby change viewers' perceptions about the prevalence of specific behaviors in real life (Mead et al. 2014). This has been demonstrated in regard to health behaviors such as smoking. However, the theory of normative social behavior also suggests that group identity aspiration (i.e., the desire to emulate members of a group) and perceived similarity with the group can increase modeling of observed behaviors directly. Importantly, this type of moral change does not require an emotional mediator such as admiration, awe, or anger in order to be effective. Instead, it works primarily via prevalence and sanction assumptions, which are driven mainly by exposure. Therefore, in this model of moral change specific character behaviors and types may be less important than overall, cumulative exposure (see also Bilandzic, this volume, on moral cultivation).

Moral Understanding

We have argued that characters may shift moral understanding in viewers via *mechanisms of character engagement*. What exactly do we mean by "moral understanding"? We mean the extent to which viewers may come to a new or previously unrealized moral conclusion after deliberation, rumination, or experience with narrative. There is ample evidence that media narratives function as a *moral laboratory* (cf. Ricoeur 1983) in which viewers can explore moral issues without facing the consequences of their moral decisions (see Krijnen 2011). As Bandura noted, the fictional world is a place full of violence, unfortunate events, and calamity, more than we would ever encounter in our own lives. Additionally, media narratives portray the past, present, and future actions of characters, and as a result we can see their motives, behaviors, and consequences with a clarity that is denied us in real life (Hoffner and Cantor 1991). Yet characters present us with a more objective evaluative standard than we use on ourselves. It may be extremely difficult for an individual to acknowledge that they behaved inappropriately, but such condemnation toward media characters, and others in general, flows without such restrictions.

Thus, characters aid us by demonstrating "concrete cases, engaging and exercising our emotions and imagination, our powers of perceptual discrimination, moral understanding, and reflection, in ways that sustain and potentially enlarge our capacity for moral judgment" (Carroll 2000, 368–369). For example, Eden et al. (2017) found that moral rumination (i.e., deliberating on the moral outcomes) of a narrative could be sparked by moral conflict within a character. Moreover, Kleemans et al. (2017) found that moral inflection or change toward characters occurred when viewers were most engaged. This process of moral deliberation and understanding may take place most often when we are confronted with morals different from our own, as Dant (2012, 42) argues: a viewer does not have to agree "with the moral premises of the characters in a television show and may actually be alerted to the moral issues implicit [in the narrative] precisely because he or she does not agree." Similarly, van Ommen, Daalmans, and Weijers (2014) found that watching the main character in *House*, a medical drama, commit moral transgressions encouraged moral deliberation and growth among medical students, as well as provided a strong ethical example for deliberation in the classroom.

Moral rumination and deliberation can lead to moral understanding and change. For example, Krijnen (2011) found that television, regardless of the genre, sparked moral deliberation and moral insight in viewers, sometimes leading to prolonged discussions in a period of moral reflection after viewing. Grizzard et al. (2014) found that moral rumination led to greater moral salience in a single exposure. By serving as moral exemplars, through the mechanisms of engagement described in this chapter, media characters can stimulate moral understanding on the part of the viewer, presenting the viewer with a variety of perspectives on moral topics that provide insight into the human character and condition.

That said, the ability of characters to spark this kind of moral rumination and growth is still being explored. A focus on either the mechanisms of character engagement or the process of attitude and behavior change has perhaps directed research efforts away from understanding the entirety of the process—from person perception and emulation to growth and understanding. We have attempted to give an overview of the process, but there is more work to be done to clearly specify the overall relationship between characters in narrative and resultant moral change. We believe such efforts could have far-reaching benefits. For example, there has been recent interest from psychologists and neuroscientists in how moral norms and attitudes can be altered via exposure to dramatic personae in the news and social media, and how these attitudes can spread. We believe that understanding how media users perceive and respond to characters in narrative, and the ways in which these characters are taken as catalysts for moral understanding, could offer a more nuanced and careful examination of these important societal issues.

Works Cited

Algoe, Sara B., and Jonathan Haidt. 2009. "Witnessing Excellence in Action: The 'Other-Praising' Emotions of Elevation, Gratitude, and Admiration." *Journal of Positive Psychology* 4, no. 2: 105–127.

Bal, Mieke. 1997. *The Mottled Screen: Reading Proust Visually*. Stanford, CA: Stanford University Press.

Bandura, A., 2001a. "Social Cognitive Theory: An Agentic Perspective." *Annual Review of Psychology* 52, no. 1: 1–26.

Bandura, A., 2001b. "Theoretical Integration and Research Synthesis Essay: Social Cognitive Theory of Mass Communication." *Media psychology*, 3: 265–299.

Bartsch, Anne, Markus Appel, and Dennis Storch. 2010. "Predicting Emotions and Meta-emotions at the Movies: The Role of the Need for Affect in Audiences' Experience of Horror and Drama." *Communication Research* 37, no. 2: 167–190.

Bilandzic, Helena. 2006. "The Perception of Distance in the Cultivation Process: A Theoretical Consideration of the Relationship between Television Content, Processing Experience, and Perceived Distance." *Communication Theory* 16, no. 3: 333–355.

Busselle, Rick, and Helena Bilandzic. 2008. "Fictionality and Perceived Realism in Experiencing Stories: A Model of Narrative Comprehension and Engagement." *Communication Theory* 18, no. 2: 255–280.

Carroll, Noël. 2000. "Art and Ethical Criticism: An Overview of Recent Directions of Research." *Ethics* 110, no. 2: 350–387.

Cohen, Jonathan. 2001. "Defining Identification: A Theoretical Look at the Identification of Audiences with Media Characters." *Mass Communication & Society* 4, no. 3: 245–264.

Cupchik, Gerald C. 1997. "Identification as a Basic Problem for Aesthetic Reception." *Systemic and Empirical Approach to Literature and Culture as Theory and Application* 7: 11–22.

Daalmans, Serena, Ellen Hijmans, and Fred Wester. 2017. "From Good to Bad and Everything in Between: An Analysis of Genre Differences in the Representation of Moral Nature." *Journal of Media Ethics* 32, no. 1: 28–44.

Dant, Tim. 2012. *Television and the Moral Imaginary: Society Through the Small Screen.* New York: Springer.

De Graaf, Anneke, Hans Hoeken, José Sanders, and Johannes W. J. Beentjes. 2012. "Identification as a Mechanism of Narrative Persuasion." *Communication Research* 39, no. 6: 802–823.

Dibble, Jayson L., Tilo Hartmann, and Sarah F. Rosaen. 2016. "Parasocial Interaction and Parasocial Relationship: Conceptual Clarification and a Critical Assessment of Measures." *Human Communication Research* 42, no. 1: 21–44.

Dijksterhuis, Ap, Russell Spears, Tom Postmes, Diederik Stapel, Willem Koomen, Ad van Knippenberg, and Daan Scheepers. 1998. "Seeing One Thing and Doing Another: Contrast Effects in Automatic Behavior." *Journal of Personality and Social Psychology* 75, no. 4: 862.

Eden, Allison, Mary Beth Oliver, Ron Tamborini, Anthony Limperos, and Julia Woolley. 2014a. "Perceptions of Moral Violations and Personality Traits among Heroes and Villains." *Mass Communication and Society* 18, no. 2: 186–208.

Eden, Allison, Ron Tamborini, Matthew Grizzard, Robert Lewis, Rene Weber, and Sujay Prabhu. 2014b. "Repeated Exposure to Narrative Entertainment and the Salience of Moral Intuitions." *Journal of Communication* 64, no. 3: 501–520.

Eden, Allison, Serena Daalmans, Merel van Ommen, and Addy Weljers. 2017. "Melfi's Choice: Morally Conflicted Content Leads to Moral Rumination in Viewers." *Journal of Media Ethics* 32, no. 3: 142–153.

Eden, Allison, Ron Tamborini, Melinda Aley, Henry Goble, P. Vorderer, and C. Klimmt. 2021. "Advances in Research on the Model of Intuitive Morality and Exemplars (MIME)." In *The Oxford Handbook or Entertainment* Theory, edited by Peter Vorderer and Christoph Klimmt, 231–249.

Egri, Lajos. 1972. *The Art of Dramatic Writing: Its Basis in the Creative Interpretation of Human Motives.* New York: Simon and Schuster.

Festinger, Leon. 1954. "A Theory of Social Comparison Processes." *Human Relations* 7, no. 2: 117–140.

Green, Melanie C. 2006. "Narratives and Cancer Communication." *Journal of Communication* 56: 163–183.

Grizzard, Matthew, C., Joseph Francemone, Kaitlin Fitzgerald, Jialing Huang, and Changhyun Ahn. 2020. "Interdependence of Narrative Characters: Implications for Media Theories." *Journal of Communication* 70, no. 2: 274–301.

Grizzard, Matthew, Jialing Huang, Julia K. Weiss, Eric Robert Novotny, Kaitlin S. Fitzgerald, Changhyun Ahn, Zed Ngoh, Alexandra Plante, and Haoran Chu. 2017. "Graphic Violence as

Moral Motivator: The Effects of Graphically Violent Content in News." *Mass Communication and Society* 20, no. 6: 763–783.

Grizzard, Matthew, Jialing Huang, Kaitlin Fitzgerald, Changhyun Ahn, and Haoran Chu. 2018. "Sensing Heroes and Villains: Character-Schema and the Disposition Formation Process." *Communication Research* 45, no. 4: 479–501.

Grizzard, Matthew, Jialing Huang, Changhyun Ahn, Kaitlin Fitzgerald, C. Joseph Francemone, and Jess Walton. 2019. "The Gordian Knot of Disposition Theory." *Journal of Media Psychology: Theories, Methods, and Applications* 32, no. 2: 100–105.

Hoffner, Cynthia. 1996. "Children's Wishful Identification and Parasocial Interaction with Favorite Television Characters." *Journal of Broadcasting & Electronic Media* 40, no. 3: 389–402.

Hoffner, Cynthia, and Martha Buchanan. 2005. "Young Adults' Wishful Identification with Television Characters: The Role of Perceived Similarity and Character Attributes." *Media Psychology* 7, no. 4: 325–351.

Hoffner, Cynthia, and Joanne Cantor. 1991. "Perceiving and Responding to Mass Media Characters." In *Responding to the Screen: Reception and Reaction Processes*, edited by Jenning Bryant and Dolf Zillman, 63–101. Mahwah, NJ: Lawrence Erlbaum.

Hopp, Frederic René, Jacob Taylor Fisher, and René Weber. 2020. "A Graph-Learning Approach for Detecting Moral Conflict in Movie Scripts." *Media and Communication* 8, no. 3: 164.

Horton, Donald, and R. Richard Wohl. 1956. "Mass Communication and Para-social Interaction: Observations on Intimacy at a Distance." *Psychiatry* 19, no. 3: 215–229.

Immordino-Yang, Mary Helen, and Lesley Sylvan. 2010. "Admiration for Virtue: Neuroscientific Perspectives on a Motivating Emotion." *Contemporary Educational Psychology* 35, no. 2: 110–115.

Joyce, Nick, Jake Harwood, and Sheila Springer. 2020. "The Sweet Spot: Curvilinear Effects of Media Exemplar Typicality on Stereotype Change." *Journal of Media Psychology* 32, no. 2: 59–69.

Jung, Carl G. [1875] 2012. *Man and His Symbols*. New York: Bantam.

Kinsella, Elaine L., Timothy D. Ritchie, and Eric R. Igou. 2015. "Zeroing in on Heroes: A Prototype Analysis of Hero Features." *Journal of Personality and Social Psychology* 108, no. 1: 114.

Kleemans, Mariska, Allison Eden, Serena Daalmans, Merel van Ommen, and Addy Weijers. 2017. "Explaining the Role of Character Development in the Evaluation of Morally Ambiguous Characters in Entertainment Media." *Poetics* 60: 16–28.

Konijn, Elly A., and Johan F. Hoorn. 2005. "Some Like It Bad: Testing a Model for Perceiving and Experiencing Fictional Characters." *Media Psychology* 7, no. 2: 107–144.

Krijnen, Tonny. 2011. "Engaging the Moral Imagination by Watching Television: Different Modes of Moral Reflection." *Participations: International Journal of Audience Research* 8, no. 2: 52–73.

Lapinski, Maria Knight, and Rajiv N. Rimal. 2005. "An Explication of Social Norms." *Communication Theory* 15, no. 2: 127–147.

Mead, Erin L., Rajiv N. Rimal, Roberta Ferrence, and Joanna E. Cohen. 2014. "Understanding the Sources of Normative Influence on Behavior: The Example of Tobacco." *Social Science & Medicine* 115: 139–143.

Moyer-Gusé, Emily. 2008. "Toward a Theory of Entertainment Persuasion: Explaining the Persuasive Effects of Entertainment-Education Messages." *Communication Theory* 18, no. 3: 407–425.

Moyer-Gusé, Emily, and Katherine Dale. 2017. "Narrative Persuasion Theories." In *The International Encyclopedia of Media Effects*, edited by Patrick Rössler, Cynthia A. Hoffern, and Liesbet van Zoonen, 1–11. Chichester, West Sussex: John Wiley & Sons, Inc.

Oatley, Keith, and Elaine Duncan. 1994. "The Experience of Emotions in Everyday Life." *Cognition & Emotion* 8, no. 4: 369–381.

Oliver, Mary Beth, Helena Bilandzic, Jonathan Cohen, Arienne Ferchaud, Drew D. Shade, Erica J. Bailey, and Chun Yang. 2019. "A Penchant for the Immoral: Implications of Parasocial Interaction, Perceived Complicity, and Identification on Liking of Anti-Heroes." *Human Communication Research* 45, no. 2: 169–201.

Plantinga, Carl. 2010. "'I Followed the Rules, and They All Loved You More': Moral Judgment and Attitudes toward Fictional Characters in Film." *Midwest Studies in Philosophy* 34, no. 1: 34.

Raney, Arthur A. 2004. "Expanding Disposition Theory: Reconsidering Character Liking, Moral Evaluations, and Enjoyment." *Communication Theory* 14, no. 4: 348–369.

Raney, Arthur A. 2017. "Affective Disposition Theory." In *The International Encyclopedia of Media Effects*, edited by Patrick Rössler, Cynthia A. Hoffern, and Liesbet van Zoonen, 1–11. Chichester, West Sussex: John Wiley & Sons, Inc.

Ricoeur, Paul. 1983. "Can Fictional Narratives Be True?" In *The Phenomenology of Man and of the Human Condition*, edited by Anna-Theress Tymieniecka, 3–19. New York: Springer.

Sanders, Meghan S. 2010. "Making a Good (Bad) Impression: Examining the Cognitive Processes of Disposition Theory to Form a Synthesized Model of Media Character Impression Formation." *Communication Theory* 20, no. 2: 147–168.

Sherif, Carolyn W., and Carl I. Hovland. 1961. *Social Judgment: Assimilation and Contrast Effects in Communication and Attitude Change.* New Haven, CT: Yale University Press.

Slater, Michael D., and Donna Rouner. 2002. "Entertainment—Education and Elaboration Likelihood: Understanding the Processing of Narrative Persuasion." *Communication Theory* 12, no. 2: 173–191.

Tamborini, Ron. 2011. "Moral Intuition and Media Entertainment." *Journal of Media Psychology: Theories, Methods, and Applications* 23, no. 1: 39.

Tamborini, Ron, René Weber, Allison Eden, Nicholas David Bowman, and Matthew Grizzard. 2010. "Repeated Exposure to Daytime Soap Opera and Shifts in Moral Judgment toward Social Convention." *Journal of Broadcasting & Electronic Media* 54, no. 4: 621–640.

Trepte, Sabine. 2008. "Cultural Proximity in TV Entertainment: An Eight-country Study on the Relationship of Nationality and the Evaluation of US Prime-time Fiction." *Communications* 33: 1–25.

Tsay-Vogel, Mina, and K. Maja Krakowiak. 2019. "The Virtues and Vices of Social Comparisons: Examining Assimilative and Contrastive Emotional Reactions to Characters in a Narrative." *Motivation and Emotion* 43, no. 4: 636–647.

van de Ven, Niels, Alfred T. M. Archer, and Bart Engelen. 2019. "More Important and Surprising Actions of a Moral Exemplar Trigger Stronger Admiration and Inspiration." *Journal of Social Psychology* 159, no. 4: 383–397.

van Ommen, Merel, Serena Daalmans, and Addy Weijers. 2014. "Who is the Doctor in this House? Analyzing the Moral Evaluations of Medical Students and Physicians of *House, M.D.*" *AJOB Empirical Bioethics* 5, no. 4: 61–74.

van Ommen, Merel, Serena Daalmans, Addy Weijers, Rebecca N. H. de Leeuw, and Moniek Buijzen. 2016. "Analyzing Prisoners', Law Enforcement Agents', and Civilians' Moral Evaluations of *The Sopranos*." *Poetics* 58: 52–65.

Weijers, G. W. M. 2014. *The Craft of Screenwriting.* Den Haag: Boom Lemma.

Zillmann, Dolf. 1994. "Mechanisms of Emotional Involvement with Drama." *Poetics* 23: 33–51.

Zillmann, Dolf. 1999. "Exemplification Theory: Judging the Whole by Some of Its Parts." *Media Psychology* 1, no. 1: 69–94.

Zillmann, Dolf. 2000. "Basal Morality in Drama Appreciation." In *Moving Images, Culture and the Mind*, edited by Ib Bondebjerg, 53–63. Luton: University of Luton Press.

Zillmann, Dolf. 2002. "Exemplification Theory of Media Influence." *Media Effects: Advances in Theory and Research* 2: 19–41.

Zillmann, Dolf. 2006b. "Dramaturgy for Emotions from Fictional Narration." In *Psychology of Entertainment*, edited by Jennings Bryant and Peter Vorderer, 215–238. Mahwah, NJ: Erlbaum.

10
Movies, Examples, and Morality

The Rhetoric of Admiration

Noël Carroll

Introduction

Probably the oldest form of moral education was teaching by example,[1] and plausibly it still is one of the leading forms of ethical instruction. Confucius, Buddha, and Jesus—as well as the vast catalogue of saints in the Christian tradition—were all held up as patents to be imitated, and for the Greeks, the Homeric heroes were characters to be emulated by citizen soldiers, while aspiring philosophers had the sage Socrates as their model (Edmundson 2015; see also Warnick 2015).

In years gone by and, even now, children begin their moral education by following the lead of their parents and caregivers, learning from their behavior how to speak their language and what to do, including what it is to be moral. This ethical education is reinforced and expanded by stories, stories with characters exemplifying ideal virtues and values.[2] Though initially oral, these stories are soon amplified by pictures, including motion pictures.[3]

African American adolescents are tutored in self-respect, fortitude, and strength by the exemplary characters in films like *Sounder* and *Hidden Figures*. *Gandhi* and *Selma* aspire to teach the ethics of passive resistance primarily through their portrayals of their protagonists. And civic virtue is expounded through models like the one represented by Jimmy Stewart in *Mr. Smith Goes to Washington*.

Of course, none of this is news. It seems profoundly unobjectionable. Indeed, so obvious is it that it hardly merits comment. And for that very reason, it hasn't received that much attention. In this chapter I would like to attempt to explain the obvious—to offer a framework for accounting for the way in which moral examples function in movies in the service of moral education and understanding.[4]

I will begin by exploring what is likely to be the first framework that might be proposed for accounting for the way in which moral examples work in the movies, namely, identification. After presenting some shortcomings with that approach, I will hypothesize that the elicitation of the emotion of admiration is a key lever by means of which movie examples induce moral education and enhance moral understanding.[5]

In order to illuminate how this education transpires, I will briefly outline my view of how the emotions function—both in, so to speak, *nature* (i.e., life outside the

Noël Carroll, *Movies, Examples, and Morality* In: *Screen Stories and Moral Understanding*. Edited by: Carl Plantinga,
Oxford University Press. © Oxford University Press 2023. DOI: 10.1093/oso/9780197665664.003.0011

movies) and then in typical movies. This will enable me to introduce the concept of *criterial prefocusing,* which I maintain is the major channel of emotional communication in the movies and which I will apply to the case of admiration.[6]

Following that I will also discuss the way in which the effects of criterial prefocusing can be refined by what I call *virtue wheels.* In the course of the presentation of what might be awkwardly labeled the "criterial prefocusing cum virtue wheels" approach, I will attempt to address some apparent problems with this model.

Identification

Perhaps the reason that scant attention has been paid to the question of how moral examples function pedagogically in movies is that it is widely believed that we already know the answer, namely, identification.

I am very suspicious of this proposal for several reasons. The first is that what is meant by "identification" is exceedingly unclear. It is ambiguous. It means too many different things to too many different people. It can mean that one likes a character, or that one has had an experience similar to the character's (like a divorce), or that one just resembles the character in some way (you're both Irish or Italian), or that one wishes to be like the character (to be as suave as James Bond or as smart as Sherlock Holmes or as righteous as Wonder Woman), to name only a few possible meanings of "identification."[7]

But these different meanings can come apart. If you wish you were like the character, for example, then you do not resemble the character in that respect. If you wish to be as suave as James Bond, then you probably aren't.

Furthermore, it may be the very ambiguity of "identification" that leaves the false impression that it has broad explanatory power. Because it can mean so many different things, it can cover many *different* cases, but not because it is a single process. Rather it is a patchwork of diverging phenomena, not unified activity. It is a mess, and not an explanation of anything.

Of course, one might extract the term "identification" from common parlance and specify its meaning perspicuously. One candidate, introduced by Plato (1971), construes identification as the audience member taking on or being possessed by the self-same emotions that beset the characters in the story. That is, the portrayal of the relevant characters arouses the putatively identical emotional state in the audience.

The father is saddened by the death of his daughter; supposedly we are likewise saddened. Allegedly, in virtue of our emotional immersion in the father's plight, when confronting comparable losses in our own lives we will react as the fictional father did. That is, the example of his response to loss will serve as an affective template for us to replicate, thereby molding our moral-emotive intelligence—in this case, our ability to discriminate a certain type of loss, as well as realizing the appropriate course of action in such circumstances.

One strength of this approach is that, given the way in which it centers on the emotions, it secures a connection with morality insofar as moral understanding is very often tied to the emotions. Moreover, this approach also suggests a connection to moral behavior, since the emotions are typically motivational; that is, the emotions provide a bridge between our evaluation of a situation and our inclination to act. And furthermore, the identification model makes characters the main source of emotional arousal in stories, which is certainly germane to the case of movies.[8]

However, despite these attractions, there are problems with this notion of identification. Perhaps the leading problem is the supposition that readers, listeners, and viewers undergo the self-same emotions that the characters with whom they supposedly "identify" endure. At least as we watch the movie, it rarely seems plausible to think that we suffer the same emotion that the character does.

We watch as a father loses his daughter onscreen. Notably, the object of the father's emotion is his daughter. He is sad because he has lost his daughter. But I am not sad because I have lost my daughter. I don't have a daughter or any other brand of child. The object of my sorrow is the father, a man who has lost his daughter. I am moved by *his* suffering; he is moved by his daughter's death.

Also, he is mourning; I am not. Though the father and I are both sad, the two kinds of sadness are distinct. On the map of emotional states, the father's emotional state and mine are neighbors; they are both dysphoric. But they are not identical. They not only have a different object; they call for different behaviors. In everyday experience, I would be motivated to comfort someone like the grieving father. The father would not be motivated to comfort himself.[9]

Furthermore, if sometime after seeing the movie, a similar misfortune should befall me, it does not seem particularly likely that I will be replicating the father's feelings of sorrow in my own response to my calamity, and certainly not the emotions I felt back then for the grieving father. Indeed, it does not seem probable that I need the memory of the movie to grieve. I have my own distinctive resources and life memories.

Consequently, if there is an emotional basis to the way in which examples contribute to moral education, it is not on the basis of sharing strictly identical emotions—either in the context of watching the movie or afterward. It is not a matter of the kind of identification that Plato had in mind, since the emotional states of the characters and the audiences are not generally *identical*.

Admiration

The kinds of examples that concern us include fictional examples of actions, skills, attitudes, virtues, and even sometimes whole lives. As children, we began our moral education by observing the behavior, attitudes, character traits, and lives of our caregivers. We wanted to be like them (Olberding 2012, 33–36). We were attracted to them. We tried to emulate not only their behavior, but the mental states that gave rise to it. We typically do not emulate everything that we see. Rather we observe and emulate the examples that we find attractive.

Attraction is also the basis of our selection of various movie examples; they are models of what we would like to be. Obviously, we are not repulsed by these examples. Instead we are drawn to them. But attraction is a very broad concept. The question is what kind of attraction is relevant in those cases where the pertinent examples contribute to morality.

My proposal is that it is *admiration*. That is, the movie characters that serve as moral models are ones that inspire admiration.[10] Needless to say, when we admire someone, we are not undergoing the same emotional states as those we admire. Those characters are not admiring themselves. We probably wouldn't admire them if they did. We look up to those we admire. They do not look up to themselves. There needs to be a discrepancy or a distance between those whom we admire and ourselves.

Admiration would appear to require that those whom we admire have certain psychological traits—including emotional dispositions—that we do not already possess. Admiration is based in our desire to acquire these. Thus, admiration cannot be a matter of identification.

Admiration can obtain in two forms. First as an occurrent emotion—Atticus Finch defends Tom Robinson and, as I sit in the movie theater, my eyes tear up in admiration. But admiration can also be a standing, stable, long-term attitude or state. Just as it was yesterday, at the present moment it is true that I admire Emma Goldman. But I am not in any particular feeling state. If asked, I would report, dispassionately, that I admire Emma Goldman, whereas the admiration that I have for Atticus Finch is something I *feel* while watching the courtroom scenes in *To Kill a Mockingbird*.

For our purposes, it is the occurrent emotion of admiration that concerns us rather than the long-term variety, since movies—first and foremost—specialize in arousing the emotions on a movie-by-movie basis. If they contribute to long-term admiration at all, it will only be in virtue of the repeated arousal of occurrent emotions of the admiring sort.

Emotions in Life and in Response to Movies

Before specifying how the emotion of admiration functions in response to the characters in movies, more needs to be said about the structure and function of the emotions[11]—first in life and then in terms of the way in which the emotions function in movies both generally and then with respect to *admiration*.

As already indicated, occurrent emotions involve bodily states or feelings. Feelings, indeed, are so essential to occurrent emotions that sometimes we simply refer to emotional states as "feelings." But not all feelings are emotional states.[12] Itches are not emotional states. Emotional states involve appraisals; they are evaluative. They assess situations in terms of our vital human interests. Fear evaluates situations as perceived to be dangerous or threatening; anger, in terms of perceived wrongs or injustices done to me or mine; sadness involves the perceived apprehension of loss; and so forth.

In general, the emotions are biological, evolutionary adaptations that have been "designed" by natural selection to protect and/or enhance our vital human interests. Fear assesses a situation as dangerous which primes appropriate behavioral responses such as fighting, fleeing, or freezing, depending upon the circumstances. The emotions evaluate situations with respect to our interests. They do so quickly, especially in contrast to slower processes such as deliberation. The emotions are adaptive mechanisms, since many situations do not practically allow enough time for protracted reasoning and research. We jump back onto the sidewalk as the SUV comes hurtling at us rather than standing in the street calculating its velocity. In this way, the possession of a rapid evaluative response mechanism is of the utmost survival value.

Moreover, inasmuch as emotions involve appraisals, they are governed by criteria which determine that the features of the particular objects of the affective state need to satisfy in order to count as this emotional state rather than that one. For example, in order to qualify as an episode of fear, the object of the emotional state must be perceived to be dangerous or threatening. The appropriate object of anger must be perceived as an infringement done to me or someone allied to me. Sadness is the perception of a loss, such as of a deceased relative. Depending on your view of the emotions, these sorts of appraisals either cause or constitute the feelings associated with the emotion in question.[13]

Furthermore, these appraisals and the feelings they arouse typically motivate actions or at least dispositions to act. Fear, as already mentioned, typically motivates a fight, flight, or freeze response. Anger points us toward revenge or retribution; sadness toward mourning. Jealousy—which disposes us to perceive others as rivals for the affections of our valued ones—prompts competitive behavior. In all these cases, the emotions involve negotiating situations where various of our vital human interests are at stake in one way or another. Occurrent emotions need not only arise when our vital human interests are imperiled. That is, they are not only dysphoric. They may be euphoric as well, as in the case of joy which arises in situations where our goals are achieved in a way that invites celebratory behavior.

In everyday life, the emotions function as searchlights. They select or pick out features of the environment that call for an emotional response. The large man lumbers toward us wielding a big knife, triggering our fear alarm, since the situation meets the criterion of being threatening. Furthermore, our fear alerts us to the need to survey the prevailing circumstances, disposing us to be on the lookout for further threatening factors—such as the rest of the encroaching thug's gang. The presiding emotion shapes our attention as it evaluates it. The emotion fixes our focus and underlines its existential significance.

However, things are different at the movies. In life, our emotions filter our attention. They pick out environmental stimuli upon which we should concentrate. But movies typically are very different insofar as the screened environment has been prefocused for the audience.

That is, the emotively significant features in the array have been picked out and made salient by the moviemaking team. Our emotions do not have to pick out the knife in the hand of that big lumbering thug if it is a scene in a movie. A close-up can do that for us. Whereas in life, the emotions focus our attention. Typically, in the movies—that is, in most mass-market, audiovisual, narrative fictions—the pertinent emotional affordances have been prefocused for us.

But why do the features that the moviemakers elect to make salient usually arouse the emotional responses that the moviemakers intend? Recall: emotions are appraisals, appraisals with respect to criteria relevant to the protection and/or enhancement of vital human interests. For example, anger is predicated upon protecting me and mine from being wronged. Insofar as the movie protagonists fall into the category "of mine," the moviemaking team will be able to arouse our anger against those who wrong *our protagonists* by foregrounding the harms and impediments inflicted on those on our side—that is, by realizing the criteria appropriate to anger in such a way that they stand out, usually unmistakably.

Think of the beating that Ransom Stoddard (Jimmy Stewart) is subjected to by Liberty Valance (Lee Marvin), from whom the film derives its name. Foregrounded are not only physical harms but the disrespect and humiliation delivered by an all but pathological sadist. In this way, John Ford and his team present us with a scene that meets the criteria of wrongness required by the emotion of anger in several respects. Of course, they have achieved this because they have designed the scene in order to do precisely this. They have *criterially prefocused* it—they designed the scene so that the criteria requisite to the mobilization of anger were intentionally built into the scene in a way that couldn't be missed.

Criterially Prefocusing Admiration

Admiration is a euphoric, (occurrent) emotion. It appraises the particular objects of its attention as worthy of respect, as esteemed, as excellent, as deserving of approval or approbation. Where the admiration is moral, it is directed at virtues, good deeds, dutiful, and supererogatory behaviors, heroism for the sake of a good cause, and/or entire upright lives. Moral admiration involves a feeling;[14] it is inspiring; with respect to moral admiration, some have labeled the feeling "elevation" (Haidt 2003).

Since the criteria of appropriateness for admiration are worthiness, excellence, and approbativeness, in order to elicit admiration moviemakers must criterially prefocus characters whose personality traits, behaviors, ambitions, actions, and/or ways of being in the world satisfy those criteria.[15] In order to make this less abstract, let me present some examples from the 2019 adaptation of *Little Women* by Greta Gerwig.

Gerwig's film was both a critical and a popular success, garnering six Academy Award nominations and a take of 218.8 million dollars. It was an adaptation of a book that has never been out of print, that has been adapted for the big screen at least five times, for American television 12 times, by the BBC as a miniseries, and as a 48-episode anime version in Japan. Much seen, the book has been much loved and influencing, as the following women have testified: Simone de Beauvoir, Doris

Lessing, Cynthis Ozick, Susan Sontag, A. S. Byatt, Margaret Atwood, Nora and Delia Ephron, Barbara Kingsolver, Jane Smiley, Anne Tyler, Mary Gordon, Jhumpa Lahiri, Stephanie Meyer, Ursula Le Guin, and the writer (whoever she may be) in Elena Ferrante's *My Beautiful Friend*. Admittedly, these are all authors, but in my unscientific experience, a great many of the nonwriting women I've known also admire the "little women," most notably Jo March.[16]

Gerwig deviates from the original novel in a number of important respects. She makes the relation between Jo March and Louisa May Alcott effectively transparent. The film is, among other things, about becoming a writer. Unlike the novel, it begins with Jo standing outside a publisher's office, mustering up her courage to enter, followed almost immediately by a flashforward insert to a window display of a copy of *Little Women*. And the film ends with Jo overseeing the printing of the book and its appearance, once again, in a display window.[17]

In addition, like the real unmarried author, Louisa May Alcott, and unlike Jo in the published version, Jo is not clearly married to Professor Bhaer in Gerwig's film. That is, Gerwig avoids giving us visual evidence that Jo and Prof. Bhaer are wed, thereby allowing fans of the book to feel that a major defect of the original has been erased or, at least, dodged.

What is it that readers and viewers—writers and civilians alike—have admired so much for over 100 years? I think that it is fundamentally Jo's commitment to freedom, to be as she chooses, irrespective of social constraints—in particular irrespective of the social constraints that relegate women to certain roles rather than others, such as housewives and mothers rather than, say, writers. Jo is an example of how to live an admirable life, that is, a liberated life, which is, needless to say, one of the first orders of the business of ethics as classically conceived.

As in the novel and previous adaptations, Jo's commitment is criterially prefocused in the narrative and the dialogue. Gerwig has her say such things as "I love my liberty too much to give it up" in response to Laurie's marriage proposal. And she makes clear that this is to be understood against the backdrop of the cultural limitations that women are subjected to when she complains that women have minds, not just hearts, and that they're fit for more than love. This resistance—including undertaking to become a writer in a man's world—to dominant social norms, especially in the relevant sociohistorical contexts, is worthy of respect both in virtue of Jo's sense of justice and also of her fortitude. It shows both moral and personal resilience.

However, Gerwig does not merely tell us through speeches that Jo is committed to living free from the social bondage women suffer in Jo's world. She shows us as well. This is worked out visually in terms of Jo's *boyishness*—Jo's commitment to acting like a boy rather than being locked into playing out the prescribed social role of a girl.

To this end, for example, Gerwig criterially prefocuses Jo's athleticism. Jo is frequently shown running very energetically, as when she joyously bolts from the publisher's office, standing out from all the other pedestrians and especially from the demurely ambulating ladies. This is doubly admirable—not only for its moral rebelliousness but also for its demonstrable physicality. She's in great shape, exhibiting genuine marathon potential.

Likewise, Gerwig will have Saoirse Ronan, as Jo, playfully shove her sisters' and Laurie's shoulders as men joshingly do to express affectionate disbelief, thus behaviorally prefocusing the criterial theme of boyishness.[18] And she does this not only by gesture but also by costume. Note how the style of her hats is often male. In a number of shots, she wears a boy's hat that she has taken from Laurie; and when she negotiates her contract with her publisher for the book that we take to be *Little Women*, she wears a derby.[19] All these visual touches are designed to expand our admiration for Jo because they all have moral significance. They are, in a manner of speaking, icons of Jo's commitment to freedom as a woman in an environment where that requires courage, single-mindedness, and an ethical backbone—spiritual excellences or virtues all worthy of esteem and respect and criterially prefocused by Gerwig's narration, cinematic and otherwise.

At the same time that Jo is presented as an example of commitment to women's liberation, she is also invested with other admirable traits. She is self-sacrificing; for example, she sells her hair for 25 dollars so that her mother can go to Washington in order to minister to her wounded husband. She is very loving; consider her solicitude and caring for her sister Beth. She is charitable; she opens a school not only for privileged children but for orphans as well. By criterially prefocusing these virtues in the story, Gerwig, and Alcott before her, humanize Jo, presenting her not as a strident fanatic or saint but as a somewhat realistic example who can be admired and embraced by ordinary mortals.[20]

Undoubtedly, some will also want to add that the admiration we bestow on Jo and other heroic movie characters can be in large part attributed to the "halo effect"—our tendency to think that beautiful people are smarter and morally better simply on the grounds that they are prettier than the rest of us. Surely, this plays a role in popular movies. But it is easy to overestimate its effectiveness. Gregory Peck was probably at the height of his beauty when he played Lewt McCanles in *Duel in the Sun*, but I doubt anyone thought the character morally better or even just less ethically despicable for that.

By arousing the occurrent emotional state of moral admiration in viewers, criterial prefocusing contributes to our moral education by reinforcing and even potentially refining our powers of ethical discrimination insofar as the emotions are an important component of moral judgment. That is, criterial prefocusing may have the capacity to sustain through exercise and possibly expand our emotional intelligence.

Criterial prefocusing has this capability in part because of its selectivity. What it makes salient to the viewer are precisely the variables relevant to the intended emotion with minimal "clutter," in contrast to the "buzzing confusion" of everyday life. Furthermore, once the movie example prompts moral admiration, that very experience can become an occasion for reflection that we can use to clarify our moral understanding of what it is that is so worthy of such admiration. That is, what is it in Jo's behavior that is so excellent that it is worthy of admiration?

Moreover, the condition of movie viewing itself also makes the elicitation of the pertinent emotion frictionless because we typically have no personal interests to interfere with our assessment of what is on screen. I don't have to worry about being punched in the nose if I side with the protagonist in a fist fight. Or, with reference to *Little Women*, I don't have to fear being regarded as a social outcast if I endorse Jo's one-woman campaign for emancipation.

Nevertheless, one reason to suspect the approach that I have been recommending is to object that my account of admiration with regard to movie examples is unacceptable because what I am talking about is not really an emotion. Emotions are appraisals that cause feeling states *and* that typically motivate behaviors that are appropriate to realizing the opportunities or avoiding the impediments highlighted by the emotion in question. But it does not appear that the moral admiration of movie examples motivates any behaviors.

One reason for that is fairly obvious. There is rarely, if any, an opportunity to act on our emotions, moral or otherwise, while we are watching the movie. I can't do anything to stop the onslaught of Darth Vader and his storm troopers or to help Jo get published. Moreover, usually the motivating force of an occurrent emotion is short-lived, and it is rare that in the immediate aftermath of a movie, one will encounter a situation that might invite us to emulate our movie example.[21]

Furthermore, as already mentioned, movie examples tend to be very rarefied in terms of the number of variables they involve. Actual examples are more complex, thereby making them difficult to straightforwardly model. This may be especially the case inasmuch as in the course of daily affairs emulating the example may provoke conflicts between the values being exemplified and our own personal interests.

For these reasons, and probably more, it may seem doubtful that the admiration of movie examples will motivate behavior. But if they don't typically motivate behavior, are they really emotions?

I don't think that this anxiety is justified, and not only because it is not always and necessarily the case that emotions motivate behavior.[22] Another reason has to do with the limited notion of "behavior" that the worry presumes. I think admiration for a moral movie example may engender certain behavioral dispositions. The first is simply that we may agree with what the example exemplifies and make reference to it in subsequent conversations and arguments. We may affirm the kind of rights to a more liberated horizon of choices that Jo represents, and we may use her as an example of how women should be treated in disagreements, for instance, with older, more traditional family members.

We may become more likely to endorse and recommend the traits that Jo exemplifies.[23] We may commend Jo's modus vivendi. Agreeing, endorsing, commending, recommending, and so on are behaviors. Moreover, in doing so, we will be emulating the example's behavior, even though we are jogging a lot less than Jo does.

Also, as psychologists have pointed out, viewers may choose to watch the movie again as a form of endorsement, or to recommend that others see the movie, or even share the movie for the purpose of enabling others to admire the example (Oliver

2021; Eden and Grizzard 2021). For example, you may loan your DVD of Gerwig's *Little Women* to a friend or neighbor in order to reinforce, affirm, consolidate, or spread a communally shared, ethical feeling. All these are behaviors, even if they are not as demonstrative as fleeing from an oncoming bear.

Virtue Wheels

Criterial prefocusing is a key strategy for eliciting audience-admiration for the relevant moral examples. Deploying virtue wheels is a particularly effective way of securing criterial prefocusing through the design of the characters as the narrative unfolds. It is not a necessary supplement to the aforementioned strategies of criterial prefocusing, but it is a very frequent one—so frequent that it deserves special comment.

What is a virtue wheel? What I have in mind is the systematic design of characters for the purpose of inviting comparisons and contrasts between them in terms of their virtues (and vices). For instance, consider Kant's contrast between the moral man and the prudent man in regard to making change. And for a movie example, recall how in *The Man in the Gray Flannel Suit*, the character Tom Rath (Gregory Peck)[24] is contrasted with his boss, Ralph Hopkins (Fredric March), as a man who values family over ambition in business. This contrast is marked in a number of different ways. One way in which Rath's choice is signaled as the better (more virtuous) one is by the fact that in the fiction Hopkins loses his daughter's affections—something that causes him manifest pain and distress—while Rath joyously incorporates a new member into his family, an illegitimate son whom he fathered while he was at war (World War II) in Italy. This contrast, which is emphatically built into the evolving narrative, makes salient one of the virtues of the example, Tom Rath in this case, which the audience is intended to admire.[25]

The use of the virtue wheel is a special way of criterial prefocusing, even though other strategies of criterial prefocusing can function without it. Nevertheless, virtue wheels are extremely pervasive. Notice that in most fiction movies—indeed, in most narratives—the protagonist is being contrasted to the antagonist in terms of a salient package of virtues versus a salient package of vices. But in many cases, the comparison/contrast structure is much more complex.

For a complex deployment of the virtue wheel, consider the film *Parenthood*, which was directed by Ron Howard and written by Lowell Ganz and Babaloo Mandel.[26] The film is—as its title advertises—about parenting. In all, five generations of the Buckman family of St. Louis make an appearance; two generations are of particular importance—the generation of Frank Buckman and his wife—and the generation of their children: Gil, Helen, Susan, and Larry. Each of Frank's children have children of their own. Thus, the viewer has five different styles of parenting before her, ripe for comparison and contrast, notably: Frank's, Gil's, Helen's, Susan's, and Larry's.[27]

Furthermore, the relevant dimension which this structure foregrounds, as the title advertises, is ultimately parenthood, which, in light of what is made salient by the virtue wheels' criterial prefocusing, is to be understood in terms of who is the best parent, or who best exemplifies excellence in parenting. That is, which parent is most worthy of our admiration?

The worst parent is obviously Larry Buckman. He effectively ignores his child Cool throughout the film. In this, Larry Buckman reflects some of the parental defects that his father Frank exhibited in raising Gil. Once a year Frank would bring Gil to a baseball game only to abandon him to the care of a ballpark usher. Although never as neglectful as Larry and, by the end of the film, mindful of his mistakes, Frank is also an instance of bad parenting. He is never as bad as Larry, but, like Larry, he exemplifies selfishness as a cardinal parental vice.

Next, moving up from the bottom of this ladder of parenting types are Susan and her husband, Nathan Huffner. Actually, Nathan is the real problem here. Their daughter Patty is very bright. For that reason, Nathan decides to turn her into a prodigy. He occupies all of her time with mental exercises in math, languages, history, and physical exercises such as exotic martial arts disciplines—basically, you name it. He turns her life into a 24/7 training routine comprised of improving and edifying activities. Nathan is not neglectful, but he is also selfish, vicariously attempting to realize his own wishes through his daughter at the expense of her having a normal childhood.

Gil tries to be a good parent. But his own self-centered worries about whether he is one and whether he is causing the same anxieties he suffers in his son Kevin that his father Frank engendered in him only succeed in making Kevin more and more nervous. That is, Gil's preoccupations with his own performance anxieties infect Kevin detrimentally. Kevin is even more neurotic than Gil.

What about Helen? Initially she seems like the least likely candidate for the title of good parent. Due to her divorce, she appears to be an existential wreck. She is distracted and scatterbrained. Her relationships with her two children—her daughter Julie and her son Gary—are very rocky, at least when we first meet the family. However, over the course of the film, I think most viewers come to recognize Helen as the most admirable example of parenthood.

Why? When contrasted to the other parents, Helen is the most unselfish. She has the capability to see her children as autonomous and independent individuals, with their own wishes, desires, reasons, interests, and needs. Helen displays a willingness to accommodate her children's legitimate projects for self-realization even when they are at odds with Helen's own hopes and expectations. She supports what they are doing, even if it is not what she planned for them.

This is most evident in Helen's acceptance of her daughter Julie's marriage to Todd Higgins, the object of Helen's utmost disdain in the earlier segments of the film. Helen wanted Julie to go to college rather than becoming a mother. It is Helen's ability to adapt and adjust to her children's needs, desires, and autonomous endeavors that stands in sharp contrast to the tendencies toward selfishness, vicarious projection, and self-preoccupation exhibited by the other representatives of parenthood in the film.

This array of parenting styles functions like a display of the adjacent colors on a color wheel. Here the contrast of various shades of parenting operate in such a way that one stands out as the best, most admirable example.[28]

In this manner, the very design of the cast of characters, as set in motion by the narrative, criterially prefocuses the target of our admiration in such a way that we may reflect upon our emotional response after the film in order to isolate the ground of our emotion in a way that can yield moral understanding insofar as our emotional response in this case enables the disclosure of one of the most important virtues of parenting.

Summary

In this essay, I have proceeded under the assumption that the emotions and moral understanding are intimately connected (Damon and Colby 2015, 72).[29] This is so in at least two senses. With respect to movies, first, the moral emotions are put through their paces by the examples to which audiences are exposed, thereby reinforcing and sometimes expanding and refining our emotional intelligence (construed as a discriminatory power) with regard to the ethical domain. And second, our emotional responses to the moral examples exhibited in movies can become upon reflection objects of self-examination that can disclose to us the reasons for and/or causes of our reactions either during or subsequent to the screening, during what Peter Kivy elegantly calls its "afterlife," which we may pursue on our own or with others (1997).

In trying to identify the recurring source of our responses to the positive ethical examples we encounter in movies, I hypothesized that admiration rather than identification is the most frequent means that examples recruit in order to engage viewers morally. I then attempted to specify as crucial to this process the operation of criterial prefocusing, of which the virtue wheel represents a particularly effective recurring instance of foregrounding moral/affective affordances.

Although I have focused on positive examples of how criterial prefocusing engages audience emotions morally, it should be evident that the same strategies can be mobilized for negative effect. Evil examples can be invested with admirable affordances—the Nazi commandant can be cloaked in apparent virtues such as courageousness and selflessness. Thus, admiration can be exploited by moviemakers for good or for ill. Admiration is an indispensable lever of our moral engagement with the movies. However, a happy ending is never guaranteed.[30]

Notes

1. I use the notion of "rhetoric" in the chapter title because of its association with "persuasion." I do not mean to suggest that the strategies that I am about discuss are solely linguistic or reducible to linguistic models. Alternatively, they might be described as "devices" or "mechanisms," although that risks sounding too deterministic. Also, I prefer in general to talk about "examples" rather than "exemplars" insofar as the latter may suggest persons, like Christ, who are perfect in every way. Moral examples in movies need be only partially

exemplary; they can come with flaws as well as virtues. Moreover, although I will be primarily focusing on characters as the most relevant site of exemplification, most of what I have to say can be modified to discuss other phenomena as examples, including actions, moods, attitudes, stances, ways of life, and personality traits, and so on.

2. Sometimes these stories would suggest models of the way in which to acquire the moral victories in question through their narratives, such as John Bunyan's *The Pilgrim's Progress* ([1678] 2003). Susan Haack (2008) proposes Samuel Butler's *The Way of All Flesh* as an example of this in her article "The Ideal of Intellectual Integrity in Life and Literature," in her book *Putting Philosophy to Work: Inquiry and Its Place in Culture: Essays on Science, Religion, Law, Literature and Life* (Amherst: NY: Prometheus Books, 2008), 183–208.

    According to Linda Trinkaus Zagzebski (2017, 66), narratives are the primary way in which cultures transmit examples.

3. Throughout I will be referring to "motion pictures" or "movies," by which I do not mean to be referring to just film or cinema narrowly construed, but to every sort of moving image practice, including not only film, but broadcast television, cable television, video, CGI, and comparable moving image technologies yet to be invented.

4. The frameworks presented in this paper are in no way movie-specific. They can be found across the gamut of fictional narratives. In fact, the use of examples for the purpose of moral instruction also obtains in nonfiction narration. See, for example, Brooks (2015).

5. Although I think that admiration is key to the promotion of moral understanding, I do not think that it is the only channel of communication for soliciting moral learning through the moving image.

6. Although I rarely agree with Gilles Deleuze and Félix Guattari (1996), I do concur with their proposal that at least one office of philosophy is the creation of new concepts when needed. *Criterial prefocusing* is such an attempt.

7. The desire to become someone else by its very nature presupposes a discrepancy between the aspirant and the object of his or her aspiration.

8. This is not to deny that movies have many other channels of emotional address, including music, lighting, environments, etc.—both natural and constructed—and sound effects. Nevertheless, it seems to me that character engagement is the primary source of the audience's emotional response to the typical narrative, fiction movie. Often those other channels of communication are designed to amplify character engagement.

9. Here it may be asked, "Isn't the fact that our emotions are similar enough to warrant calling the phenomenon 'identification'?" But from my perspective, why invoke *identity* when you mean *similarity*?

10. Here I want to be clear that the kind of emotion that I am discussing is moral admiration. "Admiration" is a term that can be applied to many situations. Not all are emotional. Some may be dispassionate, bereft of feelings, like my admiration of the deduction of a theorem. However, in this essay, I am talking about the kind of admiration of moral examples that is frequently—most frequently?—accompanied by feelings, specifically feelings of inspiration, where "inspiration" is understood as at least a feeling state. As such, this species of moral admiration is an occurrent emotion.

    It should not seem strange to argue that *certain* states of admiration are emotions. Look at the behavior of the audience when they witness an athlete break a record and their response is to stand up cheering; interview them afterward about the phenomenology of their response.

11. For a fuller account of this topic, see Carroll (2008, 147–191).

12. Henceforth, by "emotion," I will mean "occurrent emotion," unless otherwise indicated.

13. For our purposes, we need not enter this debate.

14. In this I differ from admiration theorists, like Antti Kauppinen (2019), who take the object of admiration to be directed only at the whole person.

15. Earlier I asserted that emotions are linked to protecting or enhancing our vital human interests. Some may wonder exactly what vital human interest moral admiration protects or enhances. On my view, moral admiration functions toward securing our need, as social animals, to belong to an ethical community—a community wherein we share notions of what counts as right and wrong, as permissible and impermissible, as virtue and vice, and so on, if only for coordination purposes. This requires a process of education that initiates, refines, and reinforces the construction and sustaining of said ethical community, and this process relies fundamentally upon examples designed to inspire moral admiration. Thus, moral admiration contributes to social harmony or, at least, to social order.

    It should come as no surprise that the emotions are connected to sociality. Aristotle acknowledges the moral dimension of the emotions when he defines anger in terms of *wrongs* done to me or mine. Here he is talking about justice which is an essentially social concept.

16. Information about the book *Little Women* in this essay is derived primarily from Rioux (2018) and Acocella (2018). Acocella (2020) also discusses Gerwig's film. The book *Little Women* was published in two parts in 1868 and 1869 by Roberts Brothers.

17. Throughout, Gerwig departs from Alcott's linear narration and, via editing, moves freely through space and time in order to criterially prefocus what is emotionally at sake. For example, by beginning as she does, Gerwig signals the centrality of Jo's ambition to be a writer and the gumption involved in pursuing it.

18. Of course, this theme is also made explicit in the dialogue, when characters like Meg point it out.

19. Even more subtle are the contrasts between Jo's attire and her sisters'—theirs, especially Amy's, feature more ribbons and frills; Jo's, more tweeds.

20. Gerwig, like Alcott but unlike previous film adaptations, provides more coverage of the courtships and marriages of Meg and Amy than do the previous, extant American movies. I suspect that one reason for this is in order to avoid alienating women readers who are less attracted to Jo's modus vivendi and more to married life. To that end, Gerwig gives us three examples of admirable marriages—Meg's, Amy's, and, of course, Marmee's.

    Some readers may wonder why I have not adduced as examples cinematic representations of Jesus. The reason is that in the mainstream movies in which Jesus appears he is more often than not the object of awe rather than admiration. Frequently he is presented offscreen and supported by music as if he is a hierophant too magnificent to behold.

21. Indeed, in many cases, even if the occasion did arise, it might be well beyond our powers to emulate the behavior of the moral examples whom we admire. Without Wonder Woman's extraordinary abilities, no viewer can hope to emulate the pacifying techniques that she deploys in order to quell violence, however laudable we find them.

22. For example, as an academic, I am sad that the great library of Alexandria was destroyed, but it does not move me to do anything about it.

23. One feature of admiration is a tendency to affirm normative support. We certainly can do that with respect to a movie. That is, we endorse the character's commitments. On normative support, see Grahle (2019).

24. Peck was an actor suited to function in the way he does in *Man in the Gray Flannel Suit* insofar as critical to his star persona was frequently that of being a decent man struggling with a difficult moral choice. Though sometimes overlooked, casting can function expressively. For further discussion of star personae, see Carroll (2013a, 2013b).

25. Rath has other virtues—like honesty—that are made salient by means of other characterological contrasts. I call this strategy "virtue *wheels*" on an analogy with color wheels, where different colors are individuated by putting them next to contrasting ones.

26. I was led to this example by Joseph F. Kupfer's (1999, 91–122) excellent treatment of the film in his fine book *Visions of Virtue in Popular Film*.

27. Todd, although not yet a parent, might also be considered as figuring in the virtue wheel insofar as he is a mentor to Garry. In this he contrasts favorably with Nathan in his commitment to treating Gary in an age-appropriate way, and he contrasts with Gil by not infecting Gary with any freighted, psychological baggage.

28. For further discussion of virtue wheels, see Carroll (2002). This article is reprinted in my anthology *Art in Three Dimensions* (Carroll 2010, 201–234). Nowadays I would prefer to speak of "moral learning" rather than "moral knowledge."

29. For further discussion of ideals, see Nicholas Rescher (1992).

30. I am very grateful to Nicholas Wolterstorff, Carl Plantinga, and the members of the Screen Stories and Moral Understanding Seminars for their comments on this chapter. I am especially indebted to Joan Acocella for her suggestions while I was writing this essay. However, I alone am responsible for its mistakes.

Works Cited

Acocella, Joan. 2018. "Ladies' Choice: What Gives *Little Women* Its Lasting Power?" *New Yorker*, August 27.

Acocella, Joan. 2020. "What's Lost and Gained in a Modern *Little Women*." *newyorker.com*, last modified February 7.

Brooks, David. 2015. *The Road to Character*. New York: Penguin Random House.

Bunyan, John. (1678) 2003. *The Pilgrim's Progress*. Mineola, NY: Dover.

Carroll, Noël. 2002. "The Wheel of Virtue: Art, Literature, and Moral Knowledge." *Journal Aesthetics and Art Criticism* 60, no. 3: 3–26.

Carroll, Noël. 2008. *The Philosophy of Motion Pictures*. Oxford: Blackwell.

Carroll, Noël. 2010. *Art in Three Dimensions*. Oxford: Oxford University Press.

Carroll, Noël. 2013a. "Character, Social Information, and the Challenge of Psychology." In *Minerva's Night Out: Philosophy, Pop Culture, and Moving Pictures*, edited by Noël Carroll, 64–81. Malden, MA: Wiley Blackwell.

Carroll, Noël. 2013b. "The Problem with Movie Stars." In *Minerva's Night Out: Philosophy, Pop Culture, and Moving Pictures*, edited by Noël Carroll, 106–121. Malden, MA: Wiley Blackwell.

Damon, William, and Anne Colby. 2015. *The Power of Ideals: The Real Story of Moral Choice*. Oxford: Oxford University Press.

Deleuze, Gilles, and Félix Guattari. 1996. *What Is Philosophy?* Translated by Hugh Tomlinson and Graham Burchell. New York: Columbia University Press.

Eden, Allison, and Matthew Grizzard. 2021. "Mechanisms of Moral Engagement via Character Effects on Moral Understanding." Paper presented at Screen Stories and Moral Understanding Seminars, February 11.

Edmundson, Mark. 2015. "Ancient Ideals." In *Self and Soul: A Defense of Ideals*, edited by Mark Edmundson, 19–134. Cambridge, MA: Harvard University Press.

Grahle, André. 2019. "Admiration as Normative Support." In *The Moral Psychology of Admiration*, edited by Alfred Archer and André Grahle, 149–164. London: Rowman and Littlefield International.

Haack, Susan. 2008. "The Ideal of Intellectual Integrity in Life and Literature." In *Putting Philosophy to Work: Inquiry and Its Place in Culture: Essays on Science, Religion, Law, Literature and Life*, edited by Susan Haack, 183–208. Amherst, NY: Prometheus Books.

Haidt, Jonathan. 2003. "Elevation and the Positive Psychology of Morality." In *Flourishing, Positive Psychology and the Life Well-Lived*, edited by C. L. M. Keyes and J. Haidt, 275–289. Washington, DC: American Psychological Association.

Kauppinen, Antti. 2019. "Ideals and Idols: On the Nature and Appropriateness of Agential Admiration." In *The Moral Psychology of Admiration*, edited by Alfred Archer and Andre Grahle, 29–44. Lanham, MD: Rowman and Littlefield.

Kivy, Peter. 1997. "The Laboratory of Fictional Truth." In *Philosophies of Art: An Essay in Differences*, edited by Peter Kivy, 121–139. New York: Cambridge University Press.

Kupfer, Joseph. 1999. *Visions of Virtue in Popular Film*. Boulder, CO: Westview Press.

Olberding, Amy. 2012. *Moral Exemplars in the Analects: The Good Person Is That*. London: Routledge.

Oliver, Mary Beth. 2021. "Morality and Media: The Role of Elevation/Inspiration." Paper presented at Screen Stories and Moral Understanding Seminars, February 13.

Plato. 1971. *Republic*, Books 2 and 3. In *Critical Theory since Plato*, edited by Hazard Adams, 19–32. New York: Harcourt Brace Jovanovich.

Rescher, Nicholas. 1992. *Ethical Idealism: An Inquiry into the Nature and Function of Ideals*. Berkeley: University of California Press.

Rioux, Anne Boyd. 2018. *Meg, Jo, Beth, Amy: The Story of* Little Women *and Why It Still Matters*. New York: Norton.

Warnick, Bryan R. 2015. *Imitation and Education: A Philosophical Inquiry into Learning by Example*. Albany: State University of New York Press.

Zagzebski, Linda Trinkaus. 2017. *Exemplarist Moral Theory*. Oxford: Oxford University Press.

PART V

THE REFLECTIVE AFTERLIFE

11
Audiences' Role in Generating Moral Understanding

Screen Stories as Sites for Interpretative Communities

James Harold

In debates over artistic interpretation, the idea that the audience has a significant role to play in determining a work's meaning is a familiar, if contentious, one. Since at least Roland Barthes (1977), scholars have taken seriously the notion that the audience member can play an active role in fixing the meaning (or at least *a* meaning) of an artwork. However, in the discussions that take place around moral learning in art, the audience's role in determining the meaning of the work is often ignored.[1] The audience is usually portrayed as a passive recipient of the moral perspectives taken up by the artwork itself, or perhaps by the artist. That is, the meaning is there to be discovered, already fully formed, in the artwork, and thus the moral learning proceeds from artwork to audience: the artwork serves as the teacher, and the audience as learner.

In this chapter, I explore the role that audiences can play in generating moral understanding from screen stories. The chapter is in three parts. In the first part, I review Jacqueline Bobo's study of Black women audience members' response to Steven Spielberg's 1985 film *The Color Purple*. I treat this as a case study of what bell hooks calls "the oppositional gaze": some Black women understood this film in ways quite different from what we might think of as the standard or proper interpretation, and these ways can be morally significant. I argue that the interpretation that Bobo's subjects offered has greater potential for positive moral understanding than the standard critical interpretation. It follows that screen stories that might be morally flawed can nonetheless be valuable aids in promoting moral understanding.

In the second part, I consider an objection to this as an account of moral understanding. If the meanings that give rise to moral understanding originate from the audience, how is it that the audience could be said to have *gained* moral understanding from the movie? Wouldn't the audience need already to have the understanding in question before they watched? I consider some possible responses before turning to a different approach, emphasizing the importance of developing new imagined versions of these stories in interpretative communities.

In the third part, I consider the role of audiences as communities making moral meanings together, including meanings that are not "in" the original artwork.

James Harold, *Audiences' Role in Generating Moral Understanding* In: *Screen Stories and Moral Understanding*. Edited by: Carl Plantinga, Oxford University Press. © Oxford University Press 2023. DOI: 10.1093/oso/9780197665664.003.0012

Drawing on Bobo's research, I discuss how audience members can coordinate with one another to generate oppositional readings of artworks. This opens up the possibility of moral understanding coming about in a new way—through different audience members learning from one another's insights and building moral understanding together. This leaves us with more interesting questions to be explored. I end with three questions about screen stories as sites for moral learning that I think deserve further discussion.

The upshot of the chapter is to emphasize a different way of thinking of the role of screen stories and moral understanding: that screen stories might serve as a *site* at which moral understanding takes place rather than as a *source* of moral understanding.[2] Given that moral activity is itself social and relational, it seems appropriate that the sources of moral understanding could be as well.

The Color Purple and the Oppositional Gaze

Steven Spielberg was a controversial choice to direct an adaptation of Alice Walker's 1982 Pulitzer Prize–and National Book Award–winning novel, *The Color Purple*. There were many reasons given for doubting whether Spielberg was the right director for this film, including his reputation for telling sentimental and crowd-pleasing stories, neither of which describe Walker's novel. Principally, however, the choice was controversial because of who Spielberg is: a straight white man. He was adapting a story written by a queer Black woman, and many questioned his ability to adapt this book in a way that would capture what made the novel so meaningful and impactful in the first place. Further, Spielberg made numerous significant changes to Walker's original novel, including reducing the long-term, loving, sexual relationship between Shug and Celie in the novel to a single kiss in the film.

The film *The Color Purple* follows Celie (played as an adult by Whoopi Goldberg) from her life as a teenage girl at the hands of the rapist she thinks is her father, to her forced marriage to the man she calls Mister (played by Danny Glover), who is also physically abusive. She is forcibly separated first from her children and later from her sister, Nettie (played by Akosua Busia). The story unfolds over several decades, showing Celie's learning to stand up for herself through her developing relationships with other women, especially a Blues singer named Shug (played by Margaret Avery), with whom she shares a deep connection, and her stepson's ex-wife, Sofia (played by Oprah Winfrey). The film ends with Celie leaving Mister, inheriting her family home, and being reunited with her sister and her children.

White film critics mostly offered praise for Spielberg's adaptation—Roger Ebert (1985) named it the best film of the year—and it was nominated for dozens of awards. However, Black film critics were less kind. Many Black critics noted important moral flaws in the film's portrayal of its Black characters (see Wilson 1986; Pinckney 1987). For example, Manthia Diawara (1993) argued that Spielberg's film takes up an attitude toward Blackness, and specifically toward the idea of the Black man, that expresses and reinforces dangerous prejudices. It does not particularly matter whether Spielberg consciously intended to put these attitudes and ideas in the film; indeed, there is reason to think that he did not do so intentionally. However, regardless of Spielberg's intentions, these racist attitudes, Diawara points out, are there in the film, and they constitute moral flaws.[3]

If the foregoing is right (and Diawara is far from alone in reading the film this way), then *The Color Purple* would not seem to be a fruitful film for promoting moral understanding. Even if the film were to have some moral virtues, it would also have numerous very serious moral flaws, and so the film would seem more likely to lead to moral error than to insight.

However, one might call into question Diawara's interpretation. It might be wrong, or, more interestingly, it might be one of a larger set of acceptable interpretations of the film. Our views about critical interpretation will constrain our views about what moral understandings a screen story can offer.[4] Disagreements about critical interpretation are deep and serious. While critical monists will insist that there can be only one correct interpretation of the work—so Diawara's view is either the correct one or it is not—critical pluralists argue that more than one interpretation might be acceptable. I will not here try to argue for critical pluralism. Others have done this ably (e.g., Stecker 1997). In what follows, I simply assume for the sake of argument that multiple acceptable interpretations, including interpretations not endorsed or foreseen by the artists, are possible.

In this case, the most important type of alternative, audience-generated interpretation for these purposes is what bell hooks famously called "the oppositional gaze"[5] (1992). hooks is interested in the problem of how Black women are portrayed in popular media—mainly in television and Hollywood movies. Her focus is on popular artworks in visual media (primarily film and television) that feature a Black female character whose agency is compromised or artificially limited. She writes:

> Talking with Black women of all ages and classes, in different areas of the United States, about their filmic looking relations, I hear again and again ambivalent responses to cinema. Only a few of the Black women I talked with remembered the pleasure of race movies, and even those who did, felt that pleasure interrupted and usurped by Hollywood. Most of the Black women I talked with were adamant that they never went to movies expecting to see compelling representations of Black femaleness. They were all acutely aware of cinematic racism—its violent erasure of Black womanhood. (119)

hooks says that many Black women simply turn away from mainstream white screen stories, as they are unable to take any pleasure from the experience.[6] But others do engage with these stories, and hooks reports that she and other Black women often use what she calls the "oppositional gaze" to transform their experience of watching these movies and television shows. The oppositional gaze involves audience members generating their own interpretations and readings of these works. In gazing back at these works, she argues, Black women can take pleasure in the new versions of these stories that they imagine (119): "We do more than resist. We create alternative texts that are not solely reactions. As critical spectators, Black women participate in a broad range of looking relations, contest, resist, revision, interrogate, and invent on multiple levels" (128).

According to hooks, some Black women creatively construct new understandings of screen stories—understandings that enable them to engage more deeply with these works. In her research, Jacqueline Bobo demonstrated how Black women audiences engaged in just this sort of revision and interrogation in their understandings of Spielberg's *The Color Purple* (1993, 1995). Bobo herself, like Diawara and many other Black film critics, is quite critical of Spielberg's adaptation. Bobo argues that Spielberg's choice to structure the film as a "universal" melodrama (he uses Dickens's *Oliver Twist* as a motif in the movie) undermines the specificity and nuance of the characters as they are portrayed in the novel. She notes the melodramatic structure and the use of comic and even slapstick moments (such as Sofia's Looney Tunes–like punches that send victims flying) that punctuate and thereby undermine many of the most serious dramatic scenes. But Bobo's detailed interviews with two different sets of Black women reveal a different way of thinking about the film, one that makes the film more enjoyable for Black women viewers and that also offers a richer and more rewarding ethical vision.

Bobo (1995, 97–102) conducted two studies, one in December 1987 in California, and the other in October 1988 in the Pacific Northwest. The subjects, all Black women, were interviewed together. There were nine women in the first group and six in the second. The second interview was conducted while they were watching a videotape of the movie. All of the women in both groups had both read the book and already seen the movie, though some had read the book only *after* having seen the movie adaptation. The women were all adults, between the ages of 30 and 60. They had grown up in different areas of the country and had different levels of educational attainment. Some of them knew one another. These research subjects by and large greatly enjoyed and admired the film, but their enjoyment was facilitated by reading the film differently than professional critics and scholars like Bobo and Diawara do.

Here is an example from Bobo's analysis that demonstrates the oppositional reading that these subjects formed in response to the film. Over and over in Bobo's interviews, subjects reported seeing the characters as more fully fleshed out than they are shown to be on screen. Consider their discussion of the dinner scene near the end of the movie, in which Celie finally confronts Mister and announces that she is leaving him. The scene ends with Celie holding a knife to Mister's throat. The subjects reported their admiration for Celie's growth as a character over the course of the film, leading her to that point. One subject said:

I had different feelings all the way through the film, because first I was very angry, then I started to feel so sad I wanted to cry because of the way Celie was being treated. It just upset me, the way she was being treated and the way she was so totally dominated. But gradually, as time went on, she began to realize that she could do something for herself, that she could start moving and progressing, that she could start reasoning and thinking things out for herself. In the end I felt a little proud of her from the way she began and the way she grew. (Quoted in Bobo 1995, 104–105)

For Bobo, as for many other critics, the development of this character arc was undermined by other elements of the film. Bobo writes that "moments of power were juxtaposed with comic and severely caricatured segments" (1995, 105–106). She notes, however, that her research subjects were able to simply ignore the elements of the film that would have undermined the effectiveness of the character development if they had focused on them: "If a viewer could physically edit the film and remove the comic routines, as it appears that the women I interviewed did mentally, then the scene featuring the women at the dinner table becomes a pivotal and empowering moment in the film" (106).

Bobo's subjects posit a reading of the movie that makes it a morally richer film than the one that Spielberg made: "As much as [having a Black filmmaker direct the movie] may have made a significant difference, the effects of the existence of the film were still important. And black women's reactions to it were a crucial part of that effect even though their reactions were themselves criticized. However, this again emphasizes that the ability of an audience to negotiate their responses is as important as the acknowledgement of their skill in doing so" (1995, 131). So Bobo's study supports the idea that audiences can be agents in making moral meanings, and those moral meanings may be of greater value than those found in the work itself.

How Can This Be Learning?

This conclusion suggests an immediate objection, at least in the context of thinking about screen stories as sources of moral understanding. If, as Bobo argues, the skill in generating the moral understanding surrounding *The Color Purple* lies with those Black women who saw it, how can moral learning occur? The audience would be both the source and the recipient of the putative learning. One cannot learn what one already knows.

One possible answer to this objection comes from Noël Carroll, who claims that that this problem—that audiences can learn the moral messages that art teaches only if they already in some sense believe those messages—is in fact quite a general one. He writes, "[M]ost of the moral beliefs that we might be said to acquire from art are things we already know and which, in fact, we must bring to the text in order to understand it" (1998, 310). We don't learn truly new ideas from artworks, according to Carroll, for two reasons: (1) the only beliefs we can pick up from art are ones that we find familiar, and (2) we cannot even understand narratives unless we share the basic moral beliefs presumed by the work. So works of art cannot by themselves be sources of moral learning.

However, Carroll offers a solution to this problem. Moral learning can be recon-
ceived as an extension and deepening of our preexisting moral understanding; this is
what he calls "clarificationism." According to this view, art can allow us to see better
the potential applications of and connections between the beliefs we already have; it
can also help us to appreciate the value and meaning of what we already know. For example, we might say that Bobo's research subjects already knew about the possibility
of moral growth before watching the movie, but the movie helped them to put their
insights together so as to understand moral growth more clearly. Artworks like *The
Color Purple* can be sources of moral learning in helping us to apply and deepen the
moral insights that we already have.

While Carroll's account works in the cases that he has in mind, I'm not sure it will
do as a response here. The difficulty in cases where the audience generates an oppositional reading of the work is that the audience is doing even more, and the work (and
artist) even less, than in the traditional case. As Bobo points out, her research subjects
are engaging in the highly skilled activity of reconstructing a version of Spielberg's
film in which Celie's character develops in a powerful and morally compelling way.
Even the elements of the film that serve to clarify or apply moral ideas seem to be generated, in large part, by the work of the audience.

A second possible explanation comes from Peter Kivy. In his discussion of how
works of literature can be sources of moral learning, Kivy (1997) suggests that readers
play a critical role in generating moral learning through their active cognitive engagement with the work both during and after reading. On Kivy's view, the "afterlife" of
reading is that period of reflection and consideration that occurs when the audience
is no longer reading but is still turning over and considering the themes and ideas in
the book. Kivy argues that such an afterlife offers an opportunity for readers to "test
hypotheses" suggested by the work in their imagination, and thus to come to know
that a particular moral claim is true, or false, and so advance our moral knowledge.

Kivy's account allows that audiences perform skilled work during and after the experience of taking in a work of art, and that work is necessary for their moral learning.
This seems consistent with Bobo's report. However, Kivy's account falls short in two
respects. First, Kivy's account is quite narrow in how he supposes that learning can
come about: the work suggests a hypothesis, and the reader's role is to test that hypothesis. On Kivy's view, the reader is not generating new, oppositional interpretations of the work, but picking up on themes that are put there by the author—or,
at any rate, that are there in the work. So Kivy still gives less agency to the audience
than Bobo does. Second, Kivy neglects to discuss the important role that *communities*
of audiences play in generating new ideas. The process that Kivy imagines is rather
solitary, and the testing occurs inside the reader's head. Carl Plantinga and Garrett
Strpko (2022) extend and adapt Kivy's view in a way that incorporates the role of
communities.

Plantinga and Strpko take Kivy's notion of the reflective afterlife and add to it the
idea of individual audience members working collectively to reflect morally on the
moral ideas in the work. They make use of Wayne Booth's notion of "coduction," a

process of discussion and conversation by which moral ideas from an artwork are elaborated and developed, to illustrate the social nature of the reflective process (1988). Plantinga and Strpko write, "This promotion of moral reflection, negotiation, and understanding is just one of many potential benefits of film and television narrative. And it occurs not merely in relation to the films themselves, but as embedded in the constantly changing social and institutional practices of a culture" (2022, 126). This, I think, is the key notion—the notion of moral reflection as a social process. What is lacking in Plantinga and Strpko's account is the idea that audiences can engage in this activity based not only on the themes and ideas from the work itself but also on themes and ideas that emerge from *alternative versions* of these works that audiences create by working together.

The Role of Audience Communities

It is not an accident that Bobo conducted her interviews in groups rather than interviewing subjects singly. Bobo argues that Black women viewing and discussing films together constitute what she calls an *interpretative community*: "Black women's challenge to cultural domination is part of an activist movement that works to improve the conditions of their lives. . . . As a group, these women make up what I have termed an interpretive community, which is strategically placed in relation to cultural works that either are created by black women or feature them in significant ways. Working together the women utilize representations of black women that they deem valuable, in productive and politically useful ways" (1995, 22). This process resembles in part Plantinga and Strpko's conception of the reflective afterlife. But it goes further in one key respect. Bobo's research subjects use screen stories as raw material ("utilize representations") in a skilled activity that results in their creating something of political value: a new, morally potent reinterpretation of an existing work. The individual women work with one another, sharing insights, arguing with one another, and exchanging ideas. This is not to say that every member of the group comes away with the same interpretation or moral understanding of the film, but that the group discussion allows for one individual's insight or response to enrich and transform another's (and vice versa). This makes it possible for true moral learning to happen, even when the artwork itself is not the source of those insights. People learn from one another.

It is worth noting that while Bobo's study was designed in such a way as to create these interpretative communities, this does not invalidate her claims. The reason that Bobo constructed her study in this way was in order to model an authentic feature of the appreciation and enjoyment of screen stories as they happen in ordinary experience. Real audiences do form interpretative communities on their own: friends and family watch films and television shows together and discuss them. Appreciating screen stories is a deeply social experience.

Consider another exchange that Bobo reports, which shows different members of the group moving ideas forward collectively. Her research subjects are discussing a scene early in the film when, just after Mister has thrown Nettie off their property, Celie prepares to shave Mister. Mister grabs her arm and says, "You cut me, and I'll kill you." Bobo's subjects disagreed about whether Celie was thinking about harming Mister in that moment, and what it would mean if she had:

WHITNEY: She does think about it.

PHYLLIS: She thinks about cutting his throat, but she also thinks about the consequences of not killing him, which is another beating. Which is more abuse.

MORGAN: I don't think that in this particular scene she even really thought about cutting his throat.

PHYLLIS: She's thinking about it; she's thinking about it now. But she's a young girl. She doesn't realize that if she cuts his throat bad enough he's not going to be able to hurt her. All she's thinking is that if she cuts his throat and he survives she's going to have to suffer the consequences.

WHITNEY: She's thinking about it now.

PHYLLIS: Even if she nicks the man. [She pauses.] It takes a lot to come out of low self-esteem. It takes a lot.

WHITNEY: But not a whole lot to get in it.

PHYLLIS: Not a whole lot to get in it, you're right. All it takes is one word, one person, somebody that you think is supposed to be caring about you, somebody that you have the impression that they define who you are. And if they tell you enough times and they treat you enough like you don't mean anything, you begin to actually believe that. (Bobo 1995, 109)

In this exchange, Phyllis, Whitney, and Morgan (not their real names) begin by arguing about Celie's motivations—what Celie really means to do and what she is considering—and move from there to a more general discussion about the relationship between self-esteem, abuse, and betrayal. The moral learning that happens here happens between and among these women. The role of Spielberg's film is to be a site for this learning, not the source.

What do I mean by a "site" for moral learning? The idea is that screen stories can provide a destination where people can gather together and discuss the same story, characters, and themes. The screen story in question is in one sense passive—it does not generate moral learning, but it gives everyone a reason to talk about moral matters in the first place, and thus offers an opportunity for groups to collectively generate alternative works that can provide such learning. The screen story is in effect a kind of gathering place where interpretative communities can work.

There are a number of questions one can ask about treating screen stories as sites for interpretative communities to engage in moral learning rather than as sources of authoritative moral teachers. First, what does it take for a screen story to be a fruitful location for these interpretative communities? Will any screen story do? Second, what, if anything, guarantees that interpretative communities will tend to generate moral truths and insights rather than falsehoods and confusion? Third, what should we say about interpretative communities and aesthetics? Do such interpretative communities engage in art-making when they generate oppositional readings? Or, if the activity is not art-making, is it in the same family?

I am not going to offer a decisive answer to these three questions here. I will instead try out some ideas as proposals for future discussion. These are tentative suggestions about how those discussions might go.

1. Why was *The Color Purple*, with all of its flaws, such a rich and fruitful site for these interpretative communities? Bobo suggests that it was the existence of *The Color Purple* at that particular time and place. In the 1980s, a major Hollywood production with a nearly all-Black cast, based on a renowned literary work by a Black woman, was unprecedented. No Hollywood studio had offered anything like it before. It was not necessarily the film's aesthetic or filmic qualities but its source material, its historical and cultural context, and its influence that made *The Color Purple* a site where serious moral conversation could happen.

So here perhaps is a feature that would make certain screen stories more conducive to serving this role. Works that are the first, or among the first, to tell a certain kind of story or portray a certain kind of character may be particularly attractive ground for interpretative communities to work in. If there is an audience that has been waiting to hear a story about a group that is not usually represented on screen, at least not in mainstream, high-budget, wide-release movies, then the first stories of that time will likely be a source of intense attention and interest from that audience: think of the reception of films like *Personal Best* (1982),[7] *Brokeback Mountain* (2005), or *Crazy Rich Asians* (2018). As Paul Taylor (this volume) notes, movies that take up controversial topics "can occasion and sustain vibrant participatory exercises in the criticism of self and society." Even when the works are flawed (aesthetically, morally, or otherwise), pent-up demand for certain kinds of stories could generate not only interest and attention but also enthusiasm for rethinking and reimagining these works.

But this is not to say that other factors are irrelevant. In some cases, we may be drawn to particular screen stories not for their cultural and historical relevance but for their aesthetic virtues.[8] And when we encounter morally problematic or troubling materials in a work that is aesthetically admirable in some way, we might be tempted to become oppositional spectators and form some of these interpretative communities. Cynthia Freeland offers the example of Roman Polanski's 1974 film *Chinatown*. The film is in many ways a simply magnificent work of neo-noir, with its surprising, twisty plot, electric performances (especially from John Huston), and famous score. But it is also deeply racist in its portrayal both of Asian characters and of the idea of the "Orient" itself. So works like *Chinatown* might end up engendering some oppositional interpretations that push back against these racist elements, and the aesthetic virtues of *Chinatown* play a role in making it as generative as it is.[9]

One might suggest that technology makes a difference and that contemporary audiences making use of social media may be more inclined to form interpretative communities. It seems entirely plausible that technology has made an impact on interpretative communities, but technology does not tell the whole story. No doubt technology makes communication easier and quicker, but long before social media existed people were forming communities around artworks that excite them. I remember as a child growing up in the 1970s joining a *Star Wars* fan club. I was sent a monthly newsletter; I collected trading cards; I visited a local "hobby shop" to talk with new people and sometimes make new friends. I was able, in other words, to be part of a community with strangers whom I connected with only through our shared love for these movies.

There are likely other qualities that make some screen stories more attractive as sites for interpretative communities to create valuable oppositional readings as well; for example, perhaps the presence of preexisting groups and institutions that focus attention on particular types of screen stories makes a difference.[10] This is not an exhaustive list.

2. Why should we believe that the influence of interpretative communities on moral learning will be positive? The cases that Bobo studies (she also looks closely at Julie Dash's 1992 film *Daughters of the Dust*) are selected in part because they facilitated morally and politically rich interpretative processes. However, there seems to be no guarantee that this would be the usual result.

There are, in addition to Bobo's apparently rather admirable interpretative communities, other kinds of interpretative communities, including communities of what the television critic Emily Nussbaum has called "bad fans" (2014). The bad fan, Nussbaum says, "views antiheroes as heroes. The archetypal bad fan shrugs off any notion of moral complexity; he fast-forwards through arguments with the nagging wife and freeze-frames the bloody whackings." The bad fan is determined to experience a work according to *his* moral view of the world, not according to the work's own moral framework, and the bad fan's moral view of the world is not an admirable one.

According to Nussbaum, the first prominent example of the bad fan can been seen in the response to the 1970s television show *All in the Family*. The creator of *All in the Family*, Norman Lear, intended that his show would satirize the main character, Archie Bunker, and ridicule his bigotry and closed-mindedness. The first episode even included a warning during the opening credits about Archie's bigotry, calling Archie's prejudices "absurd."[11] However, Nussbaum notes, many fans did not respond to the character in that way at all. To them, Archie was not an absurd caricature but a refreshing truth-teller. They saw Archie and his racist views as triumphant, regardless of how the narrative itself attempted to shape viewers' responses. Nussbaum (2019, 44–45) cites a study by Vidmar and Rokeach that looked at these contrary responses: "In 1974, the social psychologists Neil Vidmar and Milton Rokeach offered some evidence for this argument in a study published in the *Journal of Communication* using two samples, one of teenagers, the other of adults. Subjects, whether bigoted or not, found the show funny, but most bigoted viewers didn't perceive the program as satirical. They identified with Archie's perspective, saw him as winning arguments, and, 'perhaps most disturbing, saw nothing wrong with Archie's use of racial and ethnic slurs' [Vidmar and Rokeach 1974, 42]."

Many of Nussbaum's other examples of bad fans are similar: for example, audience members who admire Tony Soprano from *The Sopranos* or Walter White from *Breaking Bad*. These are main characters we are meant to see as antiheroes (Vaage 2016), villains, or what A. W. Eaton has called "rough heroes" (2010). They are characters with rich, complex inner lives who often do and say terrible things. These shows mean for us to care about these characters but not to admire them as moral exemplars.[12] We are supposed to recognize and regret their moral flaws. However, in each case, the response of certain audience members has been to overlook those flaws or even reverse them, imagining these characters' vices as virtues. Bad fans reimagine these works so that what are significant moral failings appear to be virtues.

So bad fans would be like the mirror-image of Bobo's interpretative communities. Like Bobo's communities, bad fans mentally edit and reinterpret works, but they do so in ways that make the works morally worse, not better. And bad fans can also work in communities. There seems to be no reason to assume, in other words, that oppositional readings and communities of audiences will normally or mostly serve to generate positive moral learning. Oppositional readings might instead generate moral confusion and immoral distortion, or perhaps they will change nothing at all, morally speaking. Sometimes audiences gather and reimagine works not in order to bring out a change in the moral or political ideas in the work but rather to fix a "plot hole" or reimagine some morally neutral part of the narrative.[13]

There is, I think, an even deeper worry about the idea that interpretative communities will tend to produce interpretations of screen stories that are morally better than the originals. One reason for thinking that "good fans" are good is that they may have the perspective necessary to see moral issues more fully. This view gets support from standpoint epistemology, the view that people who are marginalized politically can achieve special moral insight not readily available to others (Hartsock 1983). The Black women audience members Bobo studied may then be able to produce a deeper and more revealing moral interpretation of the film precisely because of their race and gender.

However, this seems too simple. Recall that Bobo, Diawara, and many other Black critics did not share the views of Bobo's subjects. The question of what kind of interpretation of *The Color Purple* is best from a moral or political point of view is not an easy one to answer. The various subjects do not all agree with one another; some nonexpert subjects do not agree with professional critics; and in general the idea of a morally "best" interpretation is ill-defined and perhaps dubious. A different approach might be to follow Taylor's lead in his chapter in this volume. Taylor argues that there are two types of moral understanding: moral understanding as an epistemic problem (getting the moral facts right) and moral understanding as an appropriate relationship between ethical communities.[14] Taylor claims that the latter type of moral understanding is both harder and more important. Although it seems right to say that Bobo's subjects' reimagining of *The Color Purple* would represent greater moral understanding in the first, epistemic sense, than Spielberg's own flawed conception, it feels strange to rest with that conclusion. If Taylor is right, the more important task, and I think this is precisely what scholars like Bobo are trying to do, is to take the oppositional readings and the standard readings and bring them together and talk through the differences. Ethical understanding may be achieved through a process of negotiating between differing insights and interpretations.

3. Are these interpretative communities also *aesthetic* communities? Bobo describes what she calls "mental editing" that her research subjects engage in, and remarks on the skill required to do this interpretative work. There are numerous examples of fans actually producing, singly or as parts of communities, artworks: fan fiction, fan edits and re-edits of existing properties, and all kinds of art that are more tangentially related to the original, such as tattoos and paintings of characters. Some—though certainly not all—of these artworks, like many of the re-edits, are made with moral aims in mind. (And then there are the cases where fans, by virtue of letter-writing, petition, or other forms of collective pressure, actually get producers and directors to alter their plans for serial fictional works as they are being made.) Clearly some of these activities count as art-making. If someone paints a picture, or writes a story, or writes and produces an original episode of an existing television show (as has been done dozens of times by *Star Trek* fans), these clearly count as art-making activities, even if those activities are legally dubious for copyright reasons.

But what about the merely "mental edits" that Bobo describes? If interpretative communities don't engage in the material production of works but instead reimagine and reconceive works, should we recognize this "skilled activity" as a form of aesthetic activity? Bobo's subjects produce, we might say, a *conception* of *The Color Purple* that is importantly distinct from the original. But is producing a conception the same as producing an artwork? To answer this question would require doing some metaphysics, and those sympathetic to Collingwood (1938) might be quick to agree that art proper is the conception of the work and not the mere physical execution: the "mental edit" is the important part, not the material process that follows. This claim is of course a highly contentious one, and fortunately we do not need to settle it here.

The important question in front of us is not whether interpretative communities make art, but whether interpretative communities engage in aesthetic activity. Bobo rightly recognizes that interpretative communities do hard, important, creative work in their engagement with screen stories. This work deserves and rewards our attention. As Dominic McIver Lopes (2018) has recently argued, a wide variety of practices in and around the arts display and develop aesthetic skills.

What can we conclude from all of this? The aim of this chapter has been to explore an alternative to a common way of thinking about how screen stories offer moral lessons, one in which the audience plays a more active, even oppositional role in producing moral meanings. Interpretative communities that form around certain screen stories can produce original and exciting reinterpretations of screen stories. And those reinterpretations deserve to count, at least sometimes, as aesthetic achievements and as moral achievements. This fact points us toward some further interesting questions about the moral qualities of different interpretative communities and about the aesthetic significance of this interpretative work. There is clearly a great deal more to be said.

It is significant that when screen stories serve as sites and not merely sources of moral learning, they often do so through communities of audiences. This makes a certain amount of sense. Morality, whatever else it does, helps us to relate to one another well and respectfully. So it is fitting that improving and widening our moral vision should happen in conversation with one another. We can learn from screen stories, certainly. But we can also learn from one another, and screen stories can serve to offer a site where we can have that conversation.[15]

Notes

1. With some exceptions, as we will see later.
2. Which is not to deny that a single work could not possibly serve both roles, at least with respect to different moral phenomena. I suspect such cases would be rare, however. Thanks to Carl Plantinga for pressing me to clarify this matter.
3. There is a very difficult ethical problem in saying why such flaws would be morally salient. I favor a consequentialist approach (Harold 2020), but there are many different explanations.
4. Katherine Thomson-Jones (2012) argues this point eloquently. My argument here is indebted to her insights.
5. The discussion in this section builds on the discussion of the oppositional gaze in chapter 9 of my *Dangerous Art* (Harold 2020).
6. Robert Sinnerbrink has suggested, and I think this is right, that this inability to take any pleasure in such screen stories constitutes a kind of imaginative resistance (Gendler 2000). It is an interesting question why some audiences overcome this resistance through the oppositional gaze and others do not.
7. I am grateful to Cynthia Freeland for suggesting this example and for recommending the discussion of this film's impact in Ellsworth (1990). Ellsworth's analysis of the reception of *Personal Best* by lesbian audiences shares some striking similarities as well as differences with the reception of *The Color Purple* by Black women, as described by Bobo.
8. This line of thought, as well as the *Chinatown* example, come from Cynthia Freeland in her comments on a draft of this chapter, which was presented at the Screen Stories and Moral Understanding Seminar on April 16, 2021.
9. Some philosophers have argued that works of art with deep and serious moral flaws thereby have less aesthetic value. I have argued against this claim in chapter 8 of Harold (2020).
10. I am grateful to Carl Plantinga for this suggestion. See Plantinga and Strpko (2022) for further discussion of this idea.
11. The disclaimer said, "The program you are about to see is *All in the Family*. It seeks to throw a humorous spotlight on our frailties, prejudices, and concerns. By making them a source of laughter, we hope to show—in a mature fashion—just how absurd they are."
12. Murray Smith (1995) distinguishes between works that merely align us with characters and get us to see things from their point of view, and those that encourage what he calls allegiance with those characters, encouraging us to endorse their values.

13. I am grateful to Robert Sinnerbrink for emphasizing this point.
14. Taylor's (this volume) examples of ethical communities include those "in which women matter less than men and embracing the myth of America is more important than condemning the sexual violence and social death of slavery" and those "who are brought up short by the liberties that *Hamilton* takes with its historical figures and by its willingness to prioritize nationalism over decolonization."
15. I am very grateful to the other members of the Screen Stories and Moral Understanding Seminar for their comments and questions on an earlier draft of this chapter. I want to particularly thank Cynthia Freeland, Robert Sinnerbrink, and Carl Plantinga for their detailed comments and suggestions, which were too numerous to note individually here.

Works Cited

Barthes, Roland. 1977. "The Death of the Author." Translated by Stephen Heath. In Barthes, *Image, Music, Text*, 142–148. New York: Hill and Wang.
Bobo, Jacqueline. 1993. "Reading through the Text: The Black Woman as Audience." In *Black American Cinema*, edited by Manthia Diawara 272–287. New York: Routledge.
Bobo, Jacqueline. 1995. *Black Women as Cultural Readers*. New York: Columbia University Press.
Booth, Wayne. 1988. *The Company We Keep: An Ethics of Fiction*. Berkeley: University of California Press.
Carroll, Noël. 1998. *A Philosophy of Mass Art*. New York: Oxford University Press.
Collingwood, R. G. 1938. *The Principles of Art*. Oxford: Clarendon Press.
Diawara, Manthia. 1993. "Black Spectatorship." In *Black American Cinema*, edited by Manthia Diawara, 211–220. New York: Routledge.
Eaton, A. W. 2010. "Rough Heroes of the New Hollywood." *Revue Internationale de Philosophie* 64: 511–524.
Ebert, Roger. 1985. "Review: *The Color Purple*." December 20. https://www.rogerebert.com/reviews/the-color-purple-1985.
Ellsworth, Elizabeth. 1990. "Illicit Pleasures: Feminist Spectators and *Personal Best*." In *Issues in Feminist Film Criticism*, edited by Patricia Erens, 183–196. Bloomington: Indiana University Press.
Gendler, Tamar Szabó. 2000. "The Puzzle of Imaginative Resistance." *Journal of Philosophy* 97, no. 2: 55–81.
Harold, James. 2020. *Dangerous Art: On Moral Criticisms of Artworks*. New York: Oxford University Press.
Hartsock, Nancy. 1983. "The Feminist Standpoint: Developing the Ground for a Specifically Feminist Historical Materialism." In *Discovering Reality: Feminist Perspectives on Epistemology, Metaphysics, Methodology, and the Philosophy of Science*, edited by Sandra Harding and Merrill Hintikka, 283–310. Dordrecht: D. Reidel.
hooks, bell. 1992. "The Oppositional Gaze." In *Black Looks: Race and Representation*, edited by bell hooks, 115–131. Boston: South End Press.
Kivy, Peter. 1997. "The Laboratory of Fictional Truth." In *Philosophies of Arts: An Essay in Differences*, edited by Peter Kivy, 120–139. New York: Cambridge University Press.
Lopes, Dominic McIver. 2018. *Being for Beauty: Aesthetic Agency and Value*. New York: Oxford University Press.

Nussbaum, Emily. 2014. "The Female Bad Fan." *New Yorker*. October 17. https://www.newyor ker.com/culture/cultural-comment/female-bad-fan.

Nussbaum, Emily. 2019. "Norman Lear, Archie Bunker, and the Rise of the Bad Fan." In *I Like to Watch: Arguing My Way through the TV Revolution*, edited by Emily Nussbaum, 36–47. New York: Random House.

Pinckney, Darryl. 1987. "Black Victims, Black Villains." *New York Review of Books* 34, no. 1 (January 29): 17–20.

Plantinga, Carl, and Garrett Strpko. 2023. "Moral Reflection: On the Reflective Afterlife of Screen Stories." In *What Film Is Good For: On the Ethics of Spectatorship*, edited by Julian Hanich and Martin P. Rossouw, 117–127. Berkeley: University of California Press.

Smith, Murray. 1995. *Engaging Characters: Fiction, Emotion, and the Cinema*. New York: Oxford University Press.

Stecker, Robert. 1997. *ArtWorks: Definition, Meaning, Value*. University Park: Pennsylvania State University Press.

Thomson-Jones, Katherine. 2012. "Art, Ethics, and Critical Pluralism." *Metaphilosophy* 43, no. 3: 275–293.

Vaage, Margrethe Bruun. 2016. *The Antihero in American Television*. New York: Routledge.

Vidmar, Neil, and Martin Rokeach. 1974. "Archie Bunker's Bigotry: A Study in Selective Perception and Exposure." *Journal of Communication* 24: 36–47.

Wilson, Marti. 1986. "Taking the Color out of *Purple*." *Sojourner* 11, no. 6: 32–33.

12

On Reflecting on Reflections

The Moral Afterlife and Screen Studies

Wyatt Moss-Wellington

In the past, when acquaintances have asked me what I do for a living and I let them know I'm a film and media scholar, on occasion I've had the response, "There's a job for that?" Questions such as these can precipitate an interesting conversation. One of the challenges that will often come up is to define how the research we do is different from the work of film criticism or media journalism—especially when distinguishing hermeneutic and deep reading practices from reviews. While these endeavors and their value begin to feel intrinsic after many years steeped in the conversations of screen studies, it is still a demanding task to describe the different elaborative and reflective practices of each mode of writing, what sets humanities and social sciences research apart from the knowledge generated in other extended commentaries on screen stories, from journalism to fandom, and above all the value of long-term, immersive reflections on particular media qualities and trends.

Reflection does not occur simply because a story requests it. It is an invitation that must be seized, and cultures across the planet develop social systems with the function of taking up that invitation, elaborating back from stories to make explicit connections between their imaginative provocations and our lives. I have written in the past of this as taking up a story's "invitation to play" with its ideas (Moss-Wellington 2021b). In this chapter, however, I consider film and screen media scholarship as one of these reflective institutions comprising an important component in the moral afterlife of screen stories, realizing the impact of those stories across all manner of consequential contemplations, from classroom discussions and close hermeneutics to the empirical study of our many relationships with media narratives. In "screen media scholarship" then, I refer to a continuum of practices, including teaching, publishing, conferences, mentoring, and their co-relations. All of these scholarly practices involve a removal of barriers to reflection—and often moral reflection—to see what can be done with screen stories when we take that reflection as far as we can.

In this chapter, I argue that prolonging reflection on screen stories lends itself to a revisiting of one's moral judgments, an encountering of other moral perspectives emerging from other lifeworlds, and a consequent potential to enrich moral understanding—thence, a "moral afterlife" that is possible in taking up a story's invitation to "reflective afterlife." I survey existing research into the reflective afterlife

Wyatt Moss-Wellington, *On Reflecting on Reflections* In: *Screen Stories and Moral Understanding*. Edited by: Carl Plantinga,
Oxford University Press. © Oxford University Press 2023. DOI: 10.1093/oso/9780197665664.003.0013

of narrative media to see what it can illuminate about the reflective work of scholarly screen studies. I make a more general case that the reflective afterlife, as it exists in institutions that seek to learn what happens when we extend that afterlife as far as possible, need support. During a time in which humanities disciplines are being devalued, amalgamated, and defunded, we expound the historic benefits of reflection on art and narrative media, yet we also need new arguments surveying the impact of newer media—so the conversation and its rationale update themselves, and we cannot rely on historic accounts of the merit or value of humanistic study.

I concede that the imperative to explain and re-explain the value of knowledge and discovery in the humanities and social sciences is not always productive. It has been a mainstay neoliberal strategy to deplete resources for reflection in corporatizing universities and shifting time spent on thoughtful and interrogative labor to bureaucratic and competitively profiteering (dead)ends. The case for thoughtfulness, which has been made many times over millennia, has to be made time and again. In Australia, for example, during the Covid pandemic and in the wake of tens of thousands of job losses in the university sector (Littleton and Stanford 2021), the hard-right Morrison administration doubled the cost of humanities degrees as part of their "Job-ready Graduates" reforms (Norton 2020). At historic junctures like this, disciplines like our own are forced, more defensively and less probingly, to articulate an answer to these questions: What is valuable about reflecting on stories? Why should the public pay for such reflection, and why should students learn about stories that are already percolating in their culture, contemplations of which may already be embedded in their quotidian discursive routines, rather than studying a more vocational "practice"?

There may be a wealthy history of answers to these implicit reproaches extending back thousands of years, but again the question updates itself; a proliferation of screen stories in our lives changes modes and means of narrative communication that in turn call for new kinds of reflection. Noël Carroll (2021), for instance, believes that an era of binge-watching television elides sequentially paced, reflective spaces of morally targeted discussion between episodes. This perspective, in turn, recalls Peter Kivy's initial writings on the "reflective afterlife" of narrative, and in particular literature, the reading of which is by its nature intermittent (1997, 122–123) (the term has since been applied more extensively to screen media). For Kivy, reading is "gappy," "sloppy," and never "self-contained," so that in order for the propositions drawn from its thought experiments to take shape, one must stop to recollect the emotive experience of each story (Summa-Knoop 2014, 203–204). Yet in order to make this case, we will need to define the substance—and the merits—of what we are calling "reflection." In this chapter, I show how extant research on the reflective afterlife can help us explain what it is we do in the humanities and social sciences when we discuss screen stories, the value of pulling out all the stops on elaborative reflection, sometimes over many years of study, and how such a process inevitably brings moral pointedness to cultures that may be experiencing a deficit of reflective means. Screen media scholarship takes up the invitation of screen stories, following through on their prompts to thought and realizing their offer to pursue and develop moral understanding, together.

Types of Reflective Afterlife

Several essays in this volume invoke Kivy's reflective afterlife to discuss the moral dimensions of screen stories. Kivy's term, however, is one among many that address the same potential for post-hoc thinking-through of narrative arts and their meanings. Kivy was concerned with the difference between music and fiction, and the latter's potential for thematizing life and thereby promoting its own kind of propositionally focused reflection. This potential can, of course, be extended to all narrative forms of media. Since Kivy coined the term, much has been written on the reflective afterlife of screen stories, often citing their ability to "make innovative, independent contributions to philosophy" that are specific to the medium and that one may then reflect upon (Smuts 2009, 409). On the other hand, Danielle Layne and Erik Schmidt (2019) emphasize filmic narratives as embedded within the afterlife of former modes of reflective philosophy, including Socratic dialogues and Platonic myths: here, screen stories are not the source of philosophic claims, as such, but embedded within a longer dialogic tradition, so reflection is a continuous process happening over time between claims, viscerally affecting stories, and elaborations or counterclaims drawn from stories in reflective communities. The "reflective afterlife" has been widely adopted by cognitive theorists to similarly explain how the impact of screen stories can become realized over time, as reflections may modify the schemata by which we understand both fictions and the world they refer to (Carroll 2002; Flory 2015; Vaage 2017; Plantinga 2018).[1]

While Kivy's interest was a more private and personal reflection, others extended notions of a narrative afterlife to interest in communities that mediate and extend personal reflections through everyday conversations, musing on the social spaces in which revisitations of screen stories occur. Wayne C. Booth has a term for these everyday reflective practices: "coduction" (1988, 70–74). Coduction is a portmanteau of the Latin co- (together) and ducere (to draw out), so to "draw out together" the meaning of a text. Booth speaks specifically of artistic judgments and evaluations that invite comparisons to others' interpretations, but also how such a comparison is in turn an entrée to further conversations that develop further insights (72). Localized, everyday judgments of art, then, are not important for the judgments themselves, but for what else a moral or aesthetic discourse can reveal about our world and its ethics when it is reflectively engaged by multiple participants. Coduction is a manner of social reflection that can be practiced by any two or more individuals, but it can also be fostered within institutions.

Coductive conversations can occur between wider communities as well and encompass values that are forged between people who may share cultural more than relational bonds or locality. James Harold's chapter in this volume revisits Jacqueline Bobo's (1995) work on "interpretive communities" and bell hooks's (1992) "oppositional gaze" by means of response to Kivy's model of interior reflection; both Bobo and hooks are interested in the ways in which communities collectively appropriate the meanings of texts in discussions that make sense to their own sociopolitical context. Harold's two points are that moral understanding can be developed in everyday conversations around screen media (that are by their nature reflective) and that screen stories do not provide moral understanding in themselves but rather provide a platform for developing understanding that can be of a nature not "authorized" by a text.[2] In a similar vein, a 2003 issue of *Visual Anthropology Review* addressed interpretations of HIV/AIDS documentaries across two essays by Jane Stadler and Susan Levine. While Levine writes of "the after-life of film" (2003, 60) as the power of posthoc reflection to become owned by a community and thereby acted upon in their locality, as social messages spread through interpretative acts around films, Stadler looks at the importance of facilitated, reflective discussions to realize that impact (2003, 96). Stadler argues that, equally, "films may serve to reinforce denial or high-risk behaviors modeled by protagonists rather than encouraging people to critically reflect on the decisions made by the characters and see the implications for their own lives," furnishing the need for extended reflection and facilitated discussion.

While much of this work addresses the specifics of film as a medium, Tonny Krijnen (2011) breaks down the different imaginative acts involved in moral reflections after television viewing. Her research with Marc Verboord (Krijnen and Verboord 2016) on Dutch television viewers finds that individuals of differing media preferences and motivations also differ in their appetite for reflection and the subjects they are inclined to reflect upon.[3] Crucially, they find that exposure to a greater range of media with a greater range of moral themes is associated with more reflective conversations and a greater emphasis on an ethics of care (423). There are, of course, many different kinds of screen media that devise affective novelties and inspire imagination to differing reflective ends: video games, mixed realities, and the many new storytelling modes of online media among them. I am not going to go through all of these formats here; the point is that there are a range of screen media that can inspire their own morally explorative discussions, and that as those discussions are social in nature, interpretations become shaped by the needs of a community and what might hold moral salience to that community. We cannot forget either the many (predigital) film and television scholars who have written of the value of "reflexive" modes of engagement over the past century. "Reflexivity" is a term embedded in the history of film and television studies, and it is closely related to "reflection." Finally, the diverse research cited above demonstrates the ecumenical nature of reflection across the humanities and social sciences and the ways in which disciplines can take up the offer to reciprocally reflect on others' reflections, through stories, to further their own disciplinary worlds of knowledge.

In this chapter, I am mostly interested in these institutional means for mediating personal and social reflections. I should note too that this chapter takes as given that an audience brings interpretative meaning to texts—and that even those texts that are very morally prescriptive must still have audiences to interpret meaning and potentially disagree with that prescription. This may occur internally for some (not everyone will discuss their experience) and socially for others, where those social distributions shape recollections and ergo the contours of one's own reflection. But I am also concerned with the power of screen media studies to create usefully estranging distance from those more foundational interpretations over longer periods of time.

It might not be contentious to claim that communities interpret screen stories together. It might not be contentious either to point out that in emphasizing communal interpretations, one inherently moves some identified agency away from stories and storytellers. Yet all kinds of interpretation are not equal. Interpretation (which will happen one way or another) and evaluation (which can be intuitive as much as ruminative) are not the same as active *reflection*. This is not to diminish the many places and processes of private and social interpretation in any way—there is perhaps nothing more valuable than these everyday avenues for moral dialogue where they are harnessed for reflective means and calls to political action, and not everyone will go to university and be afforded the privilege of long periods of reflection on the place of story in our lives. But I want to articulate what work in screen studies can do that other conversations around screen stories might not—and extended reflections are a part of this. Removing barriers to reflection can prompt us to move our conversations beyond the needs of our immediate community and their familiar, shared values; it can cause us to revisit those needs and compare them with the needs of other communities. The humanities and their deep readings, and social scientists' interest in how we arrive at and use moral interpretations, do have a special place not just in media interpretation but in moral understanding through extended reflection.

Moral Intuitions and Their Relation to the Reflective Afterlife

It is interesting that in our discussion of the reflective afterlife so far, we have already wandered quite close to intuitionism, where one might expect reflection not necessarily to carry us further away from our intuitions but to at least prompt a revisiting of their foundations. In particular, Harold's notion of stories as a "site of interpretation" defers to preexisting values within the interpretative community, minimizing the insights the stories can bring as they are *subject to* community values rather than articulating a capacity to change the views of those communities. Another intuitionist account of moral responses to screen stories is Carroll's "clarificationism" (1998, 327). Carroll's position, simply put, is that due to the load of preexisting beliefs and ingrained emotional responses we bring to screen media, its stories cannot change our mind or moral behavior in anything more than trivial ways—although what they can do is clarify or deepen our understanding of beliefs we already hold, including the application of those beliefs to specific circumstances, the relationships between our moral thoughts, and a recognition, through imagined scenarios, of their value. Even if we concede this, it still follows that such clarifications are likely to do their "deepening" work post hoc rather than at the moment we are responding to a story, and that such work can be advanced through institutions that ask for further clarification of the principles we have drawn from screen stories. Whether or not we can have new moral beliefs introduced in media or only test preexisting beliefs in order to learn more about them, reflection remains an important space of "deepening" (to use Carroll's term) understanding.

These perspectives—what I would call a prevailing intuitionism in cognitive discussions around screen media ethics—in turn draw from Jonathan Haidt's "social intuitionist model" (2001). Haidt suggests that while it may seem we reason our way toward moral judgments, we actually tend to fortify positions we arrive at intuitively, applying reason to justify prior intuitions. Yet even in Haidt's original article on social intuitionism, he leaves room for "private reflection," especially where one experiences conflict among multiple possible judgments, causing one to revisit intuitions and thereby modify judgments, as well as the reasoning that supports those judgments. His argument is not that reasoning toward a new judgment is impossible, just that it is not a default position, and so reasoning to protect one's socially derived, moral intuitions is more likely. He writes of the capacity for reflection, "The most widely discussed method of triggering new intuitions is role-taking (Selman 1971). Simply by putting oneself into the shoes of another person, one may instantly feel pain, sympathy, or other vicarious emotional responses.... A person comes to see an issue or dilemma from more than one side and thereby experiences multiple competing intuitions" (Haidt 2001, 819).[4] This has obvious implications for storytelling, which by its nature puts us in another's shoes. There is plenty of evidence in media psychology for moral intuitions as drivers of dispositions toward screen characters (e.g., see Eden and Tamborini 2017), and scholars working across diverse fields have long noted the influence of all sorts of framing effects on moral judgment (from Tversky and Kahneman 1981 to Sunstein 2005). However, this does not mean screen stories cannot offer a circuit-breaker to these intuitions and dispositions, nor does it negate the ability of reflective practices to move beyond the level of character judgment and elaborate into more generously minded conclusions, if one is willing to compare the relative complexity of a morally concerned narrative back to the complexity of life.[5] And that is the practice we are interested in: not what happens to us during engagement but what we *can do* postengagement, how after-the-fact moral reflections can be institutionally promoted and why they matter.

Scholarly work expands that reflective space. This may be a kind of "clarification" occurring potentially over years of research or years of a humanities degree that incorporates screen stories and interpretative, intuitive, communal, or revisited private responses to those stories; indeed, others have written of the reflective afterlife as a particularly useful launching point for a narrative-based pedagogy that "[holds] together lived experience, tensions, shifts and continuity" (Goodson and Gill 2011, 140). But I also submit that the changes in perspective that can result from prolonged reflection are profound and not trivial, no matter what we think we know when we go into a story. Intuitions might ordinarily reinforce reasonable moral standards fundamental to our living and thriving together—for instance, one might feel repulsed when watching images of violent crime—but not always. Consider cases of implicit bias, such as "racialized disgust", which screen stories can attempt to disrupt (Flory, 2015). Extended reflections offer the opportunity to revisit and "clarify" moral intuitions, to know them better, but also to find ways to extend their disruption. If we look too narrowly at the immediate "effects" of screen media rather than how it lives on in potentially reflective colloquy extending over years, those effects may seem trivial where they need not be.

Ethical agency, ergo, as Haidt originally pointed out, subsists in our capacity for "reflection," to question intuitive responses and thereby provide the impetus for *both* clarification *and* meaningful perspectival change, for moving on from moral cues that have outgrown their relevance in globally interactive cultural ecologies that evolve so rapidly. Stories can invite us to explore those changes and update, in nontrivial ways, our perspective on the world; reflective communities then take up that offer; and any reflective institutional practice that not only takes up but elongates its reflective work, I think, has a greater capacity for thoughtful change in its very discovery of what exists between the story, the community, the self, and other cultures with their own ways of thinking through the world.

So the first point to be made about all this writing on the reflective afterlife (work on everyday interpretative conversations notwithstanding) is that it describes what we do as scholars in various corners of screen studies. It is an invitation we take up on behalf of those stories, and the acceptance and continual extension of this invitation is what I address in the remainder of this chapter. In the research cited above, philosophers and social scientists reveal their own capacity to learn from other communities and what they value *through* the stories that are meaningful to them. But I will also make the case that more engagement and more discussion do not necessarily equate to more reflection—of course, one can remain highly engaged with media without feeling the need for a deep revisiting of one's intuitive judgments. So the challenge is to define *reflective* engagement more specifically, not simply to describe our many available modes of interpreting, evaluating, and revisiting media or the institutions that promote hyperengagement with screen stories, of which there are many.

Distinguishing between Reflective Institutions

As Carl Plantinga and Garrett Strpko write, working outward from Kivy's personally reflective afterlife to Booth's socially "coductive" version of this afterlife, "coduction can also be encouraged by the practices of various institutions, such as academia, professional criticism, and through social media interaction" (2023).They move through a list of various institutions that promote reflection, including academia and the ways in which scholars can propel their conversations outward to other communities through websites devoted to screen analysis, or by providing resources for pre-university education. They also mention fan sites, social media that fosters and promotes the conversations of fan communities like Reddit, video-sharing sites like

YouTube, film and TV criticism, film-viewing clubs and societies, and affordances made by the very narratives themselves that invite analysis, especially as regards morally ambiguous characters.[6]

Screen studies, film criticism, fan cultures, and online communities all have their own opportunities for (but do not necessarily oblige) moral reflection. The evaluative work of film reviewing, for instance, can be a site of projected authority (Frey 2015) more than reflection—yet critics can also comment back on the broader cultural relevance of a text, offer further analytical insights, or even participate in the creative process that is continuous between film and film commentary (Bordwell 2016; Taylor 1999). The informational and evaluative functions of reviewing can collide in ways that are unique to the form (Wyatt and Badger 1990), and some criticism is explicitly oriented toward a morally reflective mode of evaluation. Consider Emily Nussbaum's recent work on "bad fandom," which is now discussed in film and television theory (2019).

One could make a similar case about the hyperengagement of fan communities. As Karen E. Dill-Shackelford and Cynthia Vinney put it, "fandom, particularly fandom for complex drama, may be largely about the search for meaning, the clarification of values, and the quest to hone our skills and understanding," which sounds a lot like the work performed in the humanities and social sciences (2020, 8). Plantinga and Strpko note too that "the more obsessive engagement of fan culture with media texts picks up where common professional criticism ends" (2023). Fanfics can be elaborative in that they extend story worlds and their meanings, and may have moral resonance in advancing, for example, queer impulses within source and progenitor texts. Another example might be YouTube channels and other online video-sharing platforms. Plantinga and Strpko point to Dan Olson's *Folding Ideas,* which muses on the ways in which popular media texts communicate moral values; other popular channels, including Matthew Patrick and Stephanie Cordato's *The Film Theorists* and *Game Theory,* are positioned as investigations into the hidden meanings of narrative-based puzzles that are less ethically motivated. Similarly, much of screen studies comprises an ethically disengaged pursuit of understanding. Plenty of writing on film reflects on historical or aesthetic issues rather than moral issues. Consider David Bordwell's "historical poetics," his reflection on the formal aspects of film that seldom concerns morality, or writing that is oriented more toward understanding the cognitive processes of moral reasoning than evaluating moral impacts (2008).

My purpose here is not to argue that one or another approach is ethically superior, but rather to articulate the potential that screen studies has for its own manner of reflection, with its own results. Screen media scholarship—along with all the discourses generated by that scholarship, in the classroom, at lectures, in conferences and discussions—has a uniquely extended continuum of reflective practices that inform one another. Plantinga and Strpko provide a good description of these:

> Academia at all levels promotes moral reflection. Film and media courses train students to formally and thematically analyze screen stories. As pedagogical leaders,

teachers screen films and may subsequently encourage and guide student reflection towards moral dimensions, equipping students with tools for interpretation
and filling in enthymematic gaps through discussion. For instance, academic discourse may prepare students to engage with a host of morally significant social
justice issues in film, such as the politics of representation and reception. Likewise,
scholars contribute to ongoing critical conversations in the form of academic publishing, which helps identify issues of moral significance in the field and contemplate solutions (2023).

Moral evaluation is not the end in itself; rather, academic discourse discovers what
we can say about the world *through* evaluation, and *after* evaluation, over time. We
collectively reflect, evaluate, reflect on the reflection, and modify our evaluations
alongside and with respect to the knowledge of others—and we write these continual
upsets of prior positions into our theory. This process is unique. Reflection, as scholarly practice, is prolonged and careful and thereby able to discover and articulate the
results of evaluating screen media.

But what are those results? In this volume, Paul C. Taylor's chapter on his own in-
trospective afterlife around the musical *Hamilton* and its many screen-based para-
texts offers a good example of how such a reflection can work, why it is valuable, and
how we might understand its distinctiveness. He draws a difference between moral
epistemics (understanding *what* a text is communicating) and a more implicating
moral understanding of one's place within the ethics conveyed across the stories in
our culture. Taylor's work also reveals a cultural marketplace that privileges the aesthetic values of artworks like *Hamilton* to maximize their appeal against the ethical
values that may distance some audience members, for instance by keeping traumatic
histories silent and minimizing their impact—and that in this case, ethical reflection
becomes an act of resistance. Taylor observes that there is something jarring about the
specific case of *Hamilton*: slave histories seem like an odd match for the characteristic
feelings of togetherness that are so much a part of traditions of sung narrative, and
that sit strangely atop a history of colonial violence. This is an emotional togetherness
that cannot admit into its emotional palette the trauma of that violence without, in
Lin-Manuel Miranda's words, "bringing the show to a halt" (without sacrificing its appeal to an audience that includes both Barack Obama and Mike Pence (Keyes, 2019).
To reflect deeply on the ethics of media is a resistant reclaiming of art from commercial forces that, in various ways, rob that ethical commitment by keeping it silent, appealing to more by saying less.

Resistances within the arts and entertainment industry continue despite these documented commercial compromises, but Taylor notes too that "[t]he obvious reason
not to be encouraged by this is that humans routinely act in ways that belie our explicit avowals." Yet toward the end of the chapter, Taylor writes, "And now I have to
tell you that writing those words in the previous paragraph made me less interested in
watching *Hamilton* in the future." In this reference to a future self of the reflective author, not who one *is* but who one *will be*, we might locate the germ of a positive ethic,

the results of a reflective practice. Taylor's "personalist turn" considers the thinking that might lead to future resistant choices. Reflection on ethics and justice is, in essence, the tool we have to fight back.

It is difficult for cultural products to *compel* any kind of thought. But what we do with our thoughts after engaging matters to who we become. As scholars and teachers, those of us converging over reflective excursions like this book bear responsibility. What Taylor's personalist turn ultimately affirms is that fostering a reflective self is central to acts of resistance, as it reinforces the need and desire for resistance, and this matters to the work we've chosen as humanists, as social scientists, as interrogators of the causal workings of the world, and our morally charged place within it.

From Autobiographical Reminiscence to Transactive Memory Systems

Reflection intrinsically calls on memory, and understanding the place of memory in reflective practice is important to any cognitive account of how that reflection works. I have written in the past of the importance of autobiographical memory in understanding the ethics of screen stories (Moss-Wellington 2021a, 58–62); while fictive stories may not be real, our response to them is real, and our responses are rehearsed both internally and socially in the narratives we tell about that response and what it means to us. What we think and feel about fictions becomes part of our autobiographical narrative, our sense of self, and autobiographical recall is important in acts of future planning (Bluck et al. 2005, 93), and therefore our ethics—who we think we are informs what we choose to do. While this earlier account of the place of memory in screen ethics was centered on the individual understanding themselves and their moral behaviors through screen stories—perhaps in unison with others when "coductively" conversing about those stories—the socially distributive reminiscence acts of reflective communities are potentially more complex. I now present a model for considering how screen media scholarship acts as a morally charged, vastly transactive memory system.

Daniel Wegner (1987) proposed a transactive memory systems theory as a means to understand the ways in which the memory of intimate couples and small groups is interdependent; others have since applied the theory to broader organizational structures and teams (Liang, Moreland, and Argote 1995; Peltokorpi 2012). We might think of memory as being stored in the individual's mind, yet there are memory acts that we really cannot perform alone because they entail collaboration and elaborations that only two or more people can achieve together. In this way, people who share a private or professional background that requires recall can sometimes remember more together than they can alone, as one shared memory prompts another that prompts another—and there are degrees of successful transactive systems that agree to collaborate more or less effectively. When successful, such groups can overcome the typical costs of collaboration to memory. ("Collaborative inhibition" can occur where individuals fail to work together effectively on memory tasks; e.g., Meade and Gigone 2011; Barnier et al. 2018.)

Memory encoding, storage, and retrieval can all be transactive in this way when cognitive labor is divided among individuals in a group, and there are three core components to such a system: distributed knowledge (individuals know different things), metaknowledge (individuals know what others are likely to know), and effective communication (individuals can access one another's knowledge). For example, individuals in a long-term romantic partnership might recognize subject expertise in their partner and rely upon them to commit certain topics to memory ("distributed knowledge"); they might thereby have good understanding of what their partner knows ("metaknowledge"); and they might also know what to say or do to prompt their partner to retrieve specific information where it becomes relevant ("effective communication"). When it works, no one person has within them all of the knowledge; rather memory exists between people's social behaviors by which they prompt each other and recall together.

Knowledge communities in institutions that have developed over centuries, the professional work of which relies upon specialized (effectively "distributed") knowledge generation, storage, and retrieval, have similarly developed transactive memory systems not simply to calcify facts but to retrieve salient components of other, potentially distant knowledge worlds when they become relevant, and to update that knowledge to new circumstances.[7] We do not just need experts researching and filing away what they find; we need a transactive memory system of collaborative prompts to make connections between knowledge worlds and then apply the knowledge *between* specializations to deliberative discussions that carry moral weight. Tim Ingold writes that "knowledge is not built from facts that are simply there, waiting to be discovered and organized in terms of concepts and categories.... [I]t rather grows and is grown in the forge of our relations with others" (2014, 391). In universities and in academic disciplines, information and understanding are forged, accumulated, probed, and updated in the interactive spaces between colleagues, within teacher-pupil and scholar-public relations interfacing between that knowledge and lived experiences outside of the university context. This transactive memory system is a way not only to store knowledge but to socially update the relevance of that knowledge to our changing lives. Reflection is not so much just the memorizing part, but the part at the tail end of collaborative recall: turning over the knowledge together, updating it as circumstances change, and arriving at new accounts to help us with current challenges.

Transactive memory is, then, a kind of extended mind thesis (Clark and Chalmers 1998), an act that involves our minds but that cannot be performed unassisted and alone, and of course the transactions do not always happen in person but can cross between (in screen studies) stories and written reflections on those stories. This capacity is demonstrated in film reading work that reflects upon memories of narrative experiences, as when Stanley Cavell (1979) probes the meaning and value he can find in accounting not for the facts of a narrative experience but for the ways it is shaped in memory. One other element of these scholarly elaborations is our ability to reflect upon the act of reflecting (as Kivy and others do in reflecting on their responses to art, and then writing about how that reflection actually works). These reflections on reflections can do so many other things, too: prolonging reflection can lead to uncovering weirdnesses and quirks and particularities that are rewarding not for the sake of generating new knowledge but because encountering a variety of human experiences and perspectives on those experiences can further destabilize our own intuitive relationship to the cultures in which our dispositions—and our moral convictions—are generated. Over the course of years of study and debate, one might not even predict the strange little things another researcher or educator says to us, or the ideas we are introduced to that will only later become profoundly meaningful, settling into a larger worldview. One might study postcolonial theory, for instance, and years after earning one's degree the concepts crystallize as one watches a film or TV show, plays a game or shares a meme, that is founded on an unquestioned thrill of spectating violence visited upon ethnic minorities. Embedded in one's own situated media experience, recall of those concepts might help one make sense of the moral world, and perhaps even provide an articulation of what, precisely, is wrong, why we must fight for change. These insights can take a while to change our perspective over long periods of reflection, not just in clarifying our personal philosophies but perhaps, over time, changing our dispositions on things that matter to political and moral spheres.

When it works, a transactive system making *meaning* from memories of screen texts and their coductive conversations is nontrivial. For Paul Ricœur, we arrive "at expression, at meaning, and at reflection only through the continual exegesis of all the significations that come to light in the world of culture. (1978, 106). Ricœur believes this is what is achieved through hermeneutic readings in the humanities. Part of reflection is exposure and perspectival openness: agreeing that we do not know what will be useful in the future, providing the impetus to remove barriers to reflecting, and reflecting again after reflection across broader conversations, across distant worlds of knowledge. Reflection is a kind of estrangement. On encountering new ideas, new worlds in stories, we look back on a mirrored image or "reflection" of our thoughts to see the distance between us then and us now. It is also experimental, not knowing where its thoughts will lead. It may be that I am biased (I am most definitely biased), but I cannot think of any process closer to cultural memory as a dimension of human evolution, to hybridizing change, to life itself.

What Is Reflection?

My argument is rather simple: that screen studies and other narrative media scholarship in the humanities and social sciences are distinguished by their ongoing removal of barriers to reflection, those points at which reflection on screen stories might stop and we might move on. The difficult part, however, is articulating what this singular mode of reflection comprises as opposed to nonscholarly reflections, and what benefit it achieves. In our academic institutions, moral knowledge and moral understanding are developed together as a specifically systematized, transactive memory practice that does not simply commit research findings to collective memory in writings and teachings but crafts moral salience from those findings at the same time, as well as inviting reflection and revisitation. It is not only about recording facts, evidence, probabilities, or propositions drawn from those things, but sifting through the various meanings we can draw from our knowledge, ethically informing our subsequent courses of action. As a process, scholarly reflection is singular in the way it agrees to the invitation of stories to ruminate on more open-ended possibilities for understanding the world and living in it—and a world of collective challenges spanning global borders requires diverse means for codevelopment of a more mutual moral understanding, bound in the stories that cross those borders, in turn binding us to others across the world. Stories and reflections that gather observations and ideas at their best extend a mutual stake in one another's thoughts, and thereby one another's lifeworlds, our sense of being. And I hope that this metacommentative essay, itself a reflection on reflection that crosses and elaborates knowledge worlds between humanities and social science, is demonstrative of the position I take.

What is reflection, then? Although it may seem intuitive when one has been practicing it so long in one's working life, I want to draw some parameters around the term so that any textual interrogation and reflection cease to be the same thing. I think that its value lies in its prolongation: reflection takes something that has stopped and does not allow it to settle, be it a story, an idea, a sense of self, or anything else that can be mulled over. But it is also gentle. Unlike interrogation, reflection has at its heart an aim to understand through social revisitation and personal revision, not to strip away to a buried truth, but to update, to evolve with new information—and as we have seen, even in its carefulness and thoughtfulness it can promote radical resistance. Scholarly work agrees to pull out the stops on reflection. It reflects upon its reflections, which may sound like an indulgence to some, but in fact this gentle upsetting of prior settled knowledge—ideas we thought we had, once, while the world moved on—is key to living well together. It is the moral edge of reflection. It is the genesis of openness to others' worlds and the call to radical change not for its own sake, but for a mutual stake, for improving our lot together.

Notes

1. The "reflective afterlife" had its own prominent afterlife in cognitive literary studies as well, with writers such as Scott R. Stroud (2008), although my object of study here is explicitly screen studies.
2. Harold concedes, however, via debates around "bad fandom" (Nussbaum 2019; Vaage 2016), that interpretative communities can still reach antisocial and even bigoted conclusions. So the question remains: What institutional-social practices facilitate reflections with the power to destabilize these corrosive forms of moralism or build moral understanding founded on respectful engagement with others around the world? And, apropos the

question of this chapter, how can scholarly work amplify or augment such beneficial forms of engagement?

3. With thanks to Jane Stadler for drawing my attention to these essays.

4. This hint of a capacity for slow and deliberative moral reflection was expanded in Haidt's early collaborations with Joshua Greene on a "dual process model" (Greene and Haidt 2002); however, in the interests of brevity I will not diverge too far into the literature on alleged cognitive differences between utilitarian and deontological thought that followed.

5. I have made the case elsewhere that as inducements to causal thinking, it matters ethically what kinds of causes and consequences stories provide for us to discuss (Moss-Wellington 2019; 2021a, 40–53).

6. We can add to this list all manner of media old and new, from radio shows to podcasts, for example.

7. Kyle Lewis (2003) identifies three variables or "indicators" of the existence of a transactive memory system: specialization, credibility, and coordination. Scholarly institutions, I submit, have professionalized certain means for extending these aspects of collaboration. Specialization is key to dividing and distributing responsibilities to those best suited, credibility to trusting and accepting the knowledge of other specialists, and coordination to the strategies—in events, writing, and other fora for sharing ideas—for prompting and utilizing others' knowledge specializations. Transactive memory systems are important for developing new knowledge, not just retrieving old facts.

Works Cited

Barnier, Amanda J., Celia B. Harris, Thomas Morris, and Greg Savage. 2018. "Collaborative Facilitation in Older Couples: Successful Joint Remembering across Memory Tasks." *Frontiers in Psychology* 9 (December): Article 2385: 1–12.

Bluck, Susan, Nicole Alea, Tilmann Habermas, and David C. Rubin. 2005. "A TALE of Three Functions: The Self-Reported Uses of Autobiographical Memory." *Social Cognition* 23, no. 1: 91–117.

Bobo, Jacqueline. 1995. *Black Women as Cultural Readers*. New York: Columbia University Press.

Booth, Wayne C. 1988. *The Company We Keep: An Ethics of Fiction*. Berkeley: University of California Press.

Bordwell, David. 2008. *Poetics of Cinema*. Berkeley: Routledge.

Bordwell, David. 2016. *The Rhapsodes: How 1940s Critics Changed American Film Culture*. Chicago: University of Chicago Press.

Carroll, Noël. 1998. *A Philosophy of Mass Art*. New York: Oxford University Press.

Carroll, Noël. 2002. "The Wheel of Virtue: Art, Literature, and Moral Knowledge." *Journal of Aesthetics and Art Criticism* 60, no. 1 (Winter): 3–26.

Carroll, Noël. 2021. "What We've Lost with the Rise of TV Streaming." *New Statesman*, August 3. https://www.newstatesman.com/culture/2021/08/what-weve-lost-rise-tv-streaming.

Cavell, Stanley. 1979. *The World Viewed: Reflections on the Ontology of Film*. Cambridge, MA: Harvard University Press.

Clark, Andy, and David Chalmers. 1998. "The Extended Mind." *Analysis* 58, no. 1 (January): 7–19.

Dill-Shackleford, Karen E., and Cynthia Vinney. 2020. *Finding Truth in Fiction*. New York: Oxford University Press.

Eden, Allison, and Ron Tamborini. 2017. "Moral Intuitions: Morality Subcultures in Disposition Formation." *Journal of Media Psychology* 29, no. 4: 198–207.

Flory, Dan. 2015. "Imaginative Resistance, Racialized Disgust, and *12 Years a Slave*." *Film and Philosophy* 19: 75–95.

Frey, Mattias. 2015. *The Permanent Crisis of Film Criticism*. Amsterdam: Amsterdam University Press.

Goodson, Ivor F., and Scherto R. Gill. 2011. "Narrative: Learning and Living in the Community." *Counterpoints* 386: 137–153.

Greene, Joshua, and Jonathan Haidt. 2002. "How Does Moral Judgement Work?" *Trends in Cognitive Sciences* 6, no. 12: 517–523.

Haidt, Jonathan. 2001. "The Emotional Dog and Its Rational Tail." *Psychological Review* 108, no. 4: 814–834.

hooks, bell. 1992. "The Oppositional Gaze." In *Black Looks: Race and Representation*, edited by bell hooks, 115–131. Boston: South End Press.

Ingold, Tim. 2014. "That's Enough about Ethnography!" *Hau: Journal of Ethnographic Theory* 4, no. 1: 383–395.

Keyes, Elizabeth. 2019. "Broadway's *Hamilton* and the Willing Suspension of Reality-Based Moral Consciousness." *Medium*, May 18. https://medium.com/@libbyliberal/broadways-hamilton-and-the-willing-suspension-of-reality-based-moral-consciousness-f2423d98d7c2.

Kivy, Peter. 1997. "The Laboratory of Fictional Truth." In *Philosophies of Arts: An Essay in Differences*, edited by Peter Kivy, 120–139. New York: Cambridge University Press.

Krijnen, Tonny. 2011. "Engaging the Moral Imagination by Watching Television." *Participations* 8, no. 2: 52–73.

Krijnen, Tonny, and Marc Verboord. 2016. "TV Genres' Moral Value: The Moral Reflection of Segmented TV Audiences." *Social Science Journal* 53, no. 4 (May): 417–426.

Layne, Danielle A., and Erik W. Schmidt. 2019. "Pseudos, Kalos and Eikōs Mythos in Plato and Film." In *Plato and the Moving Image*, edited by Shai Biderman and Michael Weinman, 37–59. Leiden: Brill.

Levine, Susan. 2003. "Documentary Film and HIV/AIDS." *Visual Anthropology Review* 19, nos. 1–2: 57–72.

Lewis, Kyle. 2003. "Measuring Transactive Memory Systems in the Field." *Journal of Applied Psychology* 88, no. 4: 587–604.

Liang, Diane Wei, Richard Moreland, and Linda Argote. 1995. "Group versus Individual Training and Group Performance: The Mediating Role of Transactive Memory." *Personality and Social Psychology Bulletin* 21, no. 4: 384–393.

Littleton, Eliza, and Jim Stanford. 2021. "An Avoidable Catastrophe: Pandemic Job Losses in Higher Education and Their Consequences." Australia Institute, September 13. https://australiainstitute.org.au/report/an-avoidable-catastrophe.

Meade, Michelle L., and Daniel Gigone. 2011. "The Effect of Information Distribution on Collaborative Inhibition." *Memory* 19, no. 5: 417–428.

Moss-Wellington, Wyatt. 2019. *Narrative Humanism: Kindness and Complexity in Fiction and Film*. Edinburgh: Edinburgh University Press.

Moss-Wellington, Wyatt. 2021a. *Cognitive Film and Media Ethics*. New York: Oxford University Press.

Moss-Wellington, Wyatt. 2021b. "Criminals at Play: *Oedipus*, *Rope*, and Telltale's *The Walking Dead*." In "Playful Encounters." Special issue, *Culture, Theory and Critique* 62, no. 3: 208–222.

Norton, Andrew. 2020. "3 Flaws in Job-Ready Graduates Package Will Add to the Turmoil in Australian Higher Education." *The Conversation*, October 9. https://theconversation.com/

3-flaws-in-job-ready-graduates-package-will-add-to-the-turmoil-in-australian-higher-education-147740.

Nussbaum, Emily. 2019. "Norman Lear, Archie Bunker, and the Rise of the Bad Fan." In *I Like to Watch: Arguing My Way through the TV Revolution*, 36–47. New York: Random House.

Peltokorpi, Vesa. 2012. "Organizational Transactive Memory Systems." *European Psychologist* 17, no. 1: 11–20.

Plantinga, Carl R. 2018. *Screen Stories: Emotion and the Ethics of Engagement*. New York: Oxford University Press.

Plantinga, Carl, and Garrett Strpko. 2023. "Moral Reflection: On the Reflective Afterlife of Screen Stories." In *What Film Is Good For: On the Ethics of Spectatorship*, edited by Julian Hanich and Martin P. Rossouw. Berkeley: University of California Press, 117–127.

Ricœur, Paul. 1978. *The Philosophy of Paul Ricœur*. Edited by Charles E. Reagan and David Stewart. Boston: Beacon Press.

Selman, Robert L. 1971. "The Relation of Role Taking to the Development of Moral Judgment in Children." *Child Development* 42, no. 1 (March): 79–91.

Smuts, Aaron. 2009. "Film as Philosophy: In Defense of a Bold Thesis." *Journal of Aesthetics and Art Criticism* 67, no. 4 (November): 409–420.

Stadler, Jane. 2003. "Narrative, Understanding and Identification in *Steps for the Future*." *Visual Anthropology Review* 19, nos. 1–2: 86–101.

Stroud, Scott R. 2008. "Simulation, Subjective Knowledge, and the Cognitive Value of Literary Narrative." *Journal of Aesthetic Education* 42, no. 3: 19–41.

Summa-Knoop, Laura Di. 2014. "Philosophical Aesthetics." *Journal of Aesthetics and Phenomenology* 1, no. 2: 191–207.

Sunstein, Cass R. 2005. "Moral Heuristics." *Behavioral and Brain Sciences* 28, no. 4: 531–542.

Taylor, Greg. 1999. *Artists in the Audience: Cults, Camp and American Film Criticism*. Princeton, NJ: Princeton University Press.

Tversky, Amos, and Daniel Kahneman. 1981. "The Framing of Decisions and the Psychology of Choice." *Science* 211, no. 4481: 453–458.

Vaage, Margrethe Bruun. 2016. *The Antihero in American Television*. New York: Routledge.

Vaage, Margrethe Bruun. 2017. "From *The Corner* to *The Wire*: On Nonfiction, Fiction, and Truth." *Journal of Literary Theory* 11, no. 2: 255–271.

Wegner, Daniel M. 1987. "Transactive Memory: A Contemporary Analysis of the Group Mind." In *Theories of Group Behavior*, edited by Brian Mullen and George R. Goethals, 185–208. New York: Springer-Verlag.

Wyatt, Robert O., and David P. Badger. 1990. "Effects of Information and Evaluation in Film Criticism." *Journalism Quarterly* 67, no. 2 (June): 359–368.

13

The Reflective Afterlife and the Ends of Imagining

Murray Smith

Fiction, Imagination, and Belief

According to one standard framework for understanding the contrast between fiction and nonfiction, and the importance of imagination to fiction, fiction and nonfiction each depend on distinct "mood-stances"—attitudes—that authors adopt in making such works, and we appreciators reciprocally adopt in engaging with them (Wolterstorff 1980).[1] In making a nonfiction, an author or artist adopts *the assertive stance*, positioning themselves as making assertions or truth claims about the world via the nonfictional work that they author; as appreciators, to the extent that we find these assertions persuasive, we revise our beliefs accordingly. In making a fiction, by contrast, an author or artist adopts *the fictive stance*, asking us instead to imagine the contents of the fictional work that they author; we are invited to imagine the world projected by the work. We can thus summarize the framework, with its two parallel tracks, as set out in Table 13.1.

It is important to add that nonfictions globally embody the assertive stance toward what they represent, while fictions globally embody the fictive stance toward the projected worlds that they represent.[2] That is, most fictions might plausibly be regarded as a combination of assertions about the actual world alongside invitations to imagine an invented world; most nonfictions, as we will see, will in parallel include some representational contents which we are most plausibly invited to imagine rather than believe. In this sense, fictions and nonfictions are somewhat heterogeneous in their contents. Nonetheless, this heterogeneity is held in check and given structure by the fact that the underlying stances—fictive and assertive—operate globally, at least in typical examples of fictional and nonfictional works. That is, we understand that, while a good many propositions which are true in a fictional world are also true of the actual world, what matters most of all is that we are being invited to imagine the projected world.[3] Similarly, we understand that while some of the contents of a nonfiction are or might be imaginative projections rather than assertions, what is most fundamental to the work as a whole is its assertive character, and the invitation to believe its core claims that comes with its assertive character.[4]

Murray Smith, *The Reflective Afterlife and the Ends of Imagining* In: *Screen Stories and Moral Understanding*. Edited by: Carl Plantinga, Oxford University Press. © Oxford University Press 2023.
DOI: 10.1093/oso/9780197665664.003.0014

Table 13.1 Mood-stances in nonfiction and fiction

The assertive stance ▽	The fictive stance ▽
Nonfiction ▽	Fiction ▽
Belief	Imagination

It is fair to say that this framework on fiction and nonfiction is an orthodox view within analytic aesthetics, closely related to a number of Gricean accounts.[5] What all of these accounts share is the idea that the distinction between fiction and non-fiction is fundamental and depends on the contrast between imagining (prompted by fiction) and believing (prompted by nonfiction). This theory (or family of theories) has its detractors, but my own view is that it represents the right foundation for understanding fiction—and the distinction between fiction and nonfiction—while nonetheless being notably incomplete, or at least underdeveloped, in at least one important respect.

Before I explain in what respect I think the "mood-stance" account of the fiction/nonfiction distinction is incomplete, let me say a word about one way in which this framework played a very important role in film studies, when it was adopted by Carl Plantinga from Nicholas Wolterstorff's work, from the late 1980s onward. Plantinga's purpose in drawing on this framework was to get a better grip on the nature of documentary and nonfiction filmmaking. At the time, and perhaps still today in certain quarters, the field of film studies was dominated by a kind of "textualism" which, suspicious of any claim that nonfiction works might represent the world objectively, sought to collapse the distinction between fiction and nonfiction entirely. On this view, any and all (narrative) representations are fictions.[6] Marie-Laure Ryan labels this position "panfictionalism" (1997).

So the mood-stance theory was a way of reasserting the reality and significance of the distinction between fiction and nonfiction. In doing so, there was no denial in Plantinga's work that nonfictions may draw on the full panoply of stylistic and structural devices in making the assertions that characterize them—indeed this was central to his work on nonfiction. Nor was there any naïve commitment to the truth or objectivity of particular works of nonfiction; to say that a work adopts and invites the assertive stance is simply to say that that work makes assertions about the world which it (or rather its authors) invite us to believe. Those assertions might well be false, or misleading, or epistemically defective in a range of other ways.

The mood-stance account was thus deployed in film studies, then, most urgently in terms of its implications for documentary and nonfiction. The notion of the assertive stance gave us a new, deeper, and more subtle way of grasping the distinctive character of nonfictions. But what about the other, complementary thesis pertaining to fiction, namely that fictions are those representations which invite us to imagine—rather than believe—their contents?

This is where I think we encounter that aspect of the mood-stance theory which is relatively sketchy. For there is something of an asymmetry between the two branches of the argument regarding the distinction between fiction and nonfiction. The proposal that nonfictions are characterized by assertions which viewers and readers are invited to accept—by adopting new beliefs and revising existing ones—is highly informative because we already understand how fundamental beliefs are to practical reasoning and action. If nonfictions seek to furnish us with new knowledge about the world—making assertions which, if persuasive, lead to new beliefs, cascading into new attitudes and new actions—then it looks like we have quite a robust understanding of the value of nonfictions, as well as some initial criteria for discriminating good and not-so-good nonfictions. Nonfictions are valuable to the extent that their assertions are reliable, affording well-founded new beliefs and justifying the amendment of existing beliefs, thereby advancing our knowledge or understanding of the world.

Can we say anything equivalent about the fictional branch of the framework? It's not obvious that we can, absent further elaboration of the framework. Fictions invite us to imagine, rather than believe, their contents. And? Whenever I reach this point in giving an exposition of the framework to students, I feel a void opening up. What would be the point of entertaining these imaginings? We know the answer to the equivalent question in relation to beliefs; we've just examined it. The point of updating our beliefs is to track what's happening in the world (kind of important to our well-being) and to reason and act effectively within it. Comparatively little follows from the mere idea that we imagine certain things. We might say that we take delight in imagining "for its own sake" or as an end in itself. But even that much seems to flirt with circularity. Why would imagining that something is the case have a self-sufficient value? This answer certainly isn't going to be very satisfactory for anyone inclined toward a naturalistic perspective on storytelling, imagination, and the arts, for whom it will be a priority to understand how our artistic and aesthetic practices fit into our wider behavioral repertoires as evolved beings.[7]

At a minimum, it seems fair to say that the idea that fictions are those representations whose contents are to be imagined is a much less informative proposal than the one we find in the other branch of the framework, pertaining to the adoption of new beliefs on the basis of engaging with a nonfiction. And this is especially true if what we are seeking to shed light on is the capacity of fiction—fictional screen stories included—to enhance our understanding (moral or otherwise) of the world. For in saying that imagining (as prompted by works of fiction) is an end in itself, we seem to cut imagining off from other parts of our cognitive economy, or at least from our ordinary engagement with the world. And, at least on one traditional view, that's the point. That's what aesthetic "disinterest" is. In other contexts, where we want to understand what appreciating an experience for its own sake might mean, appeal to the Kantian idea is useful. But if what we want to address is the contribution that imagining might make to knowledge or understanding, then saying that "imagination is its own reward" isn't going to take us far. We need to know what the imagination is (good) for, other than for itself.[8]

Let's take a step back here and consider one way in which we might elaborate on the basic mood-stance account. So far we have the picture that nonfictions invite us to adopt beliefs on the basis of the assertions they make, while fictions invite us to imagine the fictional propositions they represent. Note that the beliefs and the fictional propositions at stake are *constitutive particular propositions*—things like "Nanook speared a fish" (a particular event that the nonfiction in question, *Nanook of the North* (1922), asserts took place) and "Dobby was killed by Bellatrix Lestrange" (a particular event that the fiction in question, *Harry Potter and the Deathly Hallows* (2007), invites us to imagine).[9] The beliefs and the imaginings are tokens rather than types, tokens embodied by the propositions constituting the projected world of the work.

In speaking of "propositions" constituting or implied by narratives, I don't mean to suggest that our experience of narratives—fictional or nonfictional, literary or screen-based—can be reduced to propositional cognition. We surely need to make space for a variety of kinds of imagery, and forms of cognition, prompted by narrative representations. Much ink has been spilled on the experiential imagining prompted by narrative works, for example.[10] Even so, narrative comprehension (in screen as much as in verbal contexts) does seem to depend on propositions. Understanding a narrative in the course of engaging with it, and recalling it afterward, involves the encoding and recall of propositions describing the actions of agents and other events of the type noted above. The content of these propositions is then held in mind with contrasting attitudes in the cases of fiction and nonfiction, respectively: the same content imagined in the case of fiction will be believed (or at least considered in light of its fitness for belief) in the case of nonfiction.[11]

A first qualification (and complication) that we might introduce here is that while fictions invite us to imagine their contents (i.e., their constitutive particular propositions), they can hardly do so without drawing on a vast background of beliefs and assumptions that we bring into play as we engage with them. The world of Harry Potter might be full of fictional particulars which are distinctive of that world, but in a great many respects it functions just like the actual world. And it is in the nature of fiction that while the distinctive features of a fictional world are typically conveyed explicitly, we generally come to understand the ways in which it resembles the actual world implicitly. The game of Quidditch and the behavior of the Golden Snitch must be set out for us; the fact that wizards require oxygen and sleep (special spells aside) we assume to be true-in-the-fiction, until such time as we are compelled to revise those assumptions—beliefs—by some indication in the fiction that these facts about the real world do not hold in the world of Harry Potter. In other words, understanding fictional worlds requires the *import* of a great many beliefs about the real world, without which they would be like Swiss cheese: full of holes—palpably full of holes.[12]

The explanation for this is that when we engage with fictions, we do so on the basis of what I term the "mimetic hypothesis" (Smith 2022, ch. 2 and Afterword, drawing on Butler 1984, 7) or what Walton (1990, 144–150) terms the "Reality Principle": as we build a fictional world in our minds—that is, as we imagine that fictional world— we work on the principle that that world is just like the real world, unless and until the fiction indicates otherwise: "Depressing piano keys is understood to have the same effect in fictional worlds that it has in the real one, so long as nothing in the directly generated fictional truths indicates otherwise. So when in Eisenstein's silent film *Potemkin* it is fictional that a person steps on the keys of a piano, it is implied that fictionally piano sounds are produced" (Walton 1990, 145). Our beliefs about the real world function as a default. And, importantly, the role of belief here is instrumental. The purpose of this large-scale importation of beliefs is to fill out the contours of the fictional world—to plug those gaps, allow it to coalesce, and give it, so to speak, im- aginative cohesion, density, and momentum. The role of belief here is to support and help realize the imaginative project. The imagining of the fictional world is still the point of the exercise, but already we see one way in which our beliefs come into play in our appreciation of fiction.[13]

So narratives are comprised of constitutive particular propositions, which we are invited to imagine (in the case of fictions) or believe (in the case of nonfictions). But we surely need to add a further component, which we can represent in Table 13.2 through an elaboration of our original Table 13.1.

What are these "implied propositional generalizations"? These are the "morals" or "messages" that stories are often thought to possess; the lesson or wisdom that they seem to embody and convey. They are "implied" because they need not be, and fre- quently are not, explicitly stated. They are generalizations in that they, precisely, gen- eralize across the class or classes of event and agent into which they fit (spearings, killings, Inuit, servants . . . the set of classes of which any given particular is a member is indefinitely large). They are types rather than tokens. And, very importantly, on both the fictional and nonfictional branches of the framework, these generalizations are assertions—usually implied, to be sure, but assertions rather than imaginings nonetheless. If the language of assertion seems out of place here, we should at least grant that, in this respect, fictions as much as nonfictions have designs on our beliefs and not only on our imaginings. They seek to impart a perspective on, or knowledge

Table 13.2 Mood-stances in nonfiction and fiction elaborated

The assertive stance ▽	The fictive stance ▽
Nonfiction ▽	Fiction ▽
Constitutive particular beliefs ▽	Constitutive particular imaginings ▽
Implied propositional generalizations	Implied propositional generalizations

about, or understanding of the actual world via the fictional worlds that they project and invite us to imagine (on the basis of their constitutive particular propositions).

In Wolterstorff's terms, what is happening here is the *transference* of beliefs, ideas, and attitudes from the fictional world projected to the real world; in Tamar Szabó Gendler's terms, the *export* of beliefs, ideas, and attitudes from the fictional to the real world (mirroring the import of certain beliefs necessary to fill out the fictional world in the first place—though of course the sets of imported and exported beliefs need not be identical).[14] Note that now we have the beginnings of an answer to the question I posed a few pages back: What's the point or purpose of imagining? Aside from the self-sufficient pleasure we might take in the act of imagining, we can see that imagining may also lead us to new beliefs about and new attitudes toward the actual world—a function of the imagination well captured by Richard Moran: "For better or for worse, we seem committed to the idea that imagination is a vehicle of knowledge of various kinds. If this is so, then in such exercises we are not taking our engagement with the world imagined (the fictional world) to be sealed off from what matters to us in the real world … imagination is not so much a peering into some other world, as a way of relating to this one" (1994, 106).

Nonfiction, Belief, and Imagination

I've been stressing the idea that the mood-stance theory, originally articulated by Wolterstorff in relation to literature and theater and developed by Plantinga in the context of film, is notably underdeveloped in at least one respect. Making assertions, nonfictions solicit beliefs; inventing imaginary agents and events, fictions prompt imaginings. But in prompting our imaginings, fictions not only draw on our existing beliefs; they may also seek to add to or reshape our beliefs via the implied propositional generalizations—the "morals" or "messages" or perhaps the "vision" or "worldview"—that they embody. To that extent, the simple two-part model—represented by the two cells with plain text in Table 13.3—has been complicated by a focus on the top right-hand cell, shaded and with italicized text, concerned with the way in which fiction intersects with belief. We would do well to attend also to the other cell that is downplayed by the basic, two-part mood-stance framework, again shaded and featuring italicized text, in which the relations between nonfiction and imagining are

Table 13.3 Interrelations among fiction, nonfiction, belief, and imagining

Fiction and imagining	*Fiction and belief (background beliefs + messages, morals: implied propositional generalizations)*
Nonfiction and imagining (counterfactuals + visualizations + aesthetic form)	Nonfiction and belief

captured. Is there anything of significance going on in this space? Does imagining play a role in our appreciation of nonfiction?

In at least one respect, it surely does. For in order to understand fully what did happen in some particular historical episode, we also need to appreciate what would have happened had certain causes been absent and events had unfolded differently. Historical explanations depend on such counterfactuals, and these counterfactuals are nothing other than nonexistent, imagined states of affair, the shadows of the events which did, in fact, occur. Bare historical chronology might not require such counter-factuals, but they will feature in any historical representation of greater "thickness" and ambition. Errol Morris's *The Thin Blue Line* (1989) leaves us to contemplate the possibility that David Harris might never have confessed and that Randall Adams might have seen out his life in jail, or more likely been executed—and not just the fact that he was exonerated, in part through the intervention of Morris in making the film. *The Thin Blue Line* is unusual only in the explicitness with which it makes the counterfactuals haunting the actual narrative—the events that did occur—explicit.[15]

So nonfictional works which recount and explain historical events prompt imag-inings in at least that minimal sense. But much more needs to be said on this topic. Noël Carroll has suggested that another sense in which the imagination is sometimes involved in the making and appreciating of nonfictional representations is in visu-alizing at least some of the events recounted: "The practice of ancient historians to invent speeches and battle details was an acknowledged convention meant to viv-idly put the events before the listener's or reader's eyes (a standard expression). It was an invitation to mentally visualize the events, rather like the more prosaic pictorial illustrations in some of our history textbooks. *It was not an invitation to entertain the occurrence of the events as unasserted*" (2016, 370, my emphasis). Carroll's point here is that the role of this convention is to help us represent to ourselves the actual events recounted by the nonfiction work in a vivid fashion, rather than to hold them in mind unasserted—that is, to imagine rather than believe them.[16] Visualizing might be extended to "perceptual imagining" more generally: the bringing to mind of events in other sensory modalities—hearing most obviously, but in certain cases also the touching, smelling, tasting, thermoception, and proprioception of (actual or coun-terfactually relevant) events. And the function of such perceptual imagining in non-fictions can be directly related to another typical feature of nonfiction films analyzed by Plantinga, who argues that "certain images and sounds [in documentary films], or sequences thereof, are meant to approximate some element of the phenomenolog-ical experience of the event, such as how it looked or sounded from a particular van-tage point, or how it was full of energetic good cheer or a strong sense of foreboding" (2005, 110). In other words, the visualizing (and, by extension, perceptual imagining) identified by Carroll is the imaginative complement to the perceptual rendering of the phenomenology of a nonfiction film's represented situations and events (see the references to Plantinga in notes 10 and 11 above).

Moreover, there is a practice in audiovisual documentaries and docudramas par-allel to the imaginative visualizing elicited by some written nonfictions, as discussed by Carroll, which blend the assertive recounting and representation of events with their speculative elaboration in the form of dramatized material going beyond the level of detail that can be plausibly corroborated through documentary evidence (e.g., the exact words uttered or gestures enacted in specific historical episodes, or the unexpressed thoughts of the agents involved rendered through the interior monologue of a voice-over). The function of such material is again arguably not that we should entertain these details as "merely imagined," as we would if engaging with them on the terms of the fictive stance, but rather that we take them to exemplify the kind of words and gestures which must have characterized the event being represented on the terms of the assertive stance (i.e., they are imaginary tokens of the same type as the real tokens they stand in for). Put schematically, we have a contrast between (1) a represented detail as imagined (represented in the mind as unasserted) and (2) a represented detail as a candidate for belief (represented in the mind as asserted, but where some of the detail is treated as a generic placeholder for a kind of detail not available to the author, functioning to make the assertively represented event more vivid).[17]

My model adds a further wrinkle: the events a nonfiction work might invite us to visualize (or otherwise perceptually imagine) encompass both those asserted by the work to have occurred as well as those counterfactually relevant happenings which form part of the explanatory fabric of the work, as discussed above through the example of *The Thin Blue Line*. That is the role of the (re)enactments of the various things that might have happened on the night that David Harris in fact shot and killed police officer Robert Wood. But, crucially, we are not being invited to represent to ourselves these counterfactual events unasserted in the same way we would if they appeared in a fictional policier, that is, to imagine rather than believe them. Rather, we are being invited to consider them as candidates for or counterparts to belief. So long as we are uncertain which of several possibilities actually obtained, they are candidates for belief; once we know which of these possibilities was realized, these events become the counterfactual counterparts of actual events—things that might have happened, but did not.

In his characterization of documentary filmmaking as the "creative treatment of actuality," John Grierson (1933, 8) was at pains to emphasize that such filmmaking should not be thought of as inherently lacking in imagination and artistry. Here we encounter still another sense in which at least some nonfictions engage the imagination. We do not engage with and learn from a "creative treatment of actuality" like Morris's film in exactly the same way as we do with a pedestrian instructional nonfiction film, such as *How to Wash Your Hands* (2020).[18] The style and form of the creative documentary will be integral to its epistemic force in a way that will not be true of the purely instrumental nonfiction. The imagination is at work here, too, though in a way that is harder to pin down than it is with respect to the role of counterfactual imagining, and vivid perceptual imagining, in narrative nonfictions.

How might this kind of imagining be conceptualized? Earlier, I eschewed the Kantian notion of aesthetic disinterest as a way of explaining the function of the imagination, at least with respect to epistemic goods like knowledge and understanding.

But a different part of Kant's account of aesthetic judgment may help us get to grips with the role of the imagination in creative nonfictions of the kind Grierson sought to describe and exemplified here by *The Thin Blue Line*. Recall that for Kant (1952), artworks engage us aesthetically when they set in motion the "free play" of understanding and imagination.[19] That is, our understanding of the work and what it represents is in part attributable to our ability to assimilate it within our existing conceptual repertoire: we can readily recognize both the type of people and events the film tells of (e.g., cops, drifters, teenage dropouts, miscarriages of justice), as well as the genres of filmmaking Morris draws upon in representing these events (testimonial documentaries, police procedurals, films noir). But Morris exceeds all of these established categories in the making of the film, and in fully appreciating his film we too are compelled to transcend the routines of ordinary cognition. The film stretches and surprises our minds, and in this way delights us. This is the sense in which, in encountering a creative nonfiction—a documentary in Grierson's sense—imagination is brought into play alongside understanding.

More particularly, the manner in which Morris represents and spins these elements together exceeds our understanding (in the Kantian sense), and is meant to exceed our understanding. By design, our imaginations are stirred: What really happened, and why? What were the real motivations of the various parties involved? What was it like to be wrongly charged and convicted, or guilty but uncharged for the murder? In this way Kant's theory encompasses the perceptual imagining and counterfactual imagining we've already encountered, but more is at stake. We are struck by Morris's imaginative use of devices typically reserved for fiction films—meticulously crafted, chiaroscuro (re)stagings of what (might have) happened on the night of the shooting, interviews in which the subjects look directly into the camera, Philip Glass's ominous score[20]—to tell a real crime story. In the case of the flat-footed instructional film *How to Wash Your Hands*, everything in the work is subordinate to the understanding, and in particular to the specific goal of getting viewers to wash their hands rigorously enough to eliminate traces of the COVID virus. Morris, by contrast, wants us not only to understand what has happened—and what might have happened as a way of sharpening our understanding of what did happen—but to appreciate and savor the way in which these events have been depicted by his film.

Note that, as a consequence, the way in which we might value a creative nonfiction differs from the blunt epistemic criterion discussed above. For such works, we will not only be concerned with the extent to which they are a reliable source of information, and thus of improving our knowledge and understanding. We value such nonfictions for their inventiveness and imaginativeness as well.

Two further questions follow from this. First, we might ask: How do these two criteria—the epistemic and the aesthetic—relate to one another? Is one dominant and the other subordinate? What of those works which succeed with respect to one of the criteria, but fail with respect to the other one? And second, bringing us squarely back to the focus of our inquiry: Does the aesthetic dimension of a work, conceived along Kantian lines, make some contribution toward its epistemic value? In particular, how does the aesthetic dimension of a work bear on its capacity to advance our moral understanding? I cannot offer anything like a full answer here, but in the next section, I make an initial suggestion.

Imagining and the Reflective Afterlife

In his recent *Imagining and Knowing*, Greg Currie (2020)—who, as I've noted, defends an account of fiction and nonfiction similar to the mood-stance theory—tackles head-on the epistemic implications of the fictive branch of the framework: In what ways can fictions, as core products of the imagination, lead to learning? Can fictions function as vehicles of knowledge? Currie considers the idea that, if appreciators of fiction (as "virtuous epistemic agents") really took the epistemic claims of fiction seriously, they would "treat fictions as parts of an interconnected informational system" (111), along with, for example, the sciences and historical nonfiction. But he acknowledges that this "just does not seem to be how we naturally engage with fiction.... [H]ow many of us seek to check what we take to be [the] message [of a work] against, say, research into social psychology?" (106) We might add, moreover, that such comparison across not just distinct sources of knowledge but distinct routes to knowledge is not part of the standard games authorized by our ordinary practices of fiction-making and consumption. Indeed the suggestion is sufficiently incongruous that Currie is able to exploit its comic potential. We might read fictions by night while reading *Behavioral and Brain Sciences* by day, but the idea that we might systematically integrate our learning from them, reading a novel or watching a movie with a pile of journal issues in place of a bag of popcorn, seems akin to category mistake.

What Currie broaches here concerns, in Peter Kivy's resonant phrase, the "reflective afterlife" of fictions (1997). And what I want to propose is that, notwithstanding Currie's doubts, there is something to the idea that fiction, on the one hand, and nonfictional scientific discourse, on the other hand, might complement one another in the pursuit of knowledge. But we need a model which acknowledges the stark differences between the two activities and our customary manner of engagement with them. The epistemic role of fiction and the imagination is best thought of, I will suggest, in terms of *the discovery of possibilities through imaginative exploration*. Fictional stories are the scaffolding enabling that exploration. The epistemic rewards of fiction may have a hypothetical character, but hypotheses are a perfectly respectable, indeed essential part of both the everyday process of knowledge acquisition and the grander and more ambitious goals of the scientific enterprise.[21] Let me now tease out this proposal by elaborating on some of its key components and terms.

Consider first the concept of *discovery*. I have in mind two particular contexts in which the term is used: in law and in (the philosophy of) science. In law, "discovery" refers to the early stage in a court case when the (putative) evidence held by both the prosecution and the defense is brought to light, and is considered an essential part of a fair and transparent trial. In the philosophy of science, the distinction between the "context of discovery" and the "context of justification" speaks to the fact that the scientific process involves different stages, and different standards may apply to those different stages of inquiry. What do these two uses of "discovery" have in common? The evidence revealed during the discovery phase of a trial may or may not prove robust, and even if robust, may or may not weigh heavily in the case. Scientific findings emerging in the context of discovery may be highly provisional; they have not yet been subjected to the more demanding standards of the context of justification. We have all witnessed a version of this epistemic journey from initial, tentative discovery to robust empirical justification in the investigation of COVID-19 and of the vaccines developed to combat it. So "discovery" in both cases points to the early stages of inquiry.

What activity naturally leads to discovery? I think there is a specific kind (or conception) of knowledge-seeking activity which fits with discovery as an epistemic end, hand in glove. And that activity is *exploration*. I don't think it is an accident when, mulling over a choice between speaking of analyzing, investigating, studying, testing, experimenting, and exploring, the earlier, more provisional, and open-ended our inquiry is, the more likely we will speak of exploration.[22] And my proposal is that, to the extent that fiction is capable of playing an epistemic role, it is in respect of *exploration in the name of discovery*, as characterized above. While it may not be plausible that we look to fiction for 24-carat knowledge—justified true beliefs, scientifically vindicated truth claims, or some other exalted conception of knowledge—it is much more plausible that we look to it for ideas, insights, and hypotheses which play a role in the (individual and collective) human journey toward enlightenment.[23]

In another passage, Currie seems much more open to this reconfigured and less rigid version of "an interconnected informational system" encompassing fiction and science: "You spend the day reading William James on the emotions; seeking a different perspective that evening, you dip into *The Golden Bowl* by brother Henry" (2020, 91). While skeptical that this movement between the scientific-philosophical and the literary-fictional will generate knowledge in any strict sense, Currie is open to the idea that it can generate *understanding*—where understanding of a domain is revealed through such things as the ability to ask relevant questions about it, raise objections to received opinion, and consider how things might be otherwise—in other words, to frame new hypotheses. Note that there is a significant connection here with the role attributed to counterfactuals and hypotheses in historical nonfictions earlier in the argument. The presence of these elements in historical nonfictions, such as *The Thin Blue Line*, is essential to their ability to deepen our understanding of the events they recount.

Strikingly, Currie (2020) is willing to grant that in many contexts, understanding in this sense is much more important—more valuable—than knowledge, narrowly conceived. "When we focus on learning, criticism, and epistemic improvement, knowing has not got much to do with it.... Virtuous learning requires an active, critical, and imaginative engagement with the material" (91–92) rather than the simple extraction, or flat-footed application, of (what I am calling) 24-carat knowledge. Here we see an echo of the point made earlier regarding creative nonfictions like *The Thin Blue Line*: part of what we value in such a film is its "imaginative engagement" with its real-world story material, evident in its form and style. And we value this imaginative engagement with the material, on this view, because it is integral to the understanding afforded by the film rather than simply as an aesthetic shell encasing an epistemic kernel. This gives us the basis of an answer to the question posed at the conclusion of the previous section, insofar as (on this view) the aesthetic dimension of a work can enhance the epistemic value of it.

What might we say about *moral* understanding in particular? That is, in what ways might screen stories cultivate understanding in the moral domain? Ted Nannicelli argues that moral understanding is achieved when we develop a grasp of the *reasons why* some moral judgment or principle is true or compelling (and not merely come to accept that the judgment or principle is true—in which case we might say we have knowledge, but not understanding, of it). Such understanding, Nannicelli argues, is most likely to develop through extended and reiterated engagement across the reflective afterlife of a work and to be achieved with the right character traits, such as commitment to learning, perceptiveness, and sensitivity, in place (the latter working in a virtuous feedback loop with moral understanding). Because moral understanding involves a grasp of the reasons for a moral judgment, practically speaking it is closely tied to "doing the right thing"—that is, to action. Summarizing part of his argument, Nannicelli writes that "understanding plausibly has intrinsic value as a cognitive achievement and instrumental value as a prompt for action. The particular instrumental value of moral understanding derives from the fact that it has the potential to motivate us—at least under certain conditions—not only to (reliably) do the right thing but to do the right thing for the right reasons" (this volume, 27). So here there is a parallel between the action-guiding moral understanding we might gain from a fiction with the practical benefits from the updated beliefs we glean from reliable nonfictions (see above, 230).

Through his examples, Nannicelli puts an emphasis on the role played by something as specific as a single shot, gesture, or line of dialogue, though always as part of a much wider and more temporally extended network of ideas embedded in the dramatic structure of a work, leading to improved moral understanding and right action. Let me add an example of my own. Consider Spike Lee's depiction of the "sympathetic racist" Sal (Danny Aiello) in *Do the Right Thing* (1989) (Flory 2008). The structure of the film invites us to build up a fund of sympathy for Sal, contrasting his patience, generosity, and general benevolence toward the Black community members who patronize his pizzeria with the hostility of his son Pino (John Turturro). Threaded through Sal's ostentatious goodness, however, are a string of micro-aggressions, which eventually culminate in the sustained racist outburst directed at Radio Raheem preceding the riot. What this structure allows us to perceive is the harm of such apparently minor incidents; more particularly, the film allows the viewer, and especially the white viewer, to experience these digs from the point of view of a Black community member. And experiencing such hostilities from the Black point of view allows us to appreciate properly their harmfulness, and thus the reason such micro-aggressions should be condemned where they occur and ideally avoided in the first place.

So the film dramatizes a somewhat subtle dimension of moral behavior, allowing us to perceive and understand it. As an individual, fictional narrative, *Do the Right Thing* cannot offer anything like a proof or robust empirical knowledge of micro-aggression as a form of racism. But to echo and vary a formula from above, it can offer us ideas, insights, and hypotheses about racist micro-aggression, which may play a role in the (individual and collective) human journey toward enlightenment in the form of improved moral understanding. *Do the Right Thing* acts as the fictional scaffolding allowing us to explore, and make discoveries within, this sector of moral space.

There is a historical version of, or dimension to, the argument that fiction may complement the scientific investigation of the world in our quest for knowledge and understanding. Prior to the rise of scientific psychology in the late 19th century, what epistemic tools were available to unlock the secrets of the human mind and human behavior? Storytelling in general, and fiction in particular, were surely important resources; that is one reason why scientific psychologists will often allude to novelists (and other artists) in order to frame their scientific findings. (Jonah Lehrer's 2011 *Proust Was a Neuroscientist* might be considered a reductio of this practice.) Before the emergence of scientific psychology, then, sophisticated narrative fiction (in the novel and, later, as the discipline of psychology came into being, in film) was among the most powerful tools for understanding the human mind. And it remains so today, albeit now sharing the space of inquiry with scientific approaches to the mind. In such a world, fiction can no long carry quite the same authority as a vehicle of insight as it once did.[24]

A final thought, which weighs on the side of Currie's skepticism regarding the epistemic powers of fiction. Artistic fictions, even if they have a serious epistemic function, still must balance this function with aesthetic considerations—or least with those aesthetic factors which, in contrast to the epistemically enhancing aesthetic aspects of *The Thin Blue Line*, do not function epistemically. In this they are unlike activities in which epistemic criteria are absolutely central and dominant. We might praise the lucidity with which the Swedish medic and statistician Hans Rosling was able to convey the findings of quantitative health science through data visualization, but the vividness of Rosling's graphs and diagrams is strictly tied and subordinate to an epistemic goal. The job of the novelist or the filmmaker is, in a sense, more complicated—for even where they seek to convey knowledge or instill understanding, their designs will be swayed by beauty, as an end in itself, as well as truth.

Let me conclude by taking stock of the overall case made by the present chapter. The mood-stance account of fiction and nonfiction, I've argued, is fundamentally correct. We do discriminate between fictions and nonfictions, in the first instance, on the basis of the different "stances" creators adopt in making them, and appreciators reciprocally adopt in engaging with them (Table 13.1). Authors of nonfictions invite us to believe the states of affairs they represent in their nonfictions, as holding true of the actual world. Fictioneers, on the other hand, invite us to imagine the states of affairs they represent in their fictions. But arguably the mood-stance account is lop-sided, to the extent that it gives us a fuller understanding of the role of nonfictions than it does of the role of fictions. While it is clear what we gain by acquiring new beliefs from nonfictions, the benefits of the imaginings prompted by fictions are (so far) not obvious.

However, the basic picture given to us by the mood-stance theory quickly becomes complicated when we recognize that fictions, while prompting us to imagine what they represent, also depend on and engage our beliefs in a variety of ways, and that nonfictions, while soliciting our assent to what they assert, also often invite us to im-agine various states of affairs alongside those they assert have occurred, and may also involve the exercise of the imagination in other ways (as summarized in Table 13.3). Additionally, both fictions and nonfictions typically give rise to implied propositional generalizations—"messages" or "morals"—bearing on the actual world (Table 13.2). At this more abstract level, fictions as much as nonfictions have designs on our beliefs, not just on our imaginings; they invite us to "export" or "transfer" ideas and attitudes from the fictional worlds they project to the real world.

What, then, is the fate of these new beliefs and attitudes in the "reflective afterlife" of a work of fiction? To what extent, and on what terms, do they become integrated with our more general, evolving understanding and knowledge of the world? A full answer to this question is well beyond the scope of this chapter, but I have proposed one way in which we might characterize the epistemic goods we derive from our en-gagement with fictions. One of the primary functions of fiction is to scaffold our ex-ploration of the space of possibilities, such that we are able to discover and formulate new hypotheses about the way the world is, or might be. The pursuits of science and of fiction will seem incommensurable if we put them into direct competition, expecting each to live up precisely to the processes and norms fit for the other. A first step, then, in crediting fiction with epistemic value lies in theorizing the distinctive route to un-derstanding, or contribution to knowledge, that it may afford. Much work remains to be done in turning that first step into the whole nine yards.

Notes

1. The framework is advanced in Nicholas Wolterstorff's (1980) *Works and Worlds of Art*, written while Wolterstorff was a faculty member at Calvin College. The notion of "mood-stances" is introduced in part 4; see in particular sections VI and VII. At Calvin, Wolterstorff taught the young Carl Plantinga (1997), who went on to employ the frame-work in his *Rhetoric and Representation in Nonfiction Film*. Plantinga introduces the framework on 16ff.

2. The notion of "world projection" is central to Wolterstorff's (1980, part 4) account.

3. Greg Currie (1990, 46) offers a very strong version of this view, when he argues that "a work is fiction iff (*a*) it is the product of a fictive intent and (*b*) if the work is true, then it is at most accidentally true." In other words, at the level of what I will term the "con-stitutive particular propositions" making up a narrative, the truth or otherwise of these

propositions is not at stake in works of fiction; in this sense, where they are true, they are only "accidentally" true. For objections, see Friend (2012).

4. Plantinga (2005) nuances his account of documentary, but assertion remains central, as conveyed in his general characterization of documentary filmmaking in this essay as "asserted veridical representation." He states, "I do not want to imply that the only illocutionary act performed in or through a documentary is assertion. There is clearly much else going on. My claim here would be that assertion is a central element of what is characteristic of the documentary, not that assertion is all there is to documentary communication" (117n31; see also 115).

5. See Currie (1990), Carroll (1997), and Stock (2017), for example; Carroll also refers to "the fictive stance," citing uses of it by Currie (1990) and Lamarque and Olsen (1994, who cite Wolterstorff in their 32n4). Neither Wolterstorff nor Plantinga refers to Grice; instead, Wolterstorff's initial points of reference include both Austin and Searle. The common point of origin among these accounts, then, is the strain of philosophy of language and "speech act theory" straddling Oxford and Berkeley, developed above all by Austin, Grice, and Searle. Plantinga (2005, 107–108) plays up the speech act connection.

6. An example from 2006: "Kuleshov's montage experiments demonstrated the fictive nature not of the image but, in any succession of them, the joins" (Rohdie 2006, 27). Any film containing edits, so the claim here goes, is "fictive" simply by virtue of those cuts. Thus any documentary containing edits should be regarded as "fictive."

7. Plantinga (2005, 107) writes, "[The assertive character of nonfiction] is typically contrasted with fiction, in which the filmmaker or writer takes a fictive stance toward the world of the work, presenting the state of affairs for our delectation, edification, education, amusement, or what have you, but not to have us believe that the state of affairs that constitute[s] the world of the work holds in the actual world." Plantinga gestures here toward various possible functions of fiction, but the passage exemplifies the asymmetry in the mood-stance theory: the essay is about nonfiction, and the characterization of fiction and its functions enters the picture only by way of brief contrast.

8. I note here that Wolterstorff (2015), in his *Art Rethought*, rejects what he calls the "Grand Narrative," or in other words, the assumption or argument that the chief purpose of the arts is "disinterested contemplation" shorn of any practical function such as social protest or memorializing. Throughout that book and briefly in his *Works and Worlds of Art* (1980, 356–367) he discusses the social functions of world projection and the representational arts generally.

9. I introduce the notion of "constitutive particular propositions"—along with the complementary concept of "implied propositional generalizations," discussed below—in Smith (2000). In the case of a fiction, these propositions comprise its "core of primary fictional truths," in Walton's (1990, 144–145) terminology; Walton also writes of propositions as constituents of fiction (36–37).

10. See Smith (2016 and [2017] 2020, chs. 4, 7, 8) and Plantinga (this volume). Plantinga (2005, 110) argues further that "the moving photograph and the sound recording [constituting a documentary] are to some degree belief-independent. Their communicative richness extends beyond the intentions of the filmmakers and leaves something for interpretation and discovery by audiences."

11. Plantinga (2005, 111) puts an emphasis on the way in which verbal and filmic nonfictions work differently with respect to propositional content. In nonfiction films, and especially

in observational documentaries, propositional content is often underdetermined; the phenomenological qualities of a represented situation may be as important as or more important than its propositional content, and there is more scope for the viewer's imaginative agency, relative to what is intended and can be controlled by the filmmaker (110). Relatedly, Plantinga distinguishes between "saying" and "showing," suggesting "that a documentary combines both, but that in either case, the documentary is intended as a reliable account of, argument about, record of, or approximation of some aspect of the actual world" (115).

12. The metaphor of "importing" beliefs into fictional worlds was introduced by Gendler (2010b) (published in its original form as a journal article in 2000).

13. Ryan (1991, 51) labels this the "Principle of Minimal Departure." Wolterstorff (1980) discusses the issue within his framework in part 3, III, "Elucidation and Extrapolation."

14. Wolterstorff (2015; this volume) develops the idea of "transference." On the export of beliefs from fictions, see Gendler (2010a, 2010b).

15. Notably Walton (1990, 145ff.) discusses counterfactuals only in relation to the Reality Principle. And there they are invoked to explain how the principle works in relation to fictions. Moreover, nothing in Walton's approach to nonfictions suggests that he sees any significant role for imagining in relation to nonfictions. He grants that one can *treat* a nonfiction as a prop in a game of make-believe—treat it as a fiction—but to the extent that we treat it on its own terms, as a nonfiction, it doesn't even count as a "representation" (the latter being, for Walton, things that prompt make-believe—imagining). Thus Walton proposes a highly revisionary concept of "representation"—more restrictive than the standard concept, insofar as nonfictions are excluded; wider than the standard concept, insofar as "natural representations" (e.g., clouds in which we see figures, à la Wollheim) are included.

16. Carroll is responding here to Friend (2012), who holds that these ancient histories invite us to hold these speeches and battle details in mind unasserted—to imagine rather than believe them.

17. Notably the point of reference for both Carroll and Friend (to whom Carroll refers) is a genre of written nonfiction: Roman histories. The notion of visualization in relation to visual nonfictions opens another can of worms: Are we able to visualize what we are already seeing? For a related discussion, see my exchange with Malcolm Turvey in Allen and Smith (1997).

18. https://www.ecdc.europa.eu/en/publications-data/video-covid-19-how-wash-your-hands.

19. Note that, in this context, we need to have in mind Kant's very specific concept of understanding as a faculty of mind, rather than the broader sense of understanding as an epistemic good in contemporary debates.

20. "Existential dread" is the expression used by Morris (Savlov 2004).

21. For Wilfrid Sellars (1962), the two are continuous: the scientific method emerges historically from ordinary knowledge acquisition.

22. A recent email: "Congratulations on bringing this project into the daylight. It can't have been easy coordinating the hugely differentiated aspects of the book. I look forward to *exploring* it when my copy arrives."

23. The emphasis on the formulation of new hypotheses, through a process of abductive reasoning, makes the work of N. R. Hanson (1958) in *Patterns of Discovery* particularly apt here.

24. Green (2010) runs a similar argument.

Works Cited

Butler, Christopher. 1984. *Interpretation, Deconstruction, and Ideology: An Introduction to Some Current Issues in Literary Theory*. Oxford: Clarendon Press.

Carroll, Noël. 1997. "Fiction, Non-fiction, and the Film of Presumptive Assertion: A Conceptual Analysis." In *Film Theory and Philosophy*, edited by Richard Allen and Murray Smith, 173–202. Oxford: Clarendon Press.

Carroll, Noël. 2016. "Fiction." In *The Routledge Companion to Philosophy of Literature*, edited by Noel Carroll and John Gibson, 359–71. New York: Routledge.

Currie, Gregory. 1990. *The Nature of Fiction*. Cambridge: Cambridge University Press.

Currie, Gregory. 2020. *Imagining and Knowing*. Oxford: Oxford University Press.

Flory, Dan. 2008. *Philosophy, Black Film, Film Noir*. University Park, Pennsylvania: Pennsylvania State University Press.

Friend, Stacie. 2012. "Fiction as a Genre." *Proceedings of the Aristotelian Society* 112, no. 2: 179–209.

Gendler, Tamar Szabó. 2010a. "Imaginative Resistance Revisited" (2006). In *Intuition, Imagination, and Philosophical Methodology*, 203–226. Oxford: Oxford University Press.

Gendler, Tamar Szabó. 2010b. "The Puzzle of Imaginative Resistance" (2000). In *Intuition, Imagination, and Philosophical Methodology*, 179–202. Oxford: Oxford University Press.

Green, Mitchell. 2010. "How and What We Can Learn from Fiction." In *A Companion to the Philosophy of Literature* edited by Garry L. Hagberg and Walter Jost, 350-66. Malden, MA: Blackwell.

Grierson, John. 1933. "The Documentary Producer." *Cinema Quarterly* 2, no. 1: 7–9.

Hanson, Norwood Russell. 1958. *Patterns of Discovery: An Inquiry into the Conceptual Foundations of Science*. Cambridge: Cambridge University Press.

Kant, Immanuel. 1952. *The Critique of Judgement* (1790). Translated by James Creed Meredith. Oxford: Clarendon Press.

Kivy, Peter. 1997. *Philosophies of Arts: An Essay in Differences*. Cambridge: Cambridge University Press.

Lamarque, Peter, and Stein Haugom Olsen. 1994. *Truth, Fiction, and Literature*. Oxford: Clarendon Press.

Lehrer, Jonah. 2011. *Proust Was a Neuroscientist*. Edinburgh: Canongate.

Moran, Richard. 1994. "The Expression of Feeling in Imagination." *Philosophical Review* 103, no. 1: 75–106.

Plantinga, Carl. 1987. "Defining Documentary: Fiction, Non-fiction, and Projected Worlds." *Persistence of Vision* 5 (Spring): 44–54.

Plantinga, Carl. 1997. *Rhetoric and Representation in Nonfiction Film*. New York: Cambridge University Press.

Plantinga, Carl. 2005. "What a Documentary Is, After All." *Journal of Aesthetics and Art Criticism* 63, no. 2: 105–117.

Rohdie, Sam. 2006. *Montage*. Manchester: Manchester University Press.

Ryan, Marie-Laure. 1991. *Possible Worlds, Artificial Intelligence, and Narrative Theory*. Bloomington: Indiana University Press.

Ryan, Marie-Laure. 1997. "Postmodernism and the Doctrine of Panfictionality." *Narrative* 5, no. 2: 165–187.

Savlov, Marc. 2004. "The Ambience of Existential Dread: Philip Glass on the 'Fog of War' Score." *Austin Chronicle*, February 20. https://www.austinchronicle.com/screens/2004-02-20/197905/.

Sellars, Wilfrid. 1962. "Philosophy and the Scientific Image of Man." In *Frontiers of Science and Philosophy*, edited by Robert G. Colodny, 35–78. Pittsburgh, PA: University of Pittsburgh Press.

Smith, Murray. 2000. "Aesthetics and the Rhetorical Power of Narrative." In *Moving Images, Culture and the Mind*, edited by Ib Bondebjerg, 157–166. Luton: University of Luton Press.

Smith, Murray. 2016. "Film, Philosophy, and the Varieties of Artistic Value." In *Current Controversies in Philosophy*, edited by Katherine Thomson-Jones, 182–201. New York: Routledge.

Smith, Murray. (2017) 2020. *Film, Art, and the Third Culture*. Oxford: Oxford University Press.

Smith, Murray. 2022. *Engaging Characters: Fiction, Emotion, and the Cinema*. 2nd ed. Oxford: Clarendon Press.

Stock, Kathleen. 2017. *Only Imagine: Fiction, Interpretation, and Imagination*. Oxford: Oxford University Press.

Walton, Kendall L. 1990. *Mimesis as Make-Believe: On the Foundations of the Representational Arts*. Cambridge, MA: Harvard University Press.

Wolterstorff, Nicholas. 1980. *Works and Worlds of Art*. Oxford: Clarendon Press.

Wolterstorff, Nicholas. 2015. *Art Rethought: The Social Practices of Art*. Oxford: Oxford University Press.

Contributors

Helena Bilandzic is a professor at the University of Augsburg. She earned her PhD in 2003 from the Ludwig-Maximilians-Universität (Munich) and her habilitation degree in 2009 from the University of Erfurt. She has taught at universities in Munich, Erfurt, Ilmenau, Berlin, Hamburg, and Friedrichshafen. Bilandzic has served as an elected member of the review board for social sciences of the German Research Foundation and serves on the editorial boards of several scholarly journals. Her current research interests include media effects related to science, the environment and health, as well as social and moral issues, narrative experience, and persuasion.

Noël Carroll is Distinguished Professor of Philosophy at the Graduate Center, City University of New York. He is the author of many books and essays in the philosophy of film, aesthetics, and the philosophy of literature, including *Philosophy and the Moving Image* (2021), *Engaging the Moving Image* (2003), and *A Philosophy of Horror, or, Paradoxes of the Heart* (1990). He has also been a journalist and has written five documentaries.

Allison Eden received her PhD from Michigan State University. She is an associate professor in the Department of Communication at Michigan State University, specializing in media entertainment research. Her work is interdisciplinary, drawing from communication and media psychology, social psychology, and neuroscience in the areas of media psychology, media entertainment, and media processing.

Matthew Grizzard received his PhD from Michigan State University and is an associate professor in the School of Communication at The Ohio State University. Situated within media psychology and mass communication, his research program examines moral judgment processes as they relate to the consumption of popular media, with a primary focus on narratives.

James Harold is a professor of philosophy at Mount Holyoke College. He is the author of *Dangerous Art: On Moral Criticism of Artworks* (2020) and editor of the *Oxford Handbook of Ethics and Art* (forthcoming). He has written widely in ethics and aesthetics, on topics such as imaginative engagement with artworks, film adaptation, and the relationship between art and moral virtue.

Frederic R. Hopp is an assistant professor of political communication at the Amsterdam School of Communication Research. He earned his PhD at the University of California, Santa Barbara. His research leverages brain imaging, computational methods, and behavioral experiments to investigate how humans create, process, and respond to moralized messages.

Wyatt Moss-Wellington is the author of *Cognitive Film and Media Ethics* (2021) and *Narrative Humanism: Kindness and Complexity in Fiction and Film* (2019) and coeditor of *ReFocus: The Films of Spike*

Jonze (2019). Moss-Wellington is also a progressive folk multi-instrumentalist and singer-songwriter with four studio albums: *The Kinder We* (2017), *Sanitary Apocalypse* (2014), *Gen Y Irony Stole My Heart* (2011), and *The Supermarket and the Turncoat* (2009).

Ted Nannicelli teaches at the University of Queensland. He is the author of *Artistic Creation and Ethical Criticism* (2020) and the editor of *Projections: The Journal for Movies and Mind*.

Mary Beth Oliver is the Bellisario Professor of Media Studies in the Department of Film/Video & Media Studies and codirector of the Media Effects Research Lab at Penn State University. She is a fellow of the International Communication Association and served as president of the organization in 2021–2022. Her research focuses on entertainment psychology and on the intersection of media with emotion and social cognition.

Carl Plantinga is a research fellow at Calvin University, where he formerly occupied the Arthur H. DeKruyter Chair of Communication. Among his books are *Alternative Realities* (2021), *Screen Stories: Emotion and the Ethics of Engagement* (2018), *Moving Viewers: American Film and the Spectator's Experience* (2009), and *Rhetoric and Representation in Nonfiction Film* (1997). He is coeditor (with Greg M. Smith) of *Passionate Views: Film, Cognition, and Emotion* (1999) and (with Paisley Livingston) of *The Routledge Companion to Philosophy and Film* (2009). Plantinga also served as president of the Society for Cognitive Studies of the Moving Image.

Robert Sinnerbrink is an associate professor of philosophy and former Australian Research Council future fellow at Macquarie University. He is the author of *New Philosophies of Film (Second Edition): An Introduction to Cinema as a Way of Thinking* (2022), *Terrence Malick: Filmmaker and Philosopher* (2019), *Cinematic Ethics: Exploring Ethical Experience through Film* (2016), *New Philosophies of Film: Thinking Images* (2011), and *Understanding Hegelianism* (2007/2014). He is also a member of the editorial boards of the journals *Film-Philosophy*, *Film and Philosophy*, and *Projections: The Journal for Movies and Mind*.

Murray Smith is a professor of film and the director of the Aesthetics Research Centre at the University of Kent. He was president of the Society for Cognitive Studies of the Moving Image from 2014 to 2017 and a Laurance S. Rockefeller fellow at Princeton University's Center for Human Values for 2017–2018. He has published widely on film, art, and aesthetics. His publications include *Film, Art, and the Third Culture: A Naturalized Aesthetics of Film* (2017; revised paperback 2020), *Trainspotting* (revised edition 2021), and *Engaging Characters: Fiction, Emotion, and the Cinema* (revised edition 2022).

Paul C. Taylor is W. Alton Jones Professor of Philosophy and chair of the Philosophy Department at Vanderbilt University. He received his undergraduate training at Morehouse College and his graduate training at the Kennedy School of Government and at Rutgers University. His research focuses primarily on social philosophy, critical race theory, American philosophy, and Africana philosophy. His books include *Black Is Beautiful: A Philosophy of Black Aesthetics*, which received the 2017 monograph prize from the American Society for Aesthetics (ASA), and *On Obama* (2016). He has recently launched the Racial Justice Humanities Lab at Vanderbilt and currently serves as the vice president (and president-elect) of the ASA.

René Weber is a professor in the Department of Communication at the University of California, Santa Barbara, and the director of UCSB's Media Neuroscience Lab (https://

medianeuroscience.org). He earned his PhD at University of Technology in Berlin and his MD, at RWTH Aachen University. He was among the first media psychology scholars to regularly use brain-imaging technology and computational approaches to investigate various media effects, from flow experiences and the appeal of entertainment, processing moralized messages, diversity and inclusion in the media, and the impact of media violence, to the persuasiveness of media campaigns.

Nicholas Wolterstorff is Noah Porter Professor Emeritus of Philosophical Theology, Yale University. He taught philosophy at Calvin College from 1959 to 1989 and at Yale University from 1989 to 2001. He has been president of the American Philosophical Association (Central Division) and of the Society of Christian Philosophers; he is a fellow of the American Academy of Arts and Sciences. Among the named lectures he has given are the Wilde Lectures (Oxford) and the Gifford Lectures (St. Andrews). He is the author of 30 books, including *Works and Worlds of Art* (1980), *Art in Action* (1980), and *Art Rethought: The Social Practices of Art* (2015).

Index

For the benefit of digital users, indexed terms that span two pages (e.g., 52–53) may, on occasion, appear on only one of those pages.

Tables are indicated by *t* following the page number